New Frontiers in Public Library Research

Edited by
Carl Gustav Johannsen
Leif Kajberg

The Scarecrow Press, Inc.
Lanham, Maryland • Toronto • Oxford
2005

SCARECROW PRESS, INC.

Published in the United States of America
by Scarecrow Press, Inc.
A wholly owned subsidiary of
The Rowman & Littlefield Publishing Group, Inc.
4501 Forbes Boulevard, Suite 200, Lanham, Maryland 20706
www.scarecrowpress.com

PO Box 317
Oxford
OX2 9RU, UK

Copyright © 2005 by Carl Gustav Johannsen and Leif Kajberg

British Library Cataloguing in Publication Information Available

Library of Congress Cataloging-in-Publication Data

Library of Congress Cataloging-in-Publication Data
New frontiers in public library research / edited by Carl Gustav Johannsen,
Leif Kajberg.
  p. cm.
 Papers originally presented at a seminar held at the Royal School of Library
and Information Science in Copenhagen, December 10-11, 2001.
 Includes bibliographical references and index.
 ISBN 0-8108-5039-7 (pbk. : alk. paper)
 1. Library science–Scandinavia–Congresses. 2. Public libraries–Scandinavia–
Congresses. 3. Library science–Research–Scandinavia–Congresses. 4. Public
libraries–Research–Scandinavia–Congresses. I. Johannsen, Carl Gustav.
II. Kajberg, Leif.
Z665.2.S34N49 2005
027.448–dc22   2004029811

♾™ The paper used in this publication meets the minimum requirements of
American National Standard for Information Sciences—Permanence of
Paper for Printed Library Materials, ANSI/NISO Z39.48-1992.
Manufactured in the United States of America.

Contents

Introduction: Public Library Research in the Nordic Countries—Issues and Perspectives

Carl Gustav Johannsen and Leif Kajberg

This book contains twenty-one new Nordic research papers on public library issues. The selection of papers has grown out of a seminar in 2001 on public library research organized by the editors of the book. The seminar—supported by a grant from NORDBOK (The Nordic Literature and Library Committee)—was held at the Royal School of Library and Information Science in Copenhagen on 10-11 December. Papers accepted for presentation at the seminar were selected on the basis of a distributed call for papers. The seminar also encompassed oral presentations by invited keynote speakers and a range of contributed papers. It concluded with a summing-up session with two invited observers, one representing practical librarianship and another coming from the academic LIS world, presenting their view of the seminar and commenting on the contents of presentations. All papers appearing in this book have been through a thorough peer reviewing and updating process.

In Nordic library and information science (LIS) education and research, there is a long-standing tradition of cooperation. Collaboration covers a wide range of activities including joint meetings and academic conferences, meetings for heads of LIS schools and joint research and development projects. In the Nordic countries, some funds for research activities are made available by national library bodies and government agencies concerned with the support of libraries and library planning and development. Moreover, some cooperative research and development projects are funded by NORDBOK and NORDINFO (Nordic Council for Scientific Information). Also, in the 1990s, grant money from the European Union was used to finance a range of state-of-the-art reviews with the majority of research activities undertaken by academic staff in LIS schools in the five Nordic countries: Denmark, Finland, Iceland, Norway and Sweden. However, the major source of funding of LIS research is not external grants but remains the LIS academic institutions themselves in that they enable their faculty members to devote part of their time to research purposes. Additionally, doctoral students contributing to the academic life in Nordic LIS departments and to the scholarly development of the LIS field are becoming more and more important for Nordic LIS research.

Only in the 1980s did institutionalization of LIS research in the Nordic countries really get off the ground, and it is only now that institutionalization of the field of LIS research in this part of the world can be said to have been completed. Indeed, the volume of library and information science research has been growing steadily over the last decade and results of these research activities are increasingly finding their way into international outlets in the field. Above all, research in such "hardcore" fields as information retrieval, information seeking, information science paradigms, informetrics, knowledge organization, domain analysis in information science and studies exploring the intellectual substance of LIS as an academic discipline have had a high profile internationally.[1]

Less well known to practicing professionals and academic communities outside the five Nordic countries are research activities in other branches of the field. For instance, there exists a strong tradition of public library research, including a solid platform of research for such themes as social and cultural contexts, collection development and media and information resources. Clearly, one reason for the somewhat modest international awareness of the more "soft" fields is actually a communication barrier: Findings of research addressing public library themes are mainly published through national or Nordic channels and media and often the Nordic languages are used. In this context, the present collection of research papers therefore aims to make this less visible part of the current research output from the Nordic LIS world more visible internationally.

Included in this volume are twelve papers by Danish authors, three Norwegian contributions and two Swedish ones, plus an article by a Finnish researcher in the field. Following the articles are the text of the keynote by Michael Buckland, School of Information Management and Systems, University of California–Berkeley, USA, and the seminar reviews by Sandra Parker, School of Information Studies at the University of Northumbria, UK, and Ruth Ørnholt, Hordaland County Library System, Norway.

We cannot claim that the included articles provide a selection that gives a fully representative picture of the breadth and diversity of current Nordic research in the field of public libraries. But taken together, the pieces and studies included here cover a range of specific themes pursued and broad areas of investigation that would serve to give LIS academics and practitioners outside the Nordic LIS world an idea of what is going on in this part of the world. It is hoped that the reader will be able to get an overall impression of the thematic priorities and the spectrum of interests. In other words, the "flavor" of research can be briefly determined.

In considering the activities reported, several perspectives could be adopted. One could be an attempt at looking at the subject coverage of the studies with a view to identifying, on one hand, areas and topics that have received a fairly high amount of interest among the researchers. Similarly, attention could be focused on trying to identify weak areas, subjects ignored or sparsely covered in the research being undertaken. Furthermore, researchers' interests and disciplinary emphases are changing. Which areas of investigation can be said to be in progress and which areas seem to be declining?

The papers are organized into six groups reflecting the variety of focus and research interests. This division also represents the structuring principle of the six parts of the book. Among the subjects, digital public libraries, of course, plays a significant role, focusing primarily on different Internet issues, including virtual reference services and digital community information services. However, new roles for libraries and librarians offered by the technological development are also addressed as pertinent research issues. This is not less true of the opening perspectives of creating closer links between traditional library functions and learning resources and processes. The article by Trine Schreiber actually considers networked study rooms and their role in creating and mediating knowledge in public library contexts. For obvious reasons, public library management in a world characterized by fast and discontinuous change has also become a key research interest shared especially by Danish and Norwegian researchers. Focus here is on leadership styles and qualifications of individual leaders and on development of leadership tools enabling public libraries to represent value and outcomes in socioeconomic terms. Migration and efforts to integrate ethnic minorities into society also influence the daily life of Nordic public libraries. It is therefore natural that a number of Danish LIS researchers have chosen to focus on multicultural public library issues. Library history studies are not a new item on the research agenda in the Nordic countries. However, there is a growing concern to reconsider the theoretical foundations of public libraries and a strong interest in public library history, not the least in Denmark. Innovative theoretical approaches to library historiography are increasingly adopted. Finally, professional identity is interesting in an age where environments, technologies and professional justifications are changing and being challenged. As mentioned above, a whole section is devoted to papers on the theory-practice interface: To what extent are LIS research relevant and useful to the practitioners and to what extent are the problems facing public libraries today actually addressed by LIS school researchers?

In a methodological perspective, empirical studies tend to maintain a share of the total amount of research undertaken in the field of public libraries. But public library researchers increasingly rely on alternative research approaches and new theoretical frameworks and philosophical perspectives find their way into current research projects in the field. An examination of the collection of research studies selected for presentation in the present volume supports the impression that the classic positivist perspective is losing ground; there are signs that the focus has shifted. Research designs seem to be more rigorous and reflect a greater degree of maturity and sophistication. A greater interest in mainstream, or universal, theoretical perspectives adapted from social science and humanities contexts is discernible throughout the range of investigations and analytical pieces presented here. Examples are hermeneutic approaches, social constructivist perspectives, discourse analysis in the sense of Michel Foucault, Pierre Bourdieu's sociological theory of culture and Etienne Wenger's learning theory. Clearly, there is an increased focus on qualitative studies and interpretative approaches and there is a growing interest in drawing upon analytical perspectives and theoretical constructs developed in other disciplines and domains. Cross-disciplinary inspiration is drawn from a variety of fields including anthropology, art history, cultural studies, philosophy, history and sociology. For instance, French and German philosophical viewpoints and perspectives have attracted the interest of some of the younger LIS research academics. One paper provides a critical examination of the "information paradigm" in mainstream library user studies and draws upon broader analytical perspectives in clarifying why people are coming to libraries and in determining the role played by the public library in everyday life. Theories and models adapted from economics are a rare thing in public library research. But the present book actually includes an example of this in that one of the authors presents a study that uses *contingent valuation* for a national-scale valuation of public libraries (Norway).

In reflecting on gaps in current research and development activities in the field, there seems to be a dearth of macro-level studies of public library developments and cross-country studies of public libraries (although a few stocktaking studies of this type funded by the European

Union have been published). Furthermore, there are rather few examples of scenarios and projects setting out to examine the role, identity and tasks of the public library in the knowledge society, dream society, postmodernist society or whatever labels you prefer. Also, there is a paucity of projects exploring library finance themes and issues in information economics and more needs to be done in the field of public libraries and lifelong learning. Moreover, some of the major challenges confronting public libraries in a society dominated by information and communication technologies lend themselves to research: Access to information, broadly, and maintenance of freedom of information and democracy in the age of dominating telecom monopolies, media conglomerates and data transmission companies provide an example. And another example: Reading in the digital society—is reading pressured by electronic media and could the public library play a role here?

Another perspective to be adopted in looking at the group of papers as a collective mirror of public library-related research undertakings in the five Nordic countries is the public library practitioner's view. One could ask: To what extent does the group of research papers presented here reflect the preferences and wishes for research as seen with the practicing professionals' eyes? Is there an overlap between the priorities set and interests articulated by the practical community and those of the academic community in the field? Are the priorities and interests of the two groups converging or is a gulf widening here? This again leads us to the relations between research and practice and the recurrent discussion of the theory versus practice dichotomy coming up in so many contexts all over the world. As editors, we have no ready-made answers at hand. Specially designed studies would be required to illuminate such issues, as there is an absence of up-to-date analysis of trends and developments in Nordic LIS research. In the same way, studies attempting to map existing needs for research in the public library field in the Nordic countries are lacking. Another interesting issue that needs clarification in this context would be the profession's view of the knowledge production in the field as well as the perceived relevance and usability of theoretical knowledge. Again, however, we have to rely on guesses and assumptions.

But overall, our impression is that although differing in some respects, the research interests of the public library community members—however blurred they may appear—and those of LIS faculty are not diverging fundamentally. There is a common ground between the two communities within the discipline, on which future discussions of research and joint approaches to the development of research agendas in the field should be based.

In the Danish public library sector, for instance, the role and functions of the existing county libraries have for some time been a major area of concern. Thus, plans for reducing the number of country libraries and establishing a few regional resource centers have been heavily discussed within the sector. Also, networking, regionally and nationally, the development of digital infrastructures for libraries at the national level and schemes for web-based access to national union catalogues are examples of issues and concerns that are attracting considerable attention in the public library sector. On the whole, there seems to be a marked collective focus on products and services, and now and then a slight sense of fascination is noticeable in the development and introduction of new systems and facilities. One could speculate if this products-and-services orientation capturing the mind of the professionals leaves less room for the *user* in the public library environment. Or put a bit differently, the profile of the average user appears more diffuse in these years. Thus, the public librarian's professional identity in the digital age and in times of organizational change with new tasks and challenges to be faced by library staff—issues that have been discussed especially in Norway and Sweden—prompts further analysis. The current phase of reorientation and challenges to be addressed is characterized by such factors as blurred demarcation lines between professionals and semiprofessionals and between public librarians and professionals from other disciplines finding their way into libraries, new management styles and tools, teamwork, and so forth.

Nordic Public Libraries, published by the Danish National Library Authority, features public library services in the Nordic countries and includes profiles of selected individual libraries in the five countries and three autonomous areas.[2] This overview and easy-to-read text continues a long and well-developed tradition of Nordic cooperation in the field of public libraries. Many LIS colleagues all over the world know about Scandinavia and the geographically, historically, socially and culturally closely related Nordic countries. Very often they think of our five countries as a unity. In many ways this is a reasonable view of our countries working together that closely in many areas, although the picture is a bit more complex. So, we have this tradition of networking, close cooperation, mutual inspiration and exchange of knowledge in the library field. Mirrored, not least, by the pages of *Scandinavian Public Library Quarterly*. But after all, you could ask, *is* there a joint Nordic understanding in the public library field? Does Nordic public librarianship—insofar as a concept like this can be said to exist—have a distinct profile or identity? This could be an interesting problem statement for a cross-country research study!

The NORDBOK seminar on public library research allowed practitioners and researchers the opportunity of exchanging views and ideas. Meetings and seminars serve as vehicles for communicating research findings to members of the profession and for discussions of the nature and profile of current research activities. However, the number of meetings gathering researchers as well as practitioners and addressing research issues or with focus on presentations of research projects has decreased over the years. In addition, today the voice of practicing professionals in public libraries and professional associations and interest groups is heard less often in matters of research. This is not to say that public library professionals are not interested in research or do not recognize the value of research in terms of informing professional practice. But previous discussion of ways of enhancing the interface between theory and practice has faded away. Also, debates on public libraries and public librarians as consumers of research produced in LIS academic settings are almost nonexistent. In recent years, faculty members in Nordic LIS schools engaging in research have oriented themselves more towards their own networks nationally and internationally. They are spending more time and energy on disseminating their research at conferences and other scholarly meetings and on writing papers for academic publication. And they are maintaining relations with academic peers. Correspondingly, less attention has been paid to interacting with the public library community. This development can be seen as a natural effect of the academization process, which has also affected Nordic LIS schools and the degree programs they are offering. But the risk is that research results, innovations, new theories and conceptual frameworks are spread mainly within closed academic networks. Moreover, researchers need to critically consider their role as communicators. One of the reasons for a mismatch between the research process and practice could be researchers' reliance on esoteric terminology, inside concepts and theoreticians not generally known by practicing professionals in presenting their projects and theories.

No doubt, this situation needs to be remedied. Efforts must be made to create formal settings for presentation of research and for feedback on research projects that involve practitioners as well as research academics. In addition to facilitating research communication, such meeting contexts should enable participants to share views on research proposals and ventilate ideas for research topics. In addition to improving communication of research by means of oral media, the existing system of written communication media, including such vehicles and publication outlets as journals, professional magazines, newsletters, books, reports, web presentations and mailing lists, should be carefully reviewed for the purpose of devising strategies for coordination and improvement. A Nordic collaborative effort in this area would seem obvious. In this context, a much welcomed Norwegian initiative aiming at bringing research and practice together should be noted. During Autumn 2002 a new research center for the study of library development issues was set up at the Faculty of Journalism, Library and Information Science at the Oslo University College. One of the stated objectives of the center is to bridge the gap between research and practice and generate research proposals of use to the profession and LIS practice. A few other initiatives at the national level could be mentioned as well. In Denmark, for instance, the Royal School of Library and Information Science has launched two series of late afternoon public lectures addressing current issues and challenges in specialized fields within the LIS discipline: the "Tuesday University" and the "Wednesday University." The target audience is practicing LIS professionals, and academic staff members and Ph.D. students at the school give the lectures. The Tuesday University considers perspectives on knowledge organization and information retrieval interaction, whereas the Wednesday University is concentrating on the research and practice interface in such areas as children's culture, collection development, cultural heritage and cultural policy.

The Copenhagen seminar provided an example of a practitioner's view of current public library research in that a Norwegian public library director, Ruth Ørnholt, was given the opportunity of summing up the seminar results and commenting on issues in research considered from the perspective of a large regional library system. She makes clear that those producing the research must think much more about the way they present their findings. Results should be made available in a form that makes them easier to grasp for public library practitioners. On the other hand, libraries must show a greater interest for what is going on in the world of research.

Sandra Parker summarized and commented on the seminar presentations from the researcher's perspective. In her review of the seminar she compares objects of research and current research interest in the United Kingdom and in the Nordic countries, reflecting, among other things, on the way they vary. In discussing salient features of Nordic public library research, she points to the strong focus on the public library's political context, public library roles and the concern with problem areas such as democracy and culture. An experienced researcher herself, Sandra Parker emphasizes the methodological implications of research and the need for developing and refining research methods.

Overall, it can be noted that there is positive climate for research in the Nordic LIS academic settings and a variety of research projects on public library issues are in progress in the Nordic countries. But on the minus side, current Nordic public library research seems to be fragmented across countries, institutional contexts and academic communities. Hence, networking, cross-country and cross-institutional approaches should be encouraged and stimulated actively. There seems to be a need for making research undertakings in the public library field more visible. Also, dissemination of information on current projects and communication of research findings to interested stakeholders and relevant target groups in other academic disciplines should be enhanced. In addition, there is a need for those in the Nordic countries pursuing research with a public library focus to present findings from their projects to LIS academic colleagues in other parts of the world and to share views and ideas with these peers. As seminar organizers and editors we consider the present book an important step in this direction and we hope that the published articles will make a substantial contribution towards these goals.

Notes

1 See, for instance, *Journal of Documentation* 56, no. 1 (January 2000): 1-90. This special issue contains a range of articles featuring selected areas of research at the Royal School of Library and Information Science. Areas highlighted in this context include information retrieval, knowledge management and paradigms and conceptual frameworks of information science.

2 Jens Thorhauge, ed., *Nordic Public Libraries: The Nordic Cultural Sphere and Its Public Libraries* (Copenhagen: The Danish National Library Authority, 2002).

Part I

DIGITAL PUBLIC LIBRARIES

Librarians' Experiences of Introducing the Internet in the Public Library: A Study in Southern California

Ulla Arvidsson

The human aspects of introducing the Internet in public library contexts and the effects on librarians' working environment are examined. The theoretical perspectives adopted in the study are twofold: organizational-institutional and social constructive. Findings from interviews conducted show that the librarians are seriously interested in making the Internet an effective tool for reference service and for the library visitors' own use. A shift in the attitude of the librarians was noted: At the beginning they were enthusiastic about the opportunities of the Internet but later on they reached a more balanced view of the potentials and problems of the Net. The study also points to the importance of allowing librarians time for Internet training and practice.

Introduction

Libraries are part of society and reflect changes that take place in society. During the last decade of the twentieth century, librarians have experienced technological change leading to reshaping of the library. Librarians have rapidly adapted to more complex technologies at the same time as they have experienced both physical and emotional stress. They have to reeducate themselves to become experts at digital information technologies. However, the same technology that facilitates global communication also challenges traditions and values of the people who use it, including librarians. Network users are confronted with problems of which the technical ones seem to be easier to solve than the human ones. A wide range of opinions and emotional experiences surrounded these issues. This turbulence of various emotions and ideas about the Internet constitutes the context within which my study was accomplished.

During the 1990s many librarians have found themselves being confronted with the issues dealing with the Internet in the library. In the United States, several studies have been performed of the Internet in public libraries. These quantitative studies by Bertot,[1] McClure,[2] and Zweizig[3] provide lots of data concerning the Internet. I will focus on the human aspects connected with the utilization of the Internet. There were two reasons for this consideration. There is, on one hand, the fact that very little has been done with respect to the human aspects associated with the Internet in public libraries, and on the other hand my own experience emanating from my professional background in librarianship.

Theoretical Perspective

In carrying out this research I decided to utilize two different theories. The first theory is an organizational and institutional theory, which is used when looking at what precedes and reasons for change. The second theory is one of sociology of knowledge. The social constructive perspective is used when dealing with change itself. The reason for basing my research on these two approaches is that my work deals with *both* development of change and how the participants experienced this change.

Methodological Perspective

When something totally new is introduced in an organization, innovation and initiation, according to March and Simon,[4] precede it. The introduction of the Internet is an example of that with regard to the public libraries in the beginning of the 1990s. March and Simon also suggest that conflict is a factor that may evoke change and in my study the conflict might be found between those librarians who are for and those who are against the Internet.

This study puts emphasis on how the Internet fits into the social world of the library, focusing on the librarians' experience of the Internet in their everyday working life. According to sociologists Berger and Luckmann, it might be possible to study the Internet as "a problem" that arises within social reality. Berger and Luckmann consider language to be a capacity of communicating meanings, which is also the way I look upon what the librarians' say in my interviews. Language not only communicates meaning and experience, it also makes it possible to preserve and transmit them.[5]

Problem Formulation

From the theoretical points of departure I formulated five questions for my study. However, in this paper I will only deal with the first question formulated as follows: How do librarians experience the introduction of the Internet in the library—in particular, as a new resource of information for reference service and as a component in the interaction with the patrons?

Choice of Method

During the last decades, qualitative methods have been used within library and information studies, in particular user studies. The users in my study are the librarians and the main focus is not on the information-seeking process, but on the changes and the experiences of them that the Internet brings about in the library.

Interviews constitute the main part of my material. The strength of interviews is, according to Kvale, that they catch many individuals' opinions of a subject and offer a picture of a multifaceted world.[6] The interviews deal with the individual's world and his or her relation to it and the purpose is to describe specific situations and actions, not general opinions. These less rigid descriptions are the strong points of qualitative research, according to Kvale.

The selection of participants in this kind of study is most commonly a goal-oriented selection where the participants provide the study with deep information about the subject. However, the disadvantage might be biased information.

Selection of Libraries and Librarians

The first step was to find libraries that already were connected to the Internet and furthermore I requested that they have been connected for at least one year. Ten libraries were selected. All librarians selected for this study had personal experience of the introduction in the library. The twenty-four librarians are, on one hand, the persons responsible for the computer departments in the libraries—"the computer gurus"—and on the other hand the librarians who actually utilize the Internet in the library. In other words, I have chosen persons who are knowledgeable about the Internet. I have made this selection intentionally and I am well aware that this fact may lead to an emphasis upon individuals with a positive attitude towards the Internet.

Analysis of the Librarians' Narratives

Introduction

In library and information science there has lately been an emphasis on user-centered studies, where the individual has been the basis for the analysis. However, although I will indeed study the individual's way to experience a phenomenon, I will identify categories from my research material and these categories are not directly tied to specific individual interviews. In performing this analysis, I will aim for a description of the categories of experiences of the phenomena that are studied. Marton states, "The description is a description of variation, a description on the collective level. In this sense individual voices are not heard."[7] Alvesson and Deetz[8] suggest three aspects concerning the language in interviews. First, language is depending on the context, which signifies that it might not have any meaning outside the circumstance in which it is produced (here the interviews). Second, they claim that language is used to cause effects. What interviewees say ought to be seen in the light of what kind of impression they want to make. Third, social norms and conventions have to be included in the interpretation. It is probable, still according to Alvesson and Deetz, that the interviewees (in this study) want to emphasize a general idea of the perfect, forward-thinking librarian. The human subjectivity of language has conse-quently to be taken into account. Sundin[9] observed that the nurses in his study, in conformity with the librarians in mine, often used "we" when asked about their own opinions and experiences. Sundin suggests, and I agree with him, that the interviewees base such responses on collective, professional norms and ideas. A librarian's identity is primarily, but not exclusively, the one of librarianship. Talja says, referring to Wetherell and Potter, that an individual has "different identities and subject posi-tions in different social contexts."[10] She maintains, to which Sundin also agrees, that as a consequence "each actor has different voices."[11] Irregularity and inconsistency do not necessarily mean that there is some kind of error in the empirical material.[12]

Categorization

My empirical material consists primarily of interviews. Language can be used for descriptions but also for understanding and interpreting. As language is not exclusively words, it is necessary to include the whole setting, the context.

From my own professional background together with the empirical material, I created four categories relative to which I studied the librarians' use of the Internet. When these categories were established I went to a deeper level, looking for variations and nuances in the librarians' opinions concerning a specific category. In that way, a number of properties were added under each category. The next step of the analysis was to create the aggregated categories, or, as I prefer to call them, dimensions. The dimensions reflect and include a wide range of very varying properties within a specific category.

In this paper I will limit my analysis to the first category only. The reason for this is the limited space allowed for this paper. This category's name is "Internet experiences," to which belong the properties: "introduction of the Internet as a community service," "ongoing training for librarians," "demands for patrons' classes," "librarians as technicians and policemen," and "changes in the library's collection." These properties constitute together the dimension *professionalism*.

The First Category and Its Properties

This category covers the Internet experiences based on the librarians' different backgrounds. They might have had positive or negative experiences of the Internet even before it found its way into the libraries. Some of the librarians already utilized the Internet at home and this circumstance influenced to some extent their attitude when they are applying their knowledge in the library.

Therefore emerged, not surprisingly, varying opinions regarding experiences of the Internet. Furthermore, the librarians sometimes presented different views during the first and the second series of interviews. Librarians now using the Internet in their library occupy a role-specific knowledge. This kind of knowledge is growing faster in today's society than general knowledge, according to Berger and Luckmann.[13] When labor is divided these researchers call it "appearing of sub universe of meanings." In the libraries new titles appear that mirror these new subuniverses. Librarians are called webmasters, electronic resource librarians, and information literacy librarians, among other things. It is possible to claim that there has been a shift in these librarians' professional identity. Even though the Internet now is available in the library, the utilization of it also depends on such human factors as the leadership's attitude towards digital information and if there is a mutually accepted service philosophy in the library. Cordell and Wootton suggest that the libraries' public services area has expanded enormously with the integration of the Internet as "the Internet is a new publishing format, communication tool, repository of information, and art form."[14]

Five properties belong to the category of Internet experiences and the first one regards the Internet as a community service. There were libraries/librarians that were willing to invest both budget money and labor to get the Internet introduced, as they strongly believed that the Internet was something good for their community.

Introduction of the Internet as a Community Service

A modernist point of view is that experiences, knowing, and feeling are important ingredients for change of human society. McCarthy points out that emotions are social objects that may both be objects of social action and encourage action (here, Internet introduction).[15] According to Himmelfarb, the Internet brings two revolutions into the library, an intellectual and a technological, which "have a symbiotic relationship to each other."[16]

At an early stage the librarians were divided into those who were enthusiastic about the Internet and those who were not very interested. We may place the enthusiastic librarians in Rogers and Shoemaker's category "early adopters" and the skeptical librarians in "the late majority."[17] The librarians in my study were individuals with a specific interest in and some knowledge of the Internet. They also had a general positive attitude towards the Internet. The librarians' personal interest was seen as essential for the continuing work with the introduction of the Internet in the library. To introduce the Internet is not exclusively about change of attitudes but also about money. Therefore, libraries that received grants did not have to struggle to force the Internet expenses into their already strained budget.

> I got access to it at home so I could start playing with it so it wouldn't be something I had to face for the first time at work.
> This (the Internet) has been a source of excitement and pride—a chance to do things in terms of expanding my own understanding and my ability to serve the public that I don't think I would have had otherwise.

It was important that there was enough time, good planning, and thorough preparations before the Internet was introduced as a reference resource. All these things facilitate the introductory phase. Support from the library director and/or the library board also helped to get the librarians started. One librarian mentioned a forward-thinking library director who actually encouraged new things. These findings are in accordance with what Klobas says about a director who wants changes in his library. He has to encourage his staff, have technical understanding but also understand human aspects. Managers also have to be sensitive to the individual's personal needs through the implementation stage.[18] My study also showed that it was of great importance that the staff felt that they had a certain degree of control in determining the future of their library.

> The library management team was aware of online development and they wanted a person at the forefront so they created the electronic services specialist.
> I feel very encouraged because he (the supervisor) has given me more time and he encourages the development and he encourages me to encourage the staff.

There were early adopters and late adopters of the Internet. Those who adopted the Internet at an early stage stated that there are always people who do not want to be involved in anything new that is going on in the library. The Internet-positive interviewees described their somewhat less enthusiastic colleagues in this way.

> There are always pockets of people who kind of resist any sort of change.
> I know one librarian who just doesn't care . . . she just isn't interested.

Some librarians were hesitant at first but realized with time and with increased experiences of the Internet how it could add to the library's supply of information allowing them to change their minds.

> Initially I was kind of reluctant . . . I would say I'm using it quite a bit more than I was in the beginning . . . quite a bit more than I thought I would use it.
> I wasn't quite sure that this is going to have a place in a public library . . . now it's always there in the back of my mind . . . it's part of my thinking.

Today people expect speed in all aspects of their lives including their use of the library. "The TV/Nintendo/fast-food generation expects more and wants it faster."[19] The visitors to the libraries seemed to show quite strong expectations and they often did not even ask *when* the library would provide the Internet but *where* the Internet station was located in the library. The librarians themselves wanted to be in the forefront regarding Internet support in the community. Some librarians expressed a strong will to utilize the Internet to change a common opinion about libraries as being static and old fashioned. March and Simon claim that upward mobility and salary increase might serve as motivation to work hard within an organization. These researchers then talk about individual compensation.[20] However, in my study, the librarians as a collective consider high status of their library as their compensation. McCarthy means that knowledge (cultural artefacts) that is produced by specialists, in this case computer-savvy librarians, might transmit value and judgments[21] and influence others.

> I think the fact that libraries have really jumped into this and offering this to the public kind of shows that we are not stuck back.
> It was a necessity to find the information to compete with other professionals in the field of being able to get information to the patrons.

With the introduction of the Internet a need for learning to use it becomes evident first by the librarians and later also by the library visitors. The following part deals with the librarians' various ways to learn how to utilize this new component in the library.

Ongoing Training for Librarians

The next property belonging to the introductory phase is "training." There was a big emphasis on both learning and training throughout the interviews. Formal external courses or instructors coming to the library giving classes are here grouped under "learning." Training means, in this case, scheduled time within the working day to practice the use of the Internet. Almost all the interviewees felt that it was important that all librarians should become familiar with this new skill. After the first opportunities of learning and training, additional training was still strongly desired. Courses gave the librarians self-assurance so they became more confident in using the Internet. The staff education decreased anxiety and increased comfort in general with technology. If we look at the Internet as an "appearing problem," in line with Berger and Luckmann,[22] we can here see that the librarians try to integrate it in the reality of their everyday life through learning to utilize it. The importance of offering *all* librarians in the library the opportunity to learn the Internet was pointed out. This step was an assurance of competence but also a morale builder and probably a cure for technostress. It also ensured that patrons had access to trained staff during all the library's opening hours.

> I've never had formal training and I feel that's a disadvantage.

> Yes, all of us have gone and they (the courses) have been exceptional so that has given us another good background . . . we have made it a concerned effort to bring all up to speed on it.

Even though this formal education seemed to be important, I noticed that hands-on training initially was the most important part of becoming an Internet user at the reference desk. There were various ways of offering "practice time" to the librarians. Some libraries scheduled time to practice the Internet within the working day. Others encouraged the staff to practice more freely: "The library encourages us to explore. We just scheduled ourselves basically for practice time."

Several librarians mentioned personal interest as a motivational factor to learn to use the Internet. They also wanted to learn it as they thought it was necessary for their work in the future.

> I learned it because I was interested and because I thought it a necessity for my work and because I think having the future sneak up on you from behind is probably not a real positive experience.

For others, it was of great importance that the public library remained an information provider that could compete with commercial institutions in offering fast and useful information. They stressed that information free of charge ought to be within reach for all citizens in the community for the sake of democracy. The librarians would neither like to be surpassed by other information "experts" nor by the teenage visitors in the library. Even though in all the surveyed libraries some kind of formal and a lot more of informal training was in progress, additional training was desired for them to be able to reach a certain level of skill and confidence.

> I'd like to attend more workshops and I'd like to benefit from other peoples' skills and techniques.

> I've noticed strong feelings for "Can we have more training so we can feel more comfortable?"

The following property deals with the education of the library patrons regarding utilization of the Internet.

Demands for Patrons' Classes

There were various ways to get the patrons started. However, first the librarians themselves wanted to be rather comfortable with the technical issues. Furthermore, they wanted to make searching, in one way or another, easy for the patrons.

> We are doing training sessions for the public . . . we set up a training center here at the library . . . we limited the sessions to a small num-

ber of people and each person actually gets a computer so it makes a big difference.

This hands-on training meant, of course, that fewer people were able to receive training but the staff at these libraries were of the opinion that it was more helpful and more useful for their patrons. Other libraries gave training to docents who then were expected to teach and help the patrons to use the Internet.

> We set up maybe six PCs—we have a docent program—and we train them in the technology so they can help the public.

Some libraries decided to utilize young people for this purpose. Students, called cyber-coaches, were able to come to the library and offer the patrons hands-on training. In return, the time the students spent in the library teaching counted as community service.

> We set up a program where people can work with the high school students for one hour and everybody has the sense that the kids know better than we do . . . it was a nice way to utilize that knowledge and they get in exchange community service awards . . . we felt it so important that it was hands-on.

There were also libraries that offered demonstrations for as many as 170 in an auditorium. Another solution was to make it compulsory for the patrons to take the course that their library offered before they even were allowed to sign up for and use the Internet.

> We require people to take a brief one-hour course and we mark their library card and they can come in and observe our rules and use the system.

Despite all these various efforts to train the library patrons there was still a lot to be done by the librarians at the reference desk. That seemed to be a rather difficult issue to deal with. The librarians felt torn between answering "real" reference questions from somebody and helping to introduce somebody to the Internet. They felt pressure from the patrons to help them get started. However, depending on the patrons' abilities and what they knew about computers in general, the librarian was not able to judge beforehand how much time it would take to get them started. Many librarians found that it was not an easy task to share the time in a fair and effective way. They tried hard to avoid letting the Internet become the main focus of attention.

Sometimes we have the luxury of flying over to the computer and show them a couple of quick steps so we help them if we can.

The librarians help if they can depending on time . . . we just don't have the staff to spend a lot of time.

It depends on how busy we are at the desk . . . we've got bookmarks arranged by subject so we'll show them how to get into a bookmark and how maybe to do a basic search on a search engine.

The next issue deals with new tasks for librarians. With the Internet in the library the librarians were expected to be able to solve technical problems and protect the computers from damage.

Librarians as Technicians and Policemen

Almost all librarians felt that there was a certain demand on them to act as technicians. Some expressed feelings of being degraded from librarian to technician. The large libraries often were able to request assistance from the community's technical support group. Some libraries had come together and established their own technical support group. These technicians had to move between the libraries, which often meant delayed help. To really make the Internet work, the librarians learned how to fix simple things themselves. However, they were simultaneously complaining about these new tasks for which they were not trained. They also believed that others than librarians should carry out the technical tasks. These situations, with random events of the new technology, often caused strong emotions among the librarians.

I believe that it dominates our time so much that we are not always able to spend as much time answering reference questions because we are so busy fixing printers . . . it just dominates our time.

The Internet has made us so busy with all this printing and the printers' malfunction . . . you know we've become technicians.

It's appropriate to answer questions how to navigate and find information but is it appropriate to answer technology questions?

I've become a technician and the use of my skills has lowered tremendously and I'm doing stuff that somebody with a high school education can do.

A few librarians experienced that they sometimes had to act as policemen concerning the Internet. There were two different reasons for that. First, young people sometimes liked to "fool" with the computers, which caused extra work for the librarians. Second, parents expected the librarians to protect children from looking at inappropriate sites on the Internet, something that the librarians strongly objected to and emphasized that it was the parents' responsibility to do that.

> I don't like the feeling like I have to be policing the behavior . . . trying to keep them from committing computer vandalism.

> The public expects us, the librarians, to police everything and that's one of our burdens . . . I feel strongly that's the parents' job to monitor what the children are looking at.

Changes of the Library's Collection

It was probably somewhat early, in 1997, to ask about the librarians' thinking regarding changes in the library collection at the libraries, although some expressed an interest in purchasing the online version of certain reference books. Sometimes, they said, the Internet version was easier to use than the printed version. However, the librarians believed that the patrons were not yet ready to read, for example, magazines on the Internet. One informant suggested that the telephone directories probably were the first to be "thrown out" from the shelves.

> We are having to take a look now carefully and reevaluate our collection and see if we would be better off using it on the Internet . . . it really makes librarians sit up and take a look at the future to see what is coming and to see how to allocate their funds to best serve the public.

> We are already looking into dropping some of our marginal subscriptions because people can get them full text (on the Internet).

Conclusion

Since the data presented above is only a small part of my study it is not possible to draw the final conclusions from that partial data set. However, I think it is possible to make some observations from this introductory phase. I found that there was a great interest among the librarians in my study to introduce the Internet in their libraries and to make it useful for the community members. The librarians revealed a strong confidence in the Internet as a good and useful resource of information for the public library. However, in later data the librarians also showed some hesitance and doubts. The librarians felt sure that the Internet was able to change the image of the library and make people see the library as a place where they might find current information in an efficient and effective way. The librarians believed that because of the Internet it would become natural for people to see them as knowledgeable information professionals. To accomplish the new tasks connected with the Internet, the librarians emphasized ongoing training both for themselves and for the patrons. Regarding changes of the library collection, the librarians showed a certain hesitance in replacing books with information from the Internet partly depending on the patrons' unreadiness for such a change and partly depending on feelings of uncertainty of the accuracy of the information coming from the Internet.

Notes

1 Charles R. McClure, John C. Bertot, and Douglas L. Zweizig, *Public Libraries and the Internet: Study Results, Policy Issues, and Recommendations. Final Report* (Washington, DC: National Commission on Libraries and Information Science, 1994).

2 John C. Bertot, Charles R. McClure, and Douglas L. Zweizig, *The 1996 National Survey of Public Libraries and the Internet: Progress and Issues. Final Report* (Washington, DC: National Commission on Libraries and Information Science, 1996).

3 John C. Bertot and Charles R. McClure, "Impacts of Public Access to the Internet through Pennsylvania Public Libraries," *Information Technology and Libraries* 16, no. 4 (December 1997): 151-64.

4 James G. March and Herbert A. Simon, *Organizations*, 2d ed. (Cambridge, MA: Blackwell Publishers, 1993).

5 Peter L. Berger and Thomas Luckmann, *The Social Construction of Reality: A Treatise in the Sociology of Knowledge* (London: The Penguin Press, 1996), 52.

6 Steinar Kvale, *Den kvalitativa forskningsintervju* (Lund: Studentlitteratur, 1997), 14.

7 Ference Marton, "Cognosco ergo sum: Reflections on Reflections," in *Reflections on Phenomenography: Toward a Methodology?* ed. Gloria Da'llAlba and Björn Hasselgren, Göteborg, Studies in Educational Sciences 109 (Göteborg: Acta Universitatis Gothoburgensis, 1996), 187.

8 Mats Alvesson and Stanley Deetz, *Kritisk samhällsvetenskaplig metod* (Lund: Studentlitteratur, 2000).

9 Olof Sundin, "Social Aspects of Professional Nurses' Information Seeking and Use: Initial Findings," in *Continuity, Culture, Competition: The Future of Library and Information Studies Education? Proceedings of the 4th British-Nordic Conference on Library and Information Studies 21-23 March 2001, Dublin, Ireland*, ed. Linda Ashcroft (Bradford: Emerald, 2002), 209-17.

10 Sanna Talja, "Constituting 'Information' and 'User' as Research Objects: A Theory of Knowledge Formation as an Alternative to the Information Man-Theory," in *Information Seeking in Context*, ed. Pertti Vakkari, Reijo Savolainen, and Brenda Dervin (London: Taylor Graham, 1997), 75.

11 Sanna Talja, "Analyzing Qualitative Interview Data: The Discourse Analytic Method," *Library and Information Science Research* 21, no. 4 (1999): 461.

12 Talja, "Analyzing Qualitative Interview Data: The Discourse Analytic Method," 465.

13 Berger and Luckman, *The Social Construction of Reality: A Treatise in the Sociology of Knowledge*, 95.

14 Rosanne M. Cordell and Nancy A. Wootton, "Institutional Policy Issues for Providing Public Internet Access," *Reference Services Review* 24, no. 1 (Spring 1996): 7.

15 E. Doyle McCarthy, *Knowledge as Culture: The New Sociology of Knowledge* (London: Routledge, 1996), 70.

16 Gertrude Himmelfarb, "Revolution in the Library," *Library Trends* 47, no. 4 (Spring 1999): 617.

17 Everett M. Rogers and Floyd F. Shoemaker, *Communications of Innovations: A Cross-Cultural Approach* (New York: The Free Press, 1971), 183-84.

18 Jane E. Klobas, "Managing Technological Change in Libraries and Information Services," *The Electronic Library* 8, no. 5 (October 1990): 346-47.

19 Carol Tenopir, "Taking Online Interaction for Granted," *Library Journal* 122, no. 20 (December 1997): 39.

20 March and Simon, *Organizations*, 2d ed., 82.

21 McCarthy, *Knowledge as Culture: The New Sociology of Knowledge*, 109.

22 Berger and Luckmann, *The Social Construction of Reality: A Treatise in the Sociology of Knowledge*, 38.

Web-Based Community Information Services in Public Libraries

Marianne Hummelshøj

This article examines public library web resources in Denmark, Norway and Sweden, with a focus on sites containing different kinds of community information. A typology of web-based community information services is developed based on the distinction between the user's context (everyday life and political participation) and communicative facilities (information, communication and transaction).

Introduction

Public libraries are important mediators of community information. For decades they are considered to be independent, neutral information providers or links between the authorities and the citizen in the Nordic countries. This influences, on one hand, which kind of information they should provide, and on the other, the facilitation or the accessibility of these resources. The question discussed in this paper is how libraries exploit their websites in the mediation of community information.

Research based on inquiries (Savolainen) shows that, regardless of the origin of the information, a great number of people turn either to their local authority or to another local institution to seek information or advice. Local access is regarded as easy access and is therefore crucial in everyday life information seeking.[1]

In relation to Savolainen's research, an investigation of the ways in which public libraries organize and offer community information services, in particular the web-based services, appears to be relevant. The focus of this paper is, first, to examine the present level of web-based community information services in public libraries, and second, to present a typology as a basis for development of such services.

A definition of community information is, however, needed for an evaluation, and for the development of a typology as well. Two different views of community information can be identified. The first focuses on the dimensions of community information to be included in a library service, whereas the second view relates to the purpose and therefore primarily to the use of community information.

An evaluation of the present practice concerning the presence of community information on library websites is carried out by means of a scheme and a checklist, a method, which has been applied to previous evaluation studies carried out by the author.[2]

The present evaluation of selected public libraries in Norway, Sweden and Denmark demonstrates the need for improving the web-based services to patrons, who are seeking information for solving their everyday life problems, or for concerning themselves with or getting involved in issues relating to their local community.

Knowledge about users' information-seeking behavior related to personal purposes, such as solving private problems, or related to information for active citizenship, is essential to development of a service. As mentioned above, Savolainen's research from 1995,[3] which is about users' information-seeking behavior in relation to *daily life*, shows that information seeking is important. His findings should therefore be taken into consideration in development of community information services from library websites.

To improve the present level of web-based community information services in public libraries, a typology explicating the different types of community services, which should be available to users, is presented. The idea of a typology for web-based services has its origin in a publication from the European Commission.[4] The basis of the typology is the discrimination between *information, communication* and *transaction* services, which has been valuable for evaluation and development of web-based reference services in general.[5] In the present study, two types of information resources are added to the typology in order to emphasize community information, namely *everyday life/survival information* and *political participation/citizens' action information* according to Leech.[6]

Community Information

Community information can be defined in different ways, depending on the view of information.

Pettigrew identifies three overlapping dimensions:

1. All information about a community that has been made to flow.
2. All information that has been made to flow within a community.
3. All information that is flowing anywhere which is useful to a community.[7]

This view considers the extent and volume of community information, which should be included and presented on library websites. The consequence is that the public library is committed to be aware of, to collect and to make available to their users all kinds of information, which are related to the community, whether it is information about the community produced within the community or information about the community generated elsewhere. Furthermore, we need to elucidate the question about the providers of community information. This is further investigated and discussed by Hummelshøj and Skovrup.[8] Their study of web-based regional information services demonstrated that only public library-controlled services were inclined to include information from voluntary organizations. They concluded that public libraries should emphasize this fact to become and to promote themselves as the most significant entry to web-based community information resources.

Leech provides a more user- and use-oriented view of community information, which is divided into two categories:

1. Survival information
2. Citizens' action information[9]

Survival information is defined as information necessary for a citizen to work on a problem; for example, looking for a solicitor or a place to go for advice. This category is comparable with the kind of information which Savolainen names *everyday life information*.[10]

Citizens' action information is defined as information that enables people to participate in local political and democratic processes. Leech emphasizes such information to be important to users. Therefore, it should be included in public libraries' community information services.

This view is related to the mediation of community information on web-based services and is incorporated in the typology (see table 5).

These two definitions of community information emerging from the studies of Pettigrew and Leech[11] are both incorporated in the check-lists used in the evaluation of public library websites as presented below.

Evaluation of Community Information Services in Public Libraries in Norway, Sweden and Denmark

As mentioned in the introduction, the purpose of this paper is to present a picture of the present level of community information services in Norwegian, Swedish and Danish public libraries. The purpose of preparing a comparative analysis of community information in Norway, Sweden and Denmark is to contribute to the exchange of experience within these three countries, which are similar as to culture and level of library services in general. The intention has also been to present an evaluation not confined to a single country representing isolated results. On the other hand, it has been the idea to draw the attention to common problems or pitfalls in the present level of public libraries' provision of web-based community information and to demonstrate how this could be improved.

Research Method

The aim of the evaluation is to investigate: first, how community information is presented; second, to what extent the web-based community information services include human support by providing value-added information resources, which imply that they are well-structured and annotated; third, to what extent interactivity is integrated; and finally, the ease of accessibility. The study of these issues is related to the general model of evaluating reference services presented by Hummelshøj and Nielsen.[12] The study was carried out in two steps. The first step was to provide a general view of available web-based services in the three countries. This was accomplished to secure an optimal selection of qualified libraries. The qualification criteria were: (1) the libraries must offer a web-based service, including a list, or lists of external services and (2) the libraries must represent the various geographic regions within each country.

The general view of libraries with their own websites in Denmark, Sweden and Norway showed the following picture:

Denmark

The Danish list[13] included 134 public libraries with own websites, which were examined, and lists of links were registered. Sixteen (12%) of these only give access to the library catalogue or include no links.

Sweden

Two hundred seventy-six Swedish public libraries[14] with own websites, which were examined like the Danish; 144 (52%) of these only provide access to the library catalogue or include no links.

Norway

The Norwegian list[15] included 158 public libraries with own websites, following the same method as in the other two countries. Sixty-one (39%) of these only give access to the library catalogue, or include no links. It should be noted that a great number of Norwegian public libraries do not yet have a website, at all.

The selected libraries' websites were examined according to the following characteristics:

1. Representation of community information
2. Value-adding
3. Interactivity
4. Accessibility

Based on the above main characteristics the following aspects were examined:

1. Representation of community information: Do the libraries include community information?
2. Value adding: Do the libraries add any kind of value (annotations or notes) to the presented links?
3. Interactivity: Do the libraries present any facility, which allows the user to submit questions?

4. Accessibility: Do the libraries present community information from the main page, or in any other logical context?

The study was carried out 26-31 March 2001 by means of three almost identical checklists. The results are presented by percentages and nominal values, separately for each country.

The Evaluation

The evaluation focuses on three levels of library services available. This division seemed to be obvious and appropriate based on the general impression of the present stage of development of the websites. The stage of development is closely related to allocation of resources. Economic and financial aspects, however, are not included in this study.

The first level focuses on the libraries' inclusion of community information *directories*, which means to what extent they include links to external directories containing community information. The point is that they may choose to include external directories instead of compiling lists of links themselves. The reason for choosing that solution could be to save resources.

The second level refers to lists of community information *resources*, which the libraries may have selected from external lists and added some value (e.g. classification and annotation), for presentation on their websites. This process is obviously more resource-consuming than the first level.

The third level is reserved for *special services* with mediation of sources that focus on the context in which the information is supposed to be used; this is the most resource-consuming job on the part of libraries in relation to the presentation of links on the websites. However, it is supposed to give the best applicability to the users.

The results from the examination of the forty-five libraries in the three countries are presented below with the number of libraries in parentheses after the percentages.

Table 1.
Level I: Community Information Directories

	Denmark	**Norway**	**Sweden**
National directories[16]	80.0% (12)	60.0% (9)	73.3% (11)
Special directories[17]	60.0% (9)	53.3% (8)	60.0% (9)
National library directories[18]	93.3% (14)	73.3% (11)	60.0% (9)
Regional library directories[19]	40.0% (6)	46.7% (7)	73.3% (11)
Local authorities' directories[20]	93.3% (14)	86.7% (13)	66.7% (10)
Local/regional commercial directories[21]	80.0% (12)	46.7% (7)	40.0% (6)

The community information directories represent lists of links, externally prepared, to be included on the websites free of charge. National directories with links to most institutions in the society are available in the three countries as seen in table 1. These directories are not, however, presented on all library websites. In addition to the national directories, a number of websites[22] are available with supplementary community information and may therefore be valuable to the users.

In Denmark, Norway and Sweden, a national directory with selected and value-added links, prepared jointly by the libraries, is available to any library, but a number of libraries neglect to include this type of directory. This is surprising. Small libraries with limited resources could provide an excellent service by linking to a well-prepared directory.

Most county libraries have prepared a regional directory with selected links on any kind of subject, including community information, but these are not included in all the libraries either.

Links to external information are either a supplement or an alternative to the information resources selected by the library itself. Considerations and decisions about the balance between links to external information directories and presentation of resources, which are selected and value added by the libraries' own staff, are important for the future development of the websites.

Table 2.
Level II: Community Information Resources

	Denmark	**Norway**	**Sweden**
National resources[23]	93.3%	93.3%	80.0%
	(14)	(14)	(12)
Regional/local resources[24]	93.3%	80.0%	60.0%
	(14)	(12)	(9)
Annotations			
Full annotation[25]	40.0%	0.0%	13.3%
	(6)	(0)	(2)
Partially annotated[26]	6.7%	6.7%	20.0%
	(1)	(1)	(3)
Notes[27]	20.0%	46.7%	26.7%
	(3)	(7)	(4)

Community information resources are links provided either at the national or local/regional level, compiled by the individual library and presented on a structured or unstructured list. It has been examined whether these lists include the most obvious government resource—for example, the Danish Parliament website.[28] The majority of libraries are inclined to do so. Some lists, however, consist of what seem to be randomly selected resources, which is not satisfactory. A list with few but carefully selected and annotated resources is more useful than a long list, which has no purpose.

The evaluation demonstrates that only few libraries do add proper annotations to the presented links. But some select a few links to be annotated or add short notes (normally one line or less) with brief information about the content.

Table 3.
Level III: Community Information Services

Denmark	**Norway**	**Sweden**
26.7% (4)	26.7% (4)	26.7% (4)

Community information services[29] are services with focus on a subject (e.g. the environment) with a number of selected links, normally from national and regional/local institutions as well. The definition of a community information service is a well-structured coherent presentation of (preferable) value-added resources about the environment, employment, social issues and so forth. These services are often promoted by a direct link from the main page. The definition of a service is, consequently, how much focus there is on specially selected and presented resources.

To prepare such services is obviously the most resource-consuming work. However, it is recommended that this amount of work is undertaken to benefit the future development of web-based community information services. The reason is that it facilitates users' information seeking by presenting the information resources in a comprehensible context, instead of lists of links, often without annotations, as it appears from table 2. Lack of annotations in these services, which is the standard, is compensated by the organization of the links and by drawing particular attention to the selection of links. They could be regarded as the first step towards a more personalized service.

Table 4.
Interactive Services

Denmark	Norway	Sweden
26.7% (4)	6.7% (1)	0.0% (0)

In this evaluation, interactivity is exclusively related to the page containing community information. The point is that users who require human advice in using the community links should be able to submit a question directly from that page without having to return to the main or any other page. It means that the normal facility for e-mail reference questions placed on some other page of the website is not included in the evaluation. The human service is perhaps the most unique service in the public library. This is the most obvious distinction between web-based commercial information services and web-based information services provided by public libraries. Therefore, this feature deserves to be accentuated.

Present Stage of Development

As it appears from table 4, the presentation of community information on public library websites in Denmark, Norway and Sweden seems to be at the same stage of development, which could be characterized as focus on *access* to web resources. This finding indicates that the libraries are predominantly focused on the *mediation of links* at the expense of providing proper *services* aimed at the users' information needs.

Services of that kind would include value adding, organization and promotion.

Public libraries *are* by a long tradition committed to provision of community information. The development of web-based community information services, however, demands new reflections about the availability and mediation of the information resources.

The findings of this study reveal the need for enhanced services. The improvements suggested are based on considerations and knowledge about potential users, emphasizing the need for reliance on human support. Furthermore, a typology of the services is presented focusing on the selection and organization of the resources to illustrate a more deliberate and proactive approach to the organization of services.

The Users

Development of comprehensible community services in public libraries should be based on research of users' information-seeking behavior. Local access to community information is, as shown by completed research studies analyzing inquiries, regarded as easy access.[30] Savolainen's research on citizens' "non-work" information seeking—as opposed to professional information seeking—presents some interesting results. He introduces two related concepts: First, *way of life*, which is defined as "the order of things which is meaningful or to which one has to adapt."[31]

The second concept, *mastery of life*, is defined as "a general preparedness to approach everyday problems in certain ways in accordance with one's values."[32]

The mastery of life may be either passive or active dependent on the social and cultural capital of the individual. Savolainen's study of two different groups—workers and teachers—revealed that (1) various information sources and channels were used in problem solving, (2) the selection and use of them was determined by such factors as availability and accessibility of the source or channel as well as by the ease of use and (3) that both groups preferred informal sources, primarily personal communication.

The concepts of *way of life* and *mastery of life* are close to Leech's two user-oriented key concepts: *survival information* and *citizens' action information*.[33]

Provision of *citizens' action information* is discussed in the report entitled *New Library: The People's Network* as well.[34] These types of information seem to be relevant to include in web-based community information services prepared by public libraries. The easy availability and accessibility of information sources is emphasized in Savolainen's study, and this is also stressed in two Danish publications[35] of which the latter is based on the results of a qualitative study. The focus of this publication is on the distinction between information poor and information strong groups in society. Maximum support to the users demands considerations about this discrimination in the development process.

Another point of view related to the design of websites is articulated by Julie Johnson, who did a survey of governmental websites and concluded that they needed much more planning and investigation on users' information needs and preparation of targeted services.[36] She also draws the attention to the way institutions present themselves on the websites, which is normally related to the institutions' own view or understanding of themselves instead of their users' expectation of the organization of available services.

The above-mentioned studies emphasize users' need for information to *solve problems* in their daily life and to appear as *active citizens* in a democratic society. These requirements should be supported by the development of web-based library community information services, which accentuate *accessibility, interactivity* and *presentation*. These ideas and views are underlying the proposed typology of community information services presented below.

EU Typology of Services on Public Websites

Furthermore, it is worthwhile to consider and draw upon another publication in developing a typology for web-based community information services. This publication is a European Commission document, which presents a typology for the development of web-based services in general and in public institutions in particular.[37]

The typology contains the following elements:

1.   Information services
2.   Communication services
3.   Transaction services

Information services are defined as "services aimed at retrieving sorted and classified information on demand (e.g. WWW sites)."[38] *Communication services* enable people "to interact with individuals (private or corporate) or groups of people (e.g. via e-mail or discussion forums)."[39] *Transaction services* facilitate people's access "to acquire products or services on-line or to submit data (e.g. government forms, voting)."[40]

This typology, which is suggested transferred to the public library sector, includes, however, no indication of any *value-adding* to these services. Nor has the publication an indication of mediation/facilitation or considerations about the users of these services.

The EU project LIBERATOR within the former Telematics Program[41] has furthermore emphasized the importance of offering one guide/service, which gives a structured access to community information resources made available by the public, private and voluntary sector. This is further discussed in Hummelshøj and Skovrup.[42]

Considerations from the mentioned studies and reports are included in the proposed typology presented below.

Typology of Community Information Services

A typology of community information services is finally presented to elucidate services proposed to be included on public libraries' websites. The three columns in table 5 distinguish *information*, *communication* and *transaction* services. The rows indicate the two types of information as presented by Leech.[43] Which information resources and which information providers (private, public or voluntary) should be included are discussed by Pettigrew, as mentioned above.[44] This is illustrated by (1) content (inclusion of links), from private, public and voluntary providers; (2) interactivity (communication and transaction); and (3) presentation of information in which the focus is on the intended use of information (survival information and citizens' action information). The model could as well be related to the concept of *networked study room* as presented by Schreiber.[45]

Table 5.
Typology of Services in a Community Information Service

	Information Services	Communication Services	Transaction Services
Everyday life (survival information)	Information resources on work, housing, education, health, culture, transport, environment, etc.	Discussion forums for questions of everyday life	Ticket reservation, course registration
		E-mail contacts with public / private and voluntary consultants	E-commerce
	Public/private and voluntary service directories		Electronic submission of forms
Political participation (citizens' action information)	Information resources from governmental institutions	Discussion forums for questions dedicated to political issues	Referenda
			Elections
	Political parties and pressure groups (local/ regional and national)	E-mail contact with politicians	Opinion polls, petitions

Conclusion and Future Perspectives

Development of community information services with maximum human support is crucial for users' access to and use of information in daily life situations and their political participation. Community information resources should be prioritized on library websites, as users have a right to expect their library to provide these resources. Public libraries should profit by their potential to provide web-based community information service. This important issue is further discussed by Audunson et al.[46] The evaluation, however, shows that a great number of libraries need to focus more on users' *use* of information and their need for *support* in terms of interactive facilities offered in a public library context. Development of more uniform library services is suggested to enable users to identify the quality and level of support, which should characterize a library website and facilitate the use of the services.

Savolainen's discussion about availability and accessibility should be emphasized. This points to the fact that knowledge about the users' information-seeking behavior and the social context is necessary for development of appropriate websites with community information as well as awareness of the kind of information needed by users as citizens in the information society.

The evaluation showed that the resources are often randomly selected and presented. The definition of and the criteria for selection of community information are therefore accentuated in order to improve the present library services.

The presented typology of community information service illustrates one way of organizing web-based community information with extensive interactivity facilities. These facilities provide human support to users who are not able to solve their daily life problems exclusively by consulting the community information services represented by the links given. Personal communication as a means for problem solving was emphasized by Savolainen as mentioned above.

The most easily available and accessible sources may, however, not necessarily solve the user's problem. Savolainen's research considered two groups of users with different qualifications for information seeking. It appears relevant to relate the difference between the two groups to the concept of *information literacy* or information competence, which is discussed in several governmental publications.[47] The concern is about the population's ability to adapt to information and communication technologies and the risk that the result will be a division in two unequal groups: one which is information literate and one which is not. The role of public libraries is, unfortunately, not in focus in these reports. The considerations are nevertheless essential to the development of any service in the public library and especially in relation to a core service like community information service.

Some libraries are, however, aware of this problem, and they are developing introduction programs dealing with information retrieval (cf. the studies reported by Arvidsson[48]), and the teaching of information skills including information retrieval has been introduced in many public schools. But obviously this is a long-term process.

More research is needed into these problems connected with the development of web-based library services as well as into the relevant educational aspects.

Notes

1 Reijo Savolainen, "Everyday Life Information Seeking: Approaching Information Seeking in the Context of 'Way of Life,'" *Library and Information Science Research* 17, no. 3 (Summer 1995): 259-94.

2 Marianne Hummelshøj and Bo Gerner Nielsen, "Folkebibliotekernes referenceservices på Internet ved starten af det nye årtusinde," *Biblioteksarbejde* 20, no. 58 (2000): 45-53.

3 Savolainen, "Everyday Life Information Seeking: Approaching Information Seeking in the Context of 'Way of Life,'" 259-94.

4 European Commission, *Public Sector Information: A Key Resource for Europe. Green Paper on Public Sector Information in the Information Society.* COM (1998) 585 final (Brussels: Commision of the European Communities, 1999).

5 Hummelshøj and Gerner Nielsen, "Folkebibliotekernes referenceservices på Internet ved starten af det nye årtusinde," 45-53.

6 Helen Leech, "Better Communities through Better Information," in *Project CIRCE and Community Information. Building Community Networks: Strategies and Experiences*, ed. Sheila Pantry (London: Library Association Publishing, 1999), 39-48.

7 Karen E. Pettigrew and Margaret Ann Wilkenson, "Control of Community information: An Analysis of Roles," *Library Quarterly* 66, no. 4 (October 1996): 373-407.

8 Marianne Hummelshøj and Nanna Skovrup, "Citizens and Mediation of Community Information in the Information Society" (paper presented at the Colloquium: Which Public Administration in the Information Society? University of Liege, Brussels, 18-19 May 2000).

9 See Leech, "Better Communities through Better Information," 39-48.

10 See Savolainen, "Everyday Life Information Seeking: Approaching Information Seeking in the Context of 'Way of Life,'" 259-94.

11 See Leech, "Better Communities through Better Information," 39-48.

12 See Hummelshøj and Gerner Nielsen, "Folkebibliotekernes referenceservices på Internet ved starten af det nye årtusinde," 45-53.

13 The Danish public libraries are available at http://www.bs.dk/index .ihtml (3 February 2003).

14 The Swedish public libraries are available at http://www.inetmedia.nu/ bibliotek/ (3 February 2003).

15 The Norwegian public libraries are available at http://www.bibsent.no/ biblioteknett/fylkesbibliotek.htm (3 February 2003).

16 www.danmark.dk (3 February 2003); www.norge.no (3 February 2003); www.sverigedirect.riksdagen.se (3 February 2003).

17 For instance www.netborger.dk (3 February 2003).

18 www.fng.dk (3 February 2003); www.bibliotek.kulturnett.no (3 February 2003); www.svesok.kb.se (3 February 2003).

19 Directories prepared by regional or county libraries, e.g. http://www .molndal.se/bibl/subject.htm (3 February 2003); http://www.trondheim.folke-bibl.no/nettet/nyttig.html (3 February 2003).

20 For example www.frederiksberg.dk (3 February 2003).

21 The commercial directories include links to tourism, authorities and businesses, e.g. http://viborg.bynet.dk (3 February 2003).

22 E.g. www.netborger.dk (3 February 2003).

23 www.folketinget.dk (3 February 2003); www.stortinget.no (3 February 2003); www.riksdagen.se (3 February 2003).

24 Normally few.

25 Information about content, an evaluation, and an instruction for use of the resource.

26 Some of the resources are presented with annotations.

27 A note is defined here as a few words about the content.

28 www.folketinget.dk (3 February 2003).

29 Subjects included in these services are, among other things, consumer services, environment and education.

30 See Savolainen, "Everyday Life Information Seeking: Approaching Information Seeking in the Context of 'Way of Life,'" 259-94.

31 Savolainen, "Everyday Life Information Seeking: Approaching Information Seeking in the Context of 'Way of Life,'" 263.

32 Savolainen, "Everyday Life Information Seeking: Approaching Information Seeking in the Context of 'Way of Life,'" 264.

33 See Leech, "Better Communities through Better Information," 39-48.

34 http://www.ukoln.ac.uk/services/lic/newlibrary/

35 Indenrigsministeriet og Kommunernes Landsforening, *Kommunerne som borgernes indgang til det offentlige Danmark: Undersøgelse af kommunernes vejviserfunktioner* (Copenhagen: Indenrigsministeriet, 1999) and Statens Information, "Kvalitativ undersøgelse vedr. offentlig information" Job nr. 13863 by Frede Jørgensen, 1997, http://www.si.dk/service/rapport/index. html (3 February 2003).

36 Julie Johnson, "Government Web Pages: The Lights Are on but Nobody Is Home," *The Electronic Library* 14, no. 2 (1996): 156.

37 See European Commission, *Public Sector Information: A Key Resource for Europe.*

38 European Commission, *Public Sector Information: A Key Resource for Europe*, 8.

39 European Commission, *Public Sector Information: A Key Resource for Europe*, 8.

40 European Commission, *Public Sector Information: A Key Resource for Europe*, 8.

41 http://thenortheast.com/liberator/index.htm (3 February 2003).

42 See Hummelshøj and Skovrup, "Citizens and Mediation of Community Information in the Information Society."

43 See Leech, "Better Communities through Better Information," 39-48.

44 See Leech, "Better Communities through Better Information," 39-48.

45 Schreiber, Trine, "The Public Library, Networked Information Resources and the Concept of Learning Center." Included as a chapter in the present book.

46 Ragnar Audunson, "Information Literacy, Public Libraries and Local Community Engagement: A European Project on the Potential of Public Libraries as Promoters of Local Participation and Viable Local Communities in Metropolitan Areas," (paper presented at the Nordic Seminar on Public Library Research, Royal School of Library and Information Science Research, Copenhagen, December 2001).

47 See, among other things, *Det Digitale Danmark: Omstilling til netværkssamfundet* (Copenhagen: Forskningsministeriet, 1999), Bilag. www.fsk.dk/cgi-bin/doc-show.cgi?doc_id=19127&leftmenu=PUBLIKATIONER (8 August 2002).

48 Ulla Arvidsson, "Librarians' Experiences of Introducing the Internet in the Public Library: A Study in Southern California." Included as a chapter in the present book.

A Poem Lovely as a Tree?
Virtual Reference Questions in
Norwegian Public Libraries

Tord Høivik

Digitization is challenging traditional reference service practices while at the same time providing new possibilities such as Virtual Reference Desks (VRDs). An empirical study was conducted of the main Norwegian VRD: Ask the Library (ATL) hosted by Oslo Public Library. The study was based on a representative sample of typical queries. One of the findings was that responses to literary questions were more factually authoritative than answers to science questions. It is advised that public libraries seek closer collaboration with scientific communities and their reference portals.

Technology and Organization

Digital Reference Work

Most reference questions are asked by users who visit the library and meet the staff in person. But libraries are normally willing to answer questions that arrive by telephone, mail or fax as well. E-mail represents an additional channel. A virtual reference desk is, from this point of view, simply a formal acceptance of the electronic possibility: the library announces its willingness to receive and respond to queries by electronic mail.

Reference librarians have often dreamed about storing questions and answers so that they could build on past experience. The obstacle is always time. Writing down queries, search strategies and responses as they occur can easily double the time needed to carry out a particular reference transaction. Our knowledge about the core of reference work—the actual content and flow of questions and answers—is therefore quite limited. This is particularly true in public libraries, with their heavy traffic and their exceptional variety of questions. Some sample studies and ad hoc surveys are carried out as a basis for library statistics and annual reports. A certain amount of research has also been done, mainly on reference quality. But as soon as e-mail comes into play, the trickle of empirical data is transformed into a torrent. E-mail systems store the transactions automatically. Oral messages become digital files. Setting up a retrieval system is a massive operation in the world of writing, but a manageable task in the world of bits. Introducing e-mail is a small step for a single library—but a big stride for the social institution. Data imply rather more than an improvement of existing services. ICT creates a platform for new services and new institutions. At the same time, existing services are threatened. Digital technologies are revolutionary in their impact. Put your ear to the ground and hear the continents rumble . . .

Fifty years ago, the card catalogue was the core technology of the library world. The transition to digital typesetting created bibliographic databases as a spin-off. Then library catalogues were automated. Today, a card catalogue is a relict. Soon they will be museum exhibits—curious artifacts from the era of print.

Traditional reference work consists of a series of bilateral consultations. The customer presents a query, which the librarian—sometimes—will clarify through an interview. The librarian, or both together, explore search tools and reference sources. The customer leaves with a specific answer or a selection of relevant materials.

Traditional reference work is opaque. Transactions are invisible to other librarians and other clients. In such closed bilateral settings, quality depends on the training and the commitment of the individual librarian. They must internalize the standards in order to sustain them. In traditional libraries, systematic teamwork was rare. But the new technology literally invites teamwork. In open digital workspaces, quality is reinforced through advice, feedback and a flexible division of labor. Our cubicles turn into open landscapes. The ecology of reference work is transformed. The combination of e-mail, databases and hypertext facilitates *distributed* services. A web-based *Virtual Reference Desk* (VRD) may accept questions from anywhere in Norway or from anywhere in the world. The workload may be distributed among different partners in different localities. Partners might choose different levels of commitment. Answers may be published on the web. A comment function can easily be added, giving readers and other librarians the opportunity to supplement or correct the information provided.

In Denmark, Sweden, Finland and Great Britain, the national VRDs are run as public library networks. The main Norwegian service—*Spør biblioteket* (Ask the Library [ATL])—is operated by the Oslo Public Library, but is promoted and financed as a national service. ATL was an early initiative; operations started in October 1997. The service offers *help with factual questions, references to relevant sources and assistance in finding web resources.*

Oslo is somewhat overrepresented: 20 percent of the questions come from the Norwegian capital, which has 10 percent of the national population. But with four-fifths of the queries coming from the rest of the country, ATL is definitely a national service. The transaction volume is around 4,000 questions a year—about the same volume as that handled by the Swedish and the British (!) services. Questions and answers are available in a web archive.

ATL is not the only VRD in Norway. By spring 2002, fifteen public libraries had established virtual reference desks. But this is a small number in a country where every single municipality (400+) has its own separate public library system. And in most cases only the first step had been taken. The fifteen libraries accept questions and provide answers, but do not offer open archives.

In addition, about thirty other institutions offered specialized reference services like *Ask a Geologist* maintained by the Norwegian Geological Survey; *Ask the Photographer*, from *Dagbladet*, a major newspaper; and *Ask Dr. Chlorophyll*, which is operated by the website House, Home & Garden. But such AskA services are much more developed in Sweden and in Denmark.

The More We Know, the More We Ask

In a highly specialized world information must be sought in bits and pieces. Every organization or enterprise, small or big, public or private, receives questions within its own field of activities. We expect carpenters to know about roof beams and butchers to know about beef. All collective actors—firms, voluntary organizations and public institutions—must be prepared to answer questions about their own products, services and fields of expertise. Large Norwegian companies, such as *Statkraft, Norsk Hydro* and *Storebrand,* have their own information divisions. The division of knowledge in society mirrors that of labor.

Providing information is an essential part of the job for most voluntary organizations. When the desire to inform, or the demand for answers, is strong, specialized agencies are set up—like the national *Government Information Service,* the *Norwegian Church Information Service, Facts about Bread, Tine Kitchen* (on dairy products) and *Heat-*

ingInfo, the information office for flexible indoor heating. Norway is a cold country. Libraries aimed at particular user groups—academic libraries, school libraries, special libraries and the National Library—also provide reference services. But they only admit relevant questions. The Norwegian National Library will only accept questions on Norway and Norwegian culture. A school library should be able to explain why the sea is salt. But you should probably go to a medical library if you want to know why your *blood* is salt.

Public libraries offer general rather than specialized reference services. ATL refuses to summarize books or to write project papers. They discourage competitions and crossword puzzles. But this does not restrict the range of questions they accept, only the fullness of the answers. If the library should offer what pupils and students really want—ready-made papers with guaranteed A grades—learning through doing would lose its meaning.

It is the lack of specialization that makes public libraries special. Their reference services are freely available to the population at large. The social contract between librarians and their customers is phrased like an open invitation. People may ask about any topic and need not give reasons why librarians should spend time and energy finding the answer. Librarians are trained to take all questions seriously, from the most trivial fact to the most resistant stumper.

The true mailman will invest hours on inscrutable Christmas cards. The true librarian will pursue a really hard question for days and weeks. Utility be damned. In these professional cultures, successful identification of trivial facts is seen as a heroic feat. Persistence shall prevail.

Economy of Time and Reuse of Data

This does not imply that all questions are answered or that all answers are satisfactory. Surveys in many countries have shown that reference quality in libraries is rather low. Researchers speak about *the 55 percent rule*: only fifty-five out of every hundred questions will receive fully adequate answers. But these surveys have focused on factual questions. Recent work[1] shows better results when the normal mix of questions is studied.

But ATL is still exceptional. More than 95 percent of all questions are answered. The quality of the answers is generally high, and the response is fast. Twenty-four hour service is the norm; customers normally receive an answer within the next working day.

High reference quality in physical libraries requires good access to reference resources, effective organization of the reference service, competent reference interviewing and time to cope with the workload.

Resources, organization and time are needed in the virtual world as well.

Time is essential. A small ad hoc survey in Oslo indicates that the average ATL question takes about forty minutes to answer. The true time cost is higher—maybe one hour—since the staff also needs overhead time: to maintain the database system, attend meetings, take care of office routines, and so forth. From an economic point of view we must also include general overhead: buildings, utilities, supplies, support staff. This implies an average cost of at least sixty euro, or dollars, per answer. I am therefore a bit worried by the new Google service (April 2002). At *Google Answers*,[2] which is a networked VRD with paid volunteers, the typical cost per answer is less than ten dollars. The virtual desk provides better service than reference face-to-face. The librarians at the public desks in the physical library cannot spend forty minutes on each patron. At the desks, the constant pressure for assistance reduces the time per patron with "serious" reference questions to about ten minutes, on the average.[3]

All reference desks could provide better services if more users were more self-reliant. Virtual reference desks try to *help the users help themselves* in two main ways: by guiding them towards independent use of web-based resources and by providing searchable databases of previous questions and answers. In Oslo, these components are still rudimentary. ATL invites customers to search for books in the library catalogue on the web. But the interface is somewhat forbidding and the help menu rather technical. Users are also asked to search in the question-and-answer database before they e-mail their queries; however, the archive is poorly developed in Norway as in most other countries. The transactions have not been thoroughly edited and indexed. Misprints are frequent. The Norwegian language creates additional obstacles to string-based retrieval. The language comes in two official flavors and has a liberal attitude to orthography.

Librarians will manage. But reference archives will only be useful to the average user if the materials are edited and organized for reuse. The American service *Ask Dr. Math* is a good example of effective reuse. Questions are graded by education level and organized by mathematical subfield (algebra, geometry, calculus, etc.). Such knowledge processing is easier within well-defined and highly structured disciplines like astronomy, mathematics, medicine and law. A similar thematic arrangement of the ordinary questions and answers that arise in daily life is far more demanding, and raises difficult issues in the areas of language processing and artificial intelligence.

The Queries: What Do People Ask?

One Hundred Norwegian Questions

Nearly six thousand reference transactions had been registered in the SBI database by mid-autumn 2001. All questions are classified by Dewey (first level). Eighty percent of the questions fall within one of five "large" Dewey groups (see table). These five each catch more than 10 percent of the questions. The five "small" Dewey groups contain 5 percent or less.

Questions to *Spør biblioteket* in 2000, by Dewey Group

Five "large" Dewey groups	Five "small" Dewey groups
24% questions about literature (800 group); 18% about history & geography (900); 15% about social sciences (300); 13% about technology (600); 12% about arts & recreation (700)	5.0% about computers, information & general reference; 4.6% about science (500); 4.5% about language (400); 3.2% about religion (200); 2.6% about philosophy & psychology (100)

One hundred reference questions were selected. The sample was stratified by Dewey groups: twenty-four questions about literature, eighteen questions about history and geography, and so on. The most recent entries available on 8 September 2001 were chosen.

By *reference* we mean queries that engage the professional compe-tence of the librarian as such. British studies of ordinary reference desks show that many questions (30-40%) are practical or administra-tive in nature: *When do you close? How should I fill in this form? Where is the Britannica?*[4] Such requests are rare, but not totally absent, in the virtual case. They are excluded from our sample.

England and Sumsion also report that librarians diverge widely in their conception of reference work. Some would include giving direc-tions and "fetching and carrying" from closed access stacks.[5] For em-pirical and comparative studies we need comparable data. "The Interna-tional Standard for Library Statistics dodges the issue."[6] A Swedish study found that only 10 percent of the work at the reference desk re-quired specific professional skills.[7]

Fortunately, most of the virtual requests are bona fide reference questions. They do require the professional expertise of librarians. The borderline cases are much more frequent in the physical setting.

Our counting unit is the question, not the transaction as a whole. Some queries include several questions. If they address the same topic, they are counted as one question, however phrased. The following is taken as one question: *Has* "Kristin Lavransdatter" [Sigrid Undset's novel] *been translated into Arabic? Which languages have translations?* But the next counts as two: *I have four questions, two on garlic and two on consumer rights.*

Classifying Reference Questions

Reference is communication. The customer questions the librarian and the librarian queries the system. Our empirical data consist of the transactions between librarians and customers. Each question is a message from a client to the library and each answer is a message from the library to a client. The transaction chain is minimal: one question and one answer.

In communication studies, messages may be classified and analyzed in many different ways. VRDs are friendly, chatty and relatively informal. Entry barriers are low. Our questions reveal much about ordinary life and people at large. A social historian would find rich materials on needs and expectations, interests and problems, topics and trends in the Norwegian population.

Here we focus on practical management. All general reference services need mechanisms for sorting and allocating queries. Like patients entering a hospital, questions must be distributed on departments and specialists.

We distinguish three broad categories:

1. *Topical questions:* Users request information about a subject, theme or topic.
2. *Factual questions:* Users request factual answers to concrete and specific questions.
3. *Document questions:* Users require factual information about specific documents, usually in order to retrieve the documents.

The boundaries are, of course, approximate. *Who was governor in Bergen in 1616?* is clearly a factual question. But those who wonder *why the sea is salt* may need an explanation of *how* water moves between skies, land and ocean. The factual answer requires a topical context.

Questions about specific works are frequent. We include all questions that refer to a particular work or text, in the category *document search.* By works we also mean individual articles, poems, quotes, songs, musical compositions, pictures, films, and so on.

Among the one hundred questions, the distribution was as follows: Topical questions constituted about one-half of the transactions whereas document questions constituted about one-third. Factual questions constituted about one-sixth. A study of one hundred reference questions at Oslo Public Library five years ago, before the virtual service opened, gave roughly the same results: topical searches, 56 percent; document searches, 27 percent; factual searches, 17 percent.[8] But we know from British studies that the relative proportions of categories may vary quite a bit between libraries.[9]

Topical Questions: Subdivisions

Norway is a fractured country. Mountains and valleys, lakes and islands, fiords and forests cut across the landscape. Public administration is equally divided. The country contains 435 municipalities, each with its own autonomous library system. Most are tiny. Only a hundred systems serve more than ten thousand inhabitants. Our public libraries have strong local roots. Each system must build its own local collection and be prepared to answer questions about local history, society and culture. Questions that deal with typically local topics, or *local searches*, form a meaningful subcategory. Seen from the outside, such queries look highly specialized. But the public library system is well prepared to respond through its fine-grained municipal network.

Public libraries could also be described as literary institutions. Their primary user groups are children and readers of fiction. Their general mission is to *promote enlightenment, education and other cultural activities*.[10] But the activities tend to be literary and artistic rather than political, social or scientific. Parliament has given libraries a central role in promoting Norwegian fiction.

Library education attracts book lovers (80% female students) rather than knowledge managers (either gender). The curriculum of the library school in Oslo, which had a monopoly of training till a few years ago, still encourages a humanistic approach to library and information science. This means that *literary searches*, or questions that deal with literary subjects, also form a meaningful subcategory. Librarians bring a particular expertise to literary topics. They are literate in the field of literature and attack questions about forgotten Norwegian poets with alacrity.

The remaining topical queries can be roughly divided into a broad and a narrow segment. *Broad queries* address topics that are elementary and widely known: *communism* and *witches, calligraphy* and *the late sixties*. An educated person will be aware of the issues. They belong to the common culture of our time. Relevant information is easily available. We can draw on a rich supply of encyclopedias, textbooks, mass-market handbooks and, increasingly, authoritative websites.

Narrow queries deal with topics that are of interest to a few: *the medical use of saffron*; *the programming language SIMULA*; *the color theories of Wittgenstein*. The questions could, in principle, cover the whole range of knowledge. But ATL is a general-purpose service for the general public. We would be surprised to find questions about *the toxicity of spirocyclic piperidines* or *the literary influence of Aulus Gellius in the Renaissance*. Scholars who care about such issues have better ways of finding out. Among the fifty topical questions, the overall distribution was as follows: broad queries, 44 percent; narrow queries, 28 precent; literary queries, 16 percent; local queries, 12 percent.

Factual Questions

Most of our factual questions are rather simple. The service is not oriented towards advanced questions of a technical nature, except for advanced questions in the bibliographic field. The latter we classify as document queries. The eighteen factual questions in our material come from four main areas: words and expressions (one-third), scientific, technical and medical (one-third), society and public affairs (four questions) and history.[11] The user's problem comes from the diversity of sources rather than from the difficulty of the question. For several hundred years, almanacs took care of broad information needs. General encyclopedias also serve the FAQ market—the questions people frequently ask. For a long time, Norwegians have been inveterate buyers of encyclopedias.

Households will stock up on their special fields of interest. Some play chess, and some plant roses. Some tinker with cars, while others go skiing. Every subject has its handbooks. But modern families cannot cope with the surprises—the unexpected rarely asked questions that emerge from time to time. It requires a substantial collection of handbooks, as well as expertise in their use, to respond to the full range of questions in the twenty-first century. In other words, a well-stocked library with a competent staff.

The web is beginning to make a difference. Authoritative websites, including web-based encyclopedias, are already powerful reference tools. But physical access is not the same as intellectual access. We know that many library users feel lost in the physical reference collection. They are surrounded by information but starved for answers. Factual searches on the web are both easier and more difficult than consulting reference books. Easier because we have global indexes (Google, AltaVista). More difficult because we must do the quality control ourselves.

The future, we believe, lies with more editing rather than more re-trieval on the web. The general public does not need universal access. The universe of relevant public knowledge is much, much smaller than the totality of recorded knowledge. This limited space, which we may call *the relevant web*, can to a reasonable degree be surveyed. And here public libraries can play an important role as surveyors, editors and organizers.

We do need more self-reliant users. The future belongs to refer-ence sites that combine web resources and e-mail: on one hand, well-designed portals, guides and help functions for independent searching; on the other, personal reference services based on e-mail and chatting. But the supply of portals ought to respond to a real demand. To create efficient portals to the relevant web, the library world needs to classify, count and study the questions that members of local communities actu-ally ask.

Ellen-Merete Duvold[12] makes a vital point when she defines the li-brary in terms of knowledge rather than of information. Reference work has a superficial and a deep variant. In superficial reference, we provide facts and documents on demand. In deep reference, the library gets involved in the *processes* of learning, problem solving, reflection, pro-duction and delight.

Document Questions

Document queries are factual questions that concern the formal or external properties of documents rather than their actual content. To be answered, document questions require the core competences of librari-ans and the core technology of library systems. Document retrieval is still dominated by single-media systems: one database for books, an-other for articles, a third for audiograms, a fourth for websites. The student of Kant must work with four different interfaces in order to locate monographs, essays, portraits, and maps of Kønigsberg.

Users want a much more integrated approach. With time, web technology will provide it. But the process is complex and slow. It takes decades rather than years. In the meantime, reference work must go on. Retrieval systems will improve, and many users will be better trained in their use. But personal assistance will be needed for a long, long time. The document universe is too large, too varied and too dy-namic for most users. They may learn to tackle the merely difficult questions by themselves, but for those impossible questions they will still need reference experts.

It is hardly surprising that 75 percent of the document searches concern printed media. The balance between fiction and nonfiction was approximately three to two. The document queries are factual questions that relate to specific documents. Compared with other factual questions, they tend to be quite difficult. Three examples:

> Hi! I'm looking for a 78-recording of the song "Mona" with Sven-Olof Sandberg. It was published by Parlophon in 1931 with serial no. B41807.

> I am looking for a book for young people that appeared thirty-forty years ago. It concerns a young boy who was searching for his father. I think the title was "David."

> Could you tell me who wrote the following poem, and when? "I think that I shall never see / A poem lovely as a tree . . . / Poems are made by fools like me, / But only God can make a tree."

The poem—Joyce Kilmer's *Trees*—has been translated and the quote was given in Norwegian. Only the patient development of vast catalogues over many years makes it possible to answer such questions successfully. The web does, however, open several new possibilities. Web indexes like Google and AltaVista are exceptionally effective in tracing obscure quotes. Through its website, the Norwegian Central Bureau of Statistics provides excellent access to Norwegian statistics. The extremely detailed and thoroughly cross-indexed *International Movie Data Base* makes it possible to identify old feature films from the slightest snip of information.

The Customers: Who Are They?

Work, Learning and Leisure

We participate in complex, postindustrial knowledge societies. Our questions and queries come from a variety of social situations and reflect their origin. In the project we make a distinction between three types of situations: (1) questions that emerge from working life (private or public), (2) from situations of formal learning or study (schools, colleges, universities) and (3) from the informal sphere (family, leisure, voluntary activities).

At work we are obliged to produce. Our activities are directed towards visible results. Work is shaped by necessity and those who pay have a right to demand. Questions from work life are questions that reflect the demands of production. They are asked in the hope of solving practical problems. Answers contribute to the productive process: "I work at the Department of Social Anthropology in Trondheim, where I show documentaries. Is it possible to borrow films from your institution?"

In formal learning situations we are also obliged to produce and deliver. But the work is unpaid and the products are not sold. By working on assignments, pupils and students are supposed to develop their own knowledge, skills and attitudes. Gainful employment comes later. Learning generates a different type of query: "May I get information on France, e.g. on music, geography, culture, food, wine, architecture, history, books, theater, film, wine districts, famous persons?"

At leisure we follow our own inclinations. We also face our individual problems. Leisure questions are much more varied and much less predictable than those which stem from work or school life.

ATL does not ask the user to supply a context. Still, most of them do. The content and phrasing of the question are also revealing. Most of the queries can, at least tentatively, be located within one of the three contexts. In my sample:

1. Only a handful of questions emerge from the world of work, and these came from teachers.
2. About thirty questions reflect learning tasks, and only a few of these come (probably) from students in higher education.
3. The remaining questions are related to family life, leisure and voluntary activities.

The customers consist, in other words, of two major groups: people-at-large, outside work, and pupils working on assignments.

School Questions: What Do Pupils Ask?

Youngsters at school ask predictable questions. Very few request specific facts or documents. Teachers assign manageable subjects. We find many local, literary and broad topical questions. Typical subjects that teachers like include social institutions (monarchy, confirmation), world history (the Boer War, Tut-Ankh-Amon and the mysterious curse connected with his grave), Norwegian cultural icons (the actor Bokken Lasson), Norwegian minorities (the taming of reindeer) and the local community (crime in a particular suburb of Oslo).

Oslo Public Library has provided this service for four years. It is widely used and much appreciated by pupils all over Norway. But the field is dynamic. Last year, the main website for Norwegian schools (*skolenettet.no*) launched its own virtual reference service. For the time being, only questions about *nature* from pupils in *primary schools* are accepted. But that may change.

The school system is approximately fifty times bigger, in terms of staff and budget, than the public library system. The schools can draw on a vast body of subject specialists among their teachers. But librari-

ans are—potentially—much better knowledge organizers. I hope for a
school-oriented reference service that can combine these two strengths.

Leisure Questions: What Do Adults Ask?

Queries from everyday life are much more diverse. One client needs a
do-it-yourself manual on *carpentry*. Another wants information about a
whaling expedition—his grandfather was a shipboard cook. And what
is a *Colombian necktie*? a third asks. The answer is too gruesome to be
revealed . . . Still, it is easy to identify some typical categories, which
every public librarian will recognize. The most frequent case is the
customer who needs help to trace a document—a book, an article, a
quote, a poem, a song—that is hard to find. Document searches constitute about one-half of all leisure questions. Factual questions are also
frequent: *What does the expression "to be ready as as an egg" mean?
In a hard-boiled egg, is the white stuff fat and the yellow stuff protein,
or vice versa?* Topical queries tend to be narrow rather than broad: *Do
you have information about "Norwegian Association of Bus Companies," which was established in 1914? I am looking for books on how
to build boat models in wood, preferably fishing boats.*

The questions can obviously be arranged and classified in many
different ways. But let us consider a distinction that is important for
library policies. In Norway, public libraries are institutions for public
enlightenment. But enlightenment has two faces: one practical and one
theoretical. Should we cultivate our garden or our mind?

We distinguish between knowledge intended for use and knowledge intended for insights or enjoyment. We often seek information
with an external goal in mind. We want to increase our practical
skills—for instance, in cooking, bridge or genealogical research. The
questions have an ulterior purpose: *What are the Norwegian measures
that correspond to 1 lg? 1 md? 1 qt? 1 c?* Correct answers are followed
by culinary action.

But we also seek knowledge for the sake of knowledge. We study
in order to think. We read literature, both high and low, in order to be
entertained, moved or matured. We explore topics that fascinate: Aph-
rodite, mummies or sunken ships. We meditate on the great mysteries:
death, love and ocean. *Ripeness is all.*

At the level of policy we could ask: Should libraries emphasize
practical assistance or the cultivation of the mind? At the level of statistics we could ask: What do people actually request? Our sample is too
small to deal with this question in depth, but one aspect is treated in the
next section.

VRD data are highly relevant to many other library issues. The reference logs reveal the true concerns of our users. In her paper on community information, Marianne Hummelshøj[13] makes a distinction between information for survival and information for political action. Our sample includes only a few questions of the first kind and none of the second. There are questions about political parties, but they come from pupils who are forced to ask rather than from citizens who want to act.

Between Literature and Science

Familiar and Foreign Topics

While working on the hundred questions, I also looked at the answers and was struck by a certain difference between literary and scientific responses. The answers to literary questions revealed an easy familiarity with topics and reference tools, while the scientific answers seemed more tentative and remote. Compare the two responses below:

> Where can I find the text of Mozart's *Requiem* in Norwegian, preferably facing the Latin text?

> On "The Requiem Web," a personal website, you will find the Latin text with an English translation. . . . The Requiem mass is still used by the Catholic church—in Norway as well—so you will find the Norwegian as well as the Latin text in the missal. . . . Our music section is preparing a collection of the most important liturgical Latin texts in Norwegian translation. This will be ready sometime this autumn.

> I am doing a project on carbon fibers and have problems in finding information about their composition (structure, chemistry). . . . Could you help me with information on the web?

> Hi! There was not much on the web, but you could take a look at this link, maybe it it will help. . . . I found a little in this book: Kofstad, Per, *Uorganisk kjem: En innføring i grunnstoffenes kjemi (Inorganic Chemistry: An Introduction to the Chemistry of the Elements).* . . . You should also be able to use McGraw-Hill's *Encyclopedia of Science and Technology*, New York, 1992, which is available here in the library.

Both answers are helpful, but the first is much more confident than the second. In the carbon fiber case, good web information was available (e.g. on Vince Kelly's *Carbon Fiber* homepage).

To explore this difference more systematically, we selected ten demanding scientific queries (Dewey group 500) without checking the answers. For every question we picked a matching literary question (group 800) that had, in our judgment, at least the same level of difficulty. Then we compared the answers pair by pair.

In every case we found the literary answers to be qualitatively better, in some cases by a small and in other cases by a large margin. In other words, those who ask questions about literary topics will, on the whole, get better and fuller responses than those who ask questions about scientific topics. The scientific answers are not wrong, but they are less complete and less balanced than the literary ones.

Science Education in Crisis

That public libraries are shaped by a literary rather than a scientific culture is hardly a very new observation. But it is interesting to see familiarity and distance manifest them in concrete verbal behavior. Is this a library problem? If public libraries are defined as cultural institutions in a narrow sense, with particular responsibilities towards local history, fiction and the arts, we cannot expect the staff to be equally up to date in science, technology and medicine.

But if users who ask scientific questions receive weaker answers, we face an educational problem. The sciences are in trouble. In secondary school, young people avoid subjects that depend on mathematical skills—mathematics, informatics, physics and chemistry. Their teachers did the same twenty years ago. Mathematics is a *discipline* in both senses of the word. It has a tightly integrated inner structure, and it can only be mastered through persistence. Its rigor fits badly in with a youth culture that favors variation, communication and intense experience.

Libraries could do much more to stimulate scientific interests. But other actors are also active. Academic communities organize their own virtual reference desks. Sweden and Denmark have come far, with big and well-run services such as Ask a Researcher (*Fråga en forskare*), Ask about Science (*Spørg Naturvidenskaben*), Ask Lund about Mathematics (*Fråga Lund om matematik*) and Ask Stella (*Spørg Stella*) about astronomy. In the United States, we find several hundred subject-oriented reference services. A national network between libraries and these AskA services is emerging. In Norway the process has been much slower.

In March 2002 we found eight active scientific VRDs in Norway: (1) *Ask a geologist*, Norwegian Geological Survey; (2) *Ask a paleontologist*, Paleontological Museum, University of Oslo; (3) *You ask and we answer*, Geophysical Institute, University of Bergen (covers the subjects of meteorology and oceanography); (4) *Ask a biologist*, Norwegian Biological Association; (5) *Ask the professor*, New Media

Planet (all subjects including humanities); (6) *Ask Lexa about nature and the environment*, School Net (website for pupils in primary school); (7) *Schrödinger's cat*, Norwegian State Television (popular program on science; answers questions on subjects presented in recent programs); and (8) *Puggandplay*, Norwegian State Television (educational program for pupils between nine and twelve years; covers math, science and Norwegian). The above services 1-4 represent academia. They are low-key operations and not very well edited. The services 5-8 include one commercial company (New Media Planet) and three initiatives in public education. These four are as well designed as the leading Swedish, Danish and American services.

The demand for information and the supply of answers is likely to grow. The potential "market" is great. ATL is a general service for a general public of 4 million citizens. It receives about 300 questions a month. Puggandplay is a specialized service, for the subjects math, science and Norwegian, aimed at 250,000 children. It receives about 1,000 questions a month. The second audience is asking fifty times as many questions (per 1,000 persons and month).

In a few years there should be a substantial number of scientific VRDs in Norway as well. They will target their services to children and youngsters and be operated by educational and scholarly communities. Our public libraries are therefore faced with a strategic choice: (1) peaceful, but uncoordinated, coexistence; (2) mutual awareness and informal division of labor; and (3) tight integration based on joint interfaces and shared databases. We suspect users would prefer the third option.

Reference as a Market

Public libraries are financed by the municipalities. Their services are free of charge. But reference increasingly works like a market. There are competing suppliers of information. Many of the new services are also free of charge. Public agencies and voluntary organizations are eager to inform the general public. Commercial actors use free services as bait. To promote their products they must reach the customer's mind. The knowledge economy is an attention economy. People must be aware that your company exists before they can judge your goods. The scarce factor is eyeballs. Free information, including free reference services, is a way of creating product visibility and brand loyalty.

The transition from industrial to knowledge-based production gives knowledge institutions a central economic role. The core competence of librarians is now in high demand. New tasks, new professions and new institutions emerge for those who can organize, retrieve and present vital knowledge. But it may be easier for librarians to change their jobs than for libraries to change their robes.

Nobody expects our public libraries to be radical—to provoke and challenge their local constituencies. But even a small practical step— conducting reference by e-mail—will give libraries a taste of the technological forces and the social processes that transform their future.

Notes

1 John V. Richardson, "Reference Is Better Than We Thought," *Library Journal* 127, no. 7 (15 April 2002): 41-42.

2 *Google Answers.* http://answers.google.com/answers/main (25 May 2002).

3 Tord Høivik, field data, March 2002.

4 Len England and John Sumsion, *Perspectives of Public Library Use: A Compendium of Survey Information* (Loughborough: Loughborough University of Technology, 1995), 118.

5 England and Sumsion, *Perspectives of Public Library Use: A Compendium of Survey Information*, 116.

6 England and Sumsion, *Perspectives of Public Library Use: A Compendium of Survey Information*, 115.

7 Tord Høivik, "Sink, Swim or Surf: The Future of Reference Work in Norwegian Public Libraries," in *Library and Information Studies: Research and Professional Practice*, ed. M. Beaulieu, E. Davenport and Niels Ole Pors (London: Taylor Graham, 1997), 54.

8 Tord Høivik, "Har veven svaret?" *Norsk tidsskrift for bibliotekforskning* no. 13 (2000): 9-25.

9 England and Sumsion, *Perspectives of Public Library Use: A Compendium of Survey Information*, 118.

10 *Act on Library Services: Act No. 108 of 20th December 1985 Including Latest Amendments of 10th January 1997*, section one. http://www.ifla.org/V/cdoc/norway.htm (15 February 2003).

11 Tord Høivik, field data, March 2002.

12 Ellen-Merete Duvold, "The Meaning of the Public Library in People's Everyday Life: Some Results from a Qualitative Study." Included as a chapter in the present book.

13 Marianne Hummelshøj, "Web-Based Community Information Services." Included as a chapter in the present book.

Implications of the Concept "Samhällsinformation" for the Public Library Field in Sweden: Reflections upon a Citizenship Information Project in the City Library of Gothenburg

Karen Nowé

Reflects upon the role of the public library as a provider of citizenship information. Reflections grew out of a two-year research project at the Gothenburg City Library, Sweden, considering ways of increasing the use of citizenship information at the library. The project group included local librarians acting as reflective practitioners. Through trial and error, practitioners identified a set of central issues related to the role, nature and potentials for change of citizenship information services. It is concluded that a new, broader Swedish term may be needed to reflect the diversity of roles of citizenship information emerging from research.

Several contributions given at a Nordic seminar on public library research in December 2001 in one way or another dealt with the role of the public library in the provision of citizenship information or community information. Hummelshøj[1] studies web-based citizenship information in Nordic public libraries, Cranfield[2] sees a role for public libraries as discussion platforms for active citizens, and Audunson, Hansson, Nagy, Ulvik and Westerheim[3] discuss an action research project aimed at enhancing the role of the public library in promoting interest in local democracy. The present article reports another project to improve citizenship information services at the city library of Gothenburg (1999-2001), but its focus lies on the reflections that have come up within the project group during the time of the project. The project group consists of librarians and researchers in the field of Library and Information Science (LIS).

The Swedish title of the project was *Från SDN till FN: Samhällsinformation på biblioteket*. This can be translated as "From Town District Committee to the United Nations: Citizenship Information in the Library." We have chosen the newer term *citizenship information* used by Marcella and Baxter[4] in their national survey of British citizenship information needs, as it appears to be more appropriate than the term *community information*; for a discussion, see below. The project *Från SDN till FN* (The Citizenship Information Project [CI] Project) was started early 1999 by a group of librarians from the department responsible for citizenship information in the city library of Gothenburg. The initiative was triggered partly by a national report (1998) claiming that many citizens in Sweden lacked the knowledge about basic democratic issues necessary for them to be able to partake actively in democracy.[5] The vision of the CI Project was to awaken interest in the rules of democracy and in civil rights and obligations as well as to attract notice to opportunities for all citizens to influence and change society. The project group developed plans for using the following means to come closer to their goal:

1. exposure
2. easily accessible media
3. the library as a public room
4. meetings on several levels
5. educational tools and an outreaching way of working

At an initial stage they defined citizenship information as "information about and from public authorities and other public sector institutions within the municipality, region, state, and the European Union, as well as international organizations." This definition was modified in a later phase. A project manager worked on the project on a full-time basis together with a project group of librarians from the library's Citizenship Information Department. At the start of the project, the project group contacted researchers at the Swedish School of Library and Information Science at the University College of Borås and the University of Gothenburg, and LIS researchers have followed the project from 1999 to 2001. The present paper is based on their final report. The LIS research group has gathered data, spread over the project period, from repeated interviews with the project group, from two questionnaire-based user surveys and through observations of project group meetings. During eight months at the end of the CI Project, the project manager and a librarian kept a logbook on their activities and their thoughts, which also has been used to analyze the CI Project.

Reflective Practitioners

The project group did not spend much time on an initial analysis of the problems addressed by the CI Project or on setting measurable goals; nevertheless, the group has succeeded in implementing many activities. Often these have been based on trial and error rather than on previous analysis and planning. This confirms the findings of Holmgren and Flodin[6] that public libraries tend to miss out on analysis and evaluation and concentrate their efforts on implementation. The most striking activities have been the installation of two "citizen terminals" in the premises, the hiring of an extra librarian entitled "citizen guide" once a week in the department and the organization every fortnight of public meetings with representatives of public authorities or of larger social movement associations, such as Amnesty International. Citizen terminals are an initiative of five civil service departments offering terminals with access to their websites through a common portal. The citizen guide's function was to especially help users with citizenship information needs. Both the function of the citizen guide and the arrangement of public meetings have been prolonged after the end of the project, which shows an internal appreciation of these activities. The public seems to have enjoyed the citizen terminals, which were often used, whereas the services of the citizen guide were less often in demand. Some of the public meetings have attracted more than a hundred participants from the public, others only a few.

Apart from these tangible results, the CI Project has resulted in changes in the views of the project group. In his classic *The Reflective Practitioner: How Professionals Think in Action,* Donald Schön[7] claims that the tacit knowledge that practitioners gain through experience is essential in real, ambivalent situations. A danger inherent in practitioners' experience can be that the work becomes more and more routine as the practitioner trusts his or her long experience instead of looking for new solutions. Then he or she may exclude new and different needs that do not fit in with his or her experience. Therefore, Schön maintains that practitioners should actively reflect on their work, for instance by pondering over problems or surprises brought on by experimenting with new ways of working. The project group in the CI Project has on many occasions acted like reflective practitioners. Because of their trial-and-error method, where they consciously allowed for the possibility of failure, they have met with problems which have caused them to question their own way of working, or, on a deeper level, the library's role as a provider of citizenship information. The failure of the "citizen guide" to attract many users with questions about citizenship information has led to a discussion about whether the time schedule for the service was right, and also about what information needs the users expect the library to satisfy. Another topic that has led to deeper reflection has been the definition of the term *samhällsinformation*. From a more or less implicit understanding that was based on the collection their own department could offer, the project group has, through analysis of user surveys and evaluation of user questions, shifted perspective to allow for a definition that is more in line with the user's understanding of the concept. This has in turn led to a discussion on the strict organization of the library according to the Swedish classification system (SAB). A central task of the reflective practitioner according to Schön is to make tacit understandings explicit. The logbooks kept by some of the project group members as well as scheduled project group meetings have proved to be important tools for reflection and discussion.

Even though there have been minor tangible effects of the CI Project in the functioning of the library, the major effects of the project are the changes in paradigm in the minds of the project group members. These effects are in the long run more influential than the visible results of the project and may affect the organization of the whole library. We have chosen to elaborate upon three issues which the CI Project group has reflected upon, and which we see as essential questions for the library field. These are: the role of the public library as a provider of citizenship information, the question of a collection-oriented versus a user-oriented paradigm and the issue of cooperation and change in the library organization.

The Role of the Library as a Provider of Citizenship Information

The city library is not the only provider of citizenship information in Gothenburg. As a part of the LIS interest in the CI Project, Bogren and Gullstrand[8] mapped the market of citizenship information providers in Gothenburg in their master's thesis. They compared the services and organization of four other providers of citizenship information on different levels: a citizens' advice bureau in a district of Gothenburg, an information department in another district, an information department for the whole city and the information department of the county administrative board. None of these saw the city library as a self-evident partner in the provision of citizenship information. The project group for the CI Project cooperated with producers of citizenship information (like public authorities and social movement associations) but did not consider contacting information providers like the above. This may have been caused by a phenomenon that has been pointed out by (among others) Ginman[9] and a report evaluating another public library project, the GÖK project.[10] GÖK is composed of the initials of Gothenburg and two Swedish towns—Örnsköldsvik and Kalmar—and the project considered redefining the services provided by a Gothenburg branch library and the central libraries of the two towns. Both found that libraries do not tend to feel that they are faced with any serious competition, and therefore do not exert themselves too much to convince their environment of the library's capacities. The study by Bogren and Gullstrand[11] showed that the other providers of citizenship information were not aware of the scope of the city library's services. It is not unreasonable to assume that the same is true of the library's direct users.

Larsson[12] discusses the different positions that information providers can have in relation to the organization they inform about and to the public they inform. The possible positions are illustrated in the following figure.

The position of information providers. After Larsson 1997, p. 239.

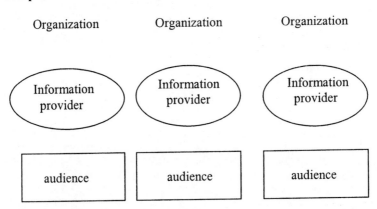

Ideally, Larsson means that the information provider is positioned at an equal distance from both organization and audience. The information providers studied by Bogren and Gullstrand[13] are all employed by the public authority they inform about, which may induce a loyalty to their organization. On the other hand, citizenship information should ideally start from the needs of the citizens, since they have the right to be informed so that they can actively partake in a democracy. The information providers are placed in a continuum, with the information department of the county administrative board being closest to its organization, and the citizen advice bureau, which works with the questions of the citizens as its point of departure, closest to the public. Still, all four providers are more connected to the municipal authorities than the library is. The library could be the neutral no man's land where authorities, associations and citizens could interact on equal conditions, and thus occupy a central position in the model. The papers by Audunson et al.[14] and Cranfield[15]—both presentations given at the Nordic LIS research seminar—stress the role of the public library as a neutral meeting place, a public sphere where citizens and politicians can meet for discussions. The experience from the CI Project suggests that this function is more important in the mediation of information from associations than in the communication of information from public authorities. Whereas meetings with representatives from associations (like Greenpeace, Attac, and Amnesty) were well attended, meetings with representatives from the municipality or from civil service departments generally attracted considerably fewer people. An explanation for this behavior could be that the threshold for contacting associations in their more "private" offices is higher than the threshold for contacting service departments or politicians. In her discussion of web-based citizenship information provided by public libraries, Hummelshøj[16] comes to a similar conclusion when she states that public libraries should include private and voluntary sources in order to offer some subsets of citizenship information that the municipal information providers do not offer.

The different services that can be offered as "citizenship information" are closely associated with the definition one gives to the concept. During the CI Project, both the project group and a random sample of users were asked to define which aspects they felt were included in the concept "citizenship information." During the autumn of 2000 a questionnaire was distributed to 150 users. A majority of the 105 respondents considered that, apart from information from and about public authorities on all levels, the following fields form part of citizenship information: environmental issues, consumer issues, information about cultural events, documents about the history of Sweden, time tables, information from local associations and on services provided by civil service departments (e.g. information about one's retirement pension, help with filling out tax forms, job announcements). Citizenship information can also be divided into information needed to influence society, and information that is offered as services by society. The respondents saw both aspects as citizenship information. The project group added background information about important events in recent history to the list.

According to the user respondents to the questionnaire and the project group members' definition, the following aspects could be part of a provision of citizenship information:

1. to provide information produced by public authorities
2. to provide information produced by associations
3. to provide background information about phenomena in society
4. to provide services from civil service departments
5. to manage specific questions as a part of the service from civil service departments
6. to arrange meetings between citizens and public authorities or associations
7. to arrange platforms for citizens to control and influence the democratic process

During the CI Project, the project group has endeavored to include all of the above functions in their service, sometimes calling in the help of other professions, like lawyers and employees of civil service departments. While this surely is possible, the question remains whether it is necessary or even wise to take on so many roles. According to Widebäck[17] the public library is forced to set clear priorities in order not to exceed its limited resources. A discussion on an e-mail list for Swedish librarians[18] revealed the apprehension of some public libraries that society tends to expect new roles for the public library (of which new aspects of citizenship information can be one) on top of their usual service, without adding resources. The issue has at least two sides: the self-image of the public library as to what their mission is and the needs of their users. If there are other organizations in the environment providing the same service in citizenship information, it could be more efficient if the public library could cooperate with this service and "provide information to the providers" instead of offering the same service to the public.

Collection or Users in the Center?

One of the most noticeable changes during the CI Project is the shift in the view of the project group on the meaning of "citizenship information." In the beginning of the CI Project, the members of the project group were asked to give their definition of what they saw as citizenship information. While they admitted that it was a vague concept, most members agreed on citizenship information being "information about and from public authorities and other public sector institutions within municipality, region, state, and the European Union, as well as international organizations." This is a definition that starts from the producers of information rather than from the needs of the citizen. To create a working definition, they agreed on citizenship information being "everything under class 'O' of the classification in the library," which excluded, among other things, consumer information from their definition. In the questionnaire mentioned above, users were asked to define citizenship information by choosing between the above definition of citizenship information and a broader one. The broader definition read as follows: "All the information I need to be able to partake actively in society and to live a satisfactory life." Of the respondents, 64.3 percent defined citizenship information as the broader alternative starting from the needs of the citizen.

In the beginning of the CI Project, there was, in other words, a gap between the project group's definition of the central concept and the users' definition. The project started from the library's collection, which, according to the project group, contained much valuable information that users were not fully aware of. Initially, the project's goal was to make the collection more easily accessible to the users while taking for granted that its contents contained the answers to the users' unidentified needs of citizenship information. This can be called a "collection-oriented attitude." During the CI Project, the project group has shifted towards a more "user-oriented attitude." This move has been inspired partly by data gathered by the project group about the users' definition of the term *citizenship information* as well as data about actual questions users put to the staff of the citizenship information department. When the project group members discussed all questions asked by the users during a week in the library department, they found that they no longer could stick to any uniform rules or guidelines to judge what was included in the concept of citizenship information. The perceived goal of the user rather than the document itself was used to decide whether the question was a need for citizenship information. A question about literature on Texas, for instance, was seen as a question that could be related to citizenship information when the user wanted to find out more about the president of the United States, but not when the user wanted to take a holiday trip to Texas. Thus, the project group abandoned the definition of citizenship information as an aspect of the documents in favor of a definition of CI with the users' needs as a frame of reference. The trial-and-error way of organizing public meetings and lectures within the CI Project resulted in a similar shift. In the beginning, the project group endeavored to select subjects for these meetings that would fit in with the existing collection at the department. This collection is organized according to the Swedish library classification system SAB. When respondents to a questionnaire about citizenship information were asked to define the concept, they gave examples of many aspects which they felt were included in the concept, and which were not part of the department's collection, for example, environmental issues. The project group started from the views of the users rather than from the contents of their collection to plan new meetings and lectures, which were not as tightly related to their collection. They started to question whether the boundaries drawn by the classification system necessarily created a logical grouping of the information from the users' point of view, and what could be done to cross these borders in order to make the information more accessible to the users. One possible way of crossing classification borders is on websites. Hummelshøj[19] points out that as a rule today's libraries need to develop strategies that put more emphasis on users' actual needs even when they design websites for citizenship information. Among other strategies, the structure of the websites and possibilities for inter-activity could be enhanced to ensure more user input.

This issue is a classic one in library and information studies, and several scholars and practitioners, among them Balslev and Rosen-qvist,[20] are convinced that we are dealing with two different paradigms, which, in the end, cannot be combined. Grönlund[21] calls them the par-ticipatory paradigm and the information delivery paradigm. Libraries following the information delivery paradigm believe that their main task is to have information at the disposal of the public, without asking which information their users need. The participatory paradigm is the newer of the two, and the principal task for libraries in this paradigm is to find out which needs their users have and to adapt their information accordingly. Even though quite a few studies have been carried out on the information needs of users, and many librarians constantly ask about users' needs in reference work, Olaisen, Djupvik and Lövhöj-den[22] believe that most inquiries have started from preconceived no-tions about user needs that have served as self-fulfilling prophesies. This is the phenomenon Schön[23] calls "over-learning"—when the prac-titioner's wide experience leads her to believe that she already knows the answer to each challenge, and therefore she does not see anything beyond the frames of her experience. In the CI Project, the project group first defined citizenship information with the classification sys-tem as a starting point. In this way, it is impossible to find results that could challenge the system, and therefore, this must be considered a collection-oriented or information delivery rather than a user-oriented approach.

A project that has worked at creating a more participatory attitude in Sweden is the GÖK project. The initiators started from their experience that public libraries exhibited a moralizing attitude, which did not correspond with a basic respect for different users' needs.[24] They also felt that it was confusing for the users that most libraries used the classification system codes as guidelines for the display of documents, since the order of the classification system does not always correspond to the users' expectations or needs. Olaisen, Djupvik and Lövhöjden[25] define this way of thinking as a system ideology as opposed to a service ideology. In a system ideology, libraries start from their internal points of view and demand that the users adapt to their system. Olaisen, Djupvik and Lövhöjden see this as a pathological state, as opposed to the service ideology, where the services offered by the library are defined by the environment—the needs of the users. On the other hand, advocates of an information delivery paradigm maintain that the participatory paradigm, where the needs of the users come before the "objective quality" of the collection, can degenerate into a populist strategy, and that the library should be a counterweight against commercial market economy. According to these voices in the evaluation of the GÖK project, the librarians' professional competence should be to maintain an objective quality in their collections; they are "people who are supposed to care about books."[26]

As an explanation underlying the collection-oriented attitude that is apparent in several library studies by, for example, Ginman,[27] Holmgren and Flodin[28] and the evaluation of the GÖK project,[29] Ginman[30] sees the close relation of libraries to public sector institutions. Because libraries are nonprofit organizations with goals hard to describe, their quality measures do not include a customer aspect. The libraries' view of their users resembles the traditional view within the public sector of citizens: the public sector offers free service, but the citizen has to adapt to the system and accept its conditions. Olaisen, Djupvik and Lövhöjden[31] argue that the internal feedback (from managers, municipality boards, etc.) is more important for the libraries than the external feedback from the users. A third cause for the internal orientation of libraries can be the homogeneous and mutually supportive professional culture within the library field, where the great value of the library for society is an axiom that is never questioned. Both Olaisen, Djupvik and Lövhöjden and the consultants evaluating the GÖK project[32] argue for this explanation. This can act as a hindrance for librarians in seeing the services of the libraries from a user's point of view, and in studying which niche the library occupies in relationship to its environment. All of these reasons we feel can be applied to some degree to the attitudes revealed in the CI Project.

The project's shift towards a more user-oriented point of view reflects the arguments by scholars in the field that libraries have to work more with service management and a service-oriented attitude in imitation of the private sector. To be able to argue for their continued existence, libraries need to adopt new measures of quality that more truthfully reflect the many goals of the library. Today, many libraries in Sweden measure their quality by the yearly number of visits to the library, and most libraries are successful according to this measure. But there should be variables measuring how well all citizens have been informed, if that is seen as an important goal, or how satisfied the users are with the service level—a viewpoint held in the report on the GÖK project.[33] Edvardsson, Karlsson and Lindström[34] propose that quality in public service organizations should always be related to all citizens' possibilities to partake in the service, and to the satisfaction of the users. They found that the possibility for users to influence services is one of the most important factors in creating satisfaction. This implies that it is important for libraries to develop their knowledge about their users as well as their cooperation with their users, as Widebäck[35] maintains. The library field should intensify a discussion on the library's role in society, and not be afraid to question even the most holy axioms. There is a need for unbiased analyses of users and user needs, both more generally and in smaller projects, as a basis for this discussion in Sweden.

The Role of Projects in Organizational Change

The shift in attitude from a more collection-centered to a more user-oriented attitude brought the project group in the CI Project up against organizational boundaries in their library. Like many other libraries, the city library of Gothenburg is organized in departments, where both the collection and the domains of responsibility of the employees follow the structure of the classification system used to categorize and display the documents. When the project group felt that they wanted to define the concept of citizenship information from the point of view of the users' expectations and needs rather than from the point of view of the classification system, they found that a considerable part of citizenship information fell outside their domain of responsibility. Consequently, the whole library should be involved, rather than one department alone, and possibly the structuring principles of the library should be reconsidered. The project group meant that it would be difficult to bring about such changes, since cooperation between the different departments was an exception rather than the rule.

Other studies of libraries' internal organization show that there is often little cooperation between different parts of the library. Ginman[36] and Holmgren and Flodin[37] have identified a possible cause of this indifference to cooperation in a lack of a clear common vision uniting all staff. Libraries are often formal organizations with several specialized task groups. This can lead to a strict division in departments with their own intermediate goals. If there is no strong common vision, the intermediate goals will seem more important than the common good of the organization, and in addition, these goals may lead in different directions. Olaisen, Djupvik and Lövhöjden[38] believe that one of the consequences of subdivision may also be that the staff, having little control over the direction of the library as a whole, may become disinterested and passive. In this book, Arvidsson[39] gives another example of the importance of strong support by library management and a feeling of control by the library staff in order to spread change through the whole system of the library.

The training and education of the librarians seems to be a key factor. Holmgren and Flodin[40] found that the deficiencies in creating a common vision may be due to the librarians' education, which until recently has been predominantly practical and has not given presumptive librarians tools for strategic planning. The consultants evaluating the GÖK project[41] also found that the Swedish library education program had mostly produced specialists, who were not used to considering problems from angles different from their own. Since 1995, the focus in Swedish LIS education has shifted towards a more comprehensive, strategic view of library and information work.

Ginman[42] claims that libraries are typically mature organizations, with built-in control systems and a strong tradition independent of the individual staff's visions. Such organizations are not known for their flexibility. One way of initiating change in mature organizations according to the evaluation of the GÖK project[43] is by setting up pilot projects: while they allow new ways of working, the risk of failure influencing the whole organization is small. Usually the success or failure of a project is not as important in itself as the lessons that can be learned from its implementation. It is of the utmost importance that these lessons be integrated into the larger organization, and for this there ought to be a plan of action from the organization's management. In the case of the CI Project, the most important lesson may be the shift in paradigm from the collection to the user already begun by project group. If there are no ways to communicate this lesson to the rest of the library, the effect of the project will be much less than it could have been.

Conclusion: The Concept *Samhällsinformation*

One broader lesson that could be drawn from the CI Project is whether the term *samhällsinformation* covers the contents that citizens and providers of information associate with it. It has proved difficult to give a uniform definition of the concept. The project group has felt that their initial definition, which identified samhällsinformation as a characteristic of the document, was insufficient to cover all user needs. A majority of a user sample viewed a more dynamic definition as more appropriate, where samhällsinformation is seen as an aspect of the user's information needs. Since the definition of samhällsinformation seems to be shifting, we wonder whether one could not coin a new concept including the dynamic and user-oriented dimension, and leave the term *samhällsinformation* to mean only "information from and/or about society institutions." A suggestion, in Swedish, for this new term could be *medborgarinformation* to emphasize the active participation of the citizen-user in the mediation of information.

A shift, both in a similar and in a contrary direction, seems to have taken place in Great Britain, where the new term *citizenship information* seems to be on its way towards replacing the older concept of *community information* in Great Britain and the United States. A search in BUBL on *community information* revealed fifty-seven hits, but none of them were published later than 1998 and most articles mentioning the concept stemmed from the 1980s. The term *citizenship information* only received eight hits, but all were published in 1999 or 2000. Most of the articles found reported on a research project on citizenship information on a national scale.[44,45] The report by Marcella and Baxter[46] from the first stage of this research project defines citizenship information in the following way: "Citizenship information is information produced by or about national and local government, government departments and public sector organizations which may be of value to the citizen either as part of everyday life or in the participation by the citizen in government and policy formulation." This definition combines both viewpoints found in the CI Project: it includes both document-oriented and user-oriented aspects. An influential definition of community information cited in several works on the subject is the one given by Donohue.[47] He states that community information service provides two types of information: survival information such as that related to health, housing, income, legal protection, economic opportunity, political rights, and so forth; and citizen action information needed for effective participation as an individual or as a member of a group in the social, political, legal, economic process. A community information service should be the agent of the citizen served rather than that of a government or business. As opposed to the shift in the understanding of samhällsinformation during the CI Project, the concept of *citizenship information* seems to have added a document-oriented dimension to a concept mainly rooted in or developing from citizen needs. A new label for samhällsinformation might make the concepts in Sweden and in Great Britain more compatible. It would be interesting to further examine the relationship between different concepts and the way the users and the providers understand the scope of *citizenship information* in Sweden and in other countries, like Great Britain and the United States.

Notes

1 Marianne Hummelshøj, "Web-Based Community Information Services in Public Libraries." Included as a chapter in the present book.

2 Andrew Cranfield, "National Identity as Cultural Policy with Emphasis on the Library as an Institution." Included as a chapter in the present book.

3 Ragnar Audunson, Joacim Hansson, Attila Nagy, Synnøve Ulvik, and Ingeborg Westerheim, "Information Literacy, Public Libraries and Local Community Engagement" (paper presented at the Nordic Seminar on Public Library Research, Copenhagen, December 2001).

4 Rita Marcella and Graeme Baxter, "The Information Needs and the Information Seeking Behaviour of a National Sample of the Population in the United Kingdom, with Special Reference to Needs Related to Citizenship." *Journal of Documentation* 55, no. 2 (1999): 159-83.

5 *Demokratirådets rapport* (Stockholm: SNS Förlag, 1998).

6 Margareta Holmgren and Barbro Flodin, *Biblioteken och folkomröstningen om EU: En studie av lokal samhällsinformation* (Stockholm: Styrelsen för psykologiskt försvar, rapport, 1996): 169-72.

7 Donald A. Schön, *The Reflective Practitioner: How Professionals Think in Action* (New York: Basic Books, 1983).

8 Hanna Bogren and Sofia Gullstrand, *Samhällsinformation i Göteborg: En jämförande studie av förmedlare av samhällsinformation* (Borås: Högskolan i Borås, Bibliotekshögskolan/Biblioteks- och informationsvetenskap, 2000).

9 Mariam Ginman, "Bibliotekens kundanpassning och flexibilitet," in *Biblioteket som serviceföretag: Kunden i centrum*, ed. Barbro Blomberg and Göran Widebäck (Stockholm: Forskningsrådsnämnden, 1992): 77-90.

10 *Evaluating the GÖK Project. The Innovative Capacity of the Swedish Library System* (Stockholm: Statens kulturråd, 1995).

11 Bogren and Gullstrand, *Samhällsinformation i Göteborg: En jämförande studie av förmedlare av samhällsinformation*.

12 Larsåke Larsson, *Tillämpad kommunikationsvetenskap* (Lund: Studentlitteratur, 1997).

13 Bogren and Gullstrand, *Samhällsinformation i Göteborg: En jämförande studie av förmedlare av samhällsinformation.*

14 Audunson et al., "Information Literacy, Public Libraries and Local Community Engagement."

15 Cranfield, "National Identity as Cultural Policy with Emphasis on the Library as an Institution."

16 Hummelshøj, "Web-Based Community Information Services: The Role of Public Libraries."

17 Göran Widebäck, "Serviceperspektiv för förnyelse," in *Biblioteket som serviceföretag: Kunden i centrum*, ed. Barbro Blomberg and Göran Widebäck. (Stockholm: Forskningsrådsnämnden, 1992): 139.

18 Biblist@segate.sunet.se (27 April 2000).

19 Hummelshøj, "Web-Based Community Information Services: The Role of Public Libraries."

20 Johannes Balslev and Kerstin Rosenqvist, *Bibliotekarien och samvete:t En rapport om nordisk bibliotekarieetik* (Köpenhamn: Nordisk Ministerråd, 1994).

21 Åke Grönlund, *Public Computer Systems, the Client-organization Encounter and the Societal Dialogue* (Umeå: Umeå universitet, institutionen för informatik, 1994): 112.

22 Johan Olaisen, Olav Djupvik and Hugo Løvhøiden, "Patologiske processer i de offentlige bibliotekssystemene." *Svensk biblioteksforskning*, no. 2 (1994): 1-17.

23 Schön, *The Reflective Practitioner: How Professionals Think in Action.*

24 Christer Bergqvist and Jan Herstad, "GÖK-projektet," in *Biblioteket som serviceföretag: Kunden i centrum*, ed. Barbro Blomberg and Göran Widebäck (Stockholm: Forskningsrådsnämnden, 1992): 31-41.

25 Olaisen, Djupvik and Løvhøiden, "Patologiske processer i de offentlige bibliotekssystemene."

26 *Evaluating the GÖK Project: The Innovative Capacity of the Swedish Library System.*

27 Ginman, "Bibliotekens kundanpassning och flexibilitet."

28 Holmgren and Flodin, *Biblioteken och folkomröstningen om EU: En studie av lokal samhällsinformation.*

29 *Evaluating the GÖK Project: The Innovative Capacity of the Swedish Library System.*

30 Ginman, "Bibliotekens kundanpassning och flexibilitet."

31 Olaisen, Djupvik and Løvhøiden, "Patologiske processer i de offentlige bibliotekssystemene."

32 *Evaluating the GÖK Project: The Innovative Capacity of the Swedish Library System.*

33 *Evaluating the GÖK Project: The Innovative Capacity of the Swedish Library System.*

34 Bo Edvardsson, Peter Karlsson and Annika Lindström, *Kvalitetskartor: Ett sätt att arbeta med kvalitetsutveckling* (Lund: Utbildningshuset/Studentlitteratur, 1996).

35 Widebäck, "Serviceperspektiv för förnyelse."

36 Ginman, "Bibliotekens kundanpassning och flexibilitet."

37 Holmgren and Flodin, *Biblioteken och folkomröstningen om EU: En studie av lokal samhällsinformation.*

38 Olaisen, Djupvik and Løvhøiden, "Patologiske processer i de offentlige bibliotekssystemene."

39 Ulla Arvidsson, "Librarians' Experiences of Introducing the Internet in the Public Library: A Study in Southern California." Included as a chapter in the present book.

40 Holmgren and Flodin, *Biblioteken och folkomröstningen om EU. En studie av lokal samhällsinformation.*

41 *Evaluating the GÖK Project: The Innovative Capacity of the Swedish Library System.*

42 Ginman, "Bibliotekens kundanpassning och flexibilitet."

43 *Evaluating the GÖK Project: The Innovative Capacity of the Swedish Library System.*

44 *Aslib Proceedings* 51, no. 4 (April 1999), http://www.aslib.co.uk/proceedings/1999/apr/index.html (10 October 2001).

45 *Aslib Proceedings* 51, no. 3 (March 2000), http://www.aslib.co.uk/proceedings/2000/mar/index.html (10 October 2001).

46 Marcella and Baxter, "The Information Needs and the Information Seeking Behaviour of a National Sample of the Population in the United Kingdom, with Special Reference to Needs Related to Citizenship."

47 Joseph C. Donohue, "Community Information Services: A Proposed Definition" (paper presented at Information Politics, the ASIS Annual Meeting, Washington D.C., 1976): 126.

Part II

LIBRARY
MANAGEMENT
AND VALUATION

The Public Library, Networked Information Resources and the Concept of Learning Center

Trine Schreiber

Discusses how a constructivistic approach to learning may change a networked information service operated by public libraries. Guidance—for many years an essential concept in public libraries—is juxtaposed with two other key concepts: Net facilitation and knowledge creation. Related to this is the theory of Etienne Wenger. Two networked subject-specific information resources in Danish public libraries are examined and analyzed in relation to the above concepts. The analysis points to ways in which the constructivistic viewpoint may affect the form and content of networked information resources in the future.

Introduction

Information and communication technologies (ICTs) offer a variety of possible alternatives to deliver and coordinate learning activities. It is quite clear that the new technology will play a central part in shaping future activities of the libraries to meet the needs of lifelong learning. ICTs are expected to play a central strategic role in helping many libraries achieve their targets for cost-effective access for users and expansion of their services.[1]

In line with these trends, the Danish public libraries have developed a number of networked information services jointly called "The Digital Library." However, as observed by Tord Høivik in his article in the present book, digitalization will change the practices of the reference services.[2] Furthermore, according to Marianne Hummelshøj, likewise in this book, if libraries want to meet the needs of their users, the design of the networked information resources will have to focus more on how the information is used than it has done up to now.[3] In the following, the article will go into both problems.

In the educational institutions new viewpoints of pedagogy have been introduced. Increasingly, the constructivistic viewpoint seems to be a dominant approach.[4] A central question is whether libraries have to follow the educational institutions with regard to this theory of pedagogy. Undoubtedly, it will change the form, as well as the content, of some of the services.

The constructivistic viewpoint is characterized, first, by emphasizing knowledge as a construction of the individual. This viewpoint stresses the importance of what learners bring with them to the learning situation. Thus, the learners interpret an event in the context of their previous understandings.[5] Second, the theory has a focus on the experiences of the individuals. Thereby, it emphasizes learning as an active process by recognizing the active construction of meaning, which goes on constantly as individuals interact with their environment. Kolb has modeled the constructivistic learning as a cycle in which individuals actively engage in an experience, look back upon it critically, evaluate their reactions and observations against theory and derive the implications for further experimentation.[6] Third, the theory recognizes collaboration and interaction with others as key activities. Many of the proponents of the theory stress this element because it may initiate a change in the constructions of meaning of the individuals and involve sharing perspectives. It is together with others that the meaning production is possible for the individual.[7]

Following this interpretative and experiential learning theory, the knowledge of the learner is not a kind of "reproduction" of the knowledge of the tutor. Instead of being a reproduction, the aim of learning of the individuals is to develop interpretations of the world which are flexible enough to be applied successfully in forthcoming situations. Brown and Duguid have called it "actionable knowledge."[8]

Many institutions are using the ICTs to support the activities of learning. Many stress the importance of reflecting the concept of learning because otherwise the use of ICTs may not fulfill the objectives determined. ICTs can be used in many different ways. Thus, each of the different approaches to pedagogy seems to presuppose their own applications. Nevertheless, it is not quite clear what the constructivistic viewpoint implies considering the form and content of a networked learning and information system. There does not exist a prescription for how to build up a networked learning resource using a constructivistic theory. Instead, there are a lot of questions affecting this area. First, how can the networked learning system reflect the context of previous understanding of the individual? Second, how can the system support the active learning, where the individual interacts with his or her environment and thereby develop an active construction of meaning? Third, how do we build up opportunities for collaboration and interaction between the individuals? These kinds of questions have resulted in a market of different ICTs systems and in discussions about their advantages and disadvantages.[9]

Also, public libraries have developed and conducted experiments concerning the form and content of networked information resources using different ICTs systems. Many libraries have also been aware of the different approaches of the educational environments to pedagogy and to the concept of learning. There exists today an interest among the librarians to develop some of the networked information resources from a constructivistic viewpoint. Still, it is not very clear what kind of changes the constructivistic approach may involve for the networked information resources. Therefore, the aim of this article is to come closer to an understanding of the potentials and opportunities of this learning approach for a networked resource.

Background

If we look at libraries today, there seem to exist different understandings of the relation between the library and the new learning trends in the educational institutions.

Some libraries seem to have the impression that the educational institutions have the responsibility for offering and developing services in accordance with the constructivistic viewpoint. The constructivistic viewpoint in the educational institutions seems then to have the effect that the library goes much more online than up to now to be as flexible as possible in relation to the different kinds of activities these institutions start offering. The library wants to meet its users at new addresses on the Net, but nothing appeals to change the design of these resources, for instance developing ways to reflect the context of the individuals, to initiate active learning and to build up collaboration between individuals.

In contrast, other libraries seem to have the impression that the library too has a responsibility for developing its services in accordance to the constructivistic viewpoint. Following this understanding, the library has to change the design of the information resources. Thus, it tries to develop the networked information services into a direction where—as mentioned above—the resources in one way or another are connected to the context of the users, initiating an interaction between the individual and his or her context and supporting the collaboration between individuals.

We here want to take a closer look at this latter view held by libraries. Therefore, the aim of this article is to examine what a constructivistic concept of learning implies for the networked information resources in the public libraries. For this purpose we will examine two selected information services developed by some Danish public libraries as part of a couple of networked services called "The Digital Library." These two selected services are both websites giving the user some guidance on either Danish literature from the last part of the nineteenth and the early twentieth century or on a Danish fiction writer. Both of the websites contain texts, links, question- and information-seeking facilities, among other things.

When we examine the two websites designed by Danish public libraries in the following, a list of questions will be adhered to. The starting point is the function of guidance. During many years public libraries have emphasized guidance as a very central element in the context of the services that they offer. Therefore, the first question is how we are going to understand the concept of guidance today. What kind of communication does guidance represent? What happened when guidance is based on a computer-mediated communication? Can we change the nature of guidance so that it is offered as part of the communication on the Net?

The chosen subject, networked information resources, implies that we need to compare the concept of "guidance" with another concept, namely "net facilitation." The concept of guidance traditionally has its foundation in the face-to-face communication. But now we have to look at communication on the Net in the context of, for instance, a facility for web-based "meetings" where many people are interacting with each other or as the one-to-many communication process where the library is talking with many different people organized individually or in groups. Therefore, the second question is about how we can understand Net facilitation in relation to the guidance.

From the perspective of the constructivistic approach, both kinds of communication on the Net just mentioned are of interest to us. The first kind, the "meeting," is of interest as a way of collaboration mediated directly on the Net. The second kind, the one-to-many communication, presupposes that the learners collaborate with somebody "outside" the Net. In line with the constructivistic viewpoint, we therefore have to discuss how this "outside" context may be represented in the communication on the Net.

Learning is the pivotal point of this article. Therefore, both guidance and Net facilitation have to be related to a process of knowledge creation. A theory about knowledge creation belonging to the constructivistic approach is, for instance, Etienne Wenger's. For Wenger, if we are going to understand learning of the individual, we have to reflect the social context represented by the so-called "community of practice."[10] Thus, the third question is how we are going to understand the knowledge creation process in relation both to guidance and Net facilitation but also to the social context of the learners.

First, the article discusses each of the three concepts: guidance, Net facilitation and knowledge creation. Second, the article describes and discusses the two selected websites developed by public libraries. The intention is to estimate their content of guidance, Net facilitation and knowledge creation.

The Concept of Guidance

In 1956, Carl Thomsen, a public library leader in Denmark at that time, voiced the opinion that public libraries had to do more than just make the information accessible to the user. They also had to guide the user with the intention to develop a kind of reading, which could serve to make the observations of patrons more sharp, stimulate the creative practice of the individuals or bring up a problem for discussion. The librarian had to limit the number of books he or she referred to, because such a selection would help the user get to the process of "active reading." He called this kind of guidance "purposeful advising."[11] Through the selection of the books, the librarian creates a setting for the development of information needs and for the learning process. In other words, guidance is not just a service containing an inquiry and with some information provided as the answer. It is not just the transmission of information from the library to the user. Guidance involves a much more complicated interaction between two people than the word *transmission* is able to express.

Public libraries have not forgot the importance of guidance since the time of Carl Thomsen. In recent years, librarians have discussed the form and content of the guidance activities supporting for instance lifelong learning. Today, in connection with the development of the new networked services, guidance once again appears as a complicated concept. At first, many people think it is a simple transmission of information, but on closer inspection, they see that it presupposes an interaction of views and opinion.

On one hand, the content of guidance will always in one or another way represent some kind of a formal system (e.g. the educational system, the labor market) and, on the other hand, the guidance must also

represent the individual who needs the advice.[12] In this way, guidance
has a double function, where the one may come into conflict with the
other. In a historical perspective, public libraries have conducted a
number of discussions about how to advise the user. In fact, these discussions have been about the double function of the guidance.

The one dimension of the guidance, the representation of a formal
system, does reveal that it is not just an equal communication process
between two persons but that it may contain an element of management
as well. The librarian may influence, if not manage, the interests of the
user. At the same time, the guidance has to motivate the user to continue with his or her information project. Thus, the other dimension of
the guidance, the representation of the person seeking an advice, reflects the necessity of this motivation. Therefore, the concept of guidance involves also the effort of stimulating the active commitment on
the part of the user.

As said, Etienne Wenger has written about learning. In his book
from 1998, he discusses how to organize teaching practices with the
intention to initiate a learning process involving the individuals.[13] He
emphasizes that you cannot design learning. You can only design *for*
initiating learning.[14] Thus, we can never be sure that the guidance has
learning as its effect. We can rely on guidance only for the purpose of
initiating a learning process but without knowing the result.

Wenger represents a social constructivistic viewpoint. For him, living is a constant process of negotiation of meaning. He uses the concept
"negotiation of meaning" very generally to characterize the process by
which individuals experience the world as meaningful. Whether people
are talking, acting, thinking, solving problems or daydreaming, they are
concerned with meanings.[15] It is the process where people negotiate
and may come to an agreement on how to understand the concepts
used.

The negotiation of meaning may involve language, but it is not
limited to that. It includes all kind of social relations. The term *negotiation* means a continuous interaction of gradual achievement, and of
give-and-take. Thus, he defines the negotiation of meaning in the following way:

> The negotiation of meaning is a productive process. The negotiation
> of meaning is a process that is shaped by multiple elements and that
> affects these elements. As a result, this negotiation constantly
> changes the situations to which it gives meaning and affects all par-
> ticipants. In this process, negotiating meaning entails both interpreta-
> tion and action. In fact, this perspective does not imply a fundamental
> distinction between interpreting and acting, doing and thinking, or
> understanding and responding. All are part of the ongoing process of

negotiating meaning. . . . It constantly produces new relations with and in the world.[16]

As a negotiation of meaning, the communication presupposes at least two persons. For Wenger, the negotiation of meaning does not seem to imply an element of management for instance by a supervisor. On the other hand, he argues for a double function in relation to the design initiating the learning process. He says that learning requires *both* enough structure and continuity to accumulate experience and enough perturbation and discontinuity to continually renegotiate meaning.[17] Using Wenger's theory, we can say that guidance is helping to guarantee the structure and the continuity. Anyhow, the word *management* may be too strong for the description of the needs of structure and continuity to accumulate experience.

The negotiation of meaning is an important element of the description of the interaction between the supervisor and the learner. The function of supporting the learner will always to a considerable extent need a negotiation. In other words, guidance is a kind of communication, which in some degree has to involve a negotiation of meaning. When we design networked information resources, it can be essential to give the negotiation of meaning between the librarian and the user some place on the Net.

Both concepts, guidance and negotiation of meaning, are not developed directly in connection with computer-mediated communication. Web-based communication has another concept attached to it, namely Net facilitation. Therefore, in the following we have to compare guidance with the concept of Net facilitation.

The Concept of Net Facilitation

Net facilitation is viewed as a process and a set of functions or activities that are carried out before, during and after a web-based "meeting" to help a group achieve its objectives.[18] In 1993, Clawson and Bostrom presented a list of functions of the facilitator role. The following are some of the activities mentioned on the list: (1) keeps the group focused on outcome/task; (2) plans and designs the meeting process; (3) encourages/supports multiple perspectives; (4) presents information to the group; (5) appropriately selects and prepares technology; (6) creates and reinforces an open, positive and participative environment; and (7) promotes ownership and encourages group responsibility.

To successfully provide a networked guidance to many users at one and the same time implies application of some of the activities mentioned above. In the described situation, the activities of "keeping the group focused on the task" and "planning the meeting process" seem very necessary, but the rest of the list may also include functions of relevance.

In an article that appeared in 1997, the role of the librarian was compared with that of a facilitator in a context of networked group communication.[19] The conclusion was that some elements in the facilitator's work were of interest to the librarian in relation to the networked tasks. Functions as mentioned above, adapted from the facilitation practice, may be relevant to the librarians' role in a situation of networked learner support. Identification and translation of the needs of the group seem to be a key dimension of the facilitator role. This has to attract the attention of the librarian.

Furthermore, both roles mentioned here involve communication, identification of information needs, searching activity, evaluation of search results and the development of a systematized terminology, which all the participants understand and can make use of. The latter activity has associations to Wenger's "negotiation of meaning" discussed earlier. To develop a systematized terminology applicable for everybody in the group presupposes a negotiation of meaning.

There seems to be a difference between guidance and Net facilitation. Often, guidance is based on the clarification of the information needs of individuals, while Net facilitation generally is about how to determine the information needs of the group. Anyway, if the objective is to initiate learning the negotiation of meaning is necessary in both cases.

When libraries are developing networked information resources the intention is to deliver their services to more people than they use to do. The information-seeking facility available for accessing these resources may still be used at the level of the individual, but part of the services has to focus some attention on the needs of groups or of many people at the same time. Therefore, to some extent, the design of the networked information services must be expected to involve the activities of Net facilitation—for example, supporting multiple perspectives and creating a participative environment—and encouraging group responsibility may also be considered in this context. If a networked resource involves communication as a kind of "meeting," the design will need to allow for the last mentioned activity.

Thus, guidance and Net facilitation are different in the sense that the last concept implies the communication with many people at one and the same time, such as a "meeting" or as a "one-to-many" approach, but they are similar to each other in the sense that the negotiation of meaning is essential.

The Concept of Knowledge Creation

Now we have to look at the concept of learning. As said, the present article aims to discuss what a specific approach to learning, the constructivistic viewpoint, means for the networked information resources developed by public libraries. The theoretical viewpoint adopted here is seeing the social context and the social relations as essential to the learning process. In Etienne Wenger's theory, the social context is defined as a "community of practice." In this connection, the question is how the website can support the relation between the learner and his or her communities of practice "outside" the Net.

In the learning process the individual will always need information. In his 1949 book *The Concept of Mind*, Gilbert Ryle made a distinction between two kinds of learning. He called the learning, where the individual is asking for information, for "knowing that."[20] In this case, learning involves the accumulation of data, facts or information. On the other hand, learning also requires you to engage in a practice. Ryle has labeled this "knowing how." The concept of "knowing how" implies that the individual gets some insights into a practice, that he or she learns something about himself or herself in relation to the practice and, furthermore, that he or she learns something about the social interaction with others. In "knowing how" knowledge, social identity and social relations are mixed up. It means that knowledge cannot be isolated from the social context. In this way, "knowing how" cannot be reduced to the information of "knowing that."

A knowledge creation process builds on both "knowing that" and "knowing how." Focusing on knowledge creation, it is appears difficult to separate the first from the second. What matters is how information—and "knowing that"—can support practice: "knowing how" and reverse. Often, the purpose of a website is to capture existing knowledge within formal systems, but seen in the perspective of learning, a website like this is only half of the task. The other half is to foster communities that can constitute the social context or the practice developing the other element, namely, the "knowing how."

As explained above, Wenger enhances the negotiation of meaning as essential to learning. Wenger himself conducted a fieldwork project involving a group of medical claims processors. He is of the opinion that the negotiation of meaning between these claims processors during the daily work forms a practice. He says: "A *practice* is what these claims processors have developed in order to be able to do their job and have a satisfying experience at work."[21]

In the same text, he goes on to say that in this sense these people constitute a "community of practice." Thus, Wenger associates practice with community. Community is defined as a relatively tight-knit group of people who know each other and work together directly. They are usually a face-to-face community that continually negotiate with, communicate with and coordinate with each other directly in the course of work. He points out that communities of practice exist everywhere: "We all belong to a number of them—at work, at school, at home, in our hobbies. Some have a name, some don't. Some are recognized, some are largely invisible. We are core members of some and we belong to others more peripherally."[22]

We have to note that he is not arguing that everything anybody might call a community can be defined as practice or includes a practice; nor that everything anybody might refer to as practice is a community.[23] Often, a group that shares interests on a website is termed a community, but it is not necessarily a community of practice in Wenger's sense of the word. A practice is only the source of the coherence of a community, if there exists: (1) a mutual engagement indicating a sort of membership in the community; (2) a joint enterprise developed as a negotiated response of the participants to their situation; and (3) a shared repertoire of routines, words, tools, ways of doing things, stories, gestures, symbols or the like.

Communities of practice fulfill a number of functions in relation to the creation of knowledge. Unlike a database, they can retain knowledge in "living" ways. They can provide people with a home base that is tuned to their learning needs. They dare the social context, which a learning process requires and presupposes. Von Krogh, Ichijo and Nonaka are talking about how to find "the right context" for knowledge creation.[24] The communities of practice function something like that.

As mentioned above, it is our opinion that in developing web-based information resources, public libraries have to reflect the learning concept in the constructivistic sense of the word. Now the question is how the web-based information resources can support the relation between the learner and his or her communities of practice established "outside" the WWW context.

As pointed out, the design of the websites has to involve some of the activities of Net facilitation, for example, encourages/supports multiple perspectives and reinforces a participative environment among others. Furthermore, initiating learning means to meet the experiences and the social context of the users. Wenger gave us a concept defining the social contexts, namely the communities of practice. The only way to come closer to these communities is by developing the communication between the library and the users. The users must have the chance to describe their communities of practice in connection with their request for information. Such a presentation may provide inspiration to other users on how to use the information. In this way, a negotiation of meaning may develop. In the following, we will discuss this proposal in relation to the two selected websites.

The Two Selected Websites

A couple of years ago, the two websites studied here were established by Danish public libraries. First, *Epoke* (Epoch) arrived, in 1997, then *ForfatterNet* (AuthorNet) was launched in the years before 2000. The two networked information resources represent a kind of guidance in relation to a selected subject.[25]

Danish public libraries have joined forces in developing the national website "The Digital Library," which serves as a kind of "umbrella" website for different kinds of reference services, each with their own website. One of the two websites examined here, *ForfatterNet*, constitutes one of the main services of "The Digital Library."

Networked resources give libraries the possibility to guide many users at one and the same time. As indicated, this means that the guidance provided needs to reflect some of the characteristics of a Net facilitation effort. The design of the networked resources has to reflect the needs of many people at one and the same time. In fulfilling this objective, it has to partly open up for a negotiation of meaning between the library and the user and partly to give communities of practice some place in the communication process in one way or another.

In the following, the two websites, *Epoke* and *ForfatterNet*, are presented. In the subsequent section, we will discuss these websites from the theoretical viewpoint outlined above.

In Silkeborg, in 1997, the public library started a website with the name *Epoke*. The purpose of the website has been partly to make the Danish literature of a specific historical period accessible to more people and partly to develop new interpretations of the observed literature of the period. The website represents a kind of guidance on a selected subject.

The website contains, first, some of the texts (novels) by Danish authors from the last part of the nineteenth to the beginning of the twentieth century. Second, it contains a couple of new interpretations of these texts. In 1998, a literary historian was attached to the project as both an author and a coeditor. This person has written the new interpretations. Third, the website has links to the electronic resources of the libraries and to other Internet materials supporting in general every kind of information seeking by the user. Fourth, the website includes an information-seeking facility, where the searching procedure is based on subject, name or title as access points. Fifth, and finally, it has a question facility characterized by a mailbox.

As explained, a specific person, the literary historian, makes the efforts of interpretation. In relation to this, the question facility allows the user the possibility to write about, to comment on and to go into details on a subject.

The literary historian has regularly contributed new interpretative pieces on the novel text. In contrast to writing a book, she has had more free working conditions in the sense that each commenting and interpretative part does not need to lay end to end. Each new part may imply new approaches in relation to the main subject. Furthermore, it has been possible for her to change the text acting on information received from the users. In connection to this, unfortunately, I have no knowledge about whether the dialogue with the user has had any effect.

This website applies to a broadly defined target group, for example, both to those who generally are interested in the subject and those who are working with the subject in an educational environment.

Recently, an evaluation of the website has been undertaken. Findings from this evaluation suggest that some of the features of the site seem to be less comprehensible than other parts.[26] Some users might find part of the text difficulty to read, while other parts seem accessible to everyone.

The question facility seems to be easy to use. One of the conclusions of the evaluation mentioned is that if we look at the number of questions received, we can characterize the website as successful. Unfortunately, the evaluation study does not provide us with details on the exact number of user inquiries. Visiting counter statistics indicate that the website had 3,000-4,000 visitors per month in the year 2000. Additionally, the evaluation reports that the number of unique visitors is 1,300-1,700 per month.[27]

The evaluation study report suggests that the question facility could be developed a bit more than it is now by the publishing selected questions and answers on the Web. This would serve as a kind of Frequently Asked Questions service (FAQ service).[28]

Financially, the operation of the website has in a period been based on external funds. But its future is uncertain, because it can be difficult to continue this achievement.

In Århus, in the years before 2000, the public library system started a website for a couple of homepages about living fiction writers. This website also offers networked guidance on a selected subject. Today about forty-five public libraries in Denmark are working with this facility as a project. The website receives financial support from the Danish National Library Authority and the Danish Council for Literature.

The website has more than one objective. One is to support the dissemination of Danish literature. Another objective is to have the website serving as a vehicle for the communication between the author and the reader. Finally, there are an intention to build a tradition among the libraries of making value-added information accessible on the Web.

Each author has his or her own home page. Each of these home pages displays a sort of profile of the person in question. One of the libraries involved has produced this author profile. It contains a short biography, a bibliography, a list of literary prizes and author stipends and grants received, a brief text portraying the author and written specifically for this purpose, a sound file with the voice of the author and a mailbox facility, so that the reader has the possibility of mailing the author. Finally, the home page includes an information-seeking facility and links to other library and Internet materials.

The umbrella website for all the author-specific home pages, *ForfatterNet*.dk, has a mailbox as well where the reader can write to the libraries maintaining the service. As with the website *Epoke*, this website does not offer a FAQ service.

Often, the production of an author profile is based on the initiative of the library or—as the website invites—an author who has taken the initiative. The principle is that the local library has the responsibility of covering those authors who live in the municipality or in the neighborhood. One result of applying this principle is that there are also home pages designed for the group of authors from a specific area of the country. On some of these home pages, the library encourages the reader to suggest an author who lives in the area but who has not yet got a Web profile. In other words, the library tries to encourage the user to take an active interest in the website.

The Discussion of the Websites

Let me say at once, both websites belong to the many exciting experiments with reference services in Nordic public libraries today. The two websites offer access to many kinds of information and both try to actively make users engage themselves in the subject.

As described above, both websites provide networked guidance in relation to selected subjects. In Carl Thomsen's words, they represent a "purposeful advising effort." They try to stimulate an interest in the chosen subject and to prepare for the "active reading." However, a central question is whether communication of information is possible without a negotiation of meaning between the library and the users.

As mentioned, both websites offer a question facility. *ForfatterNet* has the facility for directing questions to both authors and libraries. Unfortunately, we do not have any knowledge about the content of the mailbox functioning on the two websites. Thus, neither of the websites displays information about the nature of the questions put by the user. Therefore, we cannot determine whether the communication taking place between library and user has the character of a negotiation of meaning.

The advice resulting from the evaluation of *Epoke* suggests that the libraries should develop a FAQ service. This kind of service would be of relevance to both sites. Such a service could not directly show us the negotiation of meaning, but it would on the other hand give the user an example of the meaning of the concepts used and serve to generally demonstrate the whole idea behind the website and the question facility.

If communication via the mailbox has had the character required, then we can conclude that the website represents the structure and the continuity of the negotiation. On the other hand, according to Wenger, the negotiation also needs perturbation and discontinuity for being considered a learning support activity. When the website represents the structure and the continuity of the negotiation, it may be difficult for the libraries to get on with the other side. However, the perturbation and discontinuity could have been handled by a communication process between library and the user performed directly on the Web or by a Net meeting involving many users and likewise transmitted directly in a WWW context.

As explained above, Net facilitation has been defined by a list of functions or activities. The websites have successfully met the performance criteria for some of these functions or activities. No doubt, both websites keep the reader "focused on the outcome" and have "planned the communication process." In the case of *Epoke*, by letting the literary historian write the text, this website maintains the focus on the outcome. In the case of *ForfatterNet* where the libraries are producing the text, the effect seems to be the same. However, by having different libraries being responsible for different parts of the text to be added, there is the risk that the focus will change. In this specific case, it does not seem to have happened.

When we move on to other functions or activities on the list of Net facilitation features, we can see that both websites "present information" to the readers and both seem—at least at the first sight—to "create an open, positive and participative environment." The element of participation may exist in the appeal for using the mailbox or writing to the author, among other things.

It is difficult to determine whether the two websites analyzed here to a greater extent could create and reinforce a participative environment and, furthermore, whether they would be able to "encourage / support multiple perspectives." For instance, the new facility for interpretation of literature in the *Epoke* project might in one way or another have involved the users. The website could have invited the users to contribute to a debate. Maybe this could have added a refreshing participative element.

The websites do not seem to reflect the change, which will happen when libraries are moving from a face-to-face communication with the user to a communication with many people at the same time. Thus, the websites do not seem to open up for the new kind of communication. The question and information-seeking facilities have the character of being services for the individual. They do not contain a facility transmitting a group communication process, a Net meeting or the communication taking place between many users and the library. This kind of communication is missing.

Wenger emphasized the community of practice as important for knowledge creation in this context. Of course, the library will not be able to establish such communities. However, the library may support the relation between the user and the community. A class or a group can be the user's community. The user may be active in, for instance, a project of a class. The evaluation report of *Epoke* describes precisely this kind of user group. Many high school classes seem to have used *Epoke* and have sent questions concerning their projects to the library and to the literary historian. Unfortunately, the user of the website does not get any information about this knowledge exchange process. However, hearing about other projects may subsequently initiate new projects.

The introduction to a practice or a social context in relation to the question received can be done in many ways. For instance, the websites could contain information about the projects of groups or of some individuals who have initiated a contact with the library. Later on, one could imagine the distribution of an abstract of the result of the projects. Information about the communities means information about the social context of the learning process of some of the users. Therefore, the presentation of groups and their projects can be of relevance not only to the group or the individual but also to the other users. Furthermore, when the library has presented the group and the problem on the Net, they can use it as the starting point for a networked discussion with others. In this way, a negotiation of meaning may start.

Another proposal is that the library at intervals invites the users to a Net meeting. It may involve all those who want to participate, or it can be a specially invited group. The library can decide the subject of these meetings and the subject can be related to problems presented earlier by a group or by the library. Before the meeting, the library can decide the duration of the discussion. It may last only a few weeks or could go on for a longer period.

What has been discussed are suggestions for how the negotiation of meaning can be organized. It can be done in many different ways. The examples are showing how the libraries can support the users' relation to their communities and how this support can be of interest of other users. By providing a forum for the presentation of some of the communities, the system indicates the importance of the individuals' previous understanding. At the same time, the library supports the individuals' interaction with their environment. Thereby, the system may stimulate an active learning process. Thus, by developing opportunities for collaboration and interaction between the individuals in some of the ways mentioned, the design of the networked resources will be changing in the direction of a constructivistic approach to learning.

Conclusion

We started by asking what the constructivistic approach to the concept of learning means for the networked information resources. The central question was: What would this approach imply for a networked resource available through the public library? To answer this question, two things have been done in this article.

First, based on the constructivistic approach three concepts have been defined, namely guidance, Net facilitation and knowledge creation. First of all, the theory of Etienne Wenger has been used in the analysis of these concepts. The discussion shows that the concept of guidance is a quite complicated kind of communication involving a negotiation of meaning. This process of reciprocal understanding needs a room or a place as part of the networked resources. Furthermore, the concept of Net facilitation also presupposes the negotiation of meaning. At the same time, this second concept makes it clear that communication changes when the service of the library is web-based and not offered as a face-to-face contact with the user. The communication with many people implies that the resources have to include facilities for discussions transmitted directly on the Web or via Net meetings, among others.

As regards the concept of knowledge creation, the assumption is that the individual's learning presupposes his or her relation to a social context or what Wenger called the community of practice. It is in the social context that knowledge is constructed either by the individual or by the group. In interacting with the environment, the individual makes his or her experiences, and the learning process may start. Therefore, it is of importance that the networked information resource is so designed that it can support the relation between the user and the social context.

Second, two websites of the public libraries have been described and examined. The one, *Epoke*, covers Danish literature in a specific historical period. The other, *ForfatterNet*, is a presentation of living fiction writers in Denmark. It has been shown that both websites have to expand their guidance in the direction of Net facilitation. Thus, they have to make room for a negotiation of meaning between library and the individual, and as part of the communication with many people at one and the same time they also have to open up for this kind of mutual process between the users themselves. This can happen, for instance, by a Net meeting or via a discussion between many users directly in a Web setting. These kinds of communication mean that the individuals develop an understanding of the meaning of the information, of the question facility and of the website in general. Furthermore, these kinds of communication processes help the individuals participate in the construction of knowledge.

An implication of the networked information services designed as part of the constructivistic approach to learning is that they have to make room for much more communication on the Net than is the case today. No doubt, we still need a lot of experience concerning the different ways of organizing communication in the direction mentioned. The starting point is networked activities such as presentation of user projects, discussion with users concerning a specific problem or Net meetings.

Finally, the need for more communication between the library and the user than the networked resources seem capable of permitting today points to an increase of the costs involved. Thus, an expansion of the services offered by the libraries by means of the ICTs does not necessary mean a cheaper library. Learning is a complicated process and the ICTs do not make it easier. They offer quite a few opportunities but not necessarily cheaper routines.

Notes

1 Philippa Levy, "Information Specialists Supporting Learning in the Networked Environment: A Review of Trends and Issues in Higher Education," *The New Review of Libraries and Lifelong Learning* 1 (2000): 36.

2 Tord Høivik, "A Poem Lovely as a Tree? Virtual Reference in Norwegian Public Libraries," in *New Frontiers in Public Library Research*, ed. Carl Gustav Johannsen and Leif Kajberg (Lanham, Md.: Scarecrow Press, 2005). Included as a chapter in the present volume.

3 Marianne Hummelshøj, "Web-Based Community Information Services in Public Libraries," in *New Frontiers in Public Library Research*, ed. Carl Gustav Johannsen and Leif Kajberg (Lanham, Md.: Scarecrow Press, 2005). Included as a chapter in the present volume.

4 Peter Brophy, "Networked Learning," *Journal of Documentation* 57, no.1 (January 2001): 136.

5 R. Driver and V. Oldham, "A Constructivist Approach to Curriculum Development in Science," *Studies in Science Education* 13 (1986): 105-22.

6 David A. Kolb, *Experiential Learning: Experience as the Source of Learning and Development* (Englewood Cliffs, N.J.: Prentice-Hall, 1984).

7 John Seely Brown and Paul Duguid, *The Social Life of Information* (Boston, Mass.: Harvard Business School Press, 2000) and Etienne Wenger, *Communities of Practice: Learning, Meaning and Identity* (Cambridge: Cambridge University Press, 1998).

8 Seely Brown and Duguid, *The Social Life of Information*, 135.

9 Lone Dirckinck-Holmsted, Håkon Tolsby, and Tom Nyvang, "E-læring systemer i arbejdsrelateret projektpædagogik," in *Udspil om læring i arbejdslivet*, ed. Knud Illeris (Roskilde: Roskilde Universitetsforlag, 2002): 123-55.

10 Wenger, *Communities of Practice: Learning, Meaning and Identity*.

11 Carl Thomsen, "Bibliotekernes målsætning i dag," *Bogens verden* 38 (1956): 325.

12 Per Lauvås and Gunnar Handal, *Vejledning og praktisk fagteori* (Århus: Klim, 1997).

13 Wenger, *Communities of Practice: Learning, Meaning and Identity*, 225ff.

14 Wenger, *Communities of Practice: Learning, Meaning and Identity*, 229.

15 Wenger, *Communities of Practice: Learning, Meaning and Identity*, 53.

16 Wenger, *Communities of Practice: Learning, Meaning and Identity*, 54.

17 Wenger, *Communities of Practice: Learning, Meaning and Identity*, 227.

18 Victoria K. Clawson and Robert P. Bostrom, "Facilitation: The Human Side of Groupware," in *Groupware '93. Proceedings of the Second Annual Commercial Groupware Conference*, ed. David D. Coleman (San Mateo: Morgan Kaufmann, 1993): 205-24.

19 Trine Schreiber and Camilla Moring, "Communicative and Organisational Competencies of the Librarian in Networked Learner Support: A Comparative Analysis of the Roles of the Facilitator and the Librarian," *Interna-*

tional Journal of Electronic Library Research 1, no. 3 (September 1997): 299-310.

20 Gilbert Ryle, *The Concept of Mind* (London: Hutchinton House, 1949).

21 Wenger, *Communities of Practice: Learning, Meaning and Identity*, 47.

22 Etienne Wenger, "Communities of Practice: The Structure of Knowledge Stewarding," in *Knowledge Horizons: The Present and the Promise of Knowledge Management*, eds. Charles Despres and Daniele Chauvel (Woburn, Mass.: Butterworth-Heinemann, 2000): 207.

23 Wenger, *Communities of Practice: Learning, Meaning and Identity*, 72.

24 Georg von Krogh, Kazuo Ichijo, and Ikujiro Nonaka, *Enabling Knowledge Creation: How to Unlock the Mystery of Tacit Knowledge and Release the Power of Innovation* (Oxford University Press, 2000).

25 The website *Epoke* has the address http://www.w-poke.dk (1 June 2002) and the website *ForfatterNet* has http://www.ForfatterNet.dk (1 June 2002).

26 Marie Louise Valeur Jaques, *Epoke—danske romaner før 1900: En internetlitteraturhistorie ved Silkeborg Bibliotek: Evalueringsrapport* (Silkeborg: The Public Library of Silkeborg, 2001). Available at: http://www.epoke.dk/epoke-rapport.pdf.

27 Valeur Jaques, *The Report of Evaluation*, 19.

28 Valeur Jaques, *The Report of Evaluation*, 4.

Valuation of Public Libraries

Svanhild Aabø

Contingent valuation (CV) implies that respondents are stating how they value a change in the provision of a nonmarket good in the form of maximum willingness to pay for an improvement or minimum compensation in order to accept a change to the worse. Findings of a CV study of public libraries in Norway show how library users, as well as non-users, value their public libraries. The estimate range of the population's valuation shows that, on the average, Norwegian households value the benefits from public libraries clearly higher than the costs of producing such library services.

Background

An objective of my research project[1] is to explore whether it is possible—by applying methods from economics—to justify that public library services are worth their costs for society, for the general public, the citizens. If this is the case, it may be an essential argument for continuous public funding of public libraries. One (of several necessary) steps towards finding an answer to this question is to examine how the *population* values public libraries—which we have done by a contingent valuation (CV) study. If the population's valuation is higher than the costs to produce the library services, this speaks for viewing public libraries as worth their price seen from the citizens' perspective. If, however, their valuation is lower than the costs, that speaks for the opposite conclusion. Such considerations are within the frames of *economic* valuation. There are, of course, other dimensions of great importance for deciding the value of public libraries—educational, social, cultural and political. My project intends to supplement research on these other dimensions.

The background for my approach to the problem is the very re-strained economic situation of the municipalities. (It seems like a contradiction: The wealthy Oil-Norway not being able to afford maintenance of schools, hospitals—or libraries—but that's where the local public sector finds itself.) Many municipalities today, in Norway as well as in other countries, face severe budget restrictions and cutbacks in funding of public services and suggestions to raise local taxes to maintain service levels are common. Public libraries are a topic in this debate.

We will here present some results from our study,[2] which appears to be the first CV study, in Norway or internationally, to elicit how a national population sample values their public libraries. National studies of public libraries and their value—using methods other than CV—have been conducted in the UK,[3] England and Wales,[4] Canada,[5] Australia[6] and in the United States.[7] CV has been used as one of several methods in cost-benefit analyses of urban public libraries in the United States.[8] These studies reflect an increasing need to develop instruments to make valid statements about the value of public libraries. The literature in library and information sciences (LIS) report studies conducted from different theoretical and methodological positions, for example, from user studies and performance measurement studies in LIS, from sociological survey research and also a few using methods from economics.[9]

The CV method was developed in environmental economics but has spread to other sectors, including the *cultural* sector, where museums,[10] theaters,[11] national television programming,[12] cultural heritage[13] and, in a few cases, libraries[14] have been valuated.

An important methodological aspect of our study is related to whether or not the respondents perceive they have *property rights* to public libraries, that is, the good to be valued. Our study shows that an overwhelming majority, 94 percent of the respondents, think they have a *right* to have access to a public library in the municipality where they live. This share is clearly higher than the percentage that said they were library users, which are only 60 percent.[15] This fact demonstrates that the Norwegian Public Library Act, which states that all municipalities must have a public library, is very well rooted in the population.[16]

Contingent valuation is a method for valuation of *nonmarketed* goods. It is a direct method, which makes it possible to value both use values and nonuse values. The *use value of libraries* can be defined as the values, which are experienced by those who, in a variety of ways, make active use of libraries. In addition to use value, economists have for the last thirty years recognized the possibility that individuals who make no active use of a public good, might, nevertheless, derive satisfaction from its mere existence, even if they never intend to make active use of it.[17] For this concept the literature uses different terms—existence value, bequest value, altruistic externalities, vicarious consumption, prestige value, consumer externalities, producer externalities, education value, option value. There are continuing discussions both about terminology, definitions and motives, but there seems to be consensus of the wider terms *nonuse value* or *passive use value*. The *nonuse values of public libraries* can be defined as the utility individuals obtain from libraries from various reasons other than their active use of them (e.g. because they are part of our cultural heritage, are important for the national literature, contribute to the general breeding and development of creativity, social criticism, esthetic and ethical abilities). The *total value of libraries* can be defined as the sum of the use values and the nonuse values.

A comprehensive assessment of public libraries should include the whole range of possible benefits that legitimately accrue from them, so that the respondents will have the options to value all aspects. Recent research has shown that people think libraries are valuable because of a variety of reasons, including reasons not motivated by own use.[18] Audunson[19] shows that an essential part of a national population sample finds that the most important tasks of public libraries are to disseminate culture and knowledge, promote equity and social justice by diminishing the digital divide, etc., and to provide library services to elderly and disabled persons.

Contingent valuation implies that respondents are asked to state their values of a change in the provision of a nonmarket good, here public libraries, in the form of maximum Willingness to Pay (WTP) for an *improvement* or minimum compensation in order to accept (Willingness to Accept [WTA]) a *change to the worse*.[20] In theory, WTP and WTA should differ only by small amounts, but studies from the last decades show that WTA estimates are often considerably higher than WTP estimates for the same good.[21] Due to this observation, when the natural setting calls for valuing WTA, one instead often chooses to estimate WTP, which is the conservative choice.[22] A special case is when the good to be valued has an inner value or a value separated from the use value and when people feel they have property rights to the good in question. In such cases, WTP can give biased estimates while WTA better expresses what economists term the "true" preferences.[23]

Methodology

Our starting point was the recognition that public libraries had nonuse values, and we suspected that the property rights issue was relevant—

but at that time we did not yet know how relevant it was. Based on these reasons we chose a research design where half of the sample was asked WTA questions and the other half WTP questions.

Previous research has shown that valuation estimates tend to be influenced by the choice of *elicitation* method, too. We chose to use two different elicitation formats to seek to correct for elicitation method effects, namely multiple bounded discrete choice (MBDC) and dissonance minimizing format (DM). Both are recent developments from environmental economics and seek to correct for overestimating of the value of the good in question and should yield conservative estimates.[24] These two formats were both adapted to scenario descriptions for WTP and WTA, respectively. We thereby developed a *four-cell* research design (see figure 1).

Figure 1. The four subsamples.

WTP – MBDC	WTP – DM
(n = 257)	(n = 250)
WTA – MBDC	WTA – DM
(n = 251)	(n = 241)

Note:

WTP   = willingness to pay
MBDC = multiple bounded discrete choice
WTA   = willingness to accept
DM   = dissonance minimizing format

The respondents were randomly distributed to these four subsamples, and each respondent belonged to only one subsample. On this basis we will have four independent estimates. This design permits tests both between and within the subsamples and on the whole sample. We can test elicitation effects between the two WTP and WTA subsamples, respectively, and we can compare WTP and WTA within the same elicitation format. All respondents were faced with two valuation questions. The first was asked in one of the two elicitation formats (MBDC or DM), the second was open-ended. Thus, we are able to test the estimates to the first and second valuation question both within each subsample and on the sample as a whole.

The survey was administered by a professional opinion company, AC Nielsen Norway, as part of their bimonthly omnibus survey (in January 2000) that collects data from a national random sample of private households. Nine hundred ninety-nine persons older than fifteen years were interviewed in their homes as representatives of their households. In addition to the library valuation part, the questionnaire contained a section on library use or nonuse, attitudes and reasons for library behavior, sections of socioeconomic and demographic information, including political attitudes, and debriefing questions to both the respondent and interviewer. The debriefing questions aimed to provide information about how the respondent perceived the valuation questions, whether they were difficult to understand or to answer, etc., and whether they serve to test the consistency of the answers. The interviewer was asked how seriously the respondent answered the questions, whether he or she was interested in or well informed about public libraries and so forth.

In the following, we will focus only on the valuation questions. They were introduced by a scenario description. The *willingness-to-pay scenario* describes a restricted economic situation, which forces the municipality leaders to suggest a choice between closing down the local library and increasing the annual local taxes. It is assumed that the Public Library Act is amended, so this will not be a violation of the law, and the local aspect of the situation is stressed—it is closing down of the library in the *present* municipality that is described, not of the whole national public library system. *Substitutes* for the closed local library are referred to, as well; for example, the alternatives are to use the library in a neighbor municipality or to buy all books and information services. *Nonsubstitutes* are also pointed out, for example, "Reach out" services to elderly and disabled, library services to kindergartens and school classes, literature mediating, which will disappear.

The *willingness-to-accept scenario* had the same restricted economic frames, but here we described a situation where the saved money—*if* the funding of the public library in the municipality was cut and the library closed down—should be used for *other* local public services that will benefit the household, that is, an indirect compensation. The respondent was asked to state which amount he or she meant had to be transferred to other public services in the municipality to compensate for the loss of closing down the library.

Findings

The respondents' answers to the valuation questions can be divided into three main types:

1. Positive responses—expressing a positive value of the library, in the form of a specific, monetary amount.
2. Zero bids—expressing that the library has no value to respondent.
3. Protest bids—responses that are generally taken to imply that respondents do not accept the question or the scenario description.

In our study, the zero bids make up from less than 10 percent to 25 percent in the four subsamples, which is a relatively low share and well inside prevailing "standards." The response distribution of the *positive* and *protest bids* to the two valuation questions is presented in figure 2.

Figure 2. Percentage of protest bids and positive bids to the two valuation questions, Q1 and Q2.

1 WTP – MBDC			2 WTP – DM		
	Q1	Q2		Q1	Q2
Protest:	5	12	Protest:	8	7
Positive:	83	72	Positive:	58	66
3 WTA – MBDC			4 WTA – DM		
	Q1	Q2		Q1	Q2
Protest:	21	33	Protest:	0	53
Positive:	60	47	Positive:	90	29

Note:
WTP   = willingness to pay
MBDC = multiple bounded discrete choice
WTA   = willingness to accept
DM   = dissonance minimizing format

In the WTP subsamples, the positive bids constitute 60-80 percent of all bids, which is a very high share. In the two WTA subsamples, the results vary significantly and there is a clear difference between the two elicitation formats. In subsample 3 (WTA – MBDC), the variation between the positive bids to first and second valuation questions (Q1 and Q2) is of the same magnitude as in the WTP subsamples, and the share of positive responses is from close to 50 percent to 60 percent. In subsample 4 (WTA – DM), however, the share of positive responses varies from as high as 90 percent in Q1, to below 30 percent in Q2.

The *protest* bids in the WTP subsamples make up between 5 percent and 12 percent, which must be considered a low fraction. In the WTA subsamples, the share of protest bids is higher, between 20 and 50 percent. Also here, there is a large difference between these two subsamples, and—again—it is the response distribution in subsample 4 that is conspicuous.

A high share of protest bids makes it more difficult to reach plausible estimates. WTA protest bids are particularly problematic because there is no way to define a plausible upper bound to the compensating demands of WTA protest voters, which complicates interpretation of the answers. For the WTP protest bids, on the other hand, there is by contrast a well-defined *lower* bound on valuation, namely zero.

We examined the WTA protest voters further, to find out whether or not they had common characteristics. Through a binary logistic regression analysis we found four statistically significant explanatory factors:

1. Library use
2. High education
3. Cultural activity level
4. Debrief variable

This debrief variable recorded whether the respondent agreed or disagreed (wholly or partly) with the following statement: "We must retain the local library regardless of the sum of budget funds saved by closing it down."

The overall results of the analysis showed that WTA protest voters are characterized by agreeing to this statement, they are library users, have high education (from university or college), but have a low cultural activity level, for example, they use few other local cultural activities than the public library. These explanatory factors indicate that among the WTA protest voters there are respondents with a high valuation of public libraries.

Protest bids can be treated in different ways. They can be:

- Excluded from the sample.
- Included in the sample.
- Given an imputed value using a Missing Value Analysis, which gives them a value in accordance with values stated by respondents with same characteristics.

In our study, we present several different valuation procedures and protest bid treatments. Below we present estimates with protest bids *excluded*, which gives conservative (low) estimates, see figure 3. In the MBDC format, two figures are given, which are derived by two different estimation techniques.

Figure 3. The range of estimates in NOK (Norwegian crowns). Mean and median with protest bids are excluded.

Mean			
Q1		**Q2**	
WTP – MBDC	WTP – DM	WTP – MBDC	WTP – DM
1500 – 980	675	425	350
WTA – MBDC	WTA – DM	WTA – MBDC	WTA – DM
2000 – 2100	1720	1500	850

Median			
Q1		**Q2**	
WTP – MBDC	WTP – DM	WTP – MBDC	WTP – DM
500 – 400	675	300	100
WTA – MBDC	WTA – DM	WTA – MBDC	WTA – DM
700 – 760	1720	400	300

Note:
WTP   = willingness to pay
MBDC = multiple bounded discrete choice
WTA   = willingness to accept
DM   = dissonance minimizing format

We observe that the range of estimates is rather wide. Some main features can be summarized as follows:

Elicitation effect is seen in the *WTP* subsamples, both between the two different elicitation formats and between the two different estimation techniques used in subsample 1 (WTP – MBDC). In the *WTA* subsamples, the elicitation effect is clearly smaller.

Comparing the estimates to the two valuation questions, Q1 and Q2, we observe a systematic difference between them, in the sense that the amounts stated to the first are considerably higher than to the second for both elicitation methods, estimation techniques, and WTA or WTP formats.

The disparity between WTP and WTA, on the other hand, is encouragingly small compared to other studies using the two approaches.

Mean and *median* are two different measures for characterizing a data material. The median is defined by half of the respondents having stated lower amounts, and the other half higher amounts. We note the big difference between mean and median, which shows that the distribution is skewed. This is typical for such estimates, in particular when the zero bids are included as they are here, because there often tends to be a concentration around zero. We note that in our data there is a fair share of respondents with a valuation so high that they draw the mean value up.

Conclusion

An aim of our study is to measure the total benefits to the citizens of Norwegian public libraries at today's service levels. Based on the WTP estimates, we are able to identify a probable minimum estimate, a *lower bound* for the population's public library valuation. This lower bound appears to be approximately 400 NOK, which is close to the average library costs per household today.

The establishment of an *upper bound* is more difficult (in particular due to the high share of WTA protest bids, especially in subsample 4), but we can assert that the upper bound of citizens' valuation of public libraries is considerably higher than the lower valuation limit—a conservative estimate is 2000 NOK, based on the WTA estimates.

We find it reasonable to conclude that the population's "true" value is clearly higher than the lower bound because there is no prior justification for rejecting WTA in our case, where an extraordinary high proportion of the respondents, 94 percent, feel they have property rights to public libraries. The property rights question is an essential argument to attach importance to the WTA estimates.

The overall conclusion from our study is that, on the average, Norwegian households value the benefits from public libraries higher than the average costs of producing such library services. The valuation will vary among public libraries in different municipalities, and from this national study conclusions cannot be drawn for each one of the different municipalities' public libraries. Our study does not answer distributional or efficiency questions from a marginal view. At a national level, however, we can conclude that the population finds public libraries well worth their price.

Notes

1 My research project "The Value of Public Libraries in Society" is financed by the Norwegian Research Council's Library Research Program and headed by Jon Strand, professor of economics at the University of Oslo, and Ragnar Audunson, professor of library and information science at Oslo University College. The project is presented and documented in several articles: Svanhild Aabø and Jon Strand, "Public Library Valuation, Nonuse Values, and Altruistic Motivations," *Library and Information Science Research* 25, no. 3 (Summer 2004): 351-72; Svanhild Aabø and Ragnar Audunson, "Rational Choice and Evaluation of Public Libraries: Can Economic Models for Valuating Non-Market Goods Be Applied to Public Libraries," *Journal of Librarianship and Information Science* 34, no. 1 (March 2002): 4-14; Svanhild Aabø, "Verdsetting av folkebibliotek," in *Det siviliserte informasjonssamfunn*, ed. Ragnar A. Audunson and Niels Windfeld Lund (Bergen: Fagbokforlaget, 2001), 246-68; Svanhild Aabø, "Citizens' Assessment of Public Libraries," *Nordisk Kulturpolitisk Tidskrift* 3 (1998): 60-82; and Svanhild Aabø, "The Value of Public Libraries in Society," *Norsk Tidsskrift for Bibliotekforskning* 9 (1997): 59-81.

2 For a comprehensive presentation, see Svanhild Aabø, "Valuing the Benefits of Public Libraries: A Contingent Valuation Study of Norwegian Public Libraries," *Information Economics and Policy* 17, no. 2 (March 2005): 175-98.

3 Anne Morris, Margaret Hawkins and John Sumsion, *The Economic Value of Public Libraries* (London: Resource: The Council for Museums, Archives and Libraries, 2001).

4 Aslib, *Review of the Public Library Service in England and Wales for the Department of National Heritage: Final Report* (London: Aslib, 1995).

5 Leslie Fitch and Jody Warner, "Dividends: The Values of Public Libraries in Canada," *The Bottom Line: Managing Library Finances* 11, no. 4 (1998): 158-79.

6 Colin Mercer, *Navigating the Economy of Knowledge: A National Survey of Users and Non-Users of State and Public Libraries: Final Report* (Brisbane: Griffith University, 1995).

7 George D'Elia, *The Roles of the Public Library in Society: The Results of a National Survey: Final Report* (Evanston, Ill.: Urban Libraries Council, 1993).

8 Bruce T. Fraser, Timothy W. Nelson and Charles R. McClure, "Describing the Economic Impacts and Benefits of Florida Public Libraries: Findings and Methodological Applications for Future Work," *Library and Information Science Research* 24 (2002): 211-33; Charles R. McClure, Bruce T. Fraser, Timothy W. Nelson and Jane B. Robbins, *Economic Benefits and Impacts from Public Libraries in the State of Florida* (Tallahassee, Fla.: Information Use Management and Policy Institute, School of Information Studies, 2001) http://dlis.dos.state.fl.us/bld/finalreport (16 July 2003); Glen E. Holt et al., *Libraries Are Valuable: Prove It!* (St. Louis: St. Louis Public Library, 2000).

Glen E. Holt, Donald Elliott, and Amonia Moore, "Placing a Value on Public Library Services," *Public Libraries* 38, no. 2 (March/April 1999): 98-108.

9 For an overview, see Aabø, "Verdsetting av folkebibliotek," 246-68.

10 Walter Santagata and Giovanni Signorello, "Contingent Valuation and Cultural Policy Design: The Case of Napoli Musei Aperti," *Journal of Cultural Economics* 24, no. 3 (September 2000): 181-204. Riccardo Scarpa, Gemma Sirchian, and Marina Bravi, "Kernel vs. Logit Modeling of Single Bounded CV Responses: Valuing Access to Architectural and Visual Arts Heritage in Italy," in *Environmental Resource Valuation: Applications of Contingent Valuation Method in Italy*, ed. Richard Bishop and Donato Romano (Dordrecht: Kluwer, 1998): 233-44. Fernand Martin, "Determining the Size of Museum Subsidies," *Journal of Cultural Economics* 18, no. 4 (1994): 255-70.

11 Hugo Roche Rivera, "The Willing-to-Pay for a Public Mixed Good: The Colon Theatre in Argentina," in *Tenth International Conference on Cultural Economics, Barcelona 14-17 June 1998, Selection of Papers C.* (1998), 197-202. Trine Bille Hansen, "The Willingness-to-Pay for the Royal Theatre in Copenhagen as a Public Good," *Journal of Cultural Economics* 21, no. 1 (1997): 1-28.

12 Franco Papandrea, "Willingness to Pay for Domestic Television Programming," *Journal of Cultural Economics* 23 (August 1999): 149-66.

13 Ståle Navrud and Richard C. Ready, *Valuing Cultural Heritage: Applying Environmental Valuation Techniques to Historic Buildings, Monuments and Artifacts* (Cheltenham: Elgar Publishing, 2002). Ståle Navrud and Jon Strand, "Social Costs and Benefits of Preserving and Restoring the Nidaros Cathedral," in *Valuing Cultural Heritage: Applying Environmental Valuation Techniques to Historic Buildings, Monuments and Artifacts*, ed. Ståle Navrud and Richard C. Ready (Cheltenham: Elgar Publishing, 2002), 31-39. Marilena Pollicino and David Maddison, "Valuing the Benefits of Cleaning Lincoln Cathedral," *Journal of Cultural Economics* 25, no. 2 (May 2001): 131-48. Catherine M. Chambers, Paul E. Chambers, and John Whitehead, "Contingent Valuation of Quasi-Public Goods: Validity, Reliability and Application to Valuing a Historic Site," *Public Finance Review* 26, no. 2 (March 1998): 137-54. Edward Morey et al., *Valuing Acid Precipitation Assessment Programme (NAPAP)* (Washington, D.C.: 1997). Richard T. Carson and others, *Contingent Valuation of the Benefits of Conserving the Fes Medina, Quantification of Non-Moroccan's Willingness to Pay* (Cambridge, Mass.: Harvard University, 1997). Maurizio Maggi, "Il valore dei beni culturali: un'applicazione empirica," in *Economia dei Beni culturali*, ed. Giorgi Brosio (Torino: La Rosa editrice, 1994), 133-70. Pascal Grosclaude and Nils C. Soguel, "Valuing Damage to Historic Buildings Using a Contingent Market: A Case Study of Road Traffic Externalities," *Journal of Environmental Planning and Management* 37, no. 3 (June 1994): 279-87.

14 Holt et al., *Libraries Are Valuable: Prove It!* 2000. Holt, Elliott, and Moore, "Placing a Value on Public Library Services," 98-108. David W. Harless and Frank R. Allen, "Using the Contingent Valuation Method to Measure Patron Benefits of Reference Desk Service in an Academic Library," *College and Research Libraries* 60, no. 1 (January 1999): 56-69.

15 Results from other recent library surveys point in the same direction, although they did not explicitly ask about perceiving property rights. In a Swedish and a Norwegian study, 80% and 74%, respectively, of the respondents in the national samples found public libraries important for the local community, whereas only 58% and 47%, respectively, were library users. See Lars Höglund, "Bibliotekens värde," in *Ljusnande framtid: SOM-undersökningen 1998*, ed. Sören Holmberg and Lennart Weibull (Gothenburg: Göteborg Universitet, 1999), 115-28 and Heidi Kristin Reppen, *Bruk av folkebibliotek 1998* (Oslo: Statistisk sentralbyrå, 1998).

16 Norwegian Directorate for Public Libraries, *Act No. 108 of 20th December 1985. The Public Library Act: Including Latest Amendments as of 11th June 1993* (Oslo: Norwegian Directorate for Public Libraries, 1985).

17 Kenneth Arrow et al., "Report of the NOAA Panel on Contingent Valuation," *Federal Register* 58, no. 10 (15 January 1993): 4601-14.

18 Ragnar A. Audunson, "Folkebibliotekenes rolle i en digital framtid," in *Det siviliserte informasjonssamfunn*, ed. Ragnar A. Audunson and Niels Windfeld Lund (Bergen: Fagbokforlaget, 2001), 206-24. Svanhild Aabø and Jon Strand, "Public Library Assessment and Motivation by Altruism" (paper presented at the 11th Conference of the Association for Cultural Economics International, Minneapolis, May 2000), 20 pages, http://www.dac.neu.edu/economics/n.alper/acei/ACEI_2000.html (27 June 2003). Höglund, "Bibliotekens värde," 115-28. Holt, Elliott, and Moore, "Placing a Value on Public Library Services," 98-108.

19 Audunson, "Folkebibliotekenes rolle i en digital framtid," 206-24.

20 For a thorough introduction to the method, see Robert Cameron Mitchell and Richard T. Carson, *Using Surveys to Value Public Goods: The Contingent Valuation Method* (Washington, D.C.: Resources for the Future, 1989); Raymond J. Kopp, Werner W. Pommerehne, and Norbert Schwarz, eds., *Determining the Value of Non-Marketed Goods: Economic, Psychological, and Policy Relevant Aspects of Contingent Valuation Methods* (Boston: Kluwer, 1997) and Ian J. Bateman and Kenneth G. Willis, eds., *Valuing Environmental Preferences: Theory and Practice of the Contingent Valuation Method in the US, EU, and Developing Countries* (Oxford: Oxford University Press, 1999). For a comprehensive bibliography of CV studies, see Richard T. Carson et al., *Bibliography of Contingent Valuation Studies and Papers* (La Jolla, Calif.: Natural Resource Damage Assessment, 1994). And for CV studies of cultural goods, see Doug Noonan, *Contingent Valuation Studies in the Arts and Culture: An Annotated Bibliography* (Chicago: The Cultural Policy Center at the University of Chicago, 2002) http://culturalpolicy.uchicago.edu/workingpapers/Noonan11.pdf (16 July 2003).

21 Gwendolyn C. Morrison, "WTP and WTA in Repeated Trial Experiments: Learning or Leading?" *Journal of Economic Psychology* 21, no. 1 (February 2000): 57-72. Gwendolyn C. Morrison, "Understanding the Disparity between WTP and WTA: Endowment Effect, Substitutability, or Imprecise Preferences," *Economic Letters* 59 (1998): 189-94. Richard W. Dubourg, Mike W. Jones-Lee, and Graham Loomes, "Imprecise Preferences and the WTP–WTA Disparity," *Journal of Risk and Uncertainty* 9, no. 2 (October 1994):

115-33. Michael W. Hanemann, "Willingness to Pay and Willingness to Accept: How Much Can They Differ?" *American Economic Review* 81, no. 3 (June 1991): 635-47. Jack L. Knetsch, "Environmental Policy Implications of Disparities between Willingness to Pay and Compensation Demanded Measures of Values," *Journal of Environmental Economics and Management* 18, no. 3 (May 1990): 227-37.

22 Arrow et al., "Report of the NOAA Panel on Contingent Valuation," 4601-14.

23 Johan Anderson, Dan Vadnjal, and Hans-Erik Uhlin, "Moral Dimensions of the WTA–WTP Disparity: An Experimental Examination," *Ecological Economics* 32, no. 1 (January 2000): 153-62. Rebecca B. Boyce et al., "An Experimental Examination of Intrinsic Values as a Source of the WTA–WTP Disparity," *American Economic Review* 82, no. 5 (December 1992): 1366-73.

24 Michael P. Welsh and Gregory L. Poe, "Elicitation Effects in Contingent Valuation: Comparisons to a Multiple Bounded Discrete Choice Approach," *Journal of Environmental Economics and Management* 36, no. 2 (September 1998): 170-85. Russell K. Blamey, Jeff W. Bennett, and Mark D. Morrison, "Yea-Saying in Contingent Valuation Surveys," *Land Economics* 75, no. 1 (February 1999): 126-41.

Between New Public Management and Ethics: Library Management under Cross-Pressure

Carl Gustav Johannsen and Niels Ole Pors

In 2001, Johannsen and Pors conducted the first major survey on leadership and leaders in Danish libraries. This article focuses on preferences towards different leadership styles. The data document that Danish library leaders are very much in favor of the soft leadership styles. The findings also reveal that the library leaders with the highest job-satisfaction are the leaders who mostly emphasize the humanistic aspects of leadership.

Introduction

This article investigates attitudes and perceptions of Danish library leaders. The purpose is to discuss to what extent Danish library leaders are oriented towards New Public Management or towards softer management styles based on ethical values. However, we are well aware that attitudes in practice might contain elements from both kinds of management philosophies. Therefore it is necessary to carefully define and explain the two opposite management concepts in question.

The empirical foundation of this study is data from a recent, comprehensive questionnaire survey[1] of 411 Danish library leaders, representing public libraries as well as research libraries. The respondents represent 265 libraries. The questionnaire contains more than 200 questions and statements on perceptions and attitudes towards future challenges, leadership styles, management tools, job satisfaction, and the like. The 73 percent response rate was quite satisfactory.

New Public Management

New public management (NPM) is a common name for a public sector reform movement. Since the 1980s NPM has highly influenced public sector policies in the Western hemisphere. However, the term is not commonly used in the library world. Indeed, NPM belongs to the vocabulary of political scientists and sociologists. In Bryson's textbook[2] on library management, the term does not even appear in the index. However, the practical social, financial and cultural consequences behind the NPM label are nevertheless observed and felt by many library leaders and staff. The NPM framework has been variously denominated as post-bureaucratic, managerialism, market-based public administration and entrepreneurial government.[3] Although NPM covers a diversity of policy ambitions and outcomes dependent on time, country, government, etc., some common basic principles lie behind. As pointed out by Lane, the Public Sector Reform drive "was initiated during the 1980s in the advanced capitalist democracies as a response to the public sector expansion process after the Second World War."[4] Some critics, however, claim that because of the different models tried around the world, it is misleading to speak about a uniform management paradigm.[5]

A common feature of most NPM efforts is the aim to shape the public sector in the form of the private, introducing the mechanisms of management and markets within government. In other words, the goal is to replace administrative, hierarchical and professional cultures by commercial, market cultures. As a post-bureaucratic paradigm, NPM presupposes that universal or generic principles of management are ascendant and already transcending national legal traditions. The radicalism of how the NPM framework is implemented differs widely from country to country. On the one extreme we find hardcore NPM countries such as UK, USA, Australia and New Zealand; at the other end, the Scandinavian countries. Although NPM was originally conceptualized as a neoliberal ideology by Reagan and Thatcher, social democratic governments in, for example, the United Kingdom and Denmark are likely to continue promoting NPM-oriented policies.

The key elements of NPM in most countries include:

- customer- and market-orientation
- competition and user-choice
- outsourcing and privatization
- contract administration and performance review
- focus on management processes

Many authors see the implementation of NPM principles as primarily a result of external pressures from central government bodies. Alternative explanations might be mobility of leaders from the private to the public sector. In Denmark, however, this latter cause does not seem to be particularly significant. Indeed we have an extraordinarily low interchange between leaders in the private and the public sector. A recent survey[6] reveals that only 9 percent of Danish private-sector top leaders have earlier work experiences from the public sector. The other way around, the figures are even smaller: Only 2 percent of the Danish public leaders have had a prior career in a private company. It should be noted that the low cross-sector mobility in Denmark is particularly low compared to other European countries and the United States. Why do so few Danish private company leaders feel attracted by a similar position in a public institution? Differences as to salary levels seem an obvious explanation. However, other causes are listed by the leaders themselves. The mentioned Danish survey indicates that it is perceived differences as to freedom of action, especially concerning human resource management, and the arbitrary and obscure political agenda that really frightens private-sector leaders from seeking leadership positions in the public sector. In other words, it is the lack of *corporate governance* that makes public management less attractive to some. What can be concluded from this evidence is that the spread of NPM ideas in Denmark is not likely to be an effect of personal mobility of leaders from one sector to another.

However, it also seems misleading to consider NPM elements as entirely a result of external pressures. Indeed, key elements of the NPM framework have been introduced into the library sector due to independent, professional developments. It is especially true regarding the ongoing trend towards user- or customer-oriented points of view. The notions of systematic evaluation, user surveys, performance measurement and quality management have all been developed within the library sector by practitioners and researchers, and it has been proven that this evolution has happened quite independently of government NPM initiatives.[7] The popularity of Total Quality Management among both librarians and library leaders in many countries illustrates how NPM principles have been introduced into the library sector as a result of pressures and initiatives not only from the outside but also from within.[8] Post-bureaucratic and post-professional traits are also clearly visible in the general and long-term evolution from an internal, output-oriented, professional, library-oriented culture to outcome, demand and customer-oriented library models. In many respects, the impact of NPM is deep.

Also, the NPM framework itself is under constant change. Thus, the relative importance of management and commercial elements changes over time. The recent Danish Libraries Act (2000),[9] for example, is influenced by NPM thinking by promoting fee-based service in public libraries, introducing financial incentives into interlibrary cooperation and abolishing the existing monopoly of librarians to leadership positions in public libraries. Here, the commercial and market-oriented aspects of NPM are promoted especially.

Many Danish library leaders will certainly hesitate to name the increased use of contracts on all organizational level a post-bureaucratic trait. Contracts rather seem to increase paperwork and bureaucracy. Nevertheless, contract administration is an important part of present NPM practices. Semilegal contracts are indeed penetrating the life of many public institutions. Libraries make no exception here. There are four-year contracts between government and major research libraries, between government and library directors, and on the individual level, annual formal agreements, negotiated through yearly appraisal interviews between the library leaders and the individual employee. Contracts are indeed being introduced as a universal and expanding form of regulation, substituting rules and trusts relations as principal organizational integrators. The negations and signing of the four-year contract between the research library and the government, the yearly appraisal interviews between manager and employee, and the monitoring of the traffic interlibrary loans and the subsequent payment now form major events in the daily organizational life of many Danish libraries.

Also, the thinking and language of librarians has been influenced by NPM principles. According to our survey,[10] 52 percent of the respondents indicate that they believe in an increased importance of competitors in the future. Many libraries today have directors, customers, products and information services instead of chief librarians, users, loans and reference desks.

Values and Ethics

What are the realistic alternatives to the NPM paradigm? Indeed, a number of actual and historical options seem available. One is a return to the classic bureaucratic model as described by the German sociologist Max Weber. Some social scientists[11] and even library leaders have pointed out that fundamental values such as the "rule of law," democracy and citizenship have been endangered by market-driven social resource allocation. Legal rights, equality, freedom of expression and protection of human rights are considered better taken care of by the rule of traditional state and bureaucracy than by the forces of the free market. Those who emphasize "rule of law" are likely to stress the risks concerning abuse of discretion in connection with post-bureaucratic reforms and decentralization.

Another alternative might be to return to "the good old days" of the library pioneers when professional values of librarianship, the library spirit, and the universal ideas of Enlightenment were held in high esteem. It was an environment where determined and enthusiastic pioneers with clear visions created great results, avoiding the traps of bureaucracy. However, the question is whether those "good old days" have ever existed? Indeed, recent studies[12] of the history of public library management in Norway and the other Nordic countries have revealed that from the very beginning the Scandinavian public library movement was heavily influenced and even dominated by the hard philosophy of *scientific management* created by the American engineer, F.W. Taylor. American management principles were not, as believed by many NPM critics in the Nordic countries, imported in the 1980s and 1990s. It was an integrated element of the public library movement when it started in the early twentieth century. A number of Danish, Swedish, and Norwegian public library pioneers, for example, Haakon Nyhuus (1866-1913), were highly influenced by North American and British ideas and practices. Among the prominent public library pioneers, it is furthermore an established fact that Melvil Dewey himself was inspired by modern management thinking in his effort to create effective and rational public libraries utilizing the latest technologies and management techniques. Library management and library economy was one of the most important subjects taught at the first library school established by Dewey.[13]

A third way, besides the two retrograde—more or less realistic—alternatives, is to address the so-called *"softer" management philosophies*. A soft management philosophy is not an established term within organization theory. Here it covers a divers multitude of different ideas and approaches stretching in time from the days of early motivation theory in the 1930s and 1940s to contemporary concepts and buzz words such as the learning organization, knowledge management, organizational culture, change management, and the like. What differentiates this heterogeneous group from NPM-oriented paradigms is probably its common humane profile. Physical and psychological needs, feelings, attitudes and basic assumptions have traditionally been the primary focus of the classic psychologist and social-psychologist management authors such as Maslow, Herzberg, McGregor,[14] Argyris, and Schein. Today, new buzzwords have been added: ethics, values, emotional intelligence, corporate culture, symbols, sense making, reflection, identity, therapy and even love. Among the gurus of this second, late-modern wave of soft management philosophies you find the names Karl E. Sveiby, Peter Senge, Karl Weick, James G. March, David Goleman and many others. In many ways, they are very different. Nevertheless, they also share a common focus on the human individual. You may go a step further and emphasize that most of these different theories have a view on the human nature in common. If the premise of NPM is *economic* man—self-interest motivates citizens—the soft models assume that trust and cooperation play the essential role. To simplify a bit, you may say that proponents of classic bureaucracy see the *state* as the key organizational model in society. NPM adherents, on the other hand, consider the *market* as an ideal social organization. Finally, we have the supporters of soft management concepts to whom the *civil society* represents an optimal form.

One essential characteristic of NPM was the aim to translate private-sector management concepts and practices into a public-sector context. However, the same can be said about most of the soft philosophies. Corporate culture, knowledge management, the learning organization and so forth have all been applied in private-sector environments, most often even before they were introduced in public institutions. It means that the public-private sector dichotomy is not particularly helpful to distinguish between NPM and value-oriented management thinking and practice. The real watershed rather seems to be between a *system*-oriented paradigm focusing on contractual or market relations and a *life-world*-oriented approach emphasizing trust, dialogue and ethical values.

To avoid a common misunderstanding, it is also important to stress that the soft principles and methods typically are seen as means to achieve certain ends; they are not goals in themselves. The soft approaches are applied in industrial contexts in the private sector in the pursuit of profit, market shares, effectiveness, efficiency and other relevant business goals. The same can be said of their use in public-sector environments where they are supposed to further institutional objectives such as customer satisfaction, increased circulation, innovation, cost-effectiveness, and also competitive advantage. Neither NPM nor soft management followers are likely to see themselves as saints or philanthropists. It is rather a question of approaching the same goals through different strategies or methods, although some times certain means become goals in themselves.

Because of the complexity and variability of the two paradigms in question, it is not feasible to ask respondents directly about their preferences as to the two paradigms. Direct and straight questions about abstract issues are likely to be considered as strange leading to survey results of low validity. Instead, we chose an indirect approach, exposing the respondents to a multitude of different questions on attitudes and perceptions towards leadership styles and roles, desired competencies, and knowledge and application of different management tools. This indirect approach, on the other hand, creates a number of problems identifying and interpreting patterns. In the next section these problems will be addressed in greater details.

Main Survey Results

Before addressing the key research question, some basic characteristics of Danish library leaders are presented. As to gender, a clear majority of the respondents are female, most prominent in public libraries, where 65 percent of the leaders are women. In research libraries, the distribution is almost fifty–fifty. It is interesting to consider the gender distribution in the context of leadership level. Among top leaders, actually, males form a slight minority. In contrast, at the middle management level 73 percent are women. The age distributions spans from 30 to 67 with an average of 51. It is remarkable that the average is about the same, independent of gender and library type. From a sociocultural perspective, it is thought provoking to notice that the generation now in power of Danish public and research libraries, in general, got their socialization during the "rebellious" years following 1968.

Some of the patterns revealed by the survey were not particularly surprising or unexpected. Thus, male leaders seem to be more likely to emphasize new technology and Internet than their female peers. In the same way, leaders from large libraries are familiar with more management tools, more focused on external stakeholders and more inclined to projects and teamwork than their colleagues from smaller units.

However, also rather unexpected patterns were found. Conspicuous and hot topics such as multi-ethnic staff, outsourcing and fee-based library services were all very low prioritized by the leaders when asked about their perception of future challenges. Also certain discrepancies between what is taught in the management literature and actual library practices were observed. Flat structures and removal of hierarchies according to the leaders themselves are occurring to a much lesser degree in practice as to be expected from statements in standard management textbooks. Indeed, 71 percent of the respondents indicate that the number of hierarchical levels has been unchanged during the last three years. Only 20 percent have experienced fewer levels, whereas 10 percent report an increase. It is also rather a myth than a reality that "everybody" does project work. In fact, respondents indicate that one-third is not using projects at all.

Analysis

Back to our initial research question: To what extent does preferences and attitudes of Danish library leaders reflect an orientation towards NPM or towards softer, value-based management ideas? We will deal with the question through data on *leadership style, knowledge and use of management tools* and *desired future qualification*.

Library leaders' use of different management styles shows a distinctive pattern. Table 1 indicates how bureaucratic and "tayloristic" methods based on commands, supervision, and control are firmly rejected by a clear majority. Cross-tabulations, furthermore, reveal that it is especially female leaders and public library leaders that most consequently reject the hard methods. On the other hand, soft management styles with values, dialogue, teamwork, motivation and mutual respect as key ingredients are used by a vast majority. Again, the female leaders seem to be stronger in their belief in the soft values than their male colleagues. Indeed, the survey results confirm the existence of a particular and distinct female style of leadership.

Table 1. The Leaders' Perception of Own Leadership Style
[in percentages]

	Not at all	To a certain degree	Yes, very much
I use dialogue and co-operation	1	12	87
I use motivation and mutual respect	2	18	80
I use attitudes and values	2	29	70
I use rules and regulations	41	58	1
I give commands	67	32	1
I use supervision and control	69	30	1

Source: Johannsen, Carl G. and Pors, Niels O., *Ledere og ledelse i danske biblioteker* (Frederiksberg: The Librarians' Union, 2001): 29-31.

A similar picture is seen when regarding preferences as to future leadership roles.[15] Turning to specific leadership roles, the following are stressed as the most important:

1. Strategist and creator of visions
2. Creator of results
3. Shaper of values and culture
4. Network builder

The roles least appreciated by the leaders were:

1. Controller
2. Rule maker
3. Subject specialist
4. Administrator

The preferences reveal that the classical bureaucratic and administrative roles are definitely in low course compared to leader- and strategist-oriented roles.

Regarding desired future qualifications (see table 2), similar preferences are seen. There are some general traits when preferred competencies are cross-tabulated with background variables such as gender, library type, leadership level and size of library. In general, the perceived need for future qualifications are highest among leaders of small units and among middle managers compared to leaders and top leaders of larger libraries.

Table 2. Desired Future Qualifications on a Scale from 1 to 7
[7 indicates the highest preference]

Change management	4.7
Value-based management	4.7
Quality management	4.6
Knowledge management	4.5
Network organization	4.3
Human resource management	4.2
Personal development	4.2
Information and communication technology (ICT)	4.2
Team management	4.2
Contract administration	4.0
Management-by-objectives (MBO)	4.0
Library professional skills	3.6
Financial management	3.4
Foreign languages	2.5

Source: Johannsen, Carl G. and Pors, Niels O., *Ledere og ledelse i danske biblioteker* (Frederiksberg: The Librarians' Union, 2001): 53-56.

The pattern revealed has certainly something to do with confidence. This observation is confirmed when regarding table 3 showing perceived knowledge of various management tools. Compared to table 2, it is evident that present knowledge of a certain management concept and perceived qualification needs are interrelated. The first column represents an interpretation concerning whether the tool seems to be mostly related to NPM or to value-based management (VBM). The picture seems to mirror the list of desired qualifications: Library leaders think they know about NPM-oriented tools. They want to learn more about managing soft values and ethics.

Table 3. The Leaders' Degree of Knowledge Concerning Various
Management Tools [in percentages]

	Tool	Comprehensive knowledge	Some knowledge	No knowledge
NPM	Corporate plans and accounts	50	46	3
NPM	Management by objectives	36	51	13
NPM	User surveys	35	60	6
NPM	Strategic planning	21	62	17
NPM	Contract management	20	48	33
NPM	Performance related salary	16	65	19
NPM	Quality systems	10	51	39
VBM	Work place assessment	39	51	10
VBM	Staff-assessment	27	58	16
VBM	Value management	15	54	31
VBM	Knowledge management	9	60	32
VBM	Knowledge and competence accounting	6	49	46
VBM	Ethical accounting	4	46	50
VBM	Image and branding	4	32	64
VBM	Environ-mental plans and accounts	3	32	65
VBM	Social accounting	2	22	76

Source: Johannsen, Carl G. and Pors, Niels O., *Ledere og ledelse i danske biblioteker* (Frederiksberg: The Librarians' Union, 2001): 45-49.

Thus, there is no discrepancy between this interpretation and the fact mentioned above that leaders mostly desire to learn about change, management, values, quality and knowledge management. Also, the particularly low prioritization of subjects like budgets and accounts and contract management seems to be consistent with the revealed knowledge pattern. Indeed, actual knowledge and preferences often point in different directions. "We already know about NPM tools, and therefore we are especially aware and curious about the human and philosophical aspects of leadership" might be a reasonable interpretation of typical library leader attitudes.

In summary, the results presented above do not show a clear picture as to the key question whether Danish library leaders are oriented towards NPM or values and ethics. As to knowledge about different management tools, there is a clear dominance of elements from the NPM toolbox. On the other hand, when reflecting about future leadership roles and styles, the preferences of the leaders show a marked attraction towards roles such as shaper of culture, strategist, and political manager and soft management styles emphasizing dialogue, motivation and creation of meaning and identity. The same pattern is seen when regarding desired needs for new competences and preferred modes of leadership. Again, the soft types are in focus. Danish leaders wish to learn about change, knowledge and value-based management and they very clearly prefer to perform their leadership through dialogue, cooperation, mutual respect and shared values.

Discussion and Interpretation

The data presented above do not provide an unambiguous answer to the initial research question as to the relative importance of NPM or values in the minds of Danish library leaders. To make sense of the data, two distinct interpretation approaches are available. You can consider NPM and value-based management as a dichotomy, as a question of either/or. This has already been done above. Alternatively, you may consider the two approaches as complementary aspects of leadership and management or as historical answers to varying environmental challenges.

Let us consider the notion of management concepts as answers to changing environmental challenges. According to Klausen,[16] four recognized drivers of organizational change have appeared since 1945: Complexity; turbulence; claims of openness, publicity and legitimacy; and increased cross-pressure. As an answer, four managerial consequences are likely to occur:

1. Increased complexity → development of professional and administrative excellence.
2. Increased uncertainty and turbulence → development of strategic overview.
3. Claims for openness, publicity and legitimacy → development of values and ethics.
4. Increased cross-pressure → development of political management and navigation.

In turn, these managerial consequences suggest certain responses in terms of need for new leadership personalities, qualifications and roles. For example, development of adequate professional and administrative expertise requires familiarity with a number of tools such as resource management, budgeting, planning and librarianship. In the same way, strategic overview is likely to be enhanced by methods and tools such as strategic management, SWOT-analysis and user surveys. Ethics and values are stimulated through dialogue and interaction oriented leadership styles and communication models emphasizing identity and meaning. Finally, political management skills are developed through political contacts and increased visibility towards the political system and other external stakeholders.

Thus, the apparently shifted focus from NPM to values among Danish library leaders might be interpreted as a response to a diversity of different challenges. In general, NPM tools seem especially adequate when addressing challenges within the area of administrative skills and political management. On the contrary, there is an ongoing discussion whether NPM, in fact, through its focus on the market mechanism, may threaten basic democratic and human rights and claims. For example, introduction of fee-based library services is supposed to influence societal values such as openness and free access to information.

A similar simple interpretation involves the classic distinction between leadership and management.[17] Management is about coping with complexity whereas leadership is coping with change. These two different functions shape the characteristic activities of management and leadership. Planning, budgeting, organizing, staffing, controlling and problem solving are the typical management activities. By contrast, leading an organization to change begins with setting a direction, aligning people, creating coalitions, motivating and inspiring by appealing to basic human needs, values and emotions. What is important to notice here is that both leadership and management are necessary for success in an increasingly complex and volatile business environment. According to this last conceptual framework, value-based management and NPM, like leadership and management, can be seen as distinctive and complementary approaches and not as mutually exclusive approaches. The preferences and perceptions of the Danish library leaders here make sense because they reflect recognition of both management and leadership as necessary parts of their work.

Conclusion

As a start of the article, two concepts—NPM and value-based management—with different origins, functions and characteristics were presented. The main purpose of the article was outlined, namely to examine to what extent perceptions and attitudes of Danish library leaders are influenced by these two main management currents.

As to preferences and future desired skills, the picture is quite clear. Leadership and value-based styles and roles are preferred to management and NPM approaches. However, the outcome of the investigations, using data from the recent Danish library management survey, did not present an unambiguous picture. As to knowledge and application of management tools, NPM tools dominate the scene. This means that we cannot infer from the data that preferences towards values originate from mere positive feelings or the fact that many leaders feel they are already familiar with NPM. In other words, we are not able to judge to what extent Danish library leaders see NPM and value-based management as two mutually exclusive and competing concepts or as complementary models reflecting the diversity of managerial challenges facing today's library leaders. What furthermore might be concluded is that in an evolutionary process, most Danish library leaders would think that the coming managerial era belongs to value-based management principles. In this respect, Danish library managers differ a bit from their private-sector colleagues.[18] The private-sector leaders are similarly firm in their belief in soft management through dialogue and motivation. However, they differ from library leaders in their more moderate rejection of rules, orders and control. Between 41 and 69 percent of the library leaders indicate that they are not at all using such management means. Among Danish private-sector leaders, the corresponding percentages lie between 27 and 33 percent. Comparing these figures might raise the question whether library managers are biased towards soft management styles or whether their one-sided views represent an adequate answer to future challenges?

Notes

1 Carl G. Johannsen and Niels O. Pors, *Ledere og ledelse i danske biblioteker* (Frederiksberg: Bibliotekarforbundet/The Librarians' Union, 2001).

2 Jo Bryson, *Effective Library and Information Centre Management.* Second Edition (Aldershot: Gower, 1999).

3 Laurence E. Lynn, "A Critical Analysis of the New Public Management," *International Public Management Journal* 1, no. 1 (1998): 107-23.

4 Jan-Erik Lane, "Introduction: Public Sector Reform: Only Deregulation, Privatization and Marketization?" in *Public Sector Reform: Rationale, Trends and Problems*, ed. Jan-Erik Lane (London: Sage, 1997): 1-16.

5 Lynn, "A Critical Analysis of the New Public Management," 107-23.

6 *Mandag Morgen* (18 February 2002): 36-39.

7 Bryson, *Effective Library and Information Centre Management*, 383-89.

8 Carl G. Johannsen, "The Use of Quality Control Principles and Methods in Library and Information Science Theory and Practice," *Libri* 42, no. 4 (1992): 283-95.

9 Biblioteksstyrelsen, *Lov om biblioteksvirksomhed* (Copenhagen: Biblioteksstyrelsen/The Danish National Library Authority, 2000).

10 Johannsen and Pors, *Ledere og ledelse i danske biblioteker*, 25.

11 Lynn, "A Critical Analysis of the New Public Management," 107-23.

12 Gunhild Salvesen, "Hva kjennetegner kvalitetsarbeidet i norske folkebibliotek?" in *Det siviliserte informasjonssamfunn: Folkebibliotekenes rolle ved inngangen til en digital tid*, ed. Ragnar A. Audunson and Niels W. Lund (Bergen: Fagbokforlaget, 2001): 269-91.

13 Salvesen, "Hva kjennetegner kvalitetsarbeidet i norske folkebibliotek?" 275.

14 Bryson, *Effective Library and Information Centre Management*, 215-28.

15 Johannsen and Pors, *Ledere og ledelse i danske biblioteker*, 34-37.

16 Kurt Klaudi Klausen, *Offentlig Organisation, Strategi og Ledelse* (Odense: Odense Universitetsforlag, 2000): 47, 108-19.

17 John P. Kotter, "What Leaders Really Do," *Harvard Business Review* 79, no. 11 (December 2001): 85-96.

18 Det Danske Ledelsesbarometer, *Dansk ledelse anno 2000: Statusrapport* (Copenhagen: Handelshøjskolen i Århus/The Aarhus School of Business and Ledernes Hovedorganisation, 2000): 46-48.

Part III

THE CHALLENGES OF THE MULTICULTURAL SOCIETY

Usability Studies and Focus Groups as Methods for Developing Digital Public Library Services in a Multiethnic Society

Ågot Berger

Recent surveys have revealed that web-based library services are very much appreciated by immigrants, making the public library one of the key integrative forces among Danish public institutions. Ågot Berger, an experienced practitioner, shows how different types of user survey approaches—focus groups and usability studies—might be combined to optimize targeted web-based library services.

Background and Overview

Migration on a world scale is growing and will probably continue to grow in the coming years. In their book *The Age of Migration*, Castles and Miller[1] analyze the changing character of the migration. They identify five trends: globalization, acceleration, differentiation, feminization and politicizing. Out of the world population of 6 billion, it is estimated that around 120 million are immigrants. According to Seeberg,[2] there are several reasons for the growing migration:

- Access to modern information and communication technology (television, mobile telephones and Internet)—many people learn about higher living standards in other parts of the world
- Uneven economic development means that a growing number of people want to seek jobs and better lives in the Western countries

- Political and religious repression and civil war create migrants in larger scale

The global migration pattern described above will certainly also influence the situation in Denmark. In 1980, 3 percent of the inhabitants in Denmark originated from foreign countries. Today the percentage is 7. Although these percentages are small compared to Germany, the United Kingdom or Sweden, the ethnic minorities will be a growing part of the Danish population, especially in the bigger cities.

What will be the consequences of this demographic development for public libraries? Does it imply a change in the library services offered to the public or is it possible to continue with "business as usual?" Here, my point is that public libraries should design a library service that is relevant for the population in the specific local area. This means that the demographic and cultural distribution should be taken into consideration. To do so, it is necessary to challenge traditional approaches to public library service, and to create new answers, new methods and new standards. It is necessary not so much because of cultural or ethnic differences but because libraries are facing user groups with social characteristics much different from traditional Danish library users. Many immigrants are poorly educated; some are even illiterate. Certainly there are also many well-educated people in the minority groups, but most of the newcomers are not. In addition, about 50 percent of people with another ethnic background than Danish are unemployed.

On the other hand, immigrants are met with some expectations from their new society. They are supposed to learn Danish, to acquire some kind of job qualifications skills enabling them to make a living. Certainly, the newcomers themselves demand the skills required, because it is their own interest to become integrated into the society as equal citizens, with equal rights and job opportunities. They can actually use the library in different ways in their efforts to become integrated in their new country.

In my paper, I focus mainly on three points:

- What characterizes the needs of Danish immigrant library users? (results from *Refuge for Integration* survey)
- Experiences and evaluation from different user study approaches in a particular ethnic minority context
- To what extent do actual library services correspond with what the ethnic minorities demand?

My background to deal with these questions is:

- Eight years of work as public librarian in Aarhus, Denmark, with special responsibilities within ethnic librarianship. Presently, head of a community library in Copenhagen and before that with the Danish Central Library for Immigrant Literature (DCLIL).

- The user study entitled *Refuge for Integration: A Study of How the Ethnic Minorities in Denmark Use the Libraries* (in Danish, *Frirum til integration*), published in 2001.[3] My part of the survey was primarily to conduct the focus-group interviews.

- Author of the book *Mangfoldighedens biblioteker* (*Libraries of Diversity*)[4] that focuses on how Danish library services to immigrants and linguistic minorities have developed over the last thirty years.

- Recent experiences in conducting a *usability test* with a group of women with minority backgrounds, preparing a tailored website for immigrant women.

Immigrant Users' Needs: Results from *Refuge for Integration*

In Denmark in 1999-2000, three cooperating libraries—the State and University Library/DCLIL, Odense County Library and the Aarhus Municipal Libraries—conducted a large-scale user survey. The final report, *Refuge for Integration*, was published in 2001. As far as I know, this survey represents the first major study of how the ethnic minorities use the libraries in the Nordic countries.

Outside the Nordic countries, there have been other significant surveys in these areas. One such study was published in the United Kingdom: the Marlene Morrison and Patrick Roach report *Public Libraries, Ethnic Diversity and Citizenship*.[5] This was an important source of inspiration for the Danish project. In their survey they conclude that public libraries seem to be threatened by being bypassed by the ethnic minorities as an essential information resource. Their interviews revealed an ambivalent attitude towards libraries. Some characterized the library as "a place on the hill," existing in splendid isolation "up there," while the community was getting on with their own business.[6] Unlike the Danish survey, Morrison and Roach also investigated nonusers.

The purpose of *Refuge for Integration* was to find out how minorities use libraries and to learn about their satisfaction with the services provided. Finally, we were also interested in their suggestions and recommendations for improving the libraries. I will elaborate on the methods applied in the following chapter.

The survey results were published (in Danish) in the spring of 2001. The main conclusions and results of *Refuge for Integration* are:

- The percentage of borrowers among ethnic minorities fairly equals the share of borrowers among the population in general. However, users from the ethnic minorities use the library more intensely than the population in general.

The library is seen as a kind of sanctuary by ethnic minorities, especially by girls, youngsters and elderly men. Of all respondents participating in the questionnaire survey, 24% indicated that they visit the library every day and 55% replied that they use it 1-2 days a week. The respective corresponding numbers for the library users in general are 4% and 32%. Especially among young immigrants a high percentage, 84%, indicated that they visit the library at least once a week. For older male users, the library plays a particularly important role as a meeting place. It is a place where they meet friends or acquaintances and read foreign newspapers and journals. 86% of the older people said that they visit the library weekly. The reason why libraries have become so popular as meeting places for ethnic minorities may be due to the fact that the atmosphere there seems to come close to what they found in the teahouses and cafes of their native countries. The library is seen as an open and noncommercial environment, in which they can freely come and go.

- The library use pattern of the minorities differs from that of the average population by being more varied and equally divided between the different services provided.

The following figures compare data from an earlier user survey with data from *Refuge for Integration*. (Results from a general user survey in Aarhus Municipal Libraries are shown in brackets.) The minority users indicated that 53% [78%] use the library for borrowing books, 42% [49%] for borrowing music, 34% [22%] for videotapes, and 50% [25%] for reading newspapers. Especially remarkable is the use of Internet, where 65% of the interviewed migrants said that they use the Internet at the library, compared to only 19% of users in general. 17% [6%] responded that they use the library as a place of sojourn, where you meet friends and so forth.

- It is mainly adults who demand and use materials in their mother tongue. They also wish to influence which books and music the libraries purchase.

Nonfiction is preferred to fiction. It is a characteristic of those nonfiction titles that account for the largest number of loans that they deal with topics related to the cultural context of the immigrants' original countries such as books on cooking, childcare, sex guidance, religion, history, and contemporary politics. Many of those interviewed indicated that they consciously seek materials that help them maintain and develop their familiarity with the history, culture, and current developments of their native country. A good provision of literature and film in their native language was important, they argued, partly for the newly arrived, and partly to ensure that children and young people acquire and maintain a knowledge of their own cultural background and identity. However, there is also an expressed need for fiction in their original language instead of translated versions. Several of those interviewed emphasized that they wanted to influence the purchasing policy regarding books and music.

- A particularly intensive library use is apparent among young people who have a minority background and are younger than eighteen.

They often develop close relationships with the staff. This means that the staff is also likely to carry out tasks, which are more or less social or educational. Not long ago, the primary worry of many public librarians was that young people were supposed to drop library use totally. Today, the opposite situation seems to be the case. However, their purpose is not so much to borrow books: it is the computer and Internet facilities that attract them. You could say that many youngsters use the libraries as a kind of alternative youth center. This tendency is considered to be something of a problem by the library staff and other users due to the noisy behavior of the young immigrants. Many of the grown-ups that I interviewed spontaneously mentioned problems of disturbance and complained that the staff accepted too high a noise level. Many users point out that the library is a place where they can find peace and a quiet environment, for example, for study purposes. Actually, many migrants live in crowded flats with many residents, visitors and relatives. Therefore, it is important, not the least from a minority point of view, to ensure that the library offers study places and other facilities.

- Children and young people mainly use materials in Danish.

Ethnic minority children and young people are likely to focus on what might provide them with a joint identity with other Danes of the same age. In fact, many of the parents interviewed expressed concern that their children will distance themselves from their own cultural background. Therefore the parents would like the libraries to support initiatives, which encourage the youngsters to seek and appreciate their own roots. When children, to a very limited extent, demand materials in their native language, it is probably due to the fact that they cannot read or write their native language. Most children only speak their mother tongue because that is the language spoken in their homes. Many of those interviewed indicated that their awareness of ethnicity has been growing during adolescence. At that time they also become interested in learning their mother tongue, feeling that bilingual skills could be an advantage that improves job options and trading relations.

- For the girls, the library is a place of refuge, a legitimate sanctuary outside the family.

In some of the more conservative ethnic communities, opportunities for girls to participate in social activities are limited compared with those for Danish girls. Apparently, libraries have become an alternative, a respectable place, where minority parents allow their daughters to stay unsupervised. In the observations during our research, it became apparent that the girls appreciated the libraries as places of refuge where they meet friends, flirt innocently with boys, or chat on the Internet, free of the, often severe, social control exercised by parents or relatives. In fact, they wanted the library to establish "secret rooms" for girls only, to prevent cousins and uncles from observing them chatting on Internet.

- There is an overall satisfaction with the libraries, but dissatisfaction with the provision of materials in native languages.

It is a common feature of all the focus interviews that the participants consider the library a pleasant place. However, critical voices maintain that the collections in mother tongue languages are too small and too old. This concerns collections of books, music, videos, etc. They also demand a rich selection of newspapers and periodicals. In Aarhus and Odense, the stock of adult books in *immigrant languages* totals 5,600 units and 4,800 units, respectively—distributed on more than ten languages. The population is 285,000 in Aarhus and 184,000 in Odense. The total holdings of books are one million in Aarhus and 825,000 in

Odense. Thus, the stock in native language represents approximately 0.5 percent of the total holdings. The corresponding percentage of citizens originating from less developed countries represents about 10 percent of the inhabitants in the two cities. A conspicuous underrepresentation of ethnic materials is hereby documented.

- General satisfaction with service and staff attitudes. More bilingual staff requested.

Both the questionnaire survey and the focus group interviews yielded a positive evaluation of both the staff and the services offered. Of sixty-one comments, thirty-six were positive, and words such as "sweet," "friendly," "helpful," "polite," "open," "funny," "competent" and "smiling" were used. Twenty-five comments were negative. Nine pointed out that the staff seemed to be too busy to help. Examples of discrimination experienced from the library staff are not found in the qualitative and quantitative data collected. In one single case, a borrower experienced discrimination from another borrower. In this case, the staff intervened on behalf of the discriminated user.

The motives for requesting more bilingual staff are both pragmatic and symbolic. In addition, bilingual staff are supposed to be knowledgeable about the problems of ethnic minorities and should therefore able to communicate better. Many of the interviewees believed that they speak Danish so well that they had not experienced any language barriers at the library. However it is widely felt that newly arrived immigrants and those who do not master the Danish language would be likely to greatly gain benefit from the available of more bilingual staff.

- The Internet is the only library service which ethnic minorities seem to use significantly more than other services.

The Internet is used by the grown-ups primarily for chat, e-mails and, to a smaller extent, information searching. Many immigrants come to read the daily newspapers from, for example, Eritrea and Sri Lanka, or in Kurdish, which are often only available on the Internet.

The desire to use the Internet for information searching seems to be decreasing by age. The fact that many young people are so fascinated by computer technology is likely to pave the way for the acquisition of further qualifications. The writing culture of the Internet means that young people using the Internet support their learning of Danish and English.

Different Approaches to Studying User Needs

The ethnic minorities do not represent a homogenous user group. Like other people, they are different in many respects: culture, language, social class, religion, education, gender, library traditions, among others. In general, library staff is not particularly familiar with the background of the different groups of minorities. This can create an atmosphere of uncertainty in the dialogue between library staff and the newcomers. Newcomers, on the other hand, often only have very few experiences with Western-style library service.

In addition, public libraries seem hesitant, and with very little experience in making user surveys targeted to this particular group. As I have mentioned before, there are very few user studies, especially in a Nordic context, to be used as role models by the libraries.

In the coming year, it is necessary to develop different methods to collect data about and analyze the expectations and needs of ethnic minorities. I will review some of the experiences I have made during the last three years in this field.

Methods Used in *Refuge for Integration*

Which method you choose when you wish to understand and explore a given field, has, of course, been the object of big discussions and scientific works. Information professionals often use authorities such as Andersen,[7] Gorman and Clayton[8] and Steinar Kvale.[9] When we were planning the *Refuge for Integration*, we assumed that an optimal way to carry out a user study was to combine quantitative methods (data from loan statistics and questionnaires) with qualitative methods of study (focus group interviews). However, to conduct a survey based on a random sample from local authority files showed up to be problematic in many respects.

Associate professor Lise Togeby from the University of Aarhus has described the particular problems in connection with conducting a survey of perceived discrimination.[10] She concludes that although there are positive Swedish experiences where acceptable response rates have been achieved, it is questionable whether costly questionnaire surveys and telephone interviews are worth the efforts. In spite of a combination of the two data collection methods, it was possible only to obtain data from 40 percent of the selected respondents. In the questionnaire survey, the average response rate was even lower—about 17 percent. One particular problem was to get reliable data on telephone numbers because of mobile phones, private numbers and the like. Reluctance to participate was only observed by 7-13 percent of the respondents.

Umit Necef, associate professor at University of Southern Denmark, directly recommended us to "forget about" questionnaire surveys. His advice was to conduct qualitative interviews with ethnic library users, asking them why other members of their minority group were not using the library.

Based on this and similar advice, we decided to prioritize focus groups in combination with a questionnaire survey conducted among library users with minority background and supplemented with loan data from the borrower register of the involved public libraries. The group to which questionnaires were administered comprised 322 users representing different ethnic minorities from six libraries. The libraries included the two main libraries in Aarhus and Odense and four branches in areas with densely migration population: Gellerup and Hasle (Aarhus) and Vollsmose and Rising (Odense). To obtain an acceptable response rate, we walked around in the library inviting users to fill in the form. In general, people were positive and willing to fill in. Some (especially some older men) had problems with writing the answers. Many seem to think that the questionnaires were too long, so they gave up filling in part of the form. That means a high proportion of "do not know" answers.

The extract of the borrowers' register of Aarhus Municipal Libraries and Odense County Library gave interesting information on the number of borrowed materials on a specific day (October 1999) added with information about age, sex, descent, local area and so forth. The statistical snapshot showed that:

- The share of borrowers in the non-Danish group fairly equals the share of borrowers belonging to the population in general.
- Women and children are to some extent underrepresented compared to borrowers with Danish background.
- Persons from different countries of origin use the libraries to a varied extent. Persons from Iran, Vietnam and Chile are fairly highly placed with regard to the share of library cards, whereas particularly Arabic-speaking groups (Palestinians, Lebanese and Iraqis) possess library cards to a much smaller extent.
- On average, patrons from ethnic minorities borrow fewer items than the population in general.

The *focus group* interviews included fifteen groups (fifty persons) representing the following communities from Odense and Aarhus: Bosnian, Iranian, Iraqi, Pakistani, Palestinian, Somali, Turkish and Vietnamese.[11] The interviews provide a huge amount of interesting data on views, opinion and recommendations that can give useful information relevant to other Nordic countries as well.

The method that we chose, by combining three different methods, enabled us to describe the users' behavior, how they use the library, and by combining with the focus groups we also got important information about attitudes and user recommendations. The number of persons interviewed was small. But in combination with the statistical data from the borrowers' register, the interview provides strong evidence confirming the trends revealed through other data collection methods.

Usability Tests in Developing a
Portal for Minority Women

For several years, libraries in Denmark have emphasized the importance of high-quality Internet sites. For the last five years, there has been specific focus on Internet as a tool and important addition to the libraries' materials support and services to ethnic minorities.

FINFO.dk—Information for Ethnic Minorities in Denmark—is the main Danish Internet service targeted to immigrants. FINFO is a joint project of the Danish Central Library for Immigrant Literature and seventy Danish Public Libraries. Working in close cooperation, the libraries involved develop and maintain a website that provides access to relevant regional and local information.

FINFO was started in 1996 as a part of Aarhus Public Libraries services to the different ethnic minorities in the area. From the very beginning it was the vision of FINFO to offer an up-to-date Internet-based service to library users from the ethnic minorities containing information about both Denmark and their home countries. The overall aim of FINFO still is to provide ethnic minorities with better access to information about rights, obligations and opportunities in the Danish society. The goal of FINFO is to present a resource guide to information about the Danish society in these languages: Danish, Albanian, Arabic, Bosnian/Croatian/Serbian, English, French, Kurdish (Kurmanji and Sorani), Persian, Tamil, Turkish, Urdu and Vietnamese. However, Sorani-Kurdish is not supported by Windows or other operative systems based on the Unicode standard. The presentation of text in Tamil and Urdu came within reach with the launching of Windows XP, which supports those languages. In combination with a glyph-rendering program—

Autoglyph—Windows XP technology will hopefully enable FINFO to activate these two additional languages during the first half of 2003. By being the first website to present several alphabets on the same technical platform, FINFO has crossed new frontiers and contributed to the development of multilingual web technology.

Usability and FINFO's Women Portal

The importance of Internet access for ethnic minorities was fully documented in *Refuge for Integration*. Immigrant women, however, seem to make much less use of both libraries and Internet than their fellow men. Indeed, women seem to be rather isolated in their homes, having, in general, limited knowledge about Danish society and the different opportunities for women. Even where their families have access to the Internet, the women rarely use it.

For these reasons, a project has been started in 2001 to develop a special web page as an integrated part of FINFO, designed by, and for, minority women. In the design process, usability methods were used as a key product development tool. The aim of the project is to make access to relevant information easier for immigrant women.

Immediately, the job seemed easy to me. As the web editor in these fields, I was responsible for pulling together relevant links from national and local authorities about hospital, food, children and other important information for newcomers. Actually, I thought that I would be able to put together relevant information on a website—without involving the users before the site was ready for testing. Initially, I had different reservations as to the usability study approach:

- Problems in finding relevant information suppliers
- The target group is not familiar with information seeking on the Internet
- I considered another test superfluous; I thought I already knew the needs of immigrant women
- I disliked the idea of a private consultant firm, UNI-C, earning money from these projects

What Is a Usability Test?

Usability implies that the user actively participates and plays a central role in the design process. The method is—as far as I know—primarily used as a tool for the design of websites. In my opinion, the method can easily be transferred to other fields such as testing OPACs and library interior design. The main strengths of the method are that you actually observe what the users do when using the system. Compared to other types of user surveys, as a designer you do not have to interpret what the users might need or demand from general statements. On the contrary, the usability approach enables you to directly observe how the users react to different solutions concerning content and interface. This characteristic of usability as a method also means that the voice of the user becomes much more prominent and binding on the designer. Indeed, usability makes the user the central figure, not the project makers, librarians, managers or the institutions involved.

The method of usability is described in further detail in several standard works including those of Molich[12] and Nielsen.[13]

The main points are:

- Optimize the product according to the users' needs
- Make sure that the product has a relevant user interface, relevant content
- Look upon yourself in the usability work as the users' "lawyer"
- Early involvement and continuing focus on users
- Test the different products together with the users all the way

We collected a focus group of nine persons representing a variety of user segments from different areas (Somalia, Pakistan, Vietnam, Estonia, El Salvador and Lebanon). Then we asked: "What do you prefer as regards content information on a web portal for immigrant women?" "What are your own, your sister's, your mother's needs?" etc. We then tested different Danish websites (e.g. danmark.dk, finfo.dk, netdoktor .dk), asking the focus group members how they would try to locate information on different topics and observing how they navigated. Finally, we made a paper prototype together with the test group. Thereafter we tested the product, made adjustments and tested it again. In addition, we had workshops with different professionals with relevant experiences concerning immigrant women, such as nurses, teachers and project workers.

The resulting design was, in many ways, different from my initial idea of the site:

- The preferred subjects were, more or less, the same.
- The women did not like the idea of, for instance, ten links about job seeking on the Internet; they preferred a selection of the best links.

- They did not want easy access to a multitude of new sites provided by different information providers. They wanted a tailored website, designed with their particular interests in mind and presented in a very easy Danish language.
- They wanted problem pages answering their specific questions on children's care, hospitals, etc., manned by a panel of professionals (e.g. lawyers, nurses, doctors).
- Whereas the different professionals emphasized the need for information on the site on duties, the immigrant women themselves preferred information on their rights.

This usability test provided us with many new problems:

- In fact, their information needs differed from what was provided by traditional library services; we librarians usually see ourselves primarily as information intermediaries, not as information producers.
- The continuation of the site after project period would involve considerable operational costs. The University and State Library in Aarhus did not plan for these costs.

A solution to the problems mentioned above has not been found. However, it seems clear that valuable experiences and resources have been gained already:

- The members of the user panel have expressed that they like to work for free; they say that "this site is our child."
- A huge amount of relevant information about Internet use and navigation problems has been collected.

Do Libraries Deliver What Ethnic Minorities Demand?

In *Refuge for Integration*, a general satisfaction with Danish public library services was documented. On some vital points, immigrants asked for changes:

- More video films for children and adults; more copies of new, popular music; better language courses
- Improved supply of materials (books, video, music, newspapers, magazines) in their native languages
- Better information on services the library can deliver to minorities
- Members of the ethnic minorities should be involved as consultants in the collection development process

- The library should be transformed into an activity center and adopt the role of a cultural communicator
- Several offered assistance to work for the library as volunteers

However, as far as I know, these specific demands have not resulted in significant changes in the way the libraries in Odense and Aarhus organize their services to the minorities. The survey results have mainly been used on a political level, documenting the important role of libraries as effective cultural integrators.

Conclusion: Different Methods, Different Influence

It has struck me, being involved in three different projects on ethnic minorities—FINFO, *Refuge for Integration* and the women portal—that the different methods applied position the users quite differently.

In FINFO, solely the project group decided subjects and main content of the portal. Certainly, members of the user group subsequently tested the portal—and their comments and suggestions were also listened to. A user group was also formed, consisting of members of different minority organizations. However, based on the experiences, I am convinced that the application of a usability approach would have resulted in quite different results and, consequently, in a quite different design of the FINFO portal.

In *Refuge for Integration*, attitudes and suggestions of the users are referred to in great detail. However, clear indications and decisions concerning future actions based on the recommendations have not been made explicit.

As to the women portal, although the results differed quite a bit from our initial ideas especially as to financial consequences after the project period, we certainly feel obliged to implement the features demanded by the immigrant girls. These features concern subjects, content and layout, including details such as where to put the index. I think that the usability method applied has contributed to our pronounced feeling of obligation.

My conclusion based on these experiences is that usability is an efficient and not very expensive method. Today it is mostly used in the construction and testing of existing websites. In the future, I see perspectives in usability on a broader level.

In my opinion, libraries do not have enough knowledge about the needs and demands of different users. In general, libraries know very little about how users would actually transform the libraries and their virtual services.

The only way to find out (if we want to give the library users real influence) is not only to ask in the regular user tests, but to rethink the way we think about "our libraries." Otherwise there is a risk, as Patrick Roach warned in his investigation of minorities and libraries, that the libraries will be bypassed in the future as an essential source of information.

Usability is a cornerstone in avoiding that development by transforming the position of the user from being an object to become the *subject* of library design in broad meaning. It is a method to transform libraries from library staff's libraries, to become the user's place.

Refuge for Integration documents the fact that Danish libraries have been rather successful in their efforts to attract immigrants. The result is that, in Denmark, without doubt, the public library is the cultural institution that is in closest touch with people from different communities.

In the context of the different user tests, test persons formulated a wide range of wishes for future library roles and activities. In general, the proposals are not limited to lending materials and providing information. Many want libraries to organize activities and events in the local communities. Others ask for support in the production of local culture, for example, supporting translations. Immigrants do not see the library as primarily an information center. Their concept of the library is broader, typically, containing a number of additional functions such as a meeting place, an activity and information center, and cultural communicator. No doubt, the growing number of ethnic minority users will challenge traditional approaches to library service. The change of the demography in all Nordic countries will have considerable influence on the changing development of the Nordic libraries in the future.

Notes

1 Stephen Castles and Mark J. Miller, *The Age of Migration* (London: Macmillan, 1998).

2 Peter Seeberg, *Migration og det moderne Mellemøsten* (Odense: Odense Universitetsforlag, 2000).

3 *Frirum til integration: En undersøgelse af de etniske minoriteters biblioteksanvendelse* (Aarhus: Aarhus Kommunes Biblioteker: 2001); available at www.aakb.dk/frirum.

4 Ågot Berger, *Mangfoldighedens biblioteker: Flersproglig biblioteks-betjening i Danmark* (Frederiksberg: Bibliotekarforbundet, 2001).

5 Marlene Morrison and Patrick Roach, *Public Libraries, Ethnic Diversity and Citizenship* (Warwick: Centre for Research in Ethnic Relations, University of Warwick, 1998).

6 Marlene Morrison and Patrick Roach, "The Place on the Hill?" *Library Association Record* 99, no. 8 (August 1997): 432-33.

7 Ib Andersen, *Den skinbarlige virkelighed: Om valg af samfunds-videnskabelige forskningsmetoder* (Frederiksberg: Samfundslitteratur, 1997).

8 G.E. Gorman and Peter Clayton, *Qualitative Research for the Information Professional: A Practical Handbook* (London: Library Association Publishing, 1997).

9 Steinar Kvale, *Interview: Een introduktion til det kvalitative forsknings-interview* (Copenhagen: Hans Reitzels Forlag, 1994).

10 Lise Togeby and Birgit Møller, *Oplevet diskrimination* (Copenhagen: Nævnet for Etnisk Ligestilling, 1999).

11 The interviews can be read in full-scale version on the website: www.aakb.dk/frirum—Bilag.

12 Rolf Molich, *Brugervenligt webdesign* (Copenhagen: Teknisk Forlag, (2000).

13 Jacob Nielsen, *Usability Engineering* (Boston, Mass.: Academic Press, 1993).

National Identity as Cultural Policy with Emphasis on the Library as an Institution

Andrew Cranfield

This paper discusses the role and character of national identity when seen in conjunction with national cultural policy. During 2000 and 2001, the former Danish Minister of Culture, Elsebeth Gerner Nielsen, stressed the importance of a renewed debate about national values in an endeavor to strengthen lost feelings of community. The Minister's policy statements on national identity are outlined, as well as her attempts to bridge the gap between a national and a global perspective. The paper also discusses three theoretical perspectives from which one can view national identity and which together form the basis for a three-tiered model that supports the Minister's political standpoint. Finally, the paper investigates the important role that public libraries can play in the development of this new policy initiative.

National Identity as Cultural Policy

At first sight the idea of national identity as a part of cultural policy seems entirely natural. Many of the institutions which reside under the Ministry of Culture, such as museums, theaters, libraries and archives, are all, to some extent, concerned with preserving a country's heritage. It is in our visits to these institutions that we, as citizens, expect to be confronted with various aspects of our common national identity, as do those tourists who seek out these institutions hoping to discover certain aspects of a nation's identity. Few, if any, would claim that institutions of this kind are in any way specifically insular in their understanding of society or that their preservation of the thoughts, writings and artistic impressions of a society could be construed as problematic. Nevertheless, the Minister of Culture's focus on the importance of an active promotion of national values and discussion of Danish identity has proved controversial. First I will discuss the underlying reasons for the Minister's statements on identity and national values in a cultural policy context and analyze the national discourses that the minister introduces. Second, I will place this discussion in a slightly wider political context.

In order to understand the debate, it is necessary to understand the way the Minister defines the concept of culture. Often culture is seen to be, more or less, synonymous with art and artistic production and, as such, encompassing a relatively small and well-defined area of life. It is in this rather narrow understanding that culture can somehow be disconnected from everyday life. The broad understanding of culture, and this is very much the definition the Minister adheres to, sees culture as what Raymond Williams once defined as *a whole way of life, material, intellectual and spiritual*[1] or as the Minister herself defines it:

> Culture indicates in language, codes and symbols what we between us perceive as the true, the good, the beautiful and the holy, and that cultural policy can be seen as the struggle for and about values which are considered desirable for human development and community life —as the struggle about attitudes to the meaning and quality of life.[2]

As we can see, the Minister defines a cultural understanding which is very much in line with Williams's definition. Once we have accepted this definition it is obviously possible to expand the areas of life, which can be included within state cultural policy. In this broader understanding, culture can be seen as an important tool for the sustainment of community and patterns of everyday life. Here, we can ask the question whether cultural understanding and cultural identity can safeguard or further develop the idea of culture as an important element in the creation of communal feelings.

In the light of the cultural emancipation—and by this I mean freedom from traditional normative institutions such as, for example, the family—which we have experienced since the 1960s, one has to concede that common cultural traits are difficult or, perhaps, even impossible to define. Political, class and gender affiliations no longer have the same position in regard to those processes that underline thoughts of common unity.

It is this cultural emancipation which is, in some respects, the final consequence of modernity, ushering in what is commonly referred to as a *crisis of identity*. Even if we accept Zygmunt Bauman's view[3] that identity has always been a problem in modernity, it is becoming increasingly clear that the breakdown of traditions and the ontological insecurity to which the sociologist Anthony Giddens refers is asking the fundamental question: To what extent can a society continue to exist without some kind of consensus on the common values and common culture on which that society is built?

It is this "state of affairs" which the Minister wishes to address. So many of the traditional institutions of identity are under siege, and globalization, whether seen as reality or part myth as Paul Hirst claims,[4] is placing the idea of the nation state and belonging to that nation in question. It is from this perspective and not from the politics of xenophobia that the Minister wishes to instigate a debate on what elements constitute the national identity. The Minister is fully aware of the fact that the Danish nation is under transformation, not least from individualization and globalization, and asks the questions: "What is to ensure solidarity? What will provide contextuality? Won't it be necessary with a common frame of reference, which can cement our society? Or are we going to accept the reduction of our nation to subcultures?"[5]

As we can see, it is, according to the Minister, not possible to build a society based on subcultures and individualistic sensibilities alone. On numerous occasions the Minister focuses on the need for factors that will bind society together—and it is here that the national perspective becomes important. Not as an instrument for more or less unsympathetic strategies of exclusion but as an answer to a threatening fragmentation of society. While accepting the minister's motives as well intended, one cannot ignore the fact that any reiteration or emphasizing of national identity is problematic in a pluralistic and multiethnic society. In recognition of this the Minister has moved the discussion into what could be termed a national/global hybrid discourse.

I will not comment on whether the Minister has been successful in this endeavor but confine myself to a discussion of the implications of this discourse. The Minister's analysis of Danish culture as we envisage it today has, according to her, emerged from a readiness towards dialogue between Danes with different cultural backgrounds and between Danes and representatives from other nations. In her view national cultural identities are forged in meetings with others and are not products of insularity. The global and the national discourse are dialectically opposed to each other, while simultaneously constructing the other, insofar as they can only be understood in complex patterns of interaction. Even if this is true we still need to understand what threat the globalization process poses to the national identity. It is my postulate that this threat can be divided schematically into three categories as outlined in table 1:

Table 1.

	Globalization	Nation State	The Perception of Threat
Sociological	The multi-cultural society, the multiethnic society, the pluralistic society	*One* homogenous people	Immigration, refugees and mass migration
Cultural	Diversity of culture with individual choice	Liberal educa-tion with its emphasis on literature, language and history	An American hegemonization of culture / The division of identity into various subcultures
Political	Political decisions taken in international and/or global arenas	*One* nation's right to self-determination based on national assemblies	The political process be-comes intangi-ble. Democratic decision-making process becomes vague

These three dimensions and their transformation from a national to a "global" culture produce a sociological, cultural and political threat. It is therefore, from a political position, necessary to bridge the gap between the two. To do this the Minister insists that a strong national identity is "a decisive factor for being able to meet other cultures with respect. We must work out who we are and who we wish to become— i.e. to be able to carry something with us into a future global context."[6]

It is this attention to the importance of having knowledge about ourselves as a people that the Minister feels is so important. It is only by obtaining this knowledge that we can, as the Minister puts it, be Danish on the basis of a multicultural background. In this hybrid discourse the global perspective and the national perspective do not discount each other but become fundamental for the understanding of the other.

This discussion also has a political angle when we look at how the right wing seems to have taken the nation state hostage for its own political purpose. The Minister of Culture is a member of the small but influential Liberal Party (*Radikale Venstre*) which has traditionally taken center stage in the Danish political arena. This party is well known for its humanitarianism and tolerance, so a political standpoint stressing the importance of a strong and vibrant national identity was not what one might expect. However, it has been, seen from the Minister's point of view, imperative to move the debate on national identity into the middle ground of the political field. The extreme right-wing parties of Europe have been successful in creating a divide between a political and intellectual elite with an international optic on the one side and a general population who do not share this enthusiasm for an internationalization of the political sphere on the other hand. If this schism between population and government is not to continue, then it is necessary to draw the discussion on national identity into an open forum, while at the same time defining national values as broadly as possible in order to prevent a fragmentation of society.

In this debate one must of course be careful not to be guilty of an overinterpretation of the Minister's examination of national identity and cultural policy. Her policy statements have not, to any great extent, been reiterated by her party colleagues or other members of the government and as such our final analysis and judgment might be one of political "speak." However, interviews in *Politiken*[7] (a daily national newspaper) with a number of opposition politicians on cultural policy show a strong emphasis on the strengthening of national identity and culture. Peter Duetoft from *CentrumDemokraterne*, also a center liberal party, talks about the necessity of protecting Danish culture by strengthening those school subjects which are seen to be "carriers of culture" such as Danish, history and the teaching of Christian Studies. Duetoft shares the Minister of Culture's belief in that only by being aware of our own identity can we be prepared to tackle these "cultural meetings." The present Minister of Culture, Brian Mikkelsen from the Danish Conservative Party, while acknowledging that all cultural value sets are relative, also wishes to safeguard Danish culture.

It is undoubtedly difficult in this discussion to separate the political debate from the cultural and cultural policy debate. The political debate is often characterized by a rather polemic attitude in which both sides put forth their preconception of the nation state and its role in modern society. In some ways the cultural debate is less controversial. Nonetheless, in order to understand how questions of national identity can be incorporated into an expansive cultural policy it is essential to consider various theoretical views of how national identities are formed and kept alive.

National Identity between the
Imagined and the Banal

In his book *Imagined Communities*, Benedict Anderson describes the nation state as follows: "It is an imagined and political community—and imagined as both inherently limited and sovereign. It is imagined because even the smallest nation will never know most of their fellow members, meet them, or even hear them, yet in the minds of each lives the image of their communion."[8] The thinking behind Anderson's theory and its ability to define a middle ground between the primordialists, who see the nation state as an ancient cultural community, and the modernists, who see the nation as a recent political construction and as a logical result of modernity, has been important in much historical research on nationalism since its publication. Anderson's argument, put somewhat simply, is that all societies will have a certain feeling of belonging and a sense of community within the boundary of a society, even with those fellow citizens whom they have never met. The nation can possibly be described as a social construction but its foundation is built upon already existing feelings of community and, as Anderson says, "Communities are to be distinguished, not by their falsity/genuineness, but by the styles in which they are imagined."[9]

Anderson underlines the emotional level of the nation state and by doing so underplays the ideological dimensions of nationalism. By ideology, I refer to the patterns of practice and belief that make existing societal arrangements appear natural, and instead he views nationalism as being more akin to the institution of the family. There exists a host of everyday events from the reading of newspapers to supporting the national football team which underline feelings of, if not solidarity, then at least of doing the same thing at the same time. Anderson does not turn a blind eye to the idea of the nation as a construction but sees the nation more as an ongoing communicative process, a narrative of cultural solidarity, which keeps the nation going based on its own myth.

Anderson's theory is enticing in that it, in part at least, removes nationalism from being based on cultural superiority to being built on cultural solidarity. However, is this idea of the *imagined communities* enough to explain how these feelings of national identity are kept alive year in and year out?

In order to fully comprehend the continual production of these feelings, it is useful to look at sociologist Michael Billig's study of banal nationalism that he describes thus:

The term banal nationalism is introduced to cover the ideological habits that enable the established nations of the West to be introduced. It is argued that these habits are not removed from everyday life, as some observers have supposed. Daily, the nation is indicated, or "flagged," in the lives of its citizenry. Nationalism, far from being an intermittent mood in established nations, is the endemic condition.[10]

Billig looks at how nationalism as ideology is not just defined by its most extreme characteristics, but also by its more common and everyday forms. Therefore, Billig is not so much interested in explaining where nationalism comes from, but more in explaining how it is constructed and reconstructed in daily life. Central to this theory is the idea that national feelings are reproduced, not by a constant and conscious "flagging of the nation" but by quiet and constant reminders of our identity—what Billig refers to as the banal. It is this almost subconscious form of national identity that Billig describes as *enhabitation*, going on to define this as the "thoughts, reactions and symbols (that) become turned into routine habits and, thus they become enhabited."[11]

Enhabitation is what makes it possible for nation states to preserve what has been fought for and won. In Billig's world it is important to understand that nationalism is not regarded as the rather illogical ideology of others, something inherently nostalgic and obsolete, but as a state of mind where "the homeland is made both present and unnoticeable by being presented as *the* context."[12] Perhaps the best example of this contextualisation can be found in the use of deixis. Here, words such as *I, we, you, here, this, the* (e.g. "we" the people, "this" nation "the" prime minister) are used constantly in everyday speech and text to remind us of who we are and not least of where we belong. We do not ask what people, whose nation or which prime minister, but we implicitly understand the context in which the deictic words are being used. Likewise so much of what we read or see on television conceptually underlines the concept of the nation—an example being the division of many daily newspapers into home news and international news. A banal example? Undoubtedly, but one that helps construct the image of the nation as central in our understanding of the world.

Neither Michael Billig nor Benedict Anderson deny that nation states are political constructions of the nineteenth century and both would probably agree with the historian Ernest Gellner in his definition of nationalism, which states that "nationalism is primarily a political principle, which holds that the political and the national unit should be congruent."[13] Both would argue, though, that this is not the whole truth.

In fact, rather than seeing these theories somehow in opposition to each other, it is useful to combine them, which is illustrated in the following model.

Table 2.

Banal nationalism	The subconscious level	e.g. the use of deixis
The nation as an imagined community	The emotional level	e.g. the feeling of solidarity during a national football match
The nation as a political construction	The rational / public level	e.g. the debate on the European Union

If one accepts the idea of nationalism working on different levels (and other levels could also be included in the above), we can see that the deconstruction of a national identity is not as easy as some believe and that feelings of community and citizenship are deeply rooted within a national context.

Public Libraries as Carriers of National Identity and Culture

Finally I wish to look at the way in which a cultural institution could work with regard to these challenges. Obviously, there are many areas that reside under the Ministry's authority from sport to opera, and each would naturally construct very different approaches to questions of identity. Some would presumably be better suited to tackling the discussion and different histories and traditions would influence decision-making strategies.

However, an institution which is dedicated to the preservation and dissemination of the literature, history and thoughts of a nation is, one would expect, well suited to putting into practice the Minister's policy initiative. It is obvious that the public library sector is viewed as an important player in this development, not least because of their central role in the local community. The public library infrastructure in Denmark means that all citizens have access to library services and the fact that roughly two-thirds of the population actually visit the library makes them well suited as "debating fora" for the Minister's thought on identity and values—the Minister has described the public library as "a genuine cultural meeting place for everyone."[14] The challenge for libraries today is to give users access to information, but also to help these users in transforming information into knowledge. At the same time libraries must actively work for the promotion of cultural values and a strengthening of the prerequisites for democratic involvement.

Public libraries are not regarded as elitist cultural institutions and therefore enjoy the trust of the general public. If discussions on identity and values are to be successful they must be integrated into the already existing structure, that is, the public library's tradition for enlightenment and democracy. In this light the role of public libraries becomes one of supporting the discussion itself rather than defining values themselves—in this scenario the process itself becomes more important than the result. It is in this role that libraries can incorporate this task within their framework and move the discussion towards a more general deliberation on a more active citizenship. One should remember that Danish library legislation states that: "The objective of the public libraries will be achieved by observing quality, comprehensiveness and topicality in the choice of materials to be made available. These criteria alone must be the decisive factors and not any religious, moral or political views which might be expressed in the material."[15]

I am in no way claiming that this somehow precludes a discussion of identity and values, but only that one must be aware of the tradition for neutrality and objectivity, which is so embedded within the public library psyche. Libraries and, not least, librarians wish to take the discussion into a more general area where the concept of civil society and active citizenship come into fruition, where active citizenship can be defined as: "(that which) involves, in the reflexive modern and democratic society, that the individual involves himself in order to take responsibility for his own and others' life situation in a democratic society."[16]

In a recent study of library usage in Denmark documented in the book *Does the Library Make a Difference?*[17] the authors, Jochumsen and Hvenegaard Rasmussen, concluded that the library is one of the few free and open public spaces left in society today. The implications of this are far reaching in that this may mean that libraries are able to tackle these issues of identity, community and active citizenship in a way that is acceptable to the public because of the position of trust they hold within local communities.

However, we should also remember that the public library sector in Denmark has had great success in acting as integrator in a pluralistic society and that this position could be sacrificed were the libraries to adopt, what one might term, an unfortunate rhetoric on national identity. Likewise libraries have traditionally been internationally orientated and therefore there might exist an inherent conflict between this perception of the institution and that of focusing on national values.

Conclusion

In conclusion, it is my belief that when the former Minister for Culture, Elsebeth Gerner Nielsen, brought national values to the forefront of the cultural debate, it was motivated by two things. First, her belief that cultural politics should be used as an instrument for binding various segments of society together, and second, that she wished to move the very delicate question of national identity to the center ground of Danish politics. The Minister has attempted to formulate a hybrid discourse, where a global perspective is not at odds with national identity and national values.

When looking at Anderson's *Imagined Communities* and Billig's *Banal Nationalism* we find two theorists who, while not discarding the theory of the national state as a political construction, point towards a rather more encompassing idea of nationalism and one which seems to be less politically charged. The model that I have shown demonstrates that national identity is not only about constructing "us" / "them" constellations.

The Minister's policy on this subject has been somewhat vague, and though funds have been allocated to projects that address questions of identity, both regional and national, it is too soon to generalize about how questions of identity might be incorporated into national policy at a more formalized level—and perhaps it never will be. However, it seems clear from the way the Minister envisages the debate that public libraries can play a central role in the discussion on what values and foundation one wishes to build one's society, although it is the process rather than the result that libraries should focus upon.

Notes

1 Raymond Williams, *Culture and Society, 1780-1950* (London and New York: Columbia University Press, 1958), 16.

2 Elsebeth Gerner Nielsen, "Det fælles og kulturpolitikken," *Kulturkontakten* 7, no. 8 (December 1998): 4.

3 Zygmunt Bauman, "From Pilgrim to Tourist, or a Short History of Identity," in *Questions of Cultural Identity*, ed. Stuart Hall and Paul du Gay (London: Sage Publications, 1996), 18-36.

4 Paul Hirst, *Globalisering, demokrati og det civile samfund* (Copenhagen: Hans Reitzels Forlag, 1997).

5 Elsebeth Gerner Nielsen, *Fællesskabets Forandring*, September 1999, http://www.kum.dk (21 October 2001)

6 Elsebeth Gerner Nielsen, *Dansk identitet i grænselandet*. Debate at Sønderborg Castle, October 1999, http://www.kum.dk (21 October 2001)

7 "På sporet af den borgerlige kulturpolitik," *Politiken*. A series of articles published in the Danish newspaper *Politiken* on 3 March 2001, 10 March 2001, 17 March 2001, 24 March 2001, 7 April 2001 and 14 April 2001.

8 Benedict Anderson, *Imagined Communities* (London and New York: Verso, 1991), 6.

9 Anderson, *Imagined Communities*, 6.

10 Michael Billig, *Banal Nationalism* (London: Sage Publications, 1995), 6.

11 Billig, *Banal Nationalism*, 42.

12 Billig, *Banal Nationalism*, 109.

13 Ernest Gellner, *Nations and Nationalism* (Cambridge: Cambridge University Press, 1987), 4.

14 Elsebeth Gerner Nielsen, *Offentlige biblioteker og informationssamfundet*, October 1999, http://www.kum.dk (21 October 2001)

15 *Lov om biblioteksvirksomhed*, Act Regarding Library Services, Act no. 340 of 17 May 2000 (Copenhagen: The Danish National Library Authority, 2001), section 2, 200, http://www.bs.dk/index.ihtml?side=http://www.bs.dk/Publikationer.ihtml?serie=11

16 Arne Carlsen, "Samspillet mellem folkeoplysning og det civile samfund," 2000, *Uddannelse*, no. 8 (October 1999), http://udd.uvm.dk/199908/udd8-8.htm (26 June 2003).

17 Henrik Jochumsen and Casper Hvenegaard Rasmussen, *Gør biblioteket en forskel?* (Copenhagen: Danmarks Biblioteksforenings Forlag, 2000).

The Intercultural Encounter between Danish Public Libraries and Ethnic Minority Users

Hans Elbeshausen and Charlotte Werther

This article presents findings from an explorative interview study aimed at determining the involvement and role of Danish public libraries in servicing ethnic minority users. The study examines the libraries' actual engagement in and potential contribution to an intercultural dialogue with ethnic minority users, and establishes that, in coping with the requirements of these users, core library functions and services receive high priority, whereas less attention is given to the communicative or interactional aspects of library work. The analysis also includes a review of the existing body of reports on library activities in relation to ethnic minority users.

Introduction

The purpose of this article is to discuss and try to conceptualize what one might call the *(cultural) encounter* or the *intercultural communication* between Danish public libraries and librarians on one hand and ethnic minority users in Denmark on the other. The article and discussion form part of a research project which set out to uncover whether and to what extent Danish public libraries have had or will have a broader role to play in engaging in intercultural dialogue with ethnic-minority users; whether, in fact, Danish public libraries are involved in intercultural and cross-cultural networks with or around ethnic minorities that aim at furthering intercultural dialogue; and whether they are engaged in what might be called *targeted (inter)cultural work.*[1]

Work on the project was started in August 2001 and the initial step taken was to conduct five explorative interviews with librarians responsible for services to ethnic minorities in order to test questions for a possible questionnaire. Four interviews were made in libraries placed in districts within Copenhagen municipality with fairly high concentrations of ethnic minority groups and one interview was made in the provincial town of Holbæk.[2]

One very preliminary conclusion to be drawn from the interviews is that a lot of effort and commitment goes into servicing ethnic minorities in Danish public libraries, but also that it is more difficult to determine to what extent *cultural work* in a broader sense takes place, or rather, that even if or when it does, it is difficult to conceptualize and describe it for practitioners and researchers alike.

During our interviews it was very suggestive that our interviewees, if asked about "cultural encounters with ethnic minorities" or "cultural work involving ethnic minorities," interpreted the question as one enquiring into their practice of having cultural events such as an evening with a novelist or a political debate. It was evident that the terms "cultural encounter" or "cultural work" in a more ethnological or anthropological sense were relatively foreign to the interviewees and that their frame of reference or interpretation was a perception of normal or standard activities in a Danish public library.

One way of conceptualizing the different activities or profiles of a Danish public library can be found in Andersson and Skot-Hansen (1994), who divide the main functions of a public library into those of information center, knowledge center, social or community center and cultural center for the purpose of analyzing the library's roles or profile in a local area. A perception of the library as a cultural center in the sense of "a setting for cultural and artistic experience and activity, including various events, exhibitions, workshops" (our translation)[3] seemed to constitute the natural frame of reference within which to interpret questions about cultural work.

Similarly, it was difficult to extract tales of cultural differences between groups of users or of situations involving communication between cultures. One possible explanation is a high degree of loyalty towards and identification with ethnic minority users among the interviewees and great reluctance to contribute to the negative press of ethnic minorities and to perceptions of "problematic"—culturally explained—behavior.

The interviews made it clear to us that investigating public libraries' cultural work[4] in the broader sense we had envisaged and their involvement in networks would most probably be impossible by means of questionnaires but would require a more interview- and case-based approach. In addition, it made us wonder whether a certain *logic* or *rationality* more or less inadvertently underlies and informs library work within this area.

Uncertainty and Lack of Predictability

One way of trying to approach the potential logic or rationality that prevails in ethnic library work is to look at the reports that, over the years, have addressed the issue of how to service this new group of users. Several reports have been made to document, evaluate and discuss the work done in Danish public libraries in relation to ethnic minority users, but they have tended to concentrate on aspects of the *core library function* of providing various types of materials or information products to ethnic minority users such as: how much and what variety of mother-tongue material can and should be provided, how much and what type of material should be provided to support Danish language acquisition and how can use of small collections be maximized by circulation between libraries. To put it differently, the chief concern is how the core professional values of neutrality, quality and topicality of materials can be achieved, also in relation to this user group; how ethnic minority users can be serviced on an equal footing with other users in the most effective way.

In contrast, there seems to be less focus in the reports on *other possible roles* libraries might play vis-à-vis ethnic minority users. However, in the most recent survey of the way ethnic minorities use the libraries in Aarhus and Odense (*Frirum til integration: En undersøgelse af de etniske minoriteters brug af bibliotekerne*, 2001, henceforth *Refuge for Integration*), one library manager concludes:

> The main challenge is the role of the library as a meeting-place, co-operation with other local authority and private-sector organizations, the information-producing library and not least [recruiting] bilingual personnel to permanent positions. . . . In addition, the task at hand is to transform the library into an interactive place of cultural encounter(s).[5] In addition to providing information and knowledge, the library can, jointly with other providers, contribute to influencing developments by initiating, supporting and participating in relevant projects within this area.[6] [Our translation.]

In many ways the above library manager seems to envisage a more *(pro)active and networking role* for the local library, but at the same time it is less clear what actual practices might be involved in realizing the vision. In general, it can be argued that many of the reports contain speculations about what libraries can and should do as to what is directly or indirectly expected of them.

The purpose of the reports and their focusing on various topics differ. Some are mere *descriptions* of what an individual library has done in order to upgrade existing services, to build up collections of materials or to purchase, to register and to update mother-tongue materials. The addressing of the problem of upgrading services or updating collections of materials indirectly reflects that the number of ethnic users increased and their demands for materials became more differentiated.[7]

Other reports are more *prescriptive*. First and foremost, they address the problem of how to make the libraries more efficient in providing services to different ethnic user groups. However, giving chief priority to efficiency may seem somewhat inconsequential if it is not linked with potentially relevant social and cultural differences between Danish and ethnic user groups or considerations that the ethnic minorities may expect something different.[8]

The reports reviewed include official documents prepared by civil servants, and reports that are *evaluative* and based on research activities. Most reports are written from what might be called a Danish perspective; only one is written by a librarian of non-Danish origin, who was responsible for setting up a library at the Islamic Cultural Center in Copenhagen.[9] Some of the reports reviewed address more specific problems such as the kind of library service needed by the children of ethnic minorities, how to organize a central library function for ethnic user groups, or how large the collections of mother tongue materials for various ethnic user groups should be. The first report was published in 1975 and the most recent one in 2001.[10] Two overall conclusions can be drawn from the reports.

First, the reports make it clear that there has been and still is a degree of *uncertainty* in Danish library circles about the scope and content of the task of providing library services to ethnic minorities and the ability of libraries and librarians to deliver. The uncertainty was directly articulated in one report: "What must not happen is that users give up frequenting the library because we, as a consequence of our uncertainty and lack of experience, are unable to provide the requested materials. Only practice counts."[11] (Our translation.)

Even if the feeling of *uncertainty and lack of experience* is not always expressed directly, it is an underlying theme in many reports. For example, in the course of the 1970s it was a very important and central concern for many librarians to find a way of ensuring that materials in various languages complied with the general standards of quality laid down by legislation. In this case, the source of the uncertainty is fairly evident: Most Danish librarians neither knew much about the cultural background of the ethnic minorities nor spoke their languages.

Another more current example is the role and relative importance of mother-tongue materials in cultural and personal identity-building. In 1999 a committee was set up by the management of the public libraries of Copenhagen to survey the service provision to ethnic minorities in Copenhagen. One conclusion of the survey was that building up collections of mother-tongue literature, especially to small ethnic groups, is to be given less priority, whereas *integrative* material such as material to support Danish language acquisition is upgraded.[12]

The Copenhagen report and its conclusions illustrate that the perceived role of, and therefore the provision by public libraries, of native language materials may be changing and that, in the future, public libraries may, to a greater extent, concentrate their effort on integrative materials and activities. The Copenhagen report also illustrates another, more general development. The impact of globalization and migration increasingly makes it more difficult for the nation-state in general and the libraries in particular to rely on well-known and traditional practices and strategies. The cultural and political environment, worldwide and in Denmark, has become increasingly unsteady, complex and unpredictable over the last twenty years.

One aspect is that, over the last thirty years, the number of different ethnic groups from so-called "tredjelande" (non-Nordic, non-EU and non-North American countries) in Denmark has increased enormously. In 1970 there were approximately 15,000 people from mainly three nations (Turkey, Pakistan and Yugoslavia). In 2000 there were about 275,000 foreigners from nonindustrialized countries in Denmark, who represented many different nations or cultures. If one focuses exclusively on countries as Afghanistan, Iraq, Iran, Lebanon, Somalia and Sri Lanka the dynamic nature and *unpredictability* of migration processes is even more telling. In 1980 about 1,000 persons from those countries lived in Denmark; in 2000 their number had increased to nearly 75,000.[13]

This development clearly contributes to reducing the *predictability* of public libraries in servicing ethnic minority users. It is relatively unpredictable when the next contingent of refugees will arrive in Denmark, how large it will be and in what part of the country it will settle (or be settled). The uncertainty resulting from the dynamic of migration processes is likely to prevail on the libraries as long as migration lasts, and the case of the Copenhagen report suggests that trying to ensure equality of access may become increasingly difficult and potentially meaningless in some situations.

On the basis of the reports, a second conclusion can be drawn: The public libraries have, in many ways, become able to solve a number problems related primarily to their *core services* such as the supply of information materials, Internet facilities or providing assistance for the retrieval of information or materials. Some of the problems addressed in the reports such as purchasing and registering material in various languages no longer seem to constitute a major problem for the libraries. The 2001 report *Refuge for Integration* documents two things: First, the public libraries have in fact been successful in attracting ethnic minority users, and second, today ethnic library users use the libraries nearly to the same degree as the Danish population. In terms of standard measures of success it can be concluded that the public library system currently functions successfully as far as the core services for ethnic minorities are concerned.

It could be argued that what the library system experienced in the 1970s was a challenge to its traditional practices from a hitherto unknown and heterogeneous user group. If the rationality and the legitimacy of the library system as a whole were to be sustained, it was necessary for the libraries to make sure that activities directed towards the new user groups were efficient and cost-effective and complied with requirements of, for example, equality of access. The end-in-view was defined in a library commission report from 1979, which stated that "as a matter of principle it is the duty of the public libraries to provide equal service to all residents in Denmark, which includes foreign workers."[14] (Our translation.)

However, from the 1970s onwards it also became increasingly debatable whether the means and strategies traditionally employed by the libraries in their service provision were always expedient in relation to the ethnic minorities and to the end-in-view of equal access. As already discussed, the context within which the libraries functioned and consequently the efficacy of means and strategies became more *uncertain* and *unpredictable*. Therefore, one of the most central goals pursued by the public libraries over the last thirty years has been to try to adapt and develop existing solutions to the new uncertain and unpredictable context and, despite uncertainty and unpredictability, to provide equality of access as laid down in consecutive library services acts and spelled out in *Udkast til betænkning* (draft report) 1979. In this situation knowledge about the efficacy of different means and strategies in pursuing this end was needed. The reports reviewed can be interpreted as a significant reflection of the libraries' struggle for more knowledge in order to negotiate the uncertainty caused by migration processes.

Overall, it can be argued that the way public libraries coped with uncertainty and lack of predictability relied on a logic or rationality that could be characterized as a *technical rationality*. Existing means, strategies and working processes in public libraries were made to function vis-à-vis the special needs and cultural and social situation of ethnic minorities.[15]

A Technical More Than a
Communicative Rationality?

In addition to aspects of the best and most efficient service provision, the reports do touch upon the cultural encounter between ethnic minorities and the Danish population. As mentioned, the most recent report points to the importance of transforming the library into an interactive cultural meeting-place. However, what is understood by cultural encounter or dialogue between minority and majority cultures, what role the encounter or dialogue is to play and what is to be gained from it, and how it is supposed to take place is fairly vague. This is an impression that has been confirmed by our interviews so far.

If we look a little more closely at the terms and concepts used in the reports, the encounter is often described as entertainment or an event arranged for or with ethnic minorities, the main element of which is the exotic or foreign nature of ethnic minority culture. Under the heading of "events" the report *De udenlandske arbejdere og folkebiblioteket* (*Foreign workers and the public library*, 1975) lists music and theater from the country of origin, possibly in the form of amateur theater linked to exhibitions. The reasoning behind such events can be seen from the following quote: "Many foreign workers miss the kind of social life represented by life around the cafes in their country of origin for which they seldom find a replacement in this country. The events or gatherings [at the library] should therefore be held in the most inviting [*hyggelig*] and relaxed atmosphere possible."[16] (Our translation.)

Within this perspective libraries are given the task of providing a substitute setting for the way guest workers were thought to associate in their country of origin, and the cultural metaphor used for that substitution is café rather than gatherings at mosques or churches. Generally, it might be argued that the perception of library events found in some reports is mainly based on an idea of *a meeting around or about culture* where what is foreign and fascinating is at the center, rather than an interactive *meeting between cultures*.

Another interesting aspect is the longevity of this conceptualization. The 1990 report *Retningslinier for flerkulturel biblioteksbetjening* describes cultural events as part of the libraries' campaign to "charm" ethnic minorities; a campaign that might take the form of "festivals" with local ethnic performers (dance, music, theater) and exhibitions of handicrafts and the tasting of ethnic cooking.[17] Again, the underlying idea is a cultural encounter based on foreignness and folklore.

During one of our interviews, cultural encounters are touched upon several times and from different perspectives. The interviewee, who is a librarian with extensive experience of servicing ethnic minority users, stresses that experience with cultural events is mixed and that the library's participation in networks is sporadic and incidental. The understanding that underlies discussions of the cultural encounter or targeted cultural work is that of "lectures or readings at the library." At the center is an aesthetic experience where literature is enlisted as a cultural eye-opener. It is not entirely clear from the interview whose eyes are to be opened. When asked to present a few dreams for the future of ethnic library work, the interviewee said: "It would be cultural events that strongly suggest [the concept of] library without being dull. To get literature into focus. . . . To be an eye-opener to literature, to give people an eye-opening experience." (Interview.)

Even if the focus is transferred from the exotic and foreign to more aesthetic elements, the conceptualization of the cultural encounter has not changed fundamentally. What is foregrounded is not the interactive cultural encounter or cultural work as a reciprocal exchange of or dialogue about cultural views, attitudes and values, but the aesthetic experience related to a literary event at the library.

As suggested previously, it seems as if there is, to some extent, a reliance among public libraries in Denmark on a conceptualization of cultural work and intercultural encounters as cultural events involving foreign, folkloristic or exotic as well as aesthetic and eye-opening elements. Overall, a *technical rather than a more communicative rationality* seems to be privileged.

Finally, it can be argued that the terminology used by the reports and, more generally, to describe the activities engaged in by Danish libraries to service ethnic minorities is also evidence of *uncertainty*. In line with the general perception of the status of new groups in Danish society, the term employed to start with was "providing services to guest workers," which later, probably as a reflection of the general societal realization that these group had settled in Denmark on a more permanent basis, gave way to "providing services to immigrants and refugees," "providing services to ethnic minorities," which again is often telescoped into "ethnic/multicultural/multilingual library service."

It can, of course, be argued that the change and relative confusion of terminology merely reflects the more general problem of *naming* newcomers to Danish society. Are they "foreigners," "new Danes," "from ethnic minorities," "immigrants," "Danes with a foreign ethnic background"? However, it is also evident that all these terms carry various connotations and contribute to different narratives about and discursive constructions of these groups, and that the usage of certain terms may arguably privilege one interpretation of what the services are, of who the users are, and what user behavior is to be expected. A term like "ethnic library service" may be said to suggest *one* homogeneous group of "ethnic" users rather than the diversity of (Danish) and ethnic users.[18] Equally, "service" or "servicing" suggests a one-way provision rather than a two-way dialogue or encounter and may reflect a *technical rather than a communicative rationality.*

This is not to claim that the way this type of library work is conceptualized determines the way the work is practiced, but merely that the terms or concepts employed may contribute to a certain understanding of the practice and/or make it difficult to imagine or conjure up different or alternative practices.

Public Libraries as a Forum for Integration?

Yet another way of looking at ethnic library work is to try to gauge what role is envisaged for public libraries in the overall process of integrating ethnic minorities in Danish society. What is the wider context within which the libraries operate?

The most recent report referred to above explicitly links public libraries and *integration* in its title: *Refuge for Integration.* One of the questions addressed in the report is the importance of the libraries in the general integration process[19] and the overall conclusion is that public libraries do indeed have an important contribution to make as a neutral mediator; in various ways, the report concludes, public libraries serve as a bridging function or tool in the integration process. In that perspective, it might be worth asking whether performing that function or role is specifically required of public libraries and/or foreseen in, for example, parliamentary legislation.

In relation to the use by ethnic minorities of the public library system in Denmark, two different parliamentary acts can be considered the legal basis for the integration process in Denmark. First, as one of the few countries in the world, Denmark has specific legislation laying down the objectives of the public libraries and the types of materials / library media and other services that are to be on offer. The most recent *Lov om Biblioteksvirksomhed*—the Library Services Act—from May 2000 confirms what was already established in its predecessors: That concerning the access to library services and the obligations placed on the public libraries no distinction may be made between the Danish majority population and ethnic minorities.[20]

Furthermore, the present Library Services Act may be said to place special emphasis on nondiscrimination in that it is no longer necessary to live in Denmark in order to use the Danish libraries. This is evident if the 2000 act is compared with its immediate predecessor from 1993, which, in section 5(2) laid down that "public libraries must service anyone with residence in Denmark" (our translation). The 2000 act makes no mention of residence and in principle anyone from all over the world can require services or borrow materials from public libraries in Denmark. It is important to underline that this obligation on the part of the libraries comprises information units not only in Danish but also in other languages.

Moreover, the Library Services Act from May 2000 lays down what ethnic library services are to be provided centrally and what services are to be left in the charge of local libraries. As a rule of thumb one can say that more "backstage" tasks in the library are to a great extent centralized, while the local libraries take care of the direct interaction and encounter with ethnic minority users. This division of responsibilities has several obvious advantages but also a few possible disadvantages.

On one hand, locating public library services primarily with local libraries means that local authorities and local citizens may potentially become more directly involved in the encounter with ethnic minorities. In theory, privileging local decision-making makes it possible to respond immediately and most adequately to local requests and needs. On the other hand, decentralization means that the library services offered to ethnic minorities (and other local users) may vary a lot depending on local political circumstances and the public opinion in the local communities. Furthermore, economic resources are generally insufficient for public libraries in Denmark to offer the same quality of library services to every ethnic minority in each local community.

Centralizing some of the library tasks means that the services offered to ethnic minorities can be run more cheaply and in a more standardized form. However, centralization may foreground *technical* solutions at the expense of *communicative or interactional* aspects of library work. One example of this difficult balance between centralized and decentralized solutions is a debate of whether the collection of ethnic minority literature housed at the Danish Central Library of Immigrant Literature and available for deposit with local libraries should be opened to local users in the Greater Copenhagen area where the library is placed. A 1996 report prepared by the Danish consultancy firm PLS Consult argued as follows:

> The interviews among public libraries very much suggest that direct contact with users contributes to strengthening and developing provision and services. For an overarching function like the Central Library of Immigrant Literature direct user contact may of course involve disadvantages. . . . However, it is the conclusion of PLS Consult that the advantages by far outweigh the disadvantages.[21]

The recommendations were not followed and the Central Library of Immigrant Literature remains closed to the general public, in contrast to the Swedish equivalent, *Det internationella Biblioteket* (The International Library), which was opened to the public in May 2000.[22]

In contrast to the Library Services Act from 2000, the Integration Act (which is the short title for the Act on Integration of Aliens in Denmark) from 1999 had no forerunner. Therefore it is perhaps interesting to outline the overall intention with the Integration Act and to describe in more detail the political circumstances under which it was conceived. In the 1990s, the Danish government was criticized persistently for not having implemented international antidiscrimination legislation in relation to ethnic minorities.[23] One example is that not until 1996 did antidiscrimination regulations within the labor market become law in Denmark. Moreover, in 2000 the Danish Government was required by the EU to implement, within the next three years, a EU directive that prohibits all discrimination of ethnic minorities and which calls for the establishment of an ethnic discrimination complaints board.[24]

At the same time the Danish immigration policy came under Europe-wide attack. Other members of EU maintained that the government's treatment of refugees was too restrictive and its rules for family reunion discriminatory. As a reaction to the sustained criticism, the then Danish Minister of the Interior, Karen Jespersen, tabled the Integration Act and presented it as the most complete and extensive piece of integration legislation worldwide. It was stressed that this act could become a model for other European countries.[25]

The prime concern of the Integration Act is not to protect from discrimination refugees and persons who come to Denmark in connection with family reunion, but to integrate different ethnic groups into the Danish society and culture. The Integration Act could therefore be interpreted as the welfare state's response to perceived integration problems, and responsibility for the integration of ethnic minorities is conceived as resting primarily with (local) political and administrative authorities, not with civil society and its organizations.

The main aspects of the integration measures outlined in the Integration Act are as follows: All persons who have entered Denmark after 1 January 1999, who are at least eighteen years of age and who do not, essentially, come from industrialized countries (cf. section 2[3] of the Act) are offered and expected to attend a comprehensive introduction program. The most important elements of the program are the acquisition of the Danish language, a course in understanding Danish society and culture, and activities which are intended to improve the immigrant's labor skills. The program is scheduled to last three years; after this period it will be decided whether the residence permit is to be made permanent or not. Another important feature of the integration measures is the creation of local integration councils[26] and a deliberative and advisory forum, the so-called Council for Ethnic Minorities. The Council acts on a national level and in each community and gives advice to local and governmental authorities. It is primarily local communities that are responsible for implementing the integration program. In addition to complying with the integration measures explicitly laid down in the Integration Act, local authorities are required to further integration by coordinating "the general effort of integration" (cf. section 3[1] and 4[1] of the Act).

The legal repository for the public libraries' involvement in integrating ethnic minorities is, as suggested, the Library Services Act and the Integration Act. In both of them the role of the local communities—and local libraries—is emphasized, whereas the actual practices involved in playing this role are not specified. On one hand, the local authorities might, in principle, request a more direct and active involvement on the part of the public libraries in local integration activities with reference to the "general effort of integration" foreseen in the Integration Act. On the other hand, the libraries might argue the case for more active involvement by the local authorities in the library service vis-à-vis ethnic minorities—in terms of money, support and appreciation—with reference to the Library Act and their, by now, accumulated experience and knowledge.

Generally, it is still in the balance whether the establishment of local integration councils and a national Council for Ethnic Minorities will eventually trigger more discussion about appropriate fora and strategies of integration, about how existing fora of integration can be utilized better and possibly how new ones can be developed. But if such a debate ensues, Danish public libraries might have important contributions to make, since they have, perhaps more or less inadvertently, come to constitute such a forum.

Conclusion

What we have tried to argue in this article is that in the encounter with a new group of ethnic minority users, the practices of Danish public libraries have come up against increasing *uncertainty* and *unpredictability*. In their attempt to ensure equal provision and equal access to ethnic minority users in this new uncertain and unpredictable environment, public libraries have, understandably, tended to concentrate on *technical solutions* and *a technical rationality* informed, perhaps, by traditions and standard practices and values within the library system and librarianship.

What we tentatively suggest is that this *technical rationality* may militate against a *communicative rationality*, which could involve different practices of intercultural dialogue and networking. One problem involved in developing a *communicative rationality* seems to be the absence of terms and concepts with which to debate it.

The public libraries are often seen as a forum or refuge for *integration* and there is no doubt that the libraries attract many ethnic minority users and, overall, deliver a high standard of service. However, it seems worth debating whether a high standard of services and a high level of user satisfaction necessarily equal integration, and to discuss to what extent and in what way public libraries are supposed to contribute to that process.

Notes

1 In Danish, we have tentatively called it "målgruppeorienteret kulturarbejde."

2 Holbæk received its first Turkish guest workers thirty years ago and the town has had a Red Cross refugee center for more than ten years; it therefore has a fairly long history of receiving immigrants and refugees along with the other large provincial towns of Vestsjællands Amt (the county of West Zealand): Ringsted, Slagelse and, to some extent, Kalundborg (interview 5 October 2001).

3 Marianne Andersson and Dorte Skot-Hansen, *Det lokale bibliotek: Afvikling eller udvikling* (Copenhagen: The Royal School of Library and Information Science, 1994), 19.

4 "Community work" or "community librarianship" might in some ways be a better rendering in English. However, the term *community librarianship* is very much rooted in and associated with a specific trend or course of action in British librarianship during the 1970s and early 1980s which "discriminated in favour of the socially and economically deprived" and "demanded . . . the proactive involvement of librarians in . . . communities," which was "questioned

by the library establishment on the grounds that it had infringed the noble tradition of neutrality within librarianship" and eventually given up (Alistair Black, *The Public Library in Britain 1914-2000* [London: The British Library, 2000], 148). Moreover, we prefer to use the term *cultural* work, since it better explains why, in a Danish context, it is more readily associated with the library as cultural center.

5 In translating the Danish word *kulturmødested* it is difficult to determine, and therefore potentially revealing of the ambiguity inherent in the word, whether the connotations are: meeting-place of cultures, place of cultural encounter(s) or perhaps cultural meeting-place/meeting-place of/for culture.

6 *Refuge for Integration: A Study of How the Ethnic Minorities in Denmark Use the Libraries* (The State and University Library, Odense Central Library and Aarhus Public Libraries, Denmark, 2001), 22; abstract and recommendations.

7 *Biblioteksbetjening af indvandrere på Avedøre Bibliotek: Rapport* (Hvidovre: Hvidovre Kommunes Biblioteker, 1982).

8 *BF's KITAB-udvalg Retningslinier for flerkulturel biblioteksbetjening* (Copenhagen: The Librarians' Union, 1990).

9 Abdullahi, Ismail, *Situationsbeskrivelse: Indvandreren og biblioteket i Danmark* (Copenhagen: Forfatteren i samarbejde med Indvandrernes Fællesråd i Danmark, 1981).

10 *De udenlandske arbejdere og folkebibliotekerne* (Copenhagen: The State Inspection of Public Libraries, 1975) and *Refuge for Integration: A Study of How the Ethnic Minorities in Denmark Use the Libraries*; abstract and recommendations.

11 *BF's KITAB-udvalg Retningslinier for flerkulturel biblioteksbetjening*, 32.

12 *Biblioteksbetjening af flygtninge og indvandrere i København: Hvem låner hvad–hvor–og hva' så?* (Copenhagen: The Copenhagen Municipal Libraries, 1999).

13 Cf. *Udlændinge 2000: En talmæssig belysning af udlændinge i Danmark*. Indenrigsministeriet Bilag A2 og Bilagstabeller. http://129.142.227 .228/publikationer/udl2000/forside.htm.

14 *Udkast til betænkning* (Copenhagen: Bibliotekskommissionen, 1979), 57.

15 It is worth mentioning that the new possibilities offered by new technology and especially the Internet have been used to develop a website, http://www.finfo.dk, which offers information in Danish, English, French and eight immigrant languages about Danish society and institutions and links to institutions, newspapers, etc., in the countries of origin. Even if it is innovative and very useful, it may be said to fall primarily within a technological logic.

16 *De udenlandske arbejdere og folkebibliotekerne*, 37.

17 *BF's KITAB-udvalg Retningslinier for flerkulturel biblioteksbetjening.*

18 Dansk Sprognævn (The Danish Language Council) suggests that, in Danish usage, both the terms "multicultural" / "multiculturalism" and "ethnic" have come to have either strongly positive or negative connotations. For adversaries of multiculturalism the term may indicate "political correctness and

restrictions against criticism of other cultures, for proponents tolerance and new and interesting opportunities and challenges." In addition, usage of the term "ethnic Dane" is now very confused in that it used to suggest emigrated Danes but is now increasingly used to indicate Danish citizens of foreign origin. (Ole Ravnholt, Dansk Sprognævn). An example of the latter usage was to be heard in Danish TV (Danmarks Radio) on 21 November 2001 where the news anchorman Morten Løkkegaard referred to the number of "ethnic Danes" who had run for election in the November 20 parliamentary and local elections.

19 *Refuge for Integration: A Study of How the Ethnic Minorities in Denmark Use the Libraries*, 6; abstract and recommendations.

20 *Udkast til betænkning.*

21 *Folkebibliotekernes Indvandrerbibliotek: Bbehov, aktiviteter og organisatorisk ramme* (Copenhagen/Århus: PLS Consult, 1996), 54.

22 In relation to the discussion of terminology and naming above, it is interesting that, prior to the opening of the International Library, the name of the library was given a lot of attention. The name Indvandrerlånecentralen—which is very similar to the present Danish name—was changed into the International Library. Another name, Världsbibliotek, was considered but rejected for various reasons, but the debate reflects a consciousness of the potential importance of what is (suggested) in a name (*Internationella Biblioteket i Stockholm: En idé om ett Världsbibliotek: Udredning* [Stockholm, 1997], 36).

23 Hans Kornø Rasmussen, *Dem og os: Det multi-kulturelle Danmark* (Aarhus: Tiderne skifter, 2000), 44.

24 Hans Kornø Rasmussen, *Dem og os: Det multi-kulturelle Danmark*, 104-5.

25 Hans Kornø Rasmussen, *Dem og os: Det multi-kulturelle Danmark*, 47.

26 For an evaluation of the forty-eight local integration councils set up so far, see *De kommunale integrationsråd: En undersøgelse af deres sammensætning, etablering, arbejde og rolle* (Copenhagen: Rådet for Etniske Minoriteter, Mellemfolkeligt Samvirke, Kommunernes Landsforening, Indenrigsministeriet, 2001); http://www.etniskeminoriteter.dk, www.ms-dan .dk, www.kl.dk, www.inm.dk.

Classification of Religious Literature: Some Thoughts on the Dilemmas of Universalism

Kasper Graarup

Using the classification of the literature of religion in the UDC as an example, the author discusses the problems of avoiding Christian bias in classification schemes. It is argued that biases cannot be eliminated altogether. Hence, the challenges for the LIS discipline are: (1) to adequately substantiate the theoretical and methodological assumptions underlying these revisions, and (2) to become aware that these theories and methods are based on ethical and political as well as on more instrumental choices.

The Problem

The following discussion of a specific problem of classification facing the public library is largely inspired (and provoked) by an interesting paper on the classification of the literature of religion presented by Vanda Broughton at the 66th IFLA Council and General Conference, Jerusalem.[1] This, however, does not imply that the criticism expressed is directed specifically at Broughton. Rather, it uses her paper as a point of departure for discussing problems of a more general and fundamental nature.

Broughton's main interest is to propose a revision of the Universal Decimal Classification (UDC) in order to avoid, as far as possible, the obvious Christian bias of the system in its present state.

It is very appropriate to try to come up with the proposals for revisions and updating that we need, since these biases can indeed be problematic: It seems to be quite obvious that the various universal classification schemes are in need of revisions and updating. This "obviousness" is manifested in the present paper in the sense that it is not being explicitly demonstrated. Those interested in the arguments are invited to consult, among others, Broughton and Graarup,[2] where I discuss the literature of religion in the Danish version of the Dewey system—DK5—and the lack of correspondence to contemporary scientific studies in religion. However, an equally important problem is to decide upon the criteria for making these revisions, to decide according to whose interests the revisions should be implemented, and to identify the relevant methodological and theoretical tools in this process: The point is that the schemes are, quite admittedly, biased, but so is every conceivable alternative! Or in the words of Stanley Fish: "You can only fight discrimination—practices that disadvantage some groups—with discrimination—practices that disadvantage some other groups."[3] In the following I shall present argumentation that suggests that even though universality is the legitimate claim of any universal classification system, universality is in fact a very difficult, even impossible, thing to obtain. I shall also suggest that in order to extend universality, as far as possible, scientific reasoning has to acknowledge its historical contingency—its ethically and politically biased foundation.

A Christian Bias

Broughton says that one of the major difficulties "in construction of a classification for the religious literature is that of avoiding bias (whether real or apparent) toward some specific religion or denomination."[4] And she continues saying that sometimes bias is impossible to avoid, and that occasionally a bias is not necessarily undesirable. It is not undesirable that, for instance, the New York Union Theological Seminary Classification exhibits a strong bias towards Roman Catholics since this system is tailored to suit a Roman Catholic collection, and she adds:

"However, a scheme intended for universal application should be as far as possible free of such imbalance and steps must be taken to eliminate it. Bias occurs, or is perceived to occur, in three main areas:

- An illogical order, or distribution of notation, that causes one system to appear as dominant
- Use of vocabulary that has a strong flavor of one system or is special to that system
- Inadequate provision of detail other than for the 'favored' religion."[5]

Through my own work with, for example, the classification scheme used in Danish public libraries—DK5—I am quite familiar with the kind of biases Broughton mentions.[6] But there are some elements in the arguments that puzzle me. Therefore I should like to ask this potentially even blasphemous question: Why is it so important to eliminate biases in universal systems? And as subsidiary questions: Do we really think that we can obtain universality? Do we think that we can replace these biases with something better suited—something better biased? And if the latter is the case, what we need then is a discussion of what a good or better bias is.

My objections to Broughton's suggestion do not so much concern the actual content of the proposed revision but are directed at the assumptions underlying the suggestions, and especially the lack of explicit considerations. A bias is perceived to occur in three main areas: illogical order of distribution, flavored vocabulary and inadequate detail in the not favored religions. These main areas seem to have in common the assumption that opposed to what is biased there is something not biased, whereas my argument is (a deconstructive one) that opposed to biased there is nothing but biased in another way. The point is that Broughton's "illogical distribution of notation," "flavored vocabulary" and "inadequate provision of detail" are not context free but "have a strong flavor of one system," namely the "system of reason": The concept of "illogical order" presupposes the concept of a logical order. But what is logic to one may very well be not so logic to another, and might indeed seem utterly illogical and emotional to a third. Or, to put it slightly different: What is illogic to Broughton could be very logic to a Christian or a Muslim, as I will demonstrate below. Likewise, "flavored" presupposes that it is possible to say something not flavored, and "inadequate" presupposes that something is universally adequate.

The suggestion is that we should try to avoid designing our universal classification systems in such a way that one religion is emphasized in comparison to other religions. But why is this? If our subject—our main class—were not religion but, for instance, biology or zoology, we would never worry ourselves not to represent the "frog" in such a way that the "horse" could take offense. Neither would it be a problem per se if the field of biology was classified in more detail than, for instance, the field of zoology. And, contrarily, if our subject or main class was literary fiction we would indeed represent the various authors and titles in such a way that it would be apparent who is important and who is not (maybe not so evident at the level of classification, but quite so in the *related* routines of acquisition, promotion and transmission of the literature). However, when we are dealing with religion, or cultural matters in general, we suddenly become very concerned not to promote one point of view at the expense of others—after all, we are not racists! And we do not want to risk any accusation of religious chauvinism or ethnocentrism. This appropriate concern is related to contemporary notions of democracy and to the various positions of "cultural relativism," which maintain that different cultures may not be valorized hierarchically, meaning that no culture may be judged superior to another. These points of view have epistemological as well as ethical and political foundations. Today, in the Western countries, religion—that is Christianity—is not *generally speaking* a self-contained and unquestionable authority. Actually, it is rather the other way around. It is not *comme il faut* to maintain that Christianity is the truth while Islam, Buddhism, Judaism and so forth are not. This view is also reflected in public library legislation at least in relation to acquisition practice, for example, in Denmark where the relevant paragraph reads that library materials should be selected regardless of religious and political claims and that selection should be carried out *only* in consideration of *quality, actuality and versatility*. The task is to establish, for instance, "quality" disregarding "flavor." The underlying assumption is parallel to Broughton's ditto: As a librarian, you have to assume the point of view of nowhere, or everywhere, something we normally reserve for God. It is thus quite plausible to say that all religions are equal and that no one religion should hold a privileged position—not in the public life in general, and neither in library. If this is our point of view—and it is the official point of view—then it is evident that it would not be appropriate if the various universal classification systems show the biases towards Christianity that they in fact do. But still, fighting religious discrimination cannot be done without discrimination, and therefore we need to take a critical look at the new discrimination before implementing it. Classification is not a goal in itself. It is a tool we use in order to obtain something. The same thing goes for the ideals of equality expressed in statements of public library purpose appearing, for instance, in public library acts, and supposedly underlying Broughton's suggestions: it is a tool we use in order to make human life better. It is—I am happy to say—beyond the scope of this paper to establish exactly what a good life is; I only want to stress the point that not even the concepts of equality, democracy, enlightenment and so forth are beyond political ambition: They are as biased as everything else, contingent, and deeply rooted in and dependent on their specific cultural history. This is in no way a trivial remark, and mainly for two reasons: (1) not all (at all) would agree, and (2) if agreed upon, this utilitarian and pragmatic approach renders everything—including "equality"—a concept the priority of which becomes relative to the consequences of its use. In other words: if legislation does not work, it must be changed. Therefore, when we consider whether the above-mentioned legislative point of view concerning acquisition is transferable to (among others) the area of classification, we *also* need to consider what is and what is not obtained by this approach. Two goals seem fairly obvious. The first is to optimize the performance of the system: to offer the best possible means (for everyone) for locating the desired documents—or if you please, the desired information. The second is of a more explicitly ethical nature: to prevent discriminations.

Ethics

The ethical ambition of the proposed revisions are, however, quite intimidated, and especially when considered from, well, an ethical point of view! I mean, why should the opinion that all religions are equal be more ethical than the opinion that Christianity is more ethical, more truthful than other religions? One could maintain that the Western attitude of earlier times that Christianity had prior rank in relation to other religions (the attitude which is reflected in the UDC as it is today) has been replaced by the modern and "rational" attitude that rationality and modernity itself (saying that *no* religion holds any truth or privileges) should hold a privileged position in relation to the various religious worldviews, including Christianity? In other words: Broughton is concerned with a system that shows a bias towards Christianity in relation to other religions, but the way in which she proposes to remedy this situation is by suggesting a system which favors a modern, secularized and even antireligious worldview in opposition to all religious point of views. We have a system that ranks Christianity high in relation to other religions, and Broughton is proposing a system which *implicitly* ranks the modern viewpoints high in relation to all religious points of view, including Christianity, graphically represented like this:

The UDC *before* the proposed revision	The UDC *after* the proposed revision
Christianity is favored compared to other religions	A secularized / modern point of view is favored compared to all religious points of view

I am not altogether sure that what Broughton proposes is an entirely bad idea, but I am pretty sure that she is doing nothing but replacing one bias with another.

To develop this point just a little further: Why would a Muslim be more content with a system that devaluates Islam in relation to secularized points of view than he would be with a system that devaluates Islam in relation to Christianity? My point is that by erasing a bias towards Christianity and replacing it with a bias towards a modern, secularized point of view, we are in fact only repeating and making sure that the dominating perception is manifested on behalf of the minorities. We are thus, and quite contrary to our intention, possibly making the system even more chauvinistic than it was before. We could say that the only news is that Christianity is now included in number of the suppressed. The relative status of Muslims is the same before and after the revision suggested by Broughton: they are still a minority and still ignored. Ignored in the sense that the views reflected are Western and not Islamic. They are Western in the sense, among other things, that the very idea of conceiving of Islam as a religion—that is, as something set apart from other societal institutions, as something which provides explanations of a religious nature, and thereby as something which has no authority on nonreligious matters such as politics and science—is a modern, Western, and in a sense even a Christian idea, or paraphrasing Broughton: *It has a strong flavor of one system.* Broughton is stretching out her hand to all the non-Christian religions of the world, but as long as she not willing to accept the *Islamic fact* that Allah created the world and according to this placing Islamic literature next to Darwin, she is not *really* taking them seriously.

Reason and Belief

This problem has been intriguingly addressed by the Islamic researcher Abdelwahab El-Affendi[7] in a discussion of, among other things, Salman Rushdie's *The Satanic Verses.*[8] Rushdie lets one of his characters criticize the biblical (and Islamic) Abraham for leaving wife and child—Hagar and Ishmael—unattended in the desert.[9] What kind of man would leave wife and child in the desert, he asks. But the Islamic response is that Abraham does not leave them unattended—he leaves them in the hand of God. Another episode that calls for modern indignation also concerns Abraham, and relates to his offering of another of his sons, Isaac.[10] The offering in which God in the very last second intervenes and replaces Isaac with a ram. What El-Affendi discusses is the impossibility of uniting an Islamic (or another religious) worldview with the modern, Western approach: An acquaintance of El-Affendi—a Marxist as he says—says that had God asked *him* to offer his son, he would never have complied. Neither would I, and neither would anybody reading this paper. El-Affendi says that this is the very reason why we are not Abraham but only ourselves. El-Affendi's point is to dispute the epistemological assumptions on which we condemn Abraham, and on which we as a consequence devaluate the opinions of the people to whom their religion is an undisputed truth. Generally speaking, El-Affendi is attacking the epistemological assumptions in accordance to which we feel justified in distinguishing between religious and scientific worldviews. The same justification that leads Broughton (and the Western scientific community) to classify Islam as a religion. El-Affendi says that the relation between belief and knowledge is not as simple as we might think: It is not so that the Islamic perspective is resting on belief while the scientific outlook refers to knowledge (this of course is not solely an "Islamic" postulate, but something which various Western philosophers of science have been pointing out for a long time). The relation between belief and knowledge is of a much more complex nature—knowledge is based on belief and vice versa—and very often what we understand as a rational and knowledge-based critique of, for instance, Abraham is not knowledge nor even belief but in fact "erroneous belief"! That is a belief that turns out to be wrong: Abraham does not leave Hagar and Ishmael to an uncertain destiny in the desert, he leaves them in the hands of God, and God takes care of them. If we follow the text—namely the bible—that is the point of origin of our critique it becomes apparent that there is empirical proof that our condemnation of what we conceive of as Abraham's blind faith is unjustified: God *does* take care of Abraham's family and Abraham *knows* that. Abraham knows that because he knows his God. Consequently, Abraham's actions rely on knowledge while our condemnation rests on erroneous belief. However, Abraham does not know everything; he only knows enough to be able to believe, as demonstrated in the story of the offering of Isaac. Abraham knows that this is God's will, and he knows that he must do it, but he does not know that it is a good thing or that everything will turn out just fine—that is what he believes and hopes. El-Affendi postulates that we would have been less condemning and more understanding towards Abraham if God had said: "*Pretend* to offer your son for my sake, and I grant you much happiness and make you and yours the greatest men on earth." Had God said that, Abraham's action would have been trivial, utilitarian and selfish, and consequently "perfectly understandable to the Rushdies of this world": We accept that man is cynical, utilitarian and selfish—such an assumption is scientific, while the assumption that man can know the truth and wants to do good is religion. According to El-Affendi, Abraham's action is based on knowledge but also on belief, and that is what makes the story unique and memorable: Abraham acts on belief, but a belief that is based on knowledge and courage.

The point of this seemingly sophistic digression into the nature of Abraham is to underline the illusionary character or at least the weakness of the argument of equality: The revision suggested by Broughton will indeed make the classification system more contemporary, but it still will not reflect an Islamic or any other religious outlook. And thus universality is not obtained. What *is* obtained is nothing but that the public library is confirming the outlook of the resourceful and dominating classes of Western society. Stanley Fish[11] identifies this problem in what he calls *the structure of liberal thought*. Liberalism defines itself against the dogmas of Christianity—the very dogmas or flavors that also Broughton wants to exorcise—and recognizes that "faction, difference, and point of view are irreducible." Still the liberal strategy—reflected in library legislation—is to "devise procedural mechanisms that are neutral with respect to point of view and therefore can serve to frame partisan debates in a non-partisan manner." This is an obvious contradiction: on one hand, we acknowledge that no transcendent point of view exists, and on the other, we act as if the public library provides just that.

The Performance of Classification Schemes in Knowledge Organization and Information Seeking

Now, let us put aside for a moment ethics and exegesis and try to look at the problem from a different angle. After all, ethics can hardly be said to be a very important contemporary way of justifying scientific—methodological and theoretical—claims. Let us look at classification from a more instrumental point of view: We do not then perceive a cultural or religious bias as a problem from an ethical point of view but because such bias makes it difficult for various users to find relevant documents. Difficult because the documents in question are filtered through a biased language and thereby misrepresented: Since Islam, Judaism, Buddhism and so forth are classified and filtered in Christian terms, the result is supposedly that (user-) questions formulated in accordance with non-Christian categories and patterns will not find—or only with great difficulty find—appropriate and relevant answers.

Various users are thinking and are formulating their questions in various ways. The main challenge of any universal classification system is to represent the materials in a way that makes it possible to handle these heterogeneous and differently formulated questions, and this is evidently not easily done—not in the general design of information systems and not in relation to classification "in isolation." By implementing the revisions suggested by Broughton, we would probably have come a little closer to perfection, implying that by making our filters less Christian and more modern we are closer to the average user. And this "getting closer" might very well be the best we can do in our everlasting craving for universal perfection in representation. But it *is* important that we do not fool ourselves into believing that by getting closer to the average, we are also serving the not-so-average, and that is the not-so-average in relation to degree of influence and not necessarily in relation to actual numbers (and thus we are linking the instrumental considerations to the ethical ditto).

What we are trying to do is to make our universal classification schemes less Christian and more modern in their bias. We do this because we believe that this will make the systems more functional, will make them perform better.

I think that in a way it is quite safe to say that the modern way of life has moved beyond the notion of a universal classification system. That this is the case is manifested in the various theories of cultural relativism and in the highly differentiated and stratified societies of today: "Islam" is one thing (probably many) to a Muslim, another thing to a Christian, a third thing to a devoted Darwinist, a fourth thing to a sociologist with the Arabian countries as his specialty, and so forth. There is no way that all the existing and potential conceptions of "Islam" or of anything else can be anticipated and fully represented in any one universal classification system.

Birger Hjørland[12] has proposed a domain analytical approach to the problem of deciding whose manners of representation should be represented. The domain analytical theory maintains that:

- The order of representation (as reflected in, for example, indexing and classification) of documents should be arranged in accordance to the knowledge potentials of these documents.
- The knowledge potentials (meaning the questions that these documents supposedly answer) should be identified by analysis of the *domain* that the information system in question is supposed to serve.

Hjørland has recently[13] proposed what he labels *eleven approaches* to domain analysis in library and information science: number two of these is to produce and evaluate classification systems and thesauri. My suggestions should be seen in this context namely as a critical evaluation of the classification of religious literature—a literature that has its roots not in one well-established domain but in many dynamic and mutually not compatible domains: If we conceive of our domain as one (e.g. Broughton's example the Roman Catholic Community) then the task is fairly straightforward, namely to identify, by analysis, the various ways of communicating, posing and answering questions in the Roman Catholic Community (for the sake of my argument we assume that we would in fact be able to delimitate this community). However, domain analysis is primarily concerned with the scientific community and its obviousness and usefulness is most significant in this area. It is quite conceivable that it is possible to identify the (most) relevant knowledge potentials of a given document if the intended users are all from the same scientific community: Even though there exists various, ongoing and mutating conflicts among researchers in same-subject fields, there *are* ways of identifying more or less stable common denominators (in the Danish Royal School of Library and Information Science, courses related to "Information Seeking and Knowledge Organization in Disciplines" are concerned with [theories and methods for] identifying these common denominators). When the problem is how to serve the scientific communities, domain analysis seems, in my view, to be equally resource demanding and unavoidable. The picture becomes somewhat distorted though when we direct our attention towards the public library. How do we identify the relevant knowledge potentials when the domain to be analyzed is the public domain—or domains—in its broadest sense? That is, how do we identify the (typical) manner of formulating questions and performing information seeking when our user is just about anybody? Controversies between researchers inside the same institutions and sharing identical fields of interests are, no matter how spectacular, incarnations of stability and predictability compared to the heterogeneity of public life.

If our problem was to provide the (most) relevant and useful access points to documents in a public database system as, for instance, the (online seeking facilities of the) Library of Congress, then we just might—at least in theory—and by using the methodology of, for example, poly-representation as proposed by Peter Ingwersen,[14] be able to identify and reflect all the relevant knowledge potentials. This methodology, of course, would have to be combined with intensive "universal" cultural analysis. Our present task is only to identify the relevant knowledge potentials in relation to the encyclopedic and mono-representational methodology of the traditional, analogue universal classification system. I shall not discuss in any detail the future existence, or possibly the future nonexistence, of classification schemes in the traditional sense. Neither is this the place to discuss whether, nor to which extent, the library of the future will have open shelves—if they will have shelves at all. I am working on the assumption that a revision of the universal classification systems is a profitable one; that it will take several years (possibly forever) before universal classification systems can, in good conscience, be termed a thing of the past. I am working on this assumption for mainly two reasons. The first is that I find it hard to imagine that it could be appropriate for real libraries, with real shelves and real books to cease to exist, and the second is that universal classification systems are still being invented and put to new uses in relation to (e.g. search engines on) the Internet. The structured indexes of Google, Yahoo, AltaVista, etc., are examples of this. As is the case with the traditional physical library, the structured indexes (universal classification systems) of the Internet are, of course, combinable with a variety of supplementary seeking facilities. Some of these are genuine to the Internet. Some are genuine to online seeking in general. The point is that these supplementary techniques, the various ways of poly representing, do *not* render irrelevant the design of the classification system itself. So, the conclusion is that though traditional universal classification systems are indeed simple and even primitive compared to the wonders of online information seeking they are still necessary. But not only are they simple and necessary, they are also, as we have seen, practically impossible. As long as the real physical documents have to stand on real physical shelves, we have to make a choice, or rather we have to make several. We have to decide who is to be our ideal user; we have to decide in accordance to whose interests should the knowledge potentials of the documents be identified? There is absolutely no way these choices can be made without at least *co* reflecting political and ethical arguments.

Conclusion

Broughton is not very explicit about her reasons for proposing her revisions. That is, she is of course explaining that the intention of the revision is to limit the Christian bias of the UDC, but she is not revealing the theoretical motivation—ethical or instrumental—for reducing this bias. It is my impression that Broughton is implicitly working on the assumption that it is our ethical duty to remedy this situation: that we are in fact ethically obliged to the non-Christian religions of the world. As we have seen, it is doubtful that by implementing Broughton's suggestions we are actually doing, for instance, the Muslims of the world a favor.

As mentioned above, I assume that generally researchers in library and information science have a more instrumental approach to the instruments of the library: Whether and how, for example, the various universal classification schemes should be revised is a decision that must be based upon an evaluation of whether or not this revision will add to the functionality of the system. The problem imbedded in this seemingly simple proposition is that functionality is dependent on which kind of user we have mind—is it a scholar of the scientific study of religion, a Muslim, or perhaps a Jehovah's Witness? The traditional universal classification system—regarded as an isolated entity—is methodologically speaking encyclopedic and mono-representational, and therefore we need to decide which kind of user we have in mind. Or in other words, we need to choose between various biases since the idea of abandoning them altogether is simply illusionary—it cannot be done. We have to make choices that are more than just "instrumental," and thereby our problem is also an ethical problem. This problem may seem like a Gordian knot, but the way out—I believe—is to recognize the illusionary character of the public library as a locus of the transcendent nonbiased point of view: The public library is there for a reason—or rather we have to recognize that we have reasons for having it there—and make these reasons influence the makeup of the systems. It is my impression that Hans Elbeshausen and Charlotte Werther[15] are touching upon problems related to this in their discussion of the public library's ability to improve integration. Elbeshausen and Werther conclude that in their attempt to ensure equal provision and equal access to ethnic minority users *the Danish public libraries have come up against increasing uncertainty and unpredictability*. The libraries have tended to focus on technical solutions—dependent on a technical rationality—and not so much on what the authors term *communicative rationality*. It is my suggestion that this being caught up in a technical rationality is closely related to the (possibly implicit) notion of the library as a transcendent, nonbiased, *automatic* provider of access. If the libraries were more willing to accept and promote their particular reasons and agendas—in this case to improve integration—and design their (technical) systems and solutions accordingly, they might acknowledge the need and usefulness of what Elbeshausen and Werther label *communicative* approaches. And likewise, if attempts to revise the universal classification system were debated in relation to the intended effect, we could possibly find ourselves in the privileged position of choosing between varieties of inspiring flavors instead of trying to escape them.

Notes

1 Vanda Broughton, "Classification for the Literature of Religion," *International Cataloguing and Bibliographic Control* 29, no. 4 (2000): 59-61. Paper presented at the 66th IFLA Council and General Conference, Jerusalem, 2000.

2 Kasper Graarup, "Religionsvidenskab på folkebiblioteket," *Totem: Tidsskrift ved institut for religionsvidenskab* 4, special issue (2001): 23-40.

3 Stanley Fish, *There Is No Such Thing as Free Speech and It's a Good Thing Too* (New York: Oxford University Press, 1994), 3.

4 Broughton, "Classification for the Literature of Religion," 59.

5 Broughton, "Classification for the Literature of Religion," 59.

6 DK5 stands for the fifth edition of the Danish version of the Dewey Decimal Classification System

7 Abdelwahab El-Affendi, "Studying My Movement: Social Science without Cynicism," *International Journal of Middle East Studies*, no. 23 (1991): 83-94.

8 Salman Rushdie, *The Satanic Verses* (New York: Viking Penguin, 1988).

9 Genesis 21, 1-21.

10 Genesis 22, 1-19.

11 Fish, *There Is No Such Thing as Free Speech and It's a Good Thing Too*, 16.

12 Birger Hjørland, *Information Seeking and Subject Representation: An Activity-Theoretical Approach to Information Science* (Westport, Conn.: Greenwood Press, 1997).

13 Birger Hjørland, "Domain Analysis in Information Science: Eleven Approaches—Traditional as Well as Innovative," *Journal of Documentation* 58, no. 4 (2002): 422-62.

14 Peter Ingwersen, "Polyrepresentation of Information Needs and Semantic Entities," in *Proceedings of the 17th ACM-SIGIR Conference on Research and Development in Information Retrieval. Dublin, Ireland, 3-6 July 1994 (Special Issue of the SIGIR Forum)*, ed. W. Bruce Croft and C.J. van Rijsbergen (London: Springer, 1994), 101-10.

15 Hans Elbeshausen and Charlotte Werther, "The Intercultural Encounter between Danish Public Libraries and Ethnic Minority Users," in *New Frontiers in Public Library Research*, ed. Carl Gustav Johannsen and Leif Kajberg (Lanham, Md.: Scarecrow Press, 2005). Included as a chapter in the present book.

Ethnic Diversity in Danish Public Libraries: Four Stories

Bo Christensen Skøtt

This article is based on the findings of a pilot study carried out in spring of 2002. The study explored the "cultural encounter" in public libraries, defined as the encounter between new Danish citizens and Danish public librarians. Three respondents—AH, KH and HK, representing three larger public libraries in Jutland—were interviewed. Four main stories grew out of the interviews conducted.

Introduction

This article reports a pilot study of the cultural encounters as they take place in public libraries in Denmark. Three librarians from three different public library systems in Jutland, the continental part of Denmark, were interviewed. The selected public librarians possessed special knowledge of ethnic librarianship. The aim of the study was to show how librarians perceive the services aimed at ethnic minorities and how these services are offered. How do these librarians talk about servicing ethnic minorities and what kind of issues do they stress? The intention is to understand how professional routines may influence the relations between professional and user.

Part one is an introduction to the political and cultural context of the pilot study. It summarizes how the field has developed throughout the last thirty years and what kind of problems public librarians, in general, are facing in the beginning of a new millennium.

Part two discusses the conceptual framework and introduces the core terminology. The key concepts are *cultural encounter, ethnicity* and *perceptions*. The cultural encounter and ethnicity are working terms used in everyday work. However, the real meaning of the terms is implicit and hidden. What do these terms actually signify and why?

Part three concentrates on what happens in the public libraries: How does the identity of the professional librarians reflect tradition and how does it influence actual behavior? My hypothesis is that the professional attitude influences both the services offered to ethnic minorities and the socialization process that takes place.

Part four contains four "stories" based on the interviews: How do they compare—what kind of similarities can be observed and what differences might be found?

Ethnic Diversity in Public Libraries

Since the late 1960s, when immigration to Denmark surpassed the emigration from the country, ethnic librarianship has been developing as a special field of interest in public libraries. The development especially took place between 1967 and 1973, when foreign, unskilled labor—guest workers, as they were called—were imported to Denmark to overcome "bottlenecks" in the labor market. Even though restrictions were introduced in 1973, immigration continued as refugees came to the country and because of subsequent family reunions in harmony with international conventions and agreements. This is not an isolated Danish phenomenon; the rest of Europe experienced similar migration patterns earlier.

At an early stage, public libraries realized that immigrants run the risk of being socially marginalized and isolated. The main groups invited were unskilled workers from Turkey and Pakistan. To prevent their isolation and to integrate them into Danish society, public libraries concentrated their efforts on them, and especially their children. By supporting the children in educating themselves and engaging in learning activities, public schools and public libraries hoped to break the social inheritance.

The Danish conception of democracy implies that librarians respect the ethnic minorities as individuals through a relativistic approach: Every individual has a right to maintain his or her cultural values and traditions as long as they do not offend any law. This is the ideological foundation of Danish public libraries. Indeed, public libraries in Denmark have quite a tradition of devoting special attention to different groups and clienteles. Children, elderly citizens, handicapped people, socially marginalized, women, unskilled workers and unemployed have, in various periods throughout the last century, been defined as special target groups that have needed and received special attention. This explains why serving new citizens is a natural thing to many public librarians. This has been done many times before. Furthermore, at this time the target group can be quite easily defined by the way they look, dress and talk. However, one major difference clearly appears in comparison with the other special clienteles mentioned above: Because society (including the public libraries) defines the ethnic minorities as having a need for special consideration, there is a risk that their democratic rights are restricted. In fact, they become exposed as clients. Some of the immigrants might fall into the above-mentioned categories; however, a majority of the immigrants get jobs and become capable of managing their lives on their own. Nevertheless, there is a risk that within the rest of the society, an image of the whole group as being in need for special attention has been already created. This again implies that individuals belonging to that group become weak, just like children, senior citizens, handicapped persons, women, illiterates and other socially marginalized individuals in various periods throughout the last century. In defining ethnic minorities as social groups in need for special attention, public libraries reproduce the dominating image of these people as clients. Although the intentions are good—to prevent negative consequences for immigrants—the effects of the above-mentioned actions, together with images being reproduced by the mass media, turn out to be quite the opposite. The prevailing image of ethnic minorities that has arisen is one of small communities not interested in being integrated into the Danish society. According to this image, they are isolated, asocial and sticking to nondemocratic values and representing traditional life perceptions.

On a national scale, the public library system has developed and continues to develop services for ethnic minorities. Whenever needed, local public libraries all over the country can order book depots of both fiction and nonfiction in native language and material supporting the teaching of Danish, Teach Yourself Danish courses and so forth by the National Immigration Library (SBIB) to complement local collections. SBIB contains and maintains collections in about fifty languages in addition to operating FINFO, the Danish web portal for immigrants and refugees.[1] Since resources are limited, SBIB cannot entirely serve its purpose, but the Immigration Library tries as hard as possible.

Only a few user studies have been conducted on how minorities use Danish public libraries. Those that have been carried out often concentrate on the amount of material circulating in minority communities and focus on how minorities use the library and what kinds of problems are appearing (such as noise and violence) and how they are dealing with these problems. Emphasis has been placed on practice, the actual efforts made to serve minorities, so as to *explain* what is going on. In the present author's opinion, these studies often fail to *understand* why things look like they do. Why do young adults from another ethnic group differ from ethnic Danes in their behaviors, for example, as to noise? Often the explanations provided are based on ethnicity, defining the behavioral patterns observed as a result of some kind of unchangeable biological essence or as inherent characteristics of these young people. One ambitious study, *Refuge for Integration*,[2] was conducted in March 2001. This study revealed some interesting results. It identifies the kind of characteristics that define ethnic minorities. As shown later, minorities are not just communities of people of an origin other than Danish. Several other characteristics have to be fulfilled to make an individual belong to a minority in need for special consideration. Actually, ethnic minorities do have the same wishes for and demands on the library services and facilities as ethnic Danes: more and newer materials such as books, papers and periodicals, video films and music, more and faster computers and electronic facilities such as Internet access, etc. Another conclusion is that diversity emerges as minorities increase their use of libraries. In fact, ethnic minorities make greater miscellaneous use of the public library's facilities. They spend more time in libraries, they make copies, surf, chat and search on the Internet, read, write, study and so forth. Especially, the use of public libraries as a whereabouts, where friends can meet without any excuse, where elder male citizens from minorities read newspapers and exchange news with fellow acquaintances, where young adult boys meet young girls and so on are emphasized. For all categories of immigrants, consider that they borrow fewer materials than ethnic Danes. Although the conclusions in *Refuge for Integration* have identified several areas that need attention, such as establishing formal contact with certain ethnic groups through newsletters, promotion of social and cultural events and activities and contact to religious organizations, nothing has happened. In fact, no further action was taken to solve the problems that were identified in the study.[3]

The Cultural Encounter

In fact, the English term *cultural encounter*—a translation of the Danish term *kulturmøde*—does not appear appropriate, since semantically the meaning of the word is "accidental meeting," "battle" or "fight."[4] A better word would be "confrontation" because it means "put face to face."[5] Nevertheless, the Danish word *kulturmøde* is often translated as *cultural encounter* and this practice will also be adhered to in this article. The cultural encounter is defined as an encounter between people of distinct ethnic origins. It does not always take place smoothly and without problems. The risk of being misunderstood leading to a negative response is always present. Whenever cultural encounters take place, it is easy to distinguish between them and us, majority against the minority. The focus is on what keeps people apart instead of what brings them together. If, on the other hand, the cultural encounter takes place without ethnicity as the focus point, the potentials are just at hand. The positive cultural encounter enables majority normative values and the perspectives of minorities, which can be very different, to be presented on equal terms and thereby discussed in a climate of mutual acceptance. The positive cultural encounter can be defined as an exchange of experience, values and meaning in a place where all other subjects are discussed but ethnicity. By ignoring ethnicity as a prerequisite of achieving a successful interaction, this hopefully appears more equal and becomes more interesting to both parties. The purpose is to qualify the life of individuals and make it more diverse. The cultural encounter is defined by former Danish Minister of Cultural Affairs Elsebeth Gerner Nielsen[6] and reflects mainstream Danish democratic ideals and egalitarian thinking with emphasis on progression, discussions and exchange of views and ideas for mutual benefit. A statement by the Danish actor Runi Lewerissa summarizes the very essence of the good encounter: "Cultures cannot meet. It is people of different cultural origin who meet, and the arts provide the best stage for an encounter of this nature because the communication is done in a common language and has a common foundation."[7]

The different uses of services made by certain ethnic minorities, especially their use of the public library as a whereabouts, worries many librarians because of the implicit social and behavioral effects (noise) this might cause. The encounter between citizen and librarian thereby develops into an encounter between layman and professional. In doing so, it creates a disordered relation. Power, as defined by Billy Ehn and Orvar Lövgren, is the right to decide what reality is.[8]

This right still lies with the librarians representing an enlightening and educating institution, which during more than a century has constituted an important pillar in Danish democracy. However, the right to define reality is staged in another way. As we will see below in discussions of the three public librarian respondents about ethnic minority groups' uses of public libraries, minority group users' interaction with library staff assumes the character of "cultural encounters." These encounters construct the image of an equal relation between the different parts involved in the servicing process. By doing so, they also legitimize the action taken by librarians. As evidenced by the interviews, professional identity is bound to the image of Danish librarians as communicators, mediators and guardians of democratic values. Socialization is seen as integration. My point is that whenever integration is conducted on behalf of traditional values instead of through discussion and contact, it means that new citizens will have to adapt to the institution and the way the majority population thinks and not vice versa. Socialization in the sense of teaching habits and customs cannot be defined as integration but must be termed assimilation. New citizens will have to accept the image of them as maintained by public libraries: a target group requiring special attention. Nevertheless, we like to think about the public libraries as operating to the benefit of the whole public, taking action and developing services for our sake.

Ethnic Diversity as Politics

The construction of ethnic minorities has been analyzed in various context and typically emerges from such contexts as the role of the mass media reproducing enemy pictures,[9] professional routines and behaviors in social work (e.g. in asylum camps) creating hierarchical power structures,[10] the frequently reported discrimination practices evidently occurring in the labor market and so forth.[11] It is asserted here that these phenomena are to be seen as effects of the unconscious norms, behaviors, values and attitudes of professionals in abovementioned areas and that the professional routines produce client mentality and inactivity on the part of the minorities considered. Thomas Hylland Eriksen, the Norwegian anthropologist, provides more explicit descriptions of the different mechanisms that represent the fundamental national values constructing an image of ethnic minorities as representatives of certain cultures of origin. He tries to identify the mechanisms active in this context by studying the ethnic minorities from an anthropological and psychological point of view. One great idea developed by Thomas Hylland Eriksen is that ethnicity has become a strategy, which in recent years more often has been applied by different minorities in their attempt to attract international political awareness. The political use of the term ethnicity has less to do with the desire for ethnic purity. It appears that the main use has been that of serving as arguments in the struggle for basic resources in high demand in society: education, welfare, social security, work, etc.[12] Ethnic identification is a factor which can be drawn on whenever the larger political or social environment, for example, the public opinion or the world society, is considered ready to perceive the image of a threatened and suppressed minority.

Ethnic identification and culture have become legitimate tools in the political struggle for power.[13]

Social Strategies

Hence, it is important to point out that individuals belonging to ethnic minorities also contribute to the creation of images and the stories about themselves as "others." According to the Danish researcher Dorte Staunæs, Ph.D. in Intercultural Communication, this happens because social positions are the results of negotiations between individuals. She describes the process based on observations made in an asylum camp in the mid-1990s:

> The asymmetric relation between residents and staff [is maintained] daily through both residents' and staff members' everyday practice. Through action taken by both sides and by the ways of (re-) structuring the contexts, staff members become fixed in their roles as aiding experts and the residents persist in theirs as helpless clients. The responsibility and authority stay in the hands of staff members in spite of objects and intentions . . . on doing the opposite.[14]

Viewing oneself and one's potential in terms of "ethnic otherness" creates a self-picture, which is determined by the here and now situation. Clients remain fixed in a social position where they are marginalized within the established society without many (if any at all) opportunities for effecting changes through self-driven initiatives. This situation produces two different perceptions of life, which Dorte Staunæs describes as ways to *open the world* or *close the world*.[15]

To Open the World

To open the world is an attempt to actively change something and by doing so to improve the conditions for developing and strengthening the social position and identity of the individual and his or her family through commitment and active involvement. But since refugees are required to stay in the asylum camps almost twenty-four hours a day having nothing to do, it is not easy for them to "open the world." In this state where passivity leads to paralyzing, it is hard for most individuals to find ways to overcome the traumatic effect of isolation.

Figure 1.

Strategies: *to open the world*
1. Create possibilities to do something (activity because of activity)
2. Construction of alternative self-pictures (new orientation)
3. External reaction (latently aggressive)
4. Win special rights (privileges)
5. Change stigmata of otherness to trademark (pride)[16]

Strategies to open the world can be seen as different mechanisms in the attempt to create alternative pictures of the self. This happens in opposition to the established society, which empirically marginalizes the individual whose situation does not leave that many opportunities for influencing one's own conditions.[17] That is why the activity itself becomes more important than the results. It is not the product but the process which provides meaning.

To Close the World

In opposition to above-mentioned perceptions, closing the world represents internal strategies which lead to resignation and passivity. The general climate in the camp is obvious because every activity requires official approval and does not per se effect an improvement of the social or occupational conditions. The string of causes has been overruled:

> But even in spite of a persistent contribution to the activities in the youth club, he had to realize that he could not improve his and his family's life conditions through work and that salary, bigger rooms and asylum are not something which can be earned, but on the contrary something one might be granted by the Danish in spite of own contributions.[18]

Dorte Staunæs concludes that despite the Danish ideal of equality, the above-mentioned social contexts contribute to the reproduction of what she calls an "asymmetric relation" between residents and professional helpers and between ethnic Danish and ethnic others.

Figure 2.

Strategies: *to close the world*
1. Self-destructive reaction patterns (internal)
2. Fundamentalism (totalitarian expressions of opinions)
3. Narrow-mindedness (reduction of complexity)
4. Isolation[19]

In contrast to the attempt to open the world and create alternative self-pictures, closing the world strategies can be explained as an uncritical acceptance of the available images and approval by the majority of the society with subsequent frustration and anger as the outcome, no matter what alternative images are created as a contrast to the established society. Whether the individual attempts to open or to close the world, the surrounding society will react by constructing and establishing different ideals, a process that also serves to develop otherness or a refugee-like mental state within the individual. The individual belonging to a minority cannot act without these constructions and relying on them he or she will reproduce and constitute the following patterns:

> "Refugee" in the sense of seeker of asylum is not something you are. On the contrary, it is something you do and someone you are made to. "Refugees" and "ethnic otherness" are terms, which are constantly constructed and are making sense through those actions or "doings" applied by different actors. Be it politicians, staff members or the refugees themselves, and others.[20]

The above-mentioned alternative strategies are linked to simultaneous time and space, which means life, lived by individuals. It is not necessarily representing any kind of cultural origin or ethnic tradition. The actual situation in which the individual is placed and in which he or she is facing uncertainty in line with the majority's conception of normality and abnormality is visualized through refugees' invention of alternatives. In other words, identity is shaped on the basis of different social influences, which is an evident reality for second- and third-generation youngsters as well.

National Capital

Another Danish Ph.D. degree holder who has published works on "Intercultural Communication," Iben Jensen, explores, on the basis of her studies of young people in Denmark, how traditional national values are included in their negotiation of social positions. Using the concept *national capital* [21] she is pointing to the representative cultural competences as essential to how we are speaking about and within subcultural communities. The conclusion drawn from her studies is that, in contrast to theories about the decline and fall of the nation state,[22] young people identify themselves with traditional national values. Each individual identifies himself or herself as representing either normative national majority cultures or alternative minority cultures in the everyday socialization process and from this process social positions are chosen and negotiated. In those contexts, the librarian is presenting herself as an individual. However, she also appears as a member of the national majority culture. This identity on the part of the librarian affects the images of minorities and leaves its stamp on the way problems are solved, what kind of behaviors can/cannot be accepted and so forth. All human action must reflect the participants' individual personalities and the situational context where action takes place. In other words, a human being will always be found behind the citizen in question and the professional behaviors and representations in the cultural encounter.

I will not claim that the special conditions in a Red Cross asylum camp in 1996 and the way it affects people's everyday lives can be generalized to those of people who left the asylum system years ago and have started on individual integration and educational programs. Nevertheless, you will find some of the same mechanisms among the nonsocialized second-generation young adults when they attempt to create alternative self-pictures. The individuals become symbolic representatives of their cultures of origin because it appears obvious and visible that they belong to foreign ethnic minorities. An individual's general identification with the whole minority, caused by the majority, often results in very rough generalizations in terms of traditionalism, antidemocracy and fundamentalism, or even worse, and reproduces negative images of the minority. The subsequent result is discrimination and exclusion. I found that some of the professional routines in the Danish public libraries studied were producing some of these effects, even if the intentions were the opposite, namely, to avoid unequal treatment and discrimination. As shown later, initially, all librarian respondents expressed their attitudes towards ethnic minorities in terms of equality, individuality, respect for different cultural and ethnic values and, to some degree, accept of diversity in behaviors. Questions asked later in the interviews revealed a discrepancy between the ideological statements and the descriptions of the actual behavior shown when interacting with members of minorities. This is true of all four accounts presented. Although the tendency observed is not as clear as shown by Dorte Staunæs in her study of asylum camp residents, it is visible.

Librarian Identity

Identity is expressed primarily through a combination of self-pictures developed and continuously reproduced by different subcultures and the image of those subcultures as it appears in society.[23] The story depicting the relations between subcultures and the surrounding world allows subcultures to express their identity both on purpose and involuntarily through terms chosen, subjects and action taken. This is one of the ways in which subcultures reflect on the relations between themselves and the rest of the society. The reputation of the subculture will always be dependent on the changing subjects articulated for discussion and on how the subculture views and acts upon these subjects. Similarly, this reputation will vary over time. In the specific context, both the new citizen and the librarian are seen as belonging to a certain subculture: the citizen to an ethnic minority and the librarian to both an ethnic majority and a professional subject field. As part of this study, I intend to examine the interview persons in order to signal and mark the professional relations with the ethnic minorities. The statements will be compared with statements from articles appearing in professional journals and magazines, especially the library periodical *Bibliotekspressen* published by the Librarians' Union in Denmark.

Cultural Encounters in the Public Library

The respondents describe the cultural encounter as an encounter between individual and *culture*. Culture, in this sense, means democracy, including freedom of speech, and the Danish society, history, religion and so forth. The interviewees thus represent an understanding of cultural encounter different from the one provided by the definition above.[24] The cultural encounter in public libraries is centered on the service provided by the professional to the ethnic minorities. The public libraries do not support interaction between citizens, socializing and mutual exchange of experience and views, neither as a part of the public library professionals' formal tasks nor within the range of informal tasks.[25] The interpersonal communication between the public librarian and citizens approaching the librarian for assistance is formal and the professional attitude makes sure that the service and personal attention on the part of the librarian is optimal and in harmony with the requirements for good practice. This means a delivery of service that is efficient and provided as fast as possible.[26] Here, the cultural encounters are of minor importance. Furthermore, it is not in the public library that people from different ethnic groups interact to get to learn each other better—nor do ethnic Danes. For this purpose other social spheres are more adequate, for example, sports, clubs, social associations, educational institutions, personal networks, hobbies and work. Lasting personal contacts between library staff members and citizens from distant ethnic minorities in everyday work are minimal. As mentioned above, children and adult male persons from minority communities often use the public library as a whereabouts, club, After School Center and the like. However, they seldom meet and socialize with people they do not know beforehand. When cultural encounters, nevertheless, happen to take place, they often occur between members of different ethnic minorities: "That they also meet other minorities and make contacts with them because they are facing some of the same problems . . . for them this really is a meeting place."[27]

It seems as if people belonging to minority populations do meet and interact because they are encountering similar problems. Yet no one can tell how lasting these connections are. Besides, to make this observation more ambiguous, things probably look different in the children's library because children do have a different social behavior. It means that they are much more direct in their ways of making contacts with strangers. This also occurs in places which are especially concerned about the public library as a cultural bridge builder between different ethnic minority groups and the majority.[28] However, in general, the cultural encounter in the public libraries between citizens or between citizen and professional seldom develops beyond occasionally formal contact: questions asked and answered. As opposed to the definition of the positive cultural encounter outlined above, the cultural encounter in the public libraries also takes place with the citizen emphasizing ethnicity as an important value. Furthermore, librarians use ethnicity to characterize the target group in question and to sharpen their professional focus. The result is focus on cultural distinction. Ethnic origin becomes a category from which the individual is defined and measured, a character trait of the citizens involved, or in terms of Dorte Staunæs's categorization, a stigmata.

Four Stories

Equality

The three respondents' general attitude concerning public library users of Danish and foreign origin is deliberately neutral and individualistic: Each individual has a wish or a problem and for meeting or solving that wish or problem the assistance of the librarian is required. Irrespective of his or her ethnic origin, a user is an individual, and as such he or she must be treated. The different terms used by the respondents in their insistence on equality vary a little. Yet all agree that the users' ethnic identity, be they Danish or foreign citizens, should be ignored. The attention should be unique because the individual standing on the opposite side of the counter has unique requirements, skills and qualifications. This issue is in focus in the daily work of the librarians.[29] The answers of the respondents all emphasize the importance of equality as a fundamental value in the relation with citizens of foreign origin. By doing so, they live up to the image of the impartial professional librarian. That image matches the one reproduced by the rest of the society: public libraries as a cornerstone of modern Danish democracy. Hence, it seems paradoxical that in spite of the principle of equality, the actual behavior of respondents results in unequal treatment. Thus, variations in the librarian's professional attention towards users should be reflected in the way it is administered and directed. The intention of putting citizens entering the library on an equal footing with each other is utopian, because neither resources nor time will be available—and because there is no need for it! In public libraries, attention towards users has become a question of service defined as verifying, storing and delivering information and entertainment instead of communication and mediation.[30] This development ensures that the clientele of the public library almost always receives what it wants, for instance, as to resources available in Danish. The problems occur when other kinds of materials are demanded, such as literature in foreign language and with foreign letters. In the late 1960s, the principles of provision of library materials were discussed. The debate centered on the extent to which the limited resources should be used to develop foreign language collections proportional with the actual size of the minority communities or to what extent other principles of prioritizing could be relied on.[31] One of the problems facing librarians today is that collections have developed very differently from place to place in the country. However, in no respect the amount of material targeted to certain minority groups is adequate compared to the proportion of minority residents in the local community. The picture varies, but in general, materials in native tongue are very poorly represented, either because no materials are available—because the origin of immigrants tends to vary over time— or because financial resources are needed in other areas.

The second issue, whether the will to serve the ethnic minorities is present or not, can be illustrated by the following observation: Ethnic librarianship often tends to be taken care of by newly employed librarians with no or limited knowledge of the area. In recent years, however, the Danish Royal School of Library and Information Science has prioritized the area by offering special courses in "Ethnic Librarianship." Still only the largest public libraries (with the exception of SBIB) can afford employing full-time librarians to serve minorities. Thus, to a great extent, servicing ethnic communities is the job of a few enthusiastic people. The interviews revealed that all three respondents were aware that equality is a utopian idea, and that reality never matches this ideal.[32] There are distinctive differences in the service provided to Danish middle-class citizens on one hand and ethnic minority group members on the other. What seems to be lacking is a discussion of whether this priority is intended and correct or whether other priorities would serve to increase ethnic minorities' use of public libraries. The attitude seems to be the following: Keep the service level for ethnic minorities status quo because right now nobody can manage to change things.

This schism appears because the self-understanding of the three respondents, and the prevalent image in society, demand librarians to serve the public equally. Yet reality turns out to be different. On the other hand, the ideal prevents the librarians from allowing variations in the amount of professional attention allotted. Differences in services offered could be interpreted as a kind of discrimination. Emphasizing their democratic conviction, the interviewees seem to have fewer worries about tolerating differences and inequalities. In doing so, inequality becomes a question of resources. However, allocation of resources is determined by municipal politics and consequently is no longer in the hands of the librarians.

Common Characteristics of Minorities

For me, and for the respondents as well, delivering library services to ethnic minorities means adopting a starting point that emphasizes the individuality of all users. Individuality and the unique character of the individual attention are as important as equality in the way respondents talk about interaction with ethnic minorities. In spite of this, all respondents express experience related to ethnic minorities as a target group or a subculture, which defines the ethnic communities as a citizen category.[33] One interesting aspect of the way respondents talk about minorities is the apparent consensus on whom to identify as ethnic minorities. Their definition is corresponding to the one presented in *Refuge for Integration:*[34]

> Most interviewees have come to Denmark as young people or adults and many were not library users in their native countries. In many of the countries from where the interviewees come, there are

limited library services, which are attached to schools or universities, and the services offered are usually limited to books. More of the interviewees mention other possibilities to get cheap access to books, e.g. secondhand bookshops, book fairs or places where books are hired out.[35]

This definition of ethnic minorities emphasizes that part of the new citizens are not from the beginning familiar with public libraries. Indeed, the very notion of a Western public library is unknown or only fragmented. The missing knowledge and the lack of socialization to these institutions occasionally result in conflicts with library staff members and other citizens using the library service. In other words, librarians define minorities the same way as all other parts of the majority society: as people from third world countries, undeveloped, non-Western oriented, with traditional perceptions of life and with missing democratic values and traditions. Furthermore, the interviewees' ideas about the use of public libraries by ethnic minorities mirror the dominating image of the society in general. It is the same image that is persistently communicated by the mass media with their current stereotypes about minority group members' countries of origin.

Similar mechanisms can be identified in the discussion about individuality. The respondents attempt to emphasize everybody's right to be treated as an individual in relation to the Danish democratic traditions. But in their personal universe, the librarians participating in the present study tend to construct ethnic minorities as a collective entity with specific characteristics. This picture either stems from personal experiences or refers to stereotypes available in society in general. On one hand, associating certain groups with common characteristics can be very useful in order to adjust services and by creating standards for handling and solving problems. On the other hand, it may also lead to problems, because individuals are different. These differences will disappear, or become less visible, when a group mentality is established. As opposed to awareness of the schism of equal treatment, the respondents do not seem to recognize the same mechanism when it comes to individual versus group mentality. Respondents' alternating between individual and common characteristics, the way they define new citizens, occurs smoothly and happens without any further considerations. An explanation for this could be the above-mentioned tradition for dividing library users into different target groups, which is practiced so routinely and almost unconsciously.

Introduction to Library Services

Within the attempt to define a specific group mentality or certain characteristics, the concern with how especially children are introduced to and educated in use of public libraries is an important issue. In general, somehow the minorities are introduced to library services in all institutions studied here as a part of their integration program. These activities mostly take place as a result of a request from a group of citizens or a class (or their teachers) and the introduction is conducted on the basis of what the individual librarians regard as necessary and pertinent information in relation to the needs of the specific group. Material supporting the learning of Danish, linguistic collections related to the new citizens' cultures of origin, the Danish web portal for immigrants (FINFO), newspapers, periodicals and so forth are resources considered essential by the three librarian respondents. According to KH, the future action plan at her institution points to the introduction of library services to immigrants as an obligatory task, which means a more offensive policy towards immigrants and not only a set of practices based on single persons' initiatives. In that way, catering also for individuals not aware of the opportunities and services offered by the public libraries is emphasized as an obligation for the librarians to deal with.[36] At the time the interviews were conducted,[37] no other principles than those mentioned in the Danish Act on Library Activities could be relied on. Official policies or general guidelines were not adopted or implemented by any of the institutions studied here. The professional services were based on a traditional understanding of the librarian's tasks in relation to the library's target population in general.

Education

There is common agreement among the respondents that children and young people have to be educated in library use. The grown-ups are mainly left in peace even though their competences and behaviors may also, from time to time, cause anxiety and uncertainty. Cultural qualifications are seen as qualifications and skills, which each individual can and will have to develop as part of his or her personal integration process. This process can be actively supported by library materials, which, for instance, provide language stimuli.[38] At the same time, all respondents express how important materials in native tongue are in the attempt to encourage children and young people to maintain the contacts to their cultural roots and to be able to communicate with relatives, friends and family within their own culture, which, however, means acquiring cultural competences of a more static character.[39] Materials

for Danish language training are of great importance in efforts to overcome the difficulties of understanding each other's language, which is
the main cause for barriers in the interaction between librarian and
citizen.[40] In respect for and acceptance of ethnic values and traditions
such as language and family structures respondents try to mediate between these two strategies. However, by using language issues as a
specific focus area, the professional practices tend to produce an asymmetric power relation between the librarian and the citizen. Again, it
might not be as visible as seen by Dorte Staunæs, but just as effective.
The accentuation of language imperfection and the cultural competences as a process leaves an impression of the relationship between
public librarians and individuals from ethnic minorities paralleling the
one that exists between teachers and their pupils. But in contrast to the
school metaphor, the relation between the librarian and the new citizens
does not have any generally stated intentions to fulfill and it becomes
accidental, fragmented and personal, because the library introduction
and teaching sessions are a matter dependent on the librarians' personal
conviction.

Socializing

Although a main point is to leave adults in peace, no respondents in the
study underestimate the effect of adults' use of libraries—on the contrary. There is great consensus that the very use, the mere entering the
public library physically on a regular basis, produces some kind of
educational change and serves to develop competences which are most
valuable from an integration point of view. Cultural competences, language, behavior, acceptance of common democratic and social rules
can, compared to the problem areas outlined above, be seen as a process[41] that develops within each individual and the longer his or her stay
in Denmark will be, the further will this transformation progress:
"When the children start school and learn more than the grown-ups, it
has something to do with their stay in the country . . . a development
has taken place."[42]
    The three respondents all agree that this kind of socialization takes
place in their respective institutions. However, they also all agree that
socialization does not occur according to a specific strategy meant to
support the integration process. They also expressed general consensus
about what normative values are and such values are considered
equivalent to those traditional behaviors, which should be accepted and
shown by new citizens.[43] At this level a common issue for all three
respondents is the focus on noise. Noise (not violent behavior, deliberately chicaneries, etc.) is singled out as a joint feature of almost all new

citizens defined as members of ethnic minorities and especially when they make use of Internet and computer facilities. Noise is also interpreted as mismatching prescribed behaviors as expected from users. Sanctions and the associated power to define what is normal and what is abnormal are put in the hands of the librarian: that means to estimate, judge and punish. The only respondent reflecting on these matters is AH who compares the situation, noise in the libraries, with the situation in the late 1970s and early 1980s where children from certain residential areas with socially maladjusted families developed alternative physically and bodily behavioral strategies in opposition to the rest of the established society.[44] Those children were unable to adjust to norms and values in the contemporary society because they lacked social possibilities and identification. Comparing AH's statements with Dorte Staunæs's observations, life perceptions, social position and self-identity are elements in a process developing on the basis of opportunities and possibilities available in society here and now, and it is a process, which is less determined by the ethnic traditions inherent in the (image of) the ethnic minority. The two other respondents talk about variations in the librarian's professional attention as a consequence of individuals' ethnic backgrounds. In an attempt to respect the individuals and their ethnic rights as a minority, self-censorship is practiced in everyday work (according to KH[45]) along with positive discrimination through greater tolerance towards unacceptable behaviors (noise, according to HK[46]).

As part of ethnically determined behaviors, physical, bodily and ideological differences are observed and accepted by the respondents. The alternative use of the public library facilities means long-time visits and more intensive use of services and facilities compared to the use made by ethnic Danes. It also means that the behavior of the ethnic minorities becomes more visible—similar observations can be found in the study entitled *Refuge for Integration*.[47] Whether ethnicity has anything to do with these alternative behavioral patterns or they are determined by other issues, for example, the social position and surroundings, take the question. My point is that youngsters, irrespective of ethnic belongings, make noise whenever they meet in larger numbers. This is an effect of their attempt to negotiate social positions within the group and gain reputation and to conquer the public space, and it forms a natural part of their mental and physical development. This has nothing to do with ethnicity. Nevertheless, the Danish youngsters have an advantage here, being brought up and socialized to the knowledge about which kind of public space to be used for what purpose and which public zones to avoid.

Unaffected by this, the attitude among the respondents is clear: For a long time, the official policy has been offensive with regard to the task of introducing immigrants to the public libraries (maybe to secure the future use and to extend libraries' activities and spheres of operation), and less attention has been paid to instructing those new citizens in the behavioral norms common to the use of public libraries. The introduction to the libraries' facilities and the instruction in the use of the libraries have suffered in the attempt to widen the group of new citizens who are using the public library in ways that are easy to measure and quantify. Also, library use instruction has been overshadowed by the efforts to make public libraries appear as understanding, tolerant and useful institutions in the integration process. But such efforts are to blame. The wish to encourage new citizens to use the public libraries has narrowed the focus on how librarians want these new citizens to behave, because establishing contacts has been given priority.[48] Behavioral norms have been expected to be common knowledge. But this is a misjudgment made by the librarians bearing in mind the above definition of minorities as strangers with regard to the use of public libraries. Many librarians have now changed their focus and try to compensate for the misunderstandings by teaching new citizens what kinds of habits and customs are appropriate.[49]

It seems as if librarians are following two strategies at the same time in their attempt to deal with noise: on one hand, a relativistic approach where action is based upon the image of ethnic minorities as special cultural entities that demand respect for traditions and ethnic values, and on the other, a compensating approach where the effect of inconsiderate practices are been solved by establishing law and order by all means, through sanctions and rewards policies. Reflections on whether these strategies are the right ones or if other means could be developed do not appear in the interviews.

The Free Public Space

Another question is whether alternative use of the public library would anyway produce alternative physical and bodily behaviors—even if shown by ethnic Danes? An often-used phrase is the public library as a public *whereabouts* defined as a place for library visitors' informal unstructured activities or a cosmopolitan environment where people stay and mingle without any other legitimate explanation than the wish to remain there. Recalling several articles in *Bibliotekspressen*, mention is frequently made of public libraries as an alternative whereabouts for ethnic minorities. The professional identity of the responding librarians is also determined by this image of the public library as a free public and democratic space for cultural encounters and intercultural sociali-zation and they take pride in this attitude. The public library as a unpre-tentious space is a dominating story told about the public libraries, both in society in general and among librarians. The physical space is com-pared with marketplaces in Southern Europe, cafés, and community meeting places or encounters and life. Yet, in contrast to such places, public libraries exhibit at least one major difference: the presence of a representative authority—the librarian. The bodily presence—(still) essential and necessary for the librarian in performing his or her work—is at the same time structuring and consolidating the authorita-tive powers present in these institutions. The ordinary librarian does act as a professional individual but not only as that. In fact, at least three different levels of representations were identified: a private (eth-nic) level, a professional (subcultural) level and an authoritative-governmental level. The contact between professional librarian and citizen is subject to more structuring effects, which are an inbuilt fea-ture of the formal powers and continue as a factor affecting the cultural encounter between the individuals. Even in the situation analyzed here, with only three respondents, their stories about professional identity show that the kind of freedom allowed in the public areas of the librar-ies are subordinated to different expectations regarding certain prede-fined behaviors and skills. The ideas and images of the majority, de-fined above as national capital, are not limited to the negotiation of social positions among youngsters. They are also activated in the li-brarians' interaction with the public. The public space made available by the libraries are free according to the traditional Danish understand-ing of what a free space can and must mean and be available for.[50] Hence, this space is also subordinated to the same conception of de-mocracy where self-controlling arrangements structure people's norma-tive behavior. Based on these traditional values and assuming that all users understand and accept them, librarians decide whether behaviors are socially acceptable and can be rewarded or if they are deviant and require sanctions. These conventional rules are developed over time, during several hundreds of years, and represent a very definite struc-ture, preconscious to most professionals.

Furthermore, several quotes from articles in the union magazine *Bibliotekspressen* and statements from all three respondents indicate anxiety about the development where public libraries try to change their tasks towards more social work: "Libraries in areas with severe social problems must be aware that they do not try to solve all the prob-lems, which the social institutions cannot manage. . . . In fact, it is the same discussion we had back in '79 when I became a librarian; at that time it was the maladjusted Danish children."[51]

To all three respondents it is important to dissociate themselves from social institutions such as After School Centers, for example, in the municipalities.

The notion of the public library as a whereabouts also represents this schism: on one hand, the librarians taking pride in being employees of a democratic institution, available to all people in society without exceptions, and on the other hand, the attempt to be distinct from institutions dealing with the social aspects of ethnic minorities. In my opinion, this distinction cannot be made. The use of public libraries has changed with the introduction of new citizens and this fact must be realized before further development can take place.

As included in the public librarian's professional identity, I identified at least four dominating stories, outlined below, which are instrumental in determining and structuring both actions and behaviors implicit in the cultural encounters in public libraries taking place between librarians and citizens of ethnic or cultural origins other than Danish.

The four stories are as follows:

1. Equality
2. Common Characteristics of Minorities
3. Socializing
4. The Free Public Space

Even if the idea of democracy expressed by the respondents is not explicit, they all speak of issues related to these four concepts included in the Danish conception of democracy: "What is communicated and mediated is the place or the spirit, which is here. It is a place where all people can stay, yes it is a place where all people can meet . . . I think it is the spirit, yes it is *that* part of the Danish culture."[52]

The activities organized to introduce and serve new citizens coming to the public libraries are mainly legitimized on the basis of notions identical to what librarians imagine that these people would need to know about the services available in the public library. This personal estimate made by the individual librarian is rooted in the images of immigrants appearing and circulating in the library world and in the rest of the society. These images are strongly tied to the ideas of ethnicity and its influence on the individual and his or her behavior and actions. In terms of democracy, freedom of speech and equality, respondents legitimize behavioral adjusting and controlling mechanisms, which can be applied when necessary. The consideration given to the other library visitors and the consideration to the librarians themselves legitimize necessary sanctions whenever normative and conventional limits are broken—but the judgment is personal, implying that the socializing effect becomes accidental, sporadic and ambiguous.

This is how the representative powers are activated and made visible in the public librarians' interaction with ethnic minorities. Uncertainty about the purpose of services to be offered to the minorities as a foreign and unknown clientele produces uncertainty about how to handle the subsequent reactions of minority group members to the services provided and their alternative library use. Hence, the traditional story about the public libraries as integrating and democratic institutions are reestablished with enlightenment, community information and education as main tasks. In Denmark, this is a story showing the historical and professional inheritance from the Northern American public libraries around the turn of the nineteenth century. In looking to the American public libraries, inspiration has also been drawn from the ways in which the aims and objectives and service ideals of the pioneering American public libraries were translated into practice. This practice necessarily involves a certain use of power.

Notes

1 FINFO, the Danish web-portal with information for immigrants and refugees, translated into eleven different languages; available at www.finfo.dk /html/default.html.

2 *Refuge for Integration: A Study of How the Ethnic Minorities in Denmark Use the Libraries*, abstract and recommendations (Aarhus: Aarhus Public Libraries, 2001).

3 Confirmed by phone calls nine months after.

4 Jens Axelsen, ed., *Dansk: Engelsk ordbog* (Copenhagen: Gyldendal, 1984).

5 Flemming Albertus, ed., Gjellerups fremmedordbog (Copenhagen: Gjellerup & Gad, 1988).

6 Anne Gitte Munck, ed., *Det gode Kulturmøde: Unge—Profilen* (Copenhagen: The Danish Ministry of Culture, 2001) and Anne Gitte Munck, ed., *Det gode Kulturmøde: Medborgeren—Profilen* (Copenhagen: The Danish Ministry of Culture, 2001), 3. Special issues of *Profilen*, the newsletter issued by the Danish Ministry of Culture but contents provided by the Danish Research and Development Centre for Adult Education (DRDC).

7 Munck, ed., *Det gode kulturmøde: Medborgeren—Profilen*, 27.

8 Billy Ehn and Orvar Lövgren, *Kulturanalyser* (Malmö: Gleerups Utbildning, 2001), among other things, 87.

9 Mustafa Hussain, Ferruh Yilmaz and Tim O'Connor, *Medierne, minoriteterne og majoriteten: En undersøgelse af nyhedsmedier og den folkelige diskurs i Danmark* (Copenhagen: Nævnet for etnisk ligestilling, 1997).

10 Dorte Staunæs, *Transitliv: Andre perspektiver på unge flygtninge* (Copenhagen: Forlaget Politisk Revy, 1998).

11 See, for instance, Hanne Folmer Schade, "Et arbejdsmarked med åbne arme," *Bibliotekspressen*, no. 11 (2000): 371.

12 Thomas Hylland Eriksen, *Kulturterrorismen: Et oppgjør med tanken om kulturell renhet* (Oslo: Spartacus forlag, 1993), 36–38.

13 Hylland Eriksen, *Kulturterrorismen: Et oppgjør med tanken om kulturell renhet*, 22.

14 Staunæs, *Transitliv: Aandre perspektiver på unge flygtninge*, 60. Author's translation.

15 Staunæs, *Transitliv: Andre perspektiver på unge flygtninge*, 76-102.

16 Staunæs, *Transitliv: Andre perspektiver på unge flygtninge*, 90-102.

17 Staunæs, *Transitliv: Andre perspektiver på unge flygtninge*, 100.

18 Staunæs, *Transitliv: Andre perspektiver på unge flygtninge*, 64. Author's translation.

19 Staunæs, *Transitliv: Andre perspektiver på unge flygtninge*, 76-89.

20 Staunæs, *Transitliv: Andre perspektiver på unge flygtninge*, 14. Author's translation.

21 Iben Jensen, *Interkulturel kommunikation: I komplekse samfund* (Frederiksberg: Roskilde Universitets Forlag, 1998), 233-34.

22 See, for instance, Søren Mørch, *Den sidste Danmarkshistorie* (Copenhagen: Gyldendal, 1996).

23 In this context, the librarians should also be understood as a professional subculture.

24 Comment by AH, an immigration librarian: "[They] see that kind of life, all among each other, all is equal, look at the librarians as people [and they] see each other, use each other, especially when it comes to the computers. . . . In some way everybody is equal when they walk inside our doors."

Comment by KH, an immigration librarian: "In the day-to-day work we only meet them if they approach us to request help or if it is a situation where we in a toilsome way have to correct their behavior . . . but that is not a meeting. . . . It all adds up to this place . . . there simply isn't time for it."

Comment by HK, head of children's department in one of the three libraries: "Many things are implied in the attendance of a user, and towards ethnic users an explanation starting from scratch is necessary. You are not raised with irony and underact and you need the time to do it. If you do it, it is very interesting, but you need to adjust to a little more patience."

25 Comment by KH: "Do they meet the Danes in the libraries? I do not think they do. . . . They meet other groups of minorities and get in contact whith them because they are dealing with the same kind of problems . . . but this is talking from a large place like this . . . maybe the situation is different in the sub-branch libraries. . . . In the day-to-day work we only meet them if they ask for help or if it is a situation where we in a toilsome way have to correct their behavior . . . but that is not a meeting. . . . It all adds up to this place . . . there simply isn't time for it."

Comment by HK: ". . . spontaneous talks between Danes and immigrants? Among children it often happens, but usually it happens between different kinds of immigrants. . . . There is a cultural meeting going on between Danish girls and the ethnic males who are making pranks with each other, but maybe they know each other from school . . . but hardly ever the other way around."

26 This is in accordance with what Hans Elbeshausen and Charlotte Werther name the "technical rationality" in the public libraries; the handling of the tasks in the public libraries is primarily a question about rationalization and developing effective working routines and to serve the public. See the article by Hans Elbeshausen and Charlotte Werther in the present book.

27 Interview with KH conducted on 15 April 2002. She futhermore points out that in connection whith cultural events organized by the library cultural meetings do occur, but they are rare.

28 Pia Møller, "Søllerøds nye udfordring," *Bibliotekspressen*, no. 4 (2002): 99-102.

29 Comment by AH: "The starting point is: here is a person standing in front of me, who needs help. Understanding language is of course a precondition, but everything else doesn't matter. It is the inquiry, that counts."

Comment by KH: "A user is a user and then it doesn't matter whether you are a Somalian, speaking Russian or Danish."

Comment by HK: "What matters is to know what that specific individual is needing: two individual inquiries can't be answered in the same way. . . . Everything for the customer and in general we offer a high level of service in terms of promotion and communication and in the other areas."

30 Directly asked, all of the three interviewed librarians agree that this is the development in the public libraries. AH categorizes 90% of all citizen's inquiries as being related to "servicing."

31 Ågot Berger, *Mangfoldighedens biblioteker: Flersproget biblioteksbetjening i Danmark* (Frederiksberg: The Librarians' Union, 2001), 89.

32 Comment by AH: "Of course we also experience it as culture—that it looks like a clash. . . . Especially in newspapers—newspapers are per definition political and we cannot . . . it is awfully difficult to tackle—sometimes there are some powerful discussions and sometimes they end well and other times we think: no, this didn't work out the way I liked it to do."

Comment by KH: "[We] . . . do not always fulfill the task the way we could have—it is especially the problems surrounding procurement; surrounding resources but primarily surrounding procurement . . . but obviously we aren't that well prepared in what we call the immigrant collection."

33 This may be caused by the nature of the questions in the interviews, that demands common features of minorities.

34 *Frirum til integration: En undersøgelse af etniske minoriteters brug af bibliotekerne: Sammenfatning og anbefalinger—udarbejdet i et samarbejde mellem Statsbiblioteket, Odense Centralbibliotek og Århus Kommunes Biblioteker* (Aarhus: Aarhus Municipal Libraries, 2001).

35 *Refuge for Integration: A Study of How the Ethnic Minorities in Denmark Use the Libraries*, 12. The respondents participating in the survey were drawn from the following ethnic communities: Arabs, Somalians, Iranians, Vietnamese and Turks (from Århus) and Arabs, Pakistanis and Bosnians (from Odense). For futher classification see *Frirum til Integration*, 7.

36 According to interview with KH conducted on 15 April 2002.

37 In the middle of April 2002.

38 All three respondents emphasize the learning of the language as an essential part of the offers to the ethnic groups in the public libraries.

39 Interview with KH conducted on 15 April 2002: ". . . but the other way round, it is equally important that we are able to give them something from their own culture—the ones who bring that culture with them into Denmark, those who have that culture within themselves."

40 Comment by AH: "Our emphasis is placed on the ability to learn the language and to understand the Danish society."

Comment by KH: "The language barrier is not found in the direct interaction because they do not address us, but to interact and mediate directly is difficult (if they don't speak the language) the library should be able to provide information on the Danish society, language courses, history and likewise."

41 Comment by AH: "But we do a lot, to talk about democracy and the right to free speech, free right to borrow material and so on . . . here you are welcome . . . we can offer everyone within your community something from your own culture, but we can also offer support so that you will get to know the Danish society, our priorities are about learning the language and understanding the Danish society."

Comment by KH: "The interaction or mediation process going on is determined by this place or its spirit. It is a place for everyone, yes, it is a place for meeting each other. . . . I think it is this kind of spirit, we probably see it is as an integral part of the Danish culture. . . . The libraries reflect the democratic culture and structure of the Danish society. . . . They are equipped with different kinds of tools to get on in this society in a way that everyone can live with—them and us."

42 Compare interview with HK conducted on 22 April 2002.

43 Comment by AH: ". . . especially the Palestinians, but those who come from these very corrupt countries and need a dictionary for an examination tomorrow, they think that if they stay around long enough, we'll find one in a drawer somewhere, put aside for a cousin that they may have. And then you have to learn, that in Denmark, when you look at our computer and it tells us that every copy has been checked out and on loan, there are not any more, these books have actually been borrowed by someone else."

Comment by KH: "The library reflects the democratic structure of the Danish society. A picture of the society. . . . And in some way or another they learn a little about social behavior . . . and how to move around in this place. . . . They are equipped with different kinds of tools to get on in this society in a way that everyone can live with—them and us."

Comment by HK: "Democracy and the free right to speak is inherent in the idea—that is the way it works for me. . . . The longer they have stayed in the country, the more socialized they have become . . . but we offer only frameworks and material for this socialization. . . . You learn: Here are other kinds of norms ruling."

44 Comment by AH: "Actually, it is the same kind of discussion we had in '79 when I started as an librarian; at that time it was the strained Danish children. . . . The shabby Danish children that are gradually being replaced by the shabby foreign children. . . . The Danish [strained] children today are almost swallowed up by the institutions, all of them."

45 Comment by KH: ". . . attention towards ethnic norms—pictures of what certain ethnic groups can 'endure'. . . there were some naked women and so on. It just catches your eyes a little too much. . . . At that time we talked a little about how to avoid shocking someone."

46 Comment by HK: "To the Danes it is an inherited tradition (that the libraries are) a quiet place, you are not allowed to make noise, something the ethnic groups never learned. The noise is considerable in the libraries. In this situation, we are saying that they are being very loud and disturbing, but if Danes were shouting in the same way and showing the same level of behavior, we would be on our guard."

47 *Refuge for Integration: A Study of How the Ethnic Minorities in Denmark Use the Libraries*, 4-5.

48 Hanne Folmer Schade, "Tæt på brugerne," *Bibliotekspressen*, no. 11 (2000): 387, includes the following observation: "We even have been so busy being tolerant and understanding that we didn't have time to tell the children which rules to obey in a library . . . most librarians [are] in fact already working on addressing that wretched business."

49 Pia Møller, "Ali og de flinke damer," *Bibliotekspressen*, no. 4 (2002): 96-98. "They try to solve the problems by relying on what has been termed consequence pedagogy."

50 Compared with the above-mentioned problems with youngsters and noise.

51 Compare interview with AH conducted on 19 April 2002. For further information see Schade, "Tæt på brugerne," 386-87 and Møller, "Ali og de flinke damer," 96-98.

52 Interview with KH conducted on 15 April 2002.

Part IV

THE HISTORICAL DIMENSION

Architecture and Design of Danish Public Libraries, 1909-1939: Between Tradition and Modernity

Nan Dahlkild

Explores the way contemporary Danish cultural debate and public library policies interacted with public library architecture and design during 1909-1939. These years were significant in the formation of the country's public library system. Thirty-five new public libraries were built, and forty-eight libraries were rebuilt. Special consideration is given to the Library of Nyborg (1939), which represents "the functional tradition." The dilemma between sensibility and objectivity in library architecture is seen from a future perspective. The quality of the experience of library architecture and design beyond a rational organization is emphasized.

Introduction

The development of the modern public library system in the Nordic countries takes its offspring in the first decades of the twentieth century. In Sweden, the Dickson Library was erected in Gothenburg in 1897 based on the inspiration from the American public libraries with their open shelves. Similarly, a series of spectacular public library buildings were constructed in Norway during the first decades of the century. In Denmark, a joint museum and library building was opened in Køge in 1889 and when this joint accommodation had became too small, the first stand-alone or self-contained Danish public library building was erected 1918-1919. Moreover, at the National Exhibition in Århus in 1909, a working exhibition library was constructed, thus both serving as a delicate expression of the culture and library policy-related ideals typical of the period around the First World War and at the same time inspiring library construction activities in the small local communities in the interwar period. In 1920, Denmark's first Public Library Act was passed. This pioneering legislation had far-reaching implications for the organization and development of public libraries including the library construction projects in the interwar period. The new Act implied the establishment of the State Inspection of Public Libraries, an institution which was entrusted with coordinating and inspecting tasks. Thomas Døssing (1882-1947) was appointed the first director of the new inspection agency. As a true pioneer in the public library field, he left his very personal stamp on the library policy of the period with adult education and enlightening efforts on the one hand and work simplification and streamlining of operations and offerings on the other, thus forming a synthesis. The Act introduced a range of grants earmarked for public libraries. These funds would be made available to public libraries provided that they satisfied the requirements of the Act calling for collections of books in libraries composed so as to ensure diversity and informational and educational aims. Projects defined for the purpose of founding or rearranging a library could count on the award of an additional one-third of the local grant. A study based mainly on reviews and mentions appearing in the Danish library periodical *Bogens Verden* ("The World of the Book") reveals that between 1919 and 1939 thirty-five new public libraries were built in Denmark. Of these new libraries eleven were constructed in the twenties, including Køge Public Library from 1919, and twenty-four in the thirties. Corresponding figures for essential newly designed library homes and rebuilt library accommodations were forty-eight, including twenty-six in the twenties and twenty-two in the thirties.

Thus, the spectacular library-building boom took place in the thirties with a considerable geographical scattering throughout the country and in different types of local communities, implying that the new library homes were located in large towns, suburbs and smaller and medium-sized towns as well as in railway towns. In Denmark, railway towns are countryside villages that expanded concurrently with the development of the national railway network during the years 1860-1920 or simply new towns that grew up around the railway stations.

The architectural expression ranged from *Skønvirke* ("Fairwork") and historical styles over Danish Classicism in the 1920s to functionalistic trends as from the mid-1930s. The Fairwork style was a trend within Danish art and architecture, which meant a break with previous historical traditions and the Classical styles. The Fairwork period is generally considered to cover the years from 1880 to 1920. It parallels the English *Arts and Crafts Movement*, the German *Jugendstil* and the French *Art Nouveau*. Just as was the case outside Denmark, Fairwork marked a reaction against the growing supply of cheap and poorly manufactured mass-produced goods made possible by industrialization.

The typical public library from that period is characterized by a Classicistic sobriety and a symmetric ground plan like a "butterfly," where a monumental entrance hall and the adult lending department are located on the central axis as a "body" with adult reading room and children's library as "wings" on each of the sides. Very often this type of library has been characterized as a "knowledge temple."

A general trend of the period studied was the development towards a greater sobriety and matter-of-factness with respect to both construction activities and building design, thus reflecting a higher priority given to the existence of a modern and goal-directed book-lending department at the expense of a library space, which—if thinking of today's practice and preferences—would be designed for visitors' social and more unstructured activities. However, typical of the libraries in the thirties were also the designing of lecture rooms and rooms for study circles. This historical development will be put into a present-time perspective later on.

Brief Review of Research

Two classic introductory presentations that cover the subject dealt with here and the period considered are Harald Hvenegaard Lassen's *The History of Danish Public Libraries, 1876-1940* published in 1962[1] and Carl Jørgensen's *Danish Library Buildings* with an introduction by Carl Thomsen that appeared in 1946.[2]

Hvenegaard Lassen's book provides a detailed and informative account of the central period in the founding history of the modern Danish public libraries. This seminal period covers the inspiration drawn from American professional practices and philosophy, with the emphasis on freely accessible libraries with open shelves, the significance of the government grants provided for by the 1920 Public Libraries Act, the establishment of the State Inspection of Public Libraries as a national agency and the development of the county library system. The exposition emphasizes the achievements of key persons such as Andreas Schack Steenberg (1854-1929), H.O. Lange (1863-1943) and Thomas Døssing (1882-1947)—all notable Danish public library pioneers—and in a literal sense it boasts an extensive index to, or inventory of, persons and geographical places. The dominating perspective provided is the progress and growth of public libraries as institutions including especially the large-scale library construction work activities of the thirties. Clearly, the sympathy lies with the central administering and controlling agencies as opposed to the so-called Book Collections Movement, which emphasized decentralizing public library activities. Very characteristic is the book's state-of-the-art survey of the public library situation in 1940 with the observation that, also from an international perspective, Denmark can now be rated as one of the best-equipped library countries.[3] Harald Hvenegaard Lassen (1886-1971) formed part of that development and as head of the Vejle Public Library he was one of the pioneers himself. After having acquired a Danish Master of Arts, M.A.-like qualification, he was sent to the United States in 1912.

Carl Jørgensen's presentation with an introduction by Carl Thomsen (1894-1971) constitutes a state-of-the-art of the interwar period public library building activities. It covers a selection of thirty-nine public library building projects that are described with the emphasis put on practical library design aspects on the basis of information collected from a questionnaire survey conducted by the State Inspection of Public Libraries. An "architectural point of view evaluation" has not been undertaken. Similarly, Carl Thomsen's contribution gives priority to practical aspects such as types of library designs, the location of different functions, rooms for study circles and public lectures, administration staff offices and need for stack room capacity, etc. The many photographs and ground plans constitute an important part of the book's documentation. Carl Jørgensen (1888-1973) had drawn five of the selected libraries himself and cooperated with the State Inspection of Public Libraries. Carl Thomsen was Head of the Århus Municipal Libraries and played a prominent role in solving a variety of coordinating tasks for the public libraries.

Published research in the field provides evidence on a reassessment of previous public library history writing. An illustrative example in this respect is Leif Emerek's historiographic piece on the foundation of the Modern Public Library in Denmark included as a chapter in a Norwegian anthology entitled *Det siviliserte informasjonssamfunn* ("The Civilized Information Society").[4] Emerek questioned the introvert nature of library history research work. Central to Emerek is a theoretical approach that emphasizes the general education and the general public-related orientation according to which modern public library service is viewed as a part of society's general modernization process. A similar study of the Norwegian library history with special emphasis on "Taylorization," which is viewed as the background of the establishment of the Norwegian State Inspection of Public Libraries, can be found in Salvesen in her article "What Are the Salient Features of Quality Work in Norwegian Public Libraries?" in the same collective volume.[5]

Library Policy, Cultural Debate and Architecture

The aim of the project presented more briefly in the present paper is to (1) investigate relationships between library history developments in Denmark occurring in the interwar period, the cultural debate during that period and trends in architecture and (2) examine the architectural expression and design patterns of Danish public libraries.

The library policy, the cultural debate and current architecture of the period in question were characterized by "The Modern Project"—however, in different ways. In a library context, Modernity manifested itself in the interaction between centralization and work simplification, rationalization, at the organizational level and the historically based general education ideas at the political level, whereas Modernism as reflected in the cultural debate to a higher degree assumed the character of an experimenting avant-garde. Also mastered by this avant-garde were, however, extensive technical insights and rationality within the context of functionalist architecture and town planning.

The development of public libraries was characterized by the Public Libraries Act (1920), the founding of the State Inspection of Public Libraries as a national government agency and the active inner circle of persons centered around State Inspection Director Thomas Døssing. The period witnessed clashes of interests between this modern general education oriented environment and the Book Collection Movement with representatives of the smaller libraries that wanted a more decentralized development with greater local influence on, among other things, book selection processes. In local community contexts, the general trend was to prefer traditional popular literature, and light fiction, in contrast to the critical and experimenting part of the literature.

During the period investigated, a close connection between current debate on culture and architecture—reflected, for instance, in the critical and Cultural Leftism oriented Danish journals such as *Kritisk Revy*, *Kulturkampen* and *Plan*—can be identified. The liberation or emancipation project maintained by the Danish Cultural Leftism broadly encompassed the Modernist literature and art, jazz, reform pedagogy and sex guidance as well as a new functionalist architecture in glass and concrete and modern town planning emphasizing light, air and space and green areas. The visions on the modern society as formulated by Functionalism implied the liberation of man from the hard physical work. Distinguished Danish architect Arne Jacobsen (1902-1971) created the White Town at Bellevue north of Copenhagen, which provides an elegant and thorough illustration of the leisure-oriented design of Functionalism. Built in the thirties, the White Town included apartments, theatre, beach bathing area and gas station. In this town, leisure time activities were democratized with space for some 12,000-15,000 inhabitants and with frameworks designed for a classless body culture. The architectural expression was white forms of ships, balconies, large glass windows and asymmetries.

However, Modernism was not universal as an architectural school in the interwar period. From the turn of the century onwards, the so-called *Skønvirke* style with its organic forms, the tortuous ornaments and refined handicraft had left its stamp on the aesthetic expression. In the first decade of the twentieth century and into the twenties, this style was continued by a movement like *Bedre Byggeskik* ("Better Architecture"), which wanted to develop and refine the Danish craftsmanship tradition and transform it into a popular architecture, frequently with historical borrowings. In this context, mention should be made of the great Grundtvig Church erected in the northern part of Copenhagen during the years 1920-1940. It stands out as a significant illustration of this school. At the same time, especially the twenties were characterized by a true Classicist oriented architecture with emphasis on sobriety, symmetry and monumentality. The architecture of C.F. Hansen (1756-1845), a leading Danish architect, sometime Director of the Royal Danish Academy of Fine Arts (1811-1818, 1821-1827, and 1830-1833), from early nineteenth century served as the great role model of this school which at the same time, however, analyzed and experimented with the rhythm of architecture. A principal work is the building of the Copenhagen Police Headquarters erected during 1918-1925, drawn inter alia by Danish architects Hack Kampmann (1856-1920) and Aage Rafn (1890-1953). Both schools can be viewed as a "modernization of the tradition."

Finally, the "Functional Tradition" completed the period. This concept was first used after the Second World War but one of the principal works of this school is the University of Aarhus, drawn by Danish architects Kay Fisker (1893-1965), C.F. Møller (1898-1988) and Povl Stegmann (1888-1944). The building work started in 1932. Briefly, this school can be characterized as a synthesis of the experiments of Modernism on one hand and the historical tradition and regional materials on the other.

From an architectural and design point of view, the rather few public library building projects dating back to the first decades of the twentieth century were characterized by *Skønvirke* and historical styles in solid versions, often with decoration and carvings. Examples include the Railway Town Exhibition Model Library in Århus from 1909, briefly outlined below, and the libraries in Silkeborg (from 1920) and Esbjerg (from 1927). Buildings and interiors from the mid-twenties and thirties were characterized by an increasing degree of simplicity and matter-of-factness. These stylistic features first evolved under the influence of the Classicism in the twenties, as was the case with, for instance, Hjørring Public Library (from 1927) and the project for a village hall with a library from 1925. Later on, the above stylistic expression materialized under the influence of Functionalism as with, for instance, the libraries in Århus (1934) and Frederiksberg (1935). In spite of the influence of Functionalism, library construction work preserved typical features from Classicism such as symmetry and monumentality. Thus, you can say that public library architecture was "delayed" or lagging behind compared to mainstream developments in contemporary architecture. Finally, Nyborg Public Library, built in 1939, nicely and precisely reflected the "Functional Tradition." In a cultural policy sense, a broader mediation and communication effort marked itself in the projecting and design of public lecture rooms and study circle facilities that can be seen as a distinct trend in the library building projects of the thirties.

In the context of Scandinavian library architecture, monumental Classicism is mirrored by, for instance, the Deichmann Library in Oslo; the transition between Classicism and Modernism finds its expression in Stockholm City Library, drawn by Swedish architect Gunnar Asplund, whereas Vyborg Public Library in the former Finnish territory of Carelia, drawn by world-famous Finnish architect Alvar Aalto, represents Modernism.

Typical of Danish library building activities in the interwar period is an ever-increasing *Neue Sachlichkeit* influence visible in the outer architecture and the inner design. Furthermore, the Classicist features of the twenties are dominating, finding their expression in tall staircases, central and symmetric entrances and symmetric furniture in lending departments and reading rooms with centrally located librarian's desks. The matter-of-factness reflected by the design can be viewed as an expression of both the simple Classicism of the twenties and the more ideologically laden Functionalism of the thirties. "Milestone library buildings" like Århus and Frederiksberg, which served as role models to other contemporary library building projects, almost take the shape of a compromise between the two schools.

Furthermore, this matter-of-factness orientation pervading current library building activities and, especially, library design practices can be viewed in the context of both the architectural expression of the period, with the developments in library policy and with the overall modernization process impacting on society. And it can be difficult to distinguish between these parallel trends illustrated by, for instance, the new objectivity in the architecture and the efforts to simplify and streamline the internal organization of libraries of that time.

Hence, it seems obvious to emphasize the more specific questions: Why can you not find any pure and advanced functionalist library building projects implemented in Denmark in the period considered here? And why did the monumental symmetry of Classicism dominate even the more modest local building projects, both in the twenties and in the thirties? This question becomes especially interesting if you—in continuation of the problem statement of the present study, and in the light of contemporary radical cultural debate—consider public library services as a part of this (cultural and social enlightenment) avant-garde. And this assumption could very well be justified, for instance, if you consider the fight for the valuable literature. So, with this dedicated general education effort in mind, would you not expect the shaping of an array of experimenting and modernist library buildings as a natural consequence? Or, reversely, should the matter-of-fact Classicism be viewed as an expression of a more conservative general education ideal, associated, on the other hand, with a modern, rational organization model?

The Railway Town Exhibition Model Library at the 1909 National Exhibition in Århus

An excellent illustration of the notion of the ideal public library is provided by the public library building which was erected and designed as a working public library at the so-called Railway Town Exhibition constituting a part of the large-scale 1909 National Exhibition in Århus. The library was built together with a village hall or community meeting place so that the use of a popular book collection (as the public library was called at that time), reading of newspapers, reading aloud sessions, song and physical exercises could be offered as activities in this "center of culture" as it was called in a contemporary outline of this early multipurpose community library.[6]

With its small gardens, the building was centrally situated in the main street of the railway town. It was laid out as an L-shaped building with the library located in the one wing and gymnasium and lecture room in the other. With its yellow walls, white windows with bars and cornices and a red tiled roof, it expressed the ideals formulated by the movement *Bedre Byggeskik*, which wanted to inform and spread the message about a more honest and better architecture based on the Danish craftsmanship tradition.

Serving as architect for this pioneering project, Johannes Magdahl Nielsen (1862-1941) drew both the building and its furniture himself. His buildings are associated with "Danish coziness in the absolute positive sense of the word."[7] In addition, a contemporary drawing showed a connection between library, lecture room and gymnasium and the pottery of the exhibition. This section could be casual but it can also be viewed as an even more distinct reflection of the relationship between manual and intellectual work, between soul and body. This relationship would smoothly match the Grundtvig-inspired Danish folk high school movement and the Fairwork tradition (for a very brief outline of N.S.F. Grundtvig's work, see below). Besides, the pottery produced pots and vases for the library.

The State and University Library in Århus made books and staff available during the exhibition period. A small green leaflet on "The Public Library of the Railway Town" authored by the director of the State and University Library of that time, Vilhelm Grundtvig (1866-1950, not to be mixed up with N.S.F. Grundtvig above), provides a detailed treatment of the design and philosophy of the model library. With its detailed library specifics, price information and many illustrations this leaflet served as a call to visitors to the exhibition to establish a similar library. In this context, it is important to mention that Grundtvig placed great emphasis on the quality of the design and decoration of the library. Grundtvig started by emphasizing that the library had "open shelves" so that "anyone can select and pick out what he wants."[8] It was a one-room library with five tables including a special children's table and a worktable for the librarian. Tables, chairs and bookcases were made from stained pinewood. Walls and ceilings were painted in light, yellowish tones. Pictures of Danish male and female writers, "literary places" and maps were hanging on the walls. On the tables and on the large bookcase there were pots and vases from the railway town's pottery.

Grundtvig emphasized that "a library and a reading room are not only a room for books but their prime purpose is to serve as a place where people should look for instruction, entertainment or rest after

having completed their work." Hence, it was important that both premises and furniture were kept in "plain, pure and harmonious lines and
colors. . . . The opportunity of creating a cozy and domestic impression
by means of pictures and other (good) artworks, flowers and the like
should be welcomed."[9] Thus, the library was thought of as more than a
vehicle merely for goal-directed general education activities. Using
present-day concepts, Grundtvig emphasized the library's function as a
social or civic place for a variety of purposes including unstructured
leisure activities and the importance of the library as the "sitting room
of the local community."

The visitors to the exhibition were allowed to check out books and
bring them into the garden after having approached the employee available throughout the daily opening hours from 10 a.m. to 7 p.m. About
70,000 visitors were recorded in the library including some 21,000 as
readers. The number of visitors to the library peaked at 2,750 on 18
July. Another activity taking place within the building was the first national Danish library meeting with several pioneering lectures being
held including, for instance, the visionary and seminal presentation on
"The Library Cause outside Copenhagen" by H.O. Lange, chief librarian, the Royal Library in Copenhagen.

Thus, the situation of the exhibition library in this idealized railway
town; the model library built together with the community center; the
library's architecture, layout, and design; and the model book collection
formed part of a total joint campaign for both a democratized architecture and a democratized reading. The values of the exhibition were defined as a continuation of those inherent in local communities existing
in the small towns and parishes, the traditional trades and the local
popular book collections thus paralleling contemporary criticism of
Industrialism and the social problems of the big cities. In this way, one
could speak about a "modernization of tradition" as an alternative to the
modernity and rationality of the big city culture.

For follow-ups on the exhibition library serving the railway town,
reference can be made to the layout of Vejen Public Library in 1916
and the 1925 proposal for a community center with inter alia local government offices and a library.[10]

Århus Municipal Libraries:
The Central Library

The history of the Århus Municipal Libraries dates back to 1869. In
1929 it was discussed whether a reorganization of library services

should be undertaken in conjunction with the State and University Library in Århus or whether a quite new independent library should be created. The latter solution was preferred and one of the few architectural competitions of the period was arranged and won by the local architects Alfred Mogensen (1900-1986) and Harald Salling Mortensen (1902-1969).

The new public library building was erected in the locality of Møllehaven opposite the previous State and University Library and it was ready for inauguration on 29 October 1934. In an architectural sense, the building ranges among the most Modernistic Danish libraries of the thirties. Nevertheless, it is characterized by Classicist symmetry. The Modernistic features especially materialized in the tall glass front of the central part, the long ribbon windows, the oblique inside concrete pillars and the plain and rational arrangement and furniture. Thus, with its twelve revolving steel armchairs with red leather upholstery and black arm and back rests, the newspaper reading room is the only true Modernistic library room from the period. There are no other known examples of application of steel tube furniture in Danish interwar period public libraries. Symmetry and monumentality constitute the Classicist features of the building.

In a library and cultural policy sense, the building attracts interest by its broadly based cultural offerings: In addition to the centrally located lending department, more reading rooms were in use along with a public lecture hall accommodating 200 people, a lecture theater with sixty-four seats as well as a larger and nine smaller study circle rooms. Each study group room housed a smaller collection of reference books, loudspeaker equipment together with tables dimensioned for up to sixteen persons.

In his inauguration address, the director of the State Inspection of Public Libraries, Thomas Døssing, pointed to the development from libraries for the low-income groups in towns and rural districts to present-day public libraries. Underlying his address was fundamental general education thinking: "During the growth period of these institutions, the unpleasant ring has disappeared from word 'people.' Some voices have been speaking about the possibility of a workers' culture. I shall not deal with this here. But shaping a popular culture seems possible if you provide access to the highest level of general education for all citizens."[11]

Nyborg Public Library

The library in Nyborg was unique both because of its situation and on grounds of its layout. Danish architects Erik Møller (b. 1909) and Flemming Lassen (1902-1984) drew the library and it was erected in 1938-1939 upon the arrangement of an architectural competition in 1935. Architectural competitions were rare in these years, but in this specific case the competition was decided on probably because of the library's special location on a peninsula between the inner part of the town and the Middle Ages castle. The library's two oblique wings made from red bricks and with red tiled roofs perfectly adjusted to the surroundings while at the same time emphasizing the connection between the low traditional provincial town houses and the monumental castle building on the rampart. Both wings immediately adjoined the moat. At the same time, Nyborg was one of the most Modernistic library building projects with absence of symmetry, a flexible layout with freely placed rooms and large glass areas. Thus, the entrance was designed as a plain glass door in an easy to overview connecting building built from glass that forms the entrance hall to the two wings of the library building. The largest wing accommodated lending department, reading room, children's library, and stack room and the smallest wing contained study circle rooms and a memorial room. Windows at eye level connected the library rooms with the surroundings. Hans J. Wegner, later on international well-known furniture architect, created the total interior, which was especially designed for Nyborg Public Library. As with the library's furniture in general, the lending department and the reading room walls were done in light maple. Tables and chairs were traditional types in simplified versions, which can be said to anticipate the range of sitting room chairs put into production by the Danish co-op movement after World War II. Lamps and signs were especially designed for the library as well.[12]

Later on, Nyborg Public Library has gained a central position in the history of Danish architecture and it is typically referred to as a chief work within the "Functional Tradition" on a par with the University of Århus. Reviews and pieces tend to emphasize the lack of monumentality and the free and easy reading room. "It should be felt just as common to visit a library as to enter a grocer's shop."[13]

Comparison

An immediate comparison of the three library examples is not feasible. The railway town exhibition library only operated for one single summer. The Main Library of the Århus Municipal Libraries System is a large public library, which from an architectural and a design perspective must be considered very typical for libraries belonging to a specific period. Finally, Nyborg Public Library is unique. Nevertheless, each in their way they can be considered as architectural expressions of significant milestones and positions in the library and cultural policy of the period studied here.

The Railway Town Exhibition model library was built together with a gym room and a local community meeting room thus serving as the small ideal town's "cultural center." The two wings constituted an angle covering a small garden setting very nicely situated and adjoining the railway town Main Street, but with modest entrances. The light interior of the library with practically located tall windows was furnished with tables, chairs and pine wood shelves and done in yellow, green and brown colors. With its potted plants and picture ornaments, the room must have appeared in an almost Carl Larsson-like rustic style. Carl Larsson (1853-1919) was one of the most beloved Swedish artists, known not least for his watercolor paintings and his pictures of the family in Sundborn, an idyllic village. Hence, the architectural expression of the model library can be viewed as a continuation of the international Arts and Crafts Movement with *Skønvirke* and, later on, *Bedre Byggeskik* as Danish offshoots emphasizing precisely honest materials and design in harmony with the local craftsmanship tradition. In terms of library and general education policy, the model library project is associated with the Danish folk high school tradition and the locally rooted Popular Book Collection Movement. Johannes Grønborg's very appreciative review of the Exhibition Library gives evidence to this observation. Johannes Grønborg (1865-1945) was the leading agitator within an association called *Danmarks Folkebogsamlinger* ("Denmark's Popular Book Collections"), a branch of the Danish public library movement.

The Main Library of the Municipality of Århus represents the technical and modern "temple of knowledge." It expresses a compromise between Classicism and Modernism, which was typical of the Danish public library architecture of the period considered here. An array of similar libraries from this period (e.g. those of Hjørring, Frederiksberg, Thisted, Kolding and Svendborg) can, both from an architectural and from a general education perspective, be viewed as small manifestations of French Revolution Architect Étienne-Louis Boullée's large library utopia conceived during the French Age of Enlightenment. Boullée (1728-1799) imagined a sequence of never-implemented projects for "sacral buildings for a metropolis." His tremendously professionally drawn and geometrically simplified schemes included, among other things, a temple devoted to reason and a large national library. The library project was of huge dimensions, characterized by symmetry, with naked walls and galleries. The library was high ceilinged and an almost infinite barrel vault opening towards the sky constituted the ceiling. The light came into the library from above, both in a metaphoric and in a concrete sense. Similarly, another French Revolution Architect, Claude-Nicolas Ledoux (1736-1806), provided the inspiration for the almost contemporary City Library in Stockholm created by Swedish architect Erik Gunnar Asplund. In addition, the Århus Municipal Libraries' Main Library expresses the technical and professional compromise between Classicism and Modernism typical of Danish library architecture during the period studied here.

Carl Jørgensen (1888-1973), who served as adviser for the State Inspection of Public Libraries, drew a practical version of this type of libraries, which materialized in Hvidovre Public Library. The adult lending department of Århus Municipal Libraries' Main Library is dominated by the centrally located circulation desk, the card catalogue and the clock placed on the central axis of the total building layout. The naked walls were pale green without decoration. As distinct from the domestic interior of the railway town exhibition library with its imaginary collections with the local community, the Århus Main Library thus represents the modern, rational and dynamic but at the same time almost anonymously designed metropolitan library.

In an architectural and cultural policy context, Nyborg Public Library forms part of tradition and modernity. The library forms part of the "Functional Tradition" and as such it marks a rupture with the monumentality trend in Danish public library architecture. Gladsaxe Public Library from 1940, drawn by Vilhelm Lauritzen (1894-1984), provides another illustration of this rupture and shares several features with Nyborg Public Library. The absence of monumentality and the genuine quality of craftsmanship reflected in the design of the building with panellings and plain, traditional furniture make the library appear unpretentious and intimate to the visitor. These characteristics point back to the Railway Town Exhibition Library and at the same time the reliance on asymmetries and glass represent innovative Modernistic features. In terms of cultural policy, Nyborg Public Library can be said to mirror the joint, national-scale support to popular culture, impacted as this culture was by the threat from the South—that means from a rearming Germany bordering on Denmark. During that time, trends in the Grundtvig Tradition, within the workers' culture movement—which, according to Julius Bomholt (1896-1969, the prominent cultural policy figure within the Danish Social Democratic Party), in the late 1930s had grown into a popular culture—as well as within Cultural Leftism converged to create a common national platform. Nikolaj Severin Frederik Grundtvig (1783-1872), famous Danish poet, hymn writer, theologian and politician, developed the seminal thinking behind general education and participative democracy, which are still influential in Danish society. Also, he developed the major ideas underlying the Danish folk high schools aimed at fostering a new type of communal spirit among the Danish people.

Conclusion and Perspectives

Considered as types, the three libraries singled out as illustrative examples here can be said to represent three tendencies within the library, general education and cultural policy of the period studied in the present article. The library of the Railway Town Exhibition can—with the reservation that the model library was defined and operated by the State and University Library of Århus—be said to represent the Popular Book Collections Movement. Both the architectural features and the chosen design point to the "library ideological values" articulated by this rural library movement, which tended to emphasize the small community's library close to its users and with the location in the ideal railway town. Also inherent in the library ideology of the Movement was the notion of local democracy as a part of a "modernized tradition" rooted in and continuing the general education activities pursued by the folk high schools.

The Main Library of the Århus Municipal Libraries System represents the prevailing type of library during the period examined and it appears as a compromise between Classicism and Functionalism. The design of the Århus Library is modern, "technical" and rational, thus matching the official library policy of the period, which combines a general public-oriented education philosophy with a rational form of organization. Also inherent in this context—that of the Århus Library—is the articulation of the key concept of popular culture but coupled with access to "the highest level of general education" as is pointed out.

In this context, the Nyborg Public Library—constituting an isolated example—represents the synthesis of the two trends above. This library has a double architectural identity: With its asymmetries, its free utilization of space and its large glass fronts it is the most Modernistic library from that period. But at the same time, with its wooden interiors and modernized versions of traditional furniture, the Nyborg Library refers back to the first public libraries of the period. Analyzed from the perspective of cultural policy as well, the Nyborg Library represents the orientation towards a popular culture with both traditional and modern elements.

Finally, as a concluding perspective, it could be interesting to reassess the trend towards "technicalization," matter-of-factness and practicality observed in the interwar period public library design with its emphasis on "targeted" and systematic book-lending activity at the expense of the inviting, kindly looking and nicely ornamented library intended to serve as the "sitting room of the local community." From a present-day and future information and media policy perspective, it seems to be without doubt that the mere process- and product-centered approach to information communication and library materials provision can hardly survive. It also seems clear that in securing their survival, public libraries, in the sense of physical institutions, will be depending on interiors of a challenging nature facilitating personal experience and enrichment. In addition, the library space made available to the clienteles to be served should possess some of the qualities that were lost in the "technicalized" and matter-of-factness oriented library design of the interwar period.

Notes

1 H. Hvenegaard Lassen, *De danske folkebibliotekers historie 1876-1940* (Copenhagen: Dansk Bibliografisk Kontor, 1962).

2 Carl Jørgensen, *Danske Biblioteksbygninger* (Copenhagen: Folkebibliotekernes Bibliografiske Kontor, 1946).

3 Hvenegaard Lassen, *De danske folkebibliotekers historie 1876-1940*, 340.

4 Leif Emerek, "At skrive bibliotekshistorie: Om grundlæggelsen af det moderne folkebibliotek i Danmark," in *Det siviliserte informasjonssamfunn: Folkebibliotekenes rolle ved inngangen til en digital tid*, ed. Ragnar A. Audunson and Niels Windfeld Lund (Bergen: Fagbokforlaget, 2001), 88-117.

5 Gunhild Salvesen, "Hva kjennetegner kvalitetsarbeidet i norske folkebibliotek?" in *Det siviliserte informasjonssamfunn: Folkebibliotekenes rolle ved inngangen til en digital tid*, ed. Ragnar A. Audunson and Niels Windfeld Lund (Bergen: Fagbokforlaget, 2001), 269-91.

6 Johs. Grønborg, *Søndagsbladet* 19, no. 40 (1909-1910): 8-9.

7 Karin Kryger, "Magdahl Nielsen, Johannes," in *Weilbach: Dansk Kunstnerleksikon*, vol. 5, ed. Sys Hartmann (Copenhagen: Munksgaard, Rosinante, 1995), 272-74.

8 Vilhelm Grundtvig, *Stationsbyens Folkebibliotek: Landsudstillingen Aarhus* (Aarhus: 1909), 3.

9 Grundtvig, *Stationsbyens Folkebibliotek*, 8.

10 Nan Dahlkild, "Biblioteket på Landsudstillingen i Århus 1909: Et arkitektur- og kulturpolitisk bygningsmanifest" (paper presented at the ARLIS Conference 2000, Stockholm, Sweden 2000).

11 "Indvielsen," *Bogens Verden* 16 (1934): 278.

12 Kjeld Vindum, "Den store moderator: spredte betragtninger omkring traditionen i nordisk arkitektur med udgangspunkt i biblioteket i Nyborg," *Undr* 23, no. 1 (1989): 20-31.

13 Lisbet Balslev Jørgensen, Hakon Lund and Hans Edvard Nørregård-Nielsen, *Magtens bolig* (Copenhagen: Gyldendal, 1980), 145.

Foreign Influence on the Development of the Danish Public Libraries with Emphasis on the Association Denmark's Popular Book Collections, 1905-1919

Martin Dyrbye

The article details how important aspects of the development of a Danish public library system were inspired by English and American models. The author shows how the main principles of today's Danish public library system, such as open shelves and free access to books, technical standardization, children's libraries and a coordinated library system, were already introduced in the early twentieth century based on Anglo-American ideas and experiences.

Introduction

In 1905, Denmark's first library association was founded—the Association Denmark's Popular Book Collections (in Danish, *Danmarks Folkebogsamlinger*)—which existed until 1919 when it merged with the Association of Danish Libraries (*Dansk Biblioteksforening*) under the new name of the Danish Library Association (*Danmarks Biblioteksforening*).

On the basis of Danish library history I will be discussing how the Association Denmark's Popular Book Collections addressed ideas, thoughts and tendencies from abroad and their importance for the development of the popular book collections in Denmark during the period 1905-1919. However, even before 1905 one of the early library "pioneers" made an important contribution in gaining information about library conditions abroad. This will also be discussed.

The foreign influence on Danish public library development during this period will be analyzed with focus on the following questions:

1. What role did library developments abroad play prior to the establishment of the Association Denmark's Popular Book Collections?
2. To what extent did foreign library developments influence decisively the establishment of the Association Denmark's Popular Book Collections?
3. To what extent can the establishment of a Danish library association and the development of an organized, professional and publicly financed library system in Denmark be seen as a result of an early exchange of ideas inspired by library developments abroad?
4. Where was foreign influence on Danish library development most prominent seen from our point of view today?

On an overall level it is interesting to point out some important examples of influences from abroad, which had decisive importance for library development in Denmark and which today can be observed in two important ways when borrowers visit and use the Danish public library system, namely:

1. That in a democratic society there is free and equal access to the library's information resources through a well-organized and cooperating library system.
2. That the public libraries have common and uniform standards and rules, that is, a common system which facilitates usage and contributes to making the materials accessible and, as a consequence, increases circulation.

Today Denmark can offer well-functioning library services, which can be seen as part of a cooperating library system.[1] Important elements of the present library system are built and based upon lessons from abroad, which were used in the early years of implementation, in the years from 1905-1919, and which in many ways was a landmark for the establishment of a homogenous library system in Denmark.

In the following I will exemplify how these foreign influences have made their mark on what we today take for granted and which must be considered of special importance for library development in Denmark. These examples concern in part library techniques but they are also illustrative of the conditions underlying the establishment of the library sector.

The Early Pioneer Years: Steenberg

In 1900, a few years before the establishment of the Association Denmark's Popular Book Collections in 1905 the library pioneer, grammar school teacher and member of the committee with responsibility for the financial support of the book collections (*Statens Komité til Understøttelse af Folkebogsamlinger*) Andreas Schack Steenberg published his book *Popular Book Collections, Their History and Organization* (*Folkebogsamlinger: Deres Historie og Indretning*).[2]

During the 1890s, Steenberg had established contacts with library professionals in Germany, England and America, partly through correspondence and partly from a visit to England in 1895. Through a Danish friend residing in England, the engineer Sigwald Müller, Steenberg was able to gain valuable knowledge about English libraries due to the fact that his friend sent cuttings from magazines concerning such matters and which Steenberg read with great interest. In 1893, Steenberg started a correspondence with the German professor, Dr. Edward Reyer, which lasted until the professor's death in 1914. From Reyer, Steenberg received the latter's book *Volksbibliotheken* (1893) which distinguished itself by containing "a complete account of the English and American libraries" and in his memoirs Steenberg described his pleasure concerning Reyer's book: "I remember very clearly my joy that evening (7th March, when the post arrived with the promised book) . . . that evening the English and American libraries became part of the Danish library efforts."[3]

Steenberg continued collecting information and knowledge of public libraries in England and "was sent reports and circulation rules from them" as well as making contact with "various librarians," among them the secretary for the English Library Association, J.Y.W. MacAlister, who was also editor of *The Library*. Other English library professionals were also prepared to help Steenberg. In 1893, Steenberg made contact with the famous American librarian C.A. Cutter who sent him "his cataloguing rules." The year after, in 1894, Steenberg published his "first major article concerning popular book collections" in *The Spectator* (*Tilskueren*) which deliberated on the fact that these book collections played a very minor role in the eyes of the Danish public as opposed to England and America "where through public debate one had assembled a range of evidence which underlined the importance that public libraries had for the common enlightenment." The point of reference for Steenberg was Reyer's aforementioned German account of the library situation in England and America and through Steenberg's article Danish readers were given an impression of the "Free

Public Libraries" as well as "the public libraries in other countries, not least North America."[4]

Two factors were of primary importance for Steenberg in stressing the excellence of the English and American libraries. First, that in these countries libraries were considered "a public matter which the state and local government should support in the same way as the schools." For Steenberg, a teacher himself, there was a clear connection between school and library, a fact which was to be underlined time and time again by the Association Denmark's Popular Book Collections. The connection between children's reading, education and the libraries' importance for the elevation of the level of education became one of the cardinal points for the members of the Association. The other factor which later also became an important precondition for their cause, and later the public libraries' advancement and success in the following one hundred years, was the principle that the public sector, at state and local level, should subsidize the good cause, namely the free and equal access for all to libraries in society.

Two years later, Steenberg was given a state grant and the opportunity to become more acquainted with the public libraries in England, including London and the surrounding area and Liverpool. During this stay the opportunity to meet library professionals arose and through them gain information about practice.

In 1897, Steenberg again visited England and his impressions from this visit and his visit in 1895 were communicated to a broader circle through articles in magazines, which were later—in 1899—collected in *Impressions from England* (*Skildringer fra England*). This book gave rise to discussions in Danish newspapers and magazines. Thanks to this determined approach in informing the public about library developments in England and America, the book collections became an item on the agenda for debate.

In the late 1890s, close contacts were established between Steenberg and Swedish library professionals who could exploit his knowledge to good effect. Steenberg's influence on and importance for the development of book collections/public libraries in the Nordic countries is furthermore underlined in that at a Nordic school meeting in 1898 in Sweden he started the debate by talking about the "library cause" even though this was not on the agenda.

This contact with foreign library professionals gave Steenberg the opportunity of traveling abroad, and he enjoyed great respect in England where he "was asked to act as signatory to the invitation to the Second International Library Conference," which was held in London in 1897. At this meeting Steenberg talked about the situation for libraries in the Nordic countries. A discussion of a library technical issue caused some debate and made quite an impression. This was the question of open shelves as opposed to closed shelves, which according to Steenberg "caused a stir." This discussion was later repeated in Denmark. At this meeting American library people made a big impression on Steenberg, who himself had the opportunity of seeing the promised land during his tour of America in 1902.[5]

The meeting in 1897 and the time spent together with English and American library people proved to be very significant for Steenberg:

> The great and friendly helpfulness that was shown to me, naturally most pronounced during my stay in America in 1902, was of the greatest importance in my work and was of great encouragement to me during the often weary circumstances under which my work was carried out. However, the greatest benefit from this meeting was the feeling that I had joined a global project and that I in my endeavors could, as an English librarian who took the floor after my own speech promised, count on help from those countries, which were further along the road with the cause than was my own country. This promise has been faithfully kept.[6]

The journeys to England and America resulted in useful contacts to library professionals, who had gained experience in library matters, which proved useful in the development of the public book collections. As well as this extensive correspondence with prominent English and American library professionals, Steenberg also maintained contact with Germans, including the aforementioned professor Reyer, and other European and Nordic library people. Contacts with foreign library people and knowledge of their experiences, especially information relating to conditions in England and America, was something that Steenberg held as contributing to the fact that he gained "an assured idea of in what direction developments should run and how a new library system should be built."

In 1899, the book collection's cause was strengthened when head of department from the Ministry of Ecclesiastical Affairs and Public Instruction A.P. Weiss and Steenberg were appointed as the only two members in the newly formed committee with responsibility for the financial support of the book collections (*Komiteen til Understøttelse af Folkebogsamlinger*) which replaced the committee for the distribution of book presents (*Komiteen til Uddeling af Boggaver*). Steenberg took on the responsibility of the day-to-day management and was responsible for practical matters in relation to this position. According to Steenberg, the condition of the book collections in the country and in the towns was miserable, even though altruistic and unpaid volunteers did great services for the popular book collections' cause. The solution to the task of improving the standard of the book collections was based on drawing upon experiences from abroad: "It became clear to me, that if we were to succeed in furthering the library cause it would be necessary to get to know the English speaking peoples' libraries in order to gain a notion of how important a well functioning library system is for a nation."[7]

Steenberg's overall purpose in working for the library cause was, in other words, to establish a library system. The prerequisite for this was the dissemination of information regarding "library techniques"—what we today think of as those professional standards which are applied to library work—as well as "that literature which is appropriate for the public libraries, not least that which is educational," that is, book and materials selection. A third important requirement for the furthering of the cause, as underlined by Steenberg, was the endeavors for the establishment of "children's libraries."[8]

In the year 1900, Steenberg published a book on the library profession which was be to used to promote the concept of the book collections, the already mentioned *Popular Book Collections, Their History and Organization*. In fact, Steenberg's book was the first Danish publication to address library technical questions since the publication of Molbech's book *Regarding Public Libraries* (*Om offentlige Biblioteker*) from 1829. In his book he called upon the knowledge he had gained from contacts with foreign library people as well as the reading of foreign library literature. In its form and content the book was reminiscent of John Cotton Dana's *Library Primer* (1899), which Steenberg does in fact make reference to.[9]

Thanks to Andreas Schack Steenberg's immense groundwork over many years, his deep knowledge and contacts both at home and abroad, he had the best qualifications for writing a textbook which based itself, on one hand, on library history and, on the other, on observations made abroad as to how library services should be formulated and organized in practice.

The most important source of inspiration for Steenberg was undoubtedly the development of "free public libraries" in England and America, and the libraries he had visited during his study trips to these countries. The task of writing the book was arduous due to the fact that it was necessary to find Danish words for a library terminology which came from abroad. All the same, Steenberg remembered the task with pleasure:

> However it was on the one hand a very pleasurable undertaking, recounting the fine library situation in England and America and it was a wonderful feeling to be able to use this experience to create order in all the material that I had, over the years, gathered together regarding

library technique. The book was really written at a good point in time in that they had in America, where I primarily collected my information, recently developed systems for the different aspects of library work.[10]

As such it was the English and American libraries that were the ideal for Steenberg and on which he built his account of how the libraries in Denmark should be designed and organized. By 1876 America already had a library association, the American Library Association, and a year later in 1877 a corresponding English association was formed, namely the Library Association of the United Kingdom. With direct inspiration from the American Library Association's election talk, Steenberg argued in his book for what he saw as the goal for the book collections: "In a few words one can express the goal that the book collections are working towards by using the American Library Association's election rhetoric: The best books for the greatest number of possible readers at the lowest expenditure."[11]

In his book Steenberg argues in favor of using the organization and development of the public libraries in England and America as an ideal picture of what the libraries should be and his book became, as such, a model for the future development of Danish libraries in the Twentieth Century, but also an important precondition for the professionalization of library work. Steenberg also underlined the fact that libraries should be free libraries and financed through public grants and free of charge, as was the case in America and England.

At the beginning of the 1900s it seemed as though the conditions for developing a better organized public library system were present. State subsidies helped to encourage the establishment of the Popular Book Collections. On top of this, thanks to Steenberg's book, "there was a useful tool for professional library work which would be of benefit to all those who were involved in the library cause."

In 1905, the work concerning organization of the book collections was strengthened with the foundation of the Association Denmark's Popular Book Collections, which was to become an extremely important coordinating forum, debating the cause of the book collections with a single voice, while at the same time defending their interests in relation to national and local government.

That the inspiration for the establishment of this association came from abroad seems likely in that Steenberg in his book repeated the American Library Association's election "speak" and underlined the fact that it had "had a very great influence on the development of the libraries."[12] Furthermore, Steenberg noted the following in regard to the role of the English Library Association: "It has had considerable influence on English library legislation during the last decades and has been of much use to the English libraries. In many parts of the country one finds local library associations."[13]

Foreign Library Developments and Their Mention in the *Danish Library Journal*

Like the library associations in America and England, the Association Denmark's Popular Book Collections also published a periodical, the *Danish Library Journal* (*Bogsamlingsbladet*) from 1906 to 1920 that served as a forum for contacts and information. This periodical gained a position of central importance for Association members as well as library professionals in general and therefore for Danish cultural life.

One of the most frequent columns in the periodical was "From Foreign Countries," but the reader also had the opportunity of gathering information about foreign library development from other articles. By systematically looking through the *Danish Library Journal* one can reveal the foreign influence on Danish library development. Altogether this foreign influence made its presence felt in two ways: (1) partly through individual persons' interest in the cause, especially in questions of "library technique" and questions relating to the organization of library work and (2) partly through the Association's own use of examples and experiences from abroad when agitating for the cause.

It is characteristic that each individual's contribution consisted, for the most part, in disseminating information on how practical library work, the solution to technical questions and the organization of libraries were carried out abroad. Contributors to discussions such as these were for the most part individuals from outside the Association's management, but who were sympathetic to the "library cause." Not least Steenberg was a regular contributor to these columns, which reflected on library development abroad. When the Association's management talked about the position abroad it was usually when an example taken from abroad could be used to further the good cause.

Collecting information from abroad came about by (1) the reading of foreign library journals and literature concerning libraries and library matters and (2) through individuals' collection of information from visits to foreign libraries and other institutions that had to do with the library world, for example, study trips to foreign library schools. Behind this dissemination of experiences from abroad was undoubtedly the view that this could contribute to solutions of possible benefit to those who were involved with libraries on a daily basis.

Inspiration and information from abroad came mainly from America, England, Norway and to a lesser extent Sweden and Germany, while information from other European countries was usually of a more general nature.

Inspiration from abroad and its influence on the Danish book collections manifested itself in two particular ways: (1) the processes involved in library work and (2) the development and organization of a coherent and professional library system, that is, a systematic structure which was based on the American and English model.

Questions of "Library Technique" and Their Solution

An examination of the *Danish Library Journal* shows that this periodical in particular was of great importance for practical library work and the propagation of this to the members of the Association Denmark's Popular Book Collections.

In fact, the Association had no obligation to its members in regard to informing them about the more technical aspects of library work and so this task was primarily handled by Association members and experts who were especially interested in these areas and contributed in writing to the Danish Library Journal for the benefit of the members.

New methods and technological possibilities were often mentioned in the Association journal. Most of those who were responsible for the day-to-day running of the Popular Book Collections had no formal library training and therefore the reading of articles in the *Danish Library Journal*, including reviews of library literature, presented an ideal opportunity to follow developments in the library world. Four of the library pioneers of the day were especially interested in questions of a more technical and professional nature and time and time again pointed to examples from abroad; these were Steenberg, chief librarian at the Royal Library, H.O. Lange and the librarians Thomas Døssing and H. Hvenegaard Lassen.[14]

The following examples are based on those factors, which today are of a general and an important nature for the users meeting with the public libraries and their use of materials and where influences from abroad were of special importance. The first of these is related to the question of physical access to materials, while the second relates to the user's possibilities of finding materials, either on his or her own or with help from the librarian.

One of the earliest examples in the *Danish Library Journal* of communicating experiences from abroad, which later had such importance for the development of the public libraries, was when Steenberg underlined the importance and the usefulness of "open shelves" in the book collections. Steenberg had followed the discussion of these matters in England and America and therefore had the necessary information to be able to discuss both the positive and negative aspects of this matter.

In an article in the *Danish Library Journal* from 1907 about the Deichmann Library in Oslo, Norway, Steenberg addressed the question of open shelves, which gave the users unlimited access to materials and because of this they learned "to appreciate the collections."[15] The year after Steenberg once again raised the question in the *Danish Library Journal* in reference to an article in the 1907 March issue of *Library Journal* and in the *Danish Library Journal*, he also mentions the fact that the libraries in Lemvig and Frederiksberg had introduced open shelves.

In spite of the extra need for space and the risk of theft, Steenberg concluded that experiences from abroad in relation to this were so positive that he could recommend "open shelves," in that user services became easier and cheaper due to the fact that less time was spent on the individual request. In conclusion Steenberg wrote concerning open shelves that "the borrowers are able, in a quite different way, to gain access to those books that they need and that they (i.e. the open shelves) have an educating effect on the borrowers, in that they become much more familiar with the collection."[16]

Danish public libraries of today have open shelves. The idea for this was born in America and in fact presented at the first international library meeting in London in 1877.[17]

Until a few years ago when the public libraries used card catalogues, the librarian and the user assumed that no matter where in the country one resided the system was built on the principles of uniformity, which saved time for the staff as well as for the user. The first move towards a common solution in the area of cataloguing was taken up around the period of the First World War, not by the Association of Denmark's Popular Book Collections but, on the contrary, by individuals who with their knowledge of the library situation abroad were able to see the benefits associated with libraries working together to save time and financial resources.

Leading library professionals of the day therefore raised the question of the benefits of uniform cataloguing in those aspects of library work, which concerned the registration of materials in regard to cataloguing and classification.[18]

Thomas Døssing posed the question in 1914 in regard to cataloguing when he, in an article in the *Danish Library Journal*, reported on experiences gained from Norway and America relating to the drawing up of subject lists and subject catalogues.[19]

The year after, at a meeting of the Danish Association of Librarians (*Bibliotekarforeningen*), Steenberg and Døssing argued for the introduction of uniform cataloguing standards. Their idea led to the appointment of a committee with responsibility for introducing changes to the Danish National Bibliography (*Dansk Bogfortegnelse*) and at the same time it was suggested that printed catalogue cards be introduced. Concerning the catalogue cards, Lange referred directly to the situation in America where printed cards were produced and sold from the Library of Congress in Washington. At the same time he suggested that *Gads Bogfortegnelse* (a publisher's book list) should be published once a week, printed on cards of the international standardized size.[20]

Moreover, Hvenegaard Lassen found that a uniform standard for these cards would be instrumental in achieving an important goal for all who wished to promote the library cause, namely a harmonious cooperation between libraries in Denmark: "By organizing our library, small or large, with a 'standardized size' whenever possible, one is instrumental in helping to facilitate library cooperation, which must be one of our primary goals."[21]

In the structure of the book collections it was of immense importance that they were given a common form of classification, so that library work was simplified and resources were used as rationally and appropriately as possible, not least in the light of the limited economic resources which were available to those who had responsibility for the day-to-day running of the collections.

Among those who lectured on the question of classification we find, not surprisingly, Steenberg and other "experts" from the committee with responsibility for the financial support of the book collections who all followed the developments abroad. For Steenberg there was no doubt that the classification system of the future had to be based on Dewey's American system, but that it had to be integrated into the Danish Popular Book Collections in a revised form. This did indeed happen after publication of a Danish *decimal classification for use in the arrangement of book collections.*[22]

Today, we take it for granted that the public libraries use the same system of classification, namely DK5, but the philosophy behind it was introduced during the First World War. This did not happen on recommendations from Denmark's Popular Book Collections, but on the contrary, it was thanks to individuals who supported the cause and who raised the question of a uniform system of classification through lectures and articles in the *Danish Library Journal*.

The new library initiatives regarding the technical aspects did not happen as a result of input from the Association Denmark's Popular Book Collections. Many of the Association's members were in fact skeptical of them or directly opposed to intervention in their business or increased state intervention. Actually the initiatives came partly from the committee with responsibility for the financial support of the book collections and partly from the people behind the Association of Danish Libraries, which was founded in 1916 and supported a "Danish Public library system based on an Anglo-American model."[23]

Examples of Influences from Abroad on the Organization of Book Collections

In relation to the overall policy which worked towards the organization of the book collections and by doing this strengthen them (by promoting a number of the main issues of the day), the term *library cause* was used during this period as the common denominator for those questions which were, both in the long term and short term, to be resolved. At a general level the Association management worked towards ensuring free and equal access to the book collections for users. The principle of free and equal access to information was, to all intent and purpose, inspired by library developments in America and England. This part of the "library cause" was regarded as one of the most important points for the Association's management, but at the same time a number of individuals, who were not involved at management level, were working for the promotion of important issues which would in time be of major significance for the work of the organization, not least in relation to the organization of book collections and later on for the public libraries. The members of the Association had the opportunity to become familiar with new ideas about the organization of a future library system through the reading of the *Danish Library Journal*.

The following examples illustrate two important issues which were influential on the organization of the Popular Book Collections and later on the development of the public libraries. The book collections' borrowers were adults, while children's reading was left to the schools and the home front. As was the case in America, Danish library people thought it important that measures were taken to improve the reading abilities of young people and this not just at school but also in a public library environment. Another important question was how the co-operation between the Popular Book Collections in the larger town libraries as well as the smaller libraries in the rural areas could be planned most constructively. The last of these questions was part of a wider discussion about the establishment of the county libraries in (at that time) eighteen Danish counties.

With regard to the organization of the Popular Book Collections, which during the period 1905-1920 gradually developed into the ancestors of our present-day public libraries, the inspiration for their organization came from abroad. Influences from abroad played an important role for the development of book collections for children, which later became children's libraries, and for the county libraries.

Children's Book Collections

Particularly one issue among the many, which the Association Denmark's Popular Book Collections acted as spokesperson for, was heavily influenced by experiences and developments from abroad. If the book collections were to be successful in their endeavors in the long term, then the library cause should not be restricted to adult borrowers but should also include the borrowers of tomorrow, that is, children and young adults.

The question of children's book collections had already been raised in 1908 by Steenberg on the basis of minutes from a lecture given by the American G. Stanley Hall and which had been published in *Library Journal*. It is especially interesting to note Hall's idea that libraries should be perceived as part of the educational system, from school to university level. This perception of the libraries won through in the Danish library system and it is today taken for granted that the educational system and the library system work closely together in many areas.[24]

One year later in 1909, the question of children's book collections as part of the system was raised once again, and at the general meeting in Århus the invited speaker was Anna A. Monrad, who had visited America and studied the library situation there. Monrad was keenly in favor of integrating children's book collections in "the big library system" and of there being professionally educated staff to undertake this task. Her speech met with "enthusiastic applause" in the assembly. This idea also met with approval from the Association Denmark's Popular Book Collections and therefore Johannes Høirup from the governing body of the Association supported the idea of "an ordinary children's collection in an ordinary public library."

Schoolmaster Grønberg called attention to the fact that there was very little literature for children and underlined the importance of the literature having to be of a kind that could capture their interest.[25]

In 1911, Steenberg reintroduced the idea of establishing children's libraries. In an article in the *Danish Library Journal* he once again made reference to the groundwork being done in America and the public libraries' attention to "children's reading—and so strong is their interest in this work that they have even introduced storytelling in their children's libraries in order to fuel the interest in reading among children." However, in Denmark one was far behind and the responsibility for children's reading rested solely with the schools, even though there were "a few Popular Book Collections which also acquire children's books." Steenberg advocated for the case of future teachers, as was the case in America, having had a thorough grounding in children's literature and at the same time looking for "that harmony" that existed between the American school system and the "library movement."[26]

Today, public libraries make great efforts to attract young borrowers to the libraries, first and foremost the fourteen to eighteen year-olds; that is, those who are too old to use the children's library while at the same time finding the adult section only marginally interesting. This problem is not new, though, and can be traced back to the time around the First World War.

In continuation of this campaigning for the establishment of children's libraries, Steenberg in 1915 recommended that a special effort be set in motion in order to attract young people to the book collections. In this way he underlined the fact that library people in the English-speaking countries had been successful in implementing a system whereby "children's books and books for young adults" were combined under the same roof as the book collections, while in Denmark the children's book collections were associated with the schools. Steenberg didn't, however, want to change the children's book collections connection to the schools, but he found it "natural that the book collections for young adults be viewed in connection with the Popular Book Collections." A "special collection for young adults" would thereby "also become an important support for those county colleges which are at present being established and those night schools which are already in operation."[27]

Both before and during the passing of the first library legislation in 1920 there was the possibility of applying for state grants for children's book collections "according to the same rules as those that applied to the adult book collections." However, they were not covered by the new legislation in that this question was referred to the "newly established Great School Commission." Nonetheless, this did not mean that the interest for this dwindled, and indeed children's librarians, including Eleonora Sørensen from Vejle and Helga Mollerup in Copenhagen, made great efforts to promote the cause of children's libraries during the interwar period.[28]

Not until the revision of the Act on government-supported libraries in 1931 did it become possible to receive state grants for independent children's libraries, and eventually in 1964 new and visionary legislation made it obligatory that local councils should run libraries with departments for children as well as for adults. The idea of independent children's libraries was raised as an important issue by the Association Denmark's Popular Book Collections prior to the First World War and inspiration for this came primarily from library developments in America and England.

County Libraries

In connection with the National Exhibition in Århus in 1909, a library meeting was held during which H.O. Lange gave a lecture "Regarding the Library Cause outside of Copenhagen." The lecture, which was later published, was extremely influential and many of the thoughts put forward by Lange were later realized. Lange argued in favor of the organization of the library system in Denmark being based on the American model. The organization should be implemented in such a way that there existed continuity between librarian, books, professional methods and premises; that is, an expression of a systems structure, as opposed to the conditions in Denmark at the time where it was primarily books and premises that were the main focus of attention while the importance of "the personal element in the library cause" was often underestimated. In the long run Lange was proved correct in that, based on the American model, courses, and later an independent education for librarians, were introduced from 1918.

At the library meeting in 1909 H.O. Lange introduced a revolutionary idea in his lecture, which would in the following years gain support from the members of the Association Denmark's Popular Book Collections and the rest of the library community. Lange put forward the idea that proper county libraries, based on the American example, be established in the eighteen Danish counties, but he was also aware of thoughts and initiatives for similar libraries which had been formulated in Denmark prior to 1909.[29]

The discussions within *Danmarks Folkebogsamlinger* regarding advantages and disadvantages of the establishment of county libraries were very heated indeed over the following years and were moreover seen in relation to the role of the State and University Library in Århus as far as the Popular Book Collections were concerned. In 1913, the Association's chairman, Jens Bjerre, raised the question and requested the support of his members for his *Suggestion for Central Libraries*, while at the same time referring to the American county libraries in California, which were his ideal.[30]

The question of the establishment of county libraries after the American model was followed up by an article by Hvenegaard Lassen in the *Danish Library Journal*, which actually introduced a new angle into the debate by underlining the fact that one could not just simply transfer concepts from abroad to a Danish context. However, this in no way excluded the possibility of seeking and receiving inspiration from abroad in order to make further progress—in some areas—than those countries which we like to compare ourselves to:

> Library conditions in Denmark cannot be directly compared to those in America. Among the differences I, in this context, should like to underline, is the fact that the Americans can draw upon much larger and better equipped town libraries when they bring reading materials to the country people, while we on the other hand all have our own parish book collections where the Americans often have to start from scratch. If we are swift in getting our district libraries systematized, then there is no reason why we should not come to be seen as a role model for a national library organization which is able to reach all; even the Americans have not come that far.[31]

H.O. Lange's idea was, after many discussions, put into practice in 1913 when the state provided funding for the establishment of county libraries. The first of these were founded in 1914 in Holbæk and Vejle, exactly in those towns where the forerunners of the county libraries had been created. Since the adoption of the 1920 library legislation county libraries have existed in Denmark, but the idea for this type of library was born in America.

Conclusion

As already shown, developments abroad, especially the Anglo-American influence, played an important role both before and after the foundation of the Association Denmark's Popular Book Collections. In the years prior to 1900 and up till 1905 the library pioneer Andreas Schack Steenberg made great efforts in following developments abroad and communicating this information through articles in newspapers and journals and, of course, not least in his pioneering work: popular book collections, their history and organization.

During the period 1905-1919 the *Danish Library Journal* became the forum where not least individuals, including prominent library pioneers, could disseminate their knowledge about library developments and new ideas from abroad, including the technical aspects of library work, to the Danish library community. This has been exemplified by the discussion about open shelves, classification and the cataloguing of materials.

When discussions arose pertaining to the overall aims of the Association Denmark's Popular Book Collections and the advancement of the library cause, then experiences from abroad were introduced into the debate. The Association management and interested individuals contributed to the debate as we have seen in the question of independent children's libraries and the establishment of county libraries. It is characteristic for these discussions that here too the library pioneers played a central role in that their insight and expertise regarding foreign developments gave the Association the kind of knowledge that neither members nor management had the possibility of cultivating in their daily work and canvassing for the cause.

From 1905 to 1919 we see the foundation of the "thinking in systems" that later became characteristic for the public libraries in Denmark. Behind this thinking lay especially the American and English conceptual understanding of the public libraries' role in relation to developments in society. Important for the breakthrough of these thoughts in the long run was that in the first legislation from 1920, inspired by Anglo-American developments, we find the establishment of uniform systems for the public libraries, that is:

1. Free, equal and unhindered access to book collections, that is, open shelves and free access to the materials.
2. Uniform classification and cataloguing rules, which saved time and money for the individual libraries while at the same time making it easier for borrowers to access information.
3. The establishment of children's libraries as a link between school and public library.
4. The construction of a coordinated public library structure based on smooth cooperation between libraries, ensured through the establishment of county libraries.

Even if there was opposition from some members of the Association Denmark's Popular Book Collections to the introduction of standardization and centralization during the establishment of the Danish public library system, it can be proved that library developments abroad, thanks to visionary library pioneers and the Association Denmark's Popular Book Collections, did have a decisive influence on the development of the Danish libraries.

Notes

1 Jørgen Svane-Mikkelsen, *The Library System in Denmark* (Copenhagen: The Royal School of Library and Information Science, 1997).

2 Andreas Schack Steenberg, *Folkebogsamlinger: Deres Historie og Indretning* (Aarhus and Copenhagen: On Commission with Jydsk Forlags-Forretning, 1900).

3 Andreas Schack Steenberg, *Erindringer fra mit Biblioteksarbejde* (Copenhagen: Græbes Bogtrykkeri, 1923), 5 ff. Published as an offprint version of several articles that appeared in *Bogens Verden* (1921-1924).

4 Steenberg, *Erindringer fra mit Biblioteksarbejde*, 6 ff.

5 Steenberg, *Erindringer fra mit Biblioteksarbejde*, 18 ff.; Jørgen Svane-Mikkelsen, "Rejsen til Amerika: Om Andreas Schack Steenbergs møde med den amerikanske biblioteksverden i 1902," in *Bag ved bøgernes bjerg: En hilsen til Mogens Iversen*, ed. Ole Harbo and Jørgen Svane-Mikkelsen (Copenhagen: The Royal School of Librarianship, 1978), 111-29.

6 Steenberg, *Erindringer fra mit Biblioteksarbejde*, 11.

7 Steenberg, *Erindringer fra mit Biblioteksarbejde*, 14 ff.

8 Steenberg, *Erindringer fra mit Biblioteksarbejde*, 14 ff.

9 Steenberg, *Folkebogsamlinger: Deres Historie og Indretning,* 95.

10 Steenberg, *Erindringer fra mit Biblioteksarbejde*, 15.

11 Steenberg, *Folkebogsamlinger: Deres Historie og Indretning,* 9.

12 Steenberg, *Folkebogsamlinger: Deres Historie og Indretning,* 50.

13 Steenberg, *Folkebogsamlinger: Deres Historie og Indretning,* 33 ff.

14 *Bogsamlingsbladet*, vols. 1906-1920.

15 *Bogsamlingsbladet*, no. 4 (1906-1907): 62-64.

16 *Bogsamlingsbladet*, no. 5 (1908): 88-89.

17 Steenberg, *Erindringer fra mit Biblioteksarbejde*, 11.

18 Erik Allerslev Jensen, *Bibliotekscentralens forhistorie og første år* (Ballerup: Bibliotekscentralens Forlag, 1979), 15-19.

19 *Bogsamlingsbladet*, no. 12 (1914): 185.

20 *Bogsamlingsbladet*, no. 12 (1918): 243; Allerslev Jensen, *Biblioteks-centralens forhistorie og første år*, 15-19.

21 *Bogsamlingsbladet*, no. 12 (1918): 244.

22 *Bogsamlingsbladet*, no. 3-4 (1915): 41-44.

23 Steffen Høgh, "Danmarks første folkebibliotekslov: Om tilblivelsen af biblioteksloven af 5. marts 1920 samt et efterspil," in *Bibliotekshistorie*, vol. 5, ed. Jørgen Svane-Mikkelsen and Steen Bille Larsen (Copenhagen: Dansk Bibliotekshistorisk Selskab, 1999), 74-98.

24 *Bogsamlingsbladet*, no. 2 (1908): 22-25.

25 *Bogsamlingsbladet* (1909-1910): 80-83.

26 *Bogsamlingsbladet*, no. 12 (1911): 209-14.

27 *Bogsamlingsbladet*, no. 7 (1915): 99.

28 H. Hvenegaard Lassen, *De danske folkebibliotekers historie 1876-1940* (Copenhagen: Dansk Bibliografisk Kontor, 1962), 304-13.

29 *Bogsamlingsbladet* (1908-1909): 49-53; Hvenegaard Lassen, *De danske folkebibliotekers historie 1876-1940*, 111-16.

30 Hvenegaard Lassen, *De danske folkebibliotekers historie 1876-1940*, 124-68; *Bogsamlingsbladet*, no. 10 (1913): 139-43.

31 *Bogsamlingsbladet*, no. 12 (1913): 185.

Institution, Modernity and Discourse: Three Perspectives on Public Library History

Laura Henriette Christine Skouvig

Today traditional approaches are being challenged by more critical and theory-oriented ways of history writing. Laura Skouvig belongs to a generation of young historians trying to innovate Danish library history. In writing the history of Danish public libraries in the period 1880-1920, she finds inspiration in the ideas of the postmodern French philosopher, Michel Foucault, and the use of discourse analysis.

Introduction

The different contributions to the session on library history at the 2001 Nordic Seminar on Public Library Research indicate that this field is still alive in the Nordic countries. And of course these projects are not the only ones—one finds several other current projects in the Nordic countries concerning public library history. How is it possible to relate these contributions to each other and to this article in a more subtle way than saying that they examine aspects on Danish library history? More important is that the contributions show the variety of possibilities when dealing with the history of libraries: Martin Dyrbye deals with the foreign influence on the Danish public library development in an organization perspective.[1] Nan Dahlkild focuses on the Danish library architecture in the period from 1909 to 1939.[2] My article examines different approaches to the Danish library history and deals only with the theoretical implications, whereas the other two studies also have an empirical basis. Looking more closely, however, I find it more interesting that the contributions separately are dealing with different relations to our notion of the public libraries. In this way, the articles concentrate

on physical elements of this notion: the persons involved (the organizations), the buildings and how this notion has been established. Even
though there is a strong focus on Denmark in the first half of the twentieth century the focus is not the same, and thus a faceted introduction
to Danish public library history is presented.

Hence, a variety of possible approaches to library history exists—
also in Denmark. In order to expand this variety, two additional perspectives on the Danish library history are presented in this article.
They form together with the seminar contributions and two articles by
the English library historian, Alistair Black, a stock of inspiration for
my considerations on the establishing of a theoretical framework for
my research project. The inspiration is twofold: On one hand, there is
an inspiration drawn from the articles by Black to seek a theoretical
framework. On the other hand, there is an inspiration coming from the
existing Danish research on the period from 1880 to 1920 on the general historical level and also on a theoretical level. The general historical level is based on the book *The History of the Danish Public Libraries 1876-1940*[3] from the early 1960s by county librarian H. Hvenegaard
Lassen (1886-1971). The theoretical level is based on the recent article
"Writing Library History: About the Foundation of the Modern Public
Library in Denmark"[4] by associate professor at the Royal School of
Library and Information Science in Denmark, Leif Emerek. As a third
perspective, the article introduces a discourse analytic approach based
on the work of the French thinker Michel Foucault. This approach is
based on my current theoretical considerations and therefore I am not
introducing a complete theoretical framework. I will, nevertheless,
examine the discourse analytic approach more broadly than the two
other aspects since I intend to apply this approach to my own field of
research. Still, the purpose of this article is not to give a high priority to
the discourse analytic approach or to launch this perspective as the only
way of dealing with library history. Instead I want to introduce the
theoretical concepts of Michel Foucault as a fruitful way of approaching library history.

My project on the Danish public libraries focuses on the period
from 1880 to 1920. This period was characterized by a sudden rise in
the debate and discussion of public libraries. Furthermore, the involvement of the state changed from the first granting of subsidies in 1880 to
the first Public Library Act in 1920. This preliminary description leaves
some very broad problems for an inquiry: How and why did public
libraries become an issue and how were they discussed? In this connection, it is essential also to incorporate the internal split in the library
movement without disparaging it or leaving it unmentioned. In my
opinion, two aspects are of major importance in the history of the Dan-

ish public libraries: (1) Which influence (if any at all) did the concept of *Bildung* and the education of the (adult) population have on the idea of the public libraries?[5] (2) How and why did the state involve itself in the establishing of the public libraries? These two aspects lead to the hypothesis of my project: The establishing of public libraries was connected with a changing view on Bildung and on the state. The Bildung was now considered to be for the entire population and not dependent on the class to which you belonged. And the Bildung was as well considered to be an area for the state and no longer a private task. The state was seen as having new areas of responsibility, including the provision of the population with an opportunity of getting access to information. In spite of the importance that the state ascribed to the development of public libraries, it seems to me that the role of the state has been underexposed analytically in the existing major presentations on the history of the public libraries in Denmark.

Black's Considerations on Library History

From which perspectives can you consider public library history in general and Danish public library history in the period from 1880 to 1920 in particular? It is obvious to start with a look at the public library as an institution and in this way the focus is directed towards a description of the progress—to study the public libraries from the "beginnings"[6] to the establishment of the institution and then a description of the activities until a certain time (often the current day of the author undertaking the study). The history of the institution can—as with history in general—be approached with a descriptive or a theoretical dimension. In the 1990s, Alistair Black in two articles discussed the position of library history as a subject of education and of research. He presents a thorough analysis of the library history discipline, considering its aim and relevance, and outlines a problem by referring to the traditional way of writing library history as the history of the institution. He considers this kind of history as outdated and too narrow,[7] because the history of the library as an institution neither incorporates the public libraries in a broader social or historical context nor sees them in a theoretical perspective.

In both articles, Black concentrates on the context. In "New Methodologies in Library History: A Manifesto for the 'New' Library History" he considers the present role of library history and is, as mentioned above, skeptical. He still defines the history of the library as an institution as a relevant approach, despite its lack of context. Black then suggests that library history, to gain more relevance, should include a social, historical context and a theoretical dimension. It is important for Black to insist on the relevance of the history of public libraries as an institution. According to him, this can only be achieved by contributing to the insights into history and society in general and by embracing a broader historical context.[8] According to Black, the main purpose of library history is (should be) "the light which past library activity can throw on wider society."[9] The theoretical dimension should be found in the dual perspective of modernity: (1) the self, its emancipation and progress, that is, an idealistic and utopian aspect and (2) control, surveillance and regulation. Black sees these two tendencies as inseparable parts of the project of modernity from the Age of Enlightenment and onwards, and they belong as such to the new theoretically based approach to the history of the library as an institution. Black insists in his 1998 article "Information and Modernity: The History of Information and the Eclipse of Library History" on providing the history of the public libraries with relevance, but he is skeptical towards the contributions made by the studies analyzing the history of the library from an institution perspective. As a new way of thinking, he wants to tie the public libraries to the field of history of information and abandon the traditional history of the library as an institution.[10]

Black's articles may serve as an introduction to understanding Danish public library history research because he defines three general ways of approaching library history: (1) a traditional descriptive history of the library as an institution, (2) a theoretically based history of the library in the light of modernity and (3) a theoretically based approach emphasizing aspects of control and surveillance. Existing Danish research on public library history has primarily exposed the two first aspects of the public library history. To illustrate these two aspects, I will concentrate on the book by H. Hvenegaard Lassen and the article by Leif Emerek. These works are also interesting because they to a very high degree reflect the utopian notion of the public libraries. Although they both see the public libraries from a utopian angle and focus on progress and development of the public libraries, major differences between their approaches exist. The work of Hvenegaard Lassen is influenced by the norm for historical writing in the 1960s and was carried out by request from the Danish Library Association. Emerek, however, presents a theoretically based and more analytic work. In this context, Hvenegaard Lassen and Emerek are, as mentioned above, used to illustrate the existing line of research—social causal explanations and the concept of Bildung as an important part of the ideological basis of the public libraries have been analyzed in other works. Consequently, my examination might be seen as one-sided. However, my intention is not to disparage the existing research but simply to explore the different perspectives on the history of the libraries.

The Public Library as an Institution

Hvenegaard Lassen's book is an illustration of the library as an institution. His presentation is characterized by a very strong focus on description and chronology of important, and perhaps less important, events concerning the progress of the library movement. This results in an abundance of names, places and dates. Unfortunately this also results in a lacking overview of the history of the Danish public libraries. The involved persons are seen as the most important element—Hvenegaard Lassen talks about the "pioneers" who founded the public libraries. One of them, H.O. Lange (1843-1963), is almost described as a prophet when giving his famous 1909 speech on the organization of the public libraries. The huge importance devoted to this speech in Danish library history is stressed by the fact that Hvenegaard Lassen not only mentions the day of the speech but also the exact hour.[11] Hvenegaard Lassen, so to speak, describes the success story of the Danish public libraries starting with the "beginnings" over the years of takeoff to the years of growth after the passing of the first Danish Public Library Act in 1920. Even though he acknowledges that not all planned results had been accomplished by 1940, the main impression is a "marvellous development" in the period from 1876 to 1940.[12] He never considers if this development was the only possible way to go. In the chapter named "The Beginnings," Hvenegaard Lassen focuses on the miserable situation of the popular book collections.[13] Although libraries existed before 1876 and several were founded in this period, their period of existence was short and they were badly equipped—which in the eyes of Hvenegaard Lassen is "a sad story of good intentions and poor results owing to lack of money and interest."[14] The situation is undoubtedly correctly described but colored by the unconscious comparison with the "present" (1962) conditions of the public libraries.

Hvenegaard Lassen's book does not seek to explain how the public libraries could become an issue on the political and societal agenda. Indeed, neither the role of the state nor the concept of Bildung is analyzed thoroughly. The role of the state is then described as being that of a financing resource with special focus on the size of the yearly subsidies. This seems also to be the most important aspect of the Public Library Act in 1920.[15] The intentions of the state by granting these subsidies are not considered critically. Hvenegaard Lassen does not analyze the concept of Bildung as such. However, he has numerous reflections on the standard of the popular book collections.[16] This standard he criticizes for being appalling—the popular book collections did not provide the users with educational literature. Hvenegaard Lassen indirectly uses the concept of Bildung in order to describe the standard of the popular book collections but not in an analytical way. In fact, it is not fair to criticize Hvenegaard Lassen for this because he did not intend to give such an explanation or analysis himself. One could assume that the concept of Bildung was common knowledge for the intended readers of the book and as such it did not need deep analysis.

Actually, Hvenegaard Lassen does mention the internal discussions and conflicts in the library movement as well as the resistance against an increasing centralization. I find it problematic, though, that he for instance rejects this resistance as "false and cheap."[17] Besides, there is no deeper explanation of the reasons for this resistance.[18] Apparently, Hvenegaard Lassen's strategy is to leave this split as unmentioned as possible or at least not to elaborate too much on it. Definitely, it is not a major theme for him, probably because he was himself involved in the discussions at that time. Hvenegaard Lassen not only writes the successful history of the Danish public libraries—he also writes the history of the winners of this internal split in quite an uncritical way.

As mentioned above, the key questions concerning the history of the public libraries are how and why they suddenly became an "issue" and an object for discussion. Furthermore, how and why they increasingly became objects of professionalization and centralization. The explanation given by Hvenegaard Lassen contains two elements: the personal element—the commitment of the pioneers—and also the fact that there was a model in the United States, which served as both a comparison and an inspiration. However, this explanation still leaves the question: How was it possible for these pioneers to gain sympathy for the public libraries? To answer this, one has to consider a historical—social—context, which Hvenegaard Lassen's book lacks. The public library movement seems to have existed without connections to society in general. The quality of Hvenegaard Lassen's book is the reinforcement of the professional identity of the librarians through the construction of a historical tradition that included key elements such as the popular book collections, the concept of Bildung and the ideas from the Anglo-American world, which in this tradition was given the designation "modern."

Public Libraries and Modernity

As an example of a theoretically based history of the public libraries I will discuss the article "Writing Library History: About the Foundation of the Modern Public Library in Denmark" by Leif Emerek. As an introduction he gives a short overview of the existing tradition of Danish public library history. According to Emerek, it is characterized by a clear focus on the commitment of the pioneers (or the founding fathers) and their contribution has been seen as the explanation of the rise of public libraries. Emerek finds it important to explain why it was possible for the pioneers to gather support for their ideas about a modern public library. However, he does not answer this question by looking at the personal commitment but by looking at a broader context.[19] Emerek establishes a context at the general historical level with phenomena like urbanization, industrialization, the working classes and the role of the state as major causes for the institutionalization of the library and the culture of the written word and the professionalization of the librarian's work. At a more specific library history level, the context considers a tradition built on the notion of reason and the bourgeois self from the Age of Enlightenment and onwards. This includes the concept of Bildung and the suggestion that the libraries were in opposition to the oral culture of the folk high school movement.[20] Finally, Emerek includes the rational way of running the public libraries, which was the heritage from the United States. Emerek stresses the concept of Bildung as the ideological basis of the public libraries. Consequently, he pays less attention to the instrumental influence from the United States. He still considers this influence of importance but emphasizes the criticism against the rationalistic view.[21]

Emerek opens up the scope for inquiry by introducing a theoretical dimension. He applies the general aspect of modernization of society from the Age of Enlightenment and onwards using Reinhart Koselleck's definition of modernity and the definition of the bourgeois public sphere and the free discussion as introduced by Jürgen Habermas. He diminishes the personal element even though he does not underestimate the contributions of the involved persons. In drawing upon the theories of Koselleck and Habermas and the perspective of modernity, Emerek establishes a context that differs from the traditional history of the public library as an institution. To him it is vital to study the reasons for the relatively successful implementation of the public libraries.[22]

Choosing this approach, the main themes of public library history are the emancipation of the bourgeois self and the development of modern society as well as the ability of the public libraries to serve as an integrator of the working classes that should now be educated. Emerek's analysis thus concerns the aim of the public libraries, which to a great extent was concentrated on an educational and supervising function through which the individual was to be educated in order to let society benefit from this stabilizing effect. As a prominent source, he emphasizes the book by A.S. Steenberg from 1900 (*Folkebogsamlinger: Deres Historie og Indretning*), because Steenberg, according to Emerek, described the Bourgeois Public Sphere, as defined by Habermas, with the participation of the educated *citoyen*. The integrating ability is then described by determining the values on which the public libraries were to be founded: a combination of the national neohumanism and the classical idea of Enlightenment. This, however, did not happen without resistance from the philanthropists within the public library movement who had a different view on the aim of the public libraries.

Considering the two aspects of modernity, which Black identifies, Emerek is almost solely dealing with the emancipating force of the public libraries even though he also mentions their integrating ability. The answer to his first question, why the pioneers could find support for their ideas about the modern public library, seems to be that the pioneers were exponents of a common agreement on the concept of Bildung. Furthermore, Emerek sees an explanation in the fact that the state aimed at an integration of the working classes in order to avoid an open class-conflict.[23] The modern public libraries served as an instrument for this integration providing a common understanding of what kind of Bildung was to be spread among the people.

This explains the success of the part of the library movement that sought a greater state invention. However, internal conflicts in the early period of the public libraries are still left without proper analysis. Emerek finds it problematic that traditional public library history covers this topic superficially. Yet he describes one of the opponents of increasing centralization as not being aware of the new historical context including industrialism and the working classes.[24] The adopted approach to modernity often results in a disparaging interpretation of the groups in the library movement that did not want state intervention and the traditional institution history will often avoid mention of this resistance. Emerek has very valuable reflections on the concept of Bildung and on the intentions of the state, but it does not seem clear to me how (and why) the concept of Bildung could play such an important role at the turn of the nineteenth century as to contribute to the establishment of the public libraries at this precise time. In Emerek's perspective, the public libraries are viewed as a part of the modernity and the reason for their establishment is to a great extent seen as a utopian measure. The questions of power, control and surveillance are, however, not in the center of his focus.

Foucault and the History of the Public Libraries

Discourse and Statements

Why is Michel Foucault of interest when dealing with a historical subject? In spite of the impact of his theories in the field of historical research in general, it seems as if they are still quite controversial. A common complaint regarding the application of the Foucaultian theoretical concepts is the opinion that they express his paranoia—especially against the medical sciences.[25] Furthermore, his theories are ambiguous, and the focus of his interest has shifted from analysis of knowledge over analysis of power to analysis of the self. There are not least several unclarified aspects—especially the relation between the subject and power, the possibilities of the individual and the question of historical determinism. I will, however, leave these questions without further comment. I still think, though, that it would be of benefit to consider the theories of Foucault as inspiration and as a theoretical context, and below I will specify my reasons.

First and foremost, his historical thinking is interesting. Normally one considers history in an evolutionary perspective, driven by either underlying structures or by events provoked by individual acts. Foucault sees history as built on discourses, and they follow each other through ruptures.[26] A discourse in the Foucaultian way is the historically and culturally given rules, which control the contents and forms of the statement. The rule of discourse means that the use of discourse results in the possession of knowledge of a certain area and that the discourse delimits the possibilities of what can be said about a given topic at a given time.[27] The discourse analysis then exposes what can positively be said about the topic, and the central issue is then: Why can something positively be said about a given topic—and not about something else? That is: How can a certain statement be expressed rather than another statement? When defining a discourse as a certain way in which you talk about the world, this means that other ways are excluded. In this way the discourse is connected to power. The discourse is a point of juncture between knowledge and power, and they both operate through this point.[28] The relation between power and knowledge is of great complexity—at best one can talk about a dual relation, where the techniques of power have been developed on the basis of the collected amount of knowledge whereas the very same techniques are exercised in connection with the gathering of knowledge.[29]

Furthermore, a historical analysis based on the Foucaultian approach to discourse analysis implies that the statement is in the focus of interest. One should focus on the particularity and the very existence of the statement. For traditional historical research based on a critical approach to the sources, this point of view indeed represents a challenge. The critical approach means that the sources are examined according to their origin and representativity in order to estimate their value: Is the source to be trusted? Does it say the truth? Is it of any relevance at all? For which purpose has it been created? These questions have no relevance to the Foucaultian approach to the document. The historian should no longer consider the context, the relevance or considerations on the value of the source. On the contrary, he or she should then deal with the document as if it were a detached monument left without any description or explanation.[30] It could easily lead to unqualified interpretations of the source material if reflections on the representativity and origin of the source are neglected in favor of a description of the document without any connection. On the other hand, it opens up a wider horizon claiming that the interesting part of a source is its very existence. Indeed, the Foucaultian discourse analysis does not aim at finding and deducing the definitive truth but at analyzing regimes of truth.

How have the theories of Michel Foucault, then, inspired my research project? I differ between (1) an overall methodological level where Foucault inspires to another way of understanding history and (2) a very practical level at which the inspiration affects the methods used in the very analysis.

At the methodological level, the starting point is in the circumstance that the statement—the source—is considered unique. Use of the term *discourse* means that the evolutionary horizon is dissolved—history is not seen as a steady progress. At the same time I am able to concentrate on the discourse's power of excluding and of discipline. This opens up the possibility of understanding history as shaped through different systems of knowledge. The analysis then focuses on the various statements about the public libraries in the period from 1880 to 1920. In this way, an analysis of the disagreements and conflicts that existed internally in the public library movement is possible. Besides, one avoids describing the progress as inevitable. Hvenegaard Lassen claims that the new public libraries in the minds of the pioneers were something quite different from the popular book collections and basically something much better—the intention was to improve the standards of the popular book collections.[31] In this way he looks at the public library history from an evolutionary angle, where the modern public libraries are seen as a progress in comparison to the popular book collections. By doing so, he creates continuity between the two "phenomena." Instead of this evolutionary perspective one can, with inspiration from Foucault, alternatively think in contrasting systems, which indicate that the popular book collections and the public libraries are different ways of thinking in systems of knowledge. In this way, the popular book collections are not the predecessors of the public libraries, but they express completely different principles. However, this does not mean that the arguments used in connection with the popular book collections cannot be used again when speaking of the public libraries. The latter ones had an entirely different purpose compared with the popular book collections and the reused arguments then had other consequences. To pursue this further, it would be obvious to analyze how different arguments or concepts—that is, the concept of Bildung—were used in the discussion about the popular book collections and in a discussion about the public libraries. This analysis could discover possible resemblances and differences in the way such arguments were used.

Discourse Analysis

In order to discuss the methodological aspects of the Foucaultian inspiration I will briefly outline the parameters that Foucault elaborates in his considerations on discourse analysis.

As mentioned above, the statement is crucial. The statement is a nondecomposable element and can be regarded as the smallest component of the discourse. As such the statement is the brick by which the discourse is constructed. The discourse can be compared to a network, where the statements are knots connected to each other by relations. The scope of a discourse analysis is to map and analyze these relations, and for the purpose of this analysis Foucault has established four types of relations which he names the rules of formation: object; subject positions (enunciative modalities); concepts; and strategies (themes/ theoretical choices). By analyzing the relations between the four rules of formation a "system of dispersion" is mapped. When this "system of dispersion" has been mapped one will find the discursive formation.[32] None of these four categories exists independently in relation to the discourse and they are not predecessors to the discourse but emerge in the discourse.

The object is what the discourse talks about. By describing the establishment of the object, focus is on the set of rules that governs its emergence (social and cultural areas—e.g. the school, church and intelligentsia). One has to consider how different authorities, which decide what can be said, delimit the object. Another category for analyzing the object is a grid of specification. This denotes systems that are able to relate different types of social categorizations. The discourse is based on the space in which the object can emerge, and at the same time it must provide the opportunity of transformation of the object. The discourse is not characterized by a stable object but by the space.[33]

The subject positions define who speaks, with what right they speak, from where they speak institutionally and how—is it an observing, listening or questioning situation? In order to understand the subject positions, it must be accepted that Foucault does not speak of a specific individual but of a position, which has to be accessed in order to say something. The subject positions and their accessibility are determinant for the possibility of the subject to speak and not the other way around.[34] The subject is constructed through different positions determined by discourse, and Foucault—as well as the structuralism—is refusing the creative individual.[35]

The concepts can be described as a "battery"[36] of categories, elements and types, and they characterize the way in which the object is spoken of. The description of the concepts concerns the various dependencies of the statements and how the field of statements is organized. The concepts have no value until they are part of the discourse.[37]

The strategies/themes are also a way in which the object is spoken of. The discourse produces theories that, compared to the objects, are narratives more extensive in scope and basic ideas. They exist in discourse in a special way which Foucault calls a strategy. The term *strategy* implies a limitation and a choice.[38] Through these strategic choices the discourse defines its limits towards other discourses.[39]

The discourse analysis then establishes the relations internally in the rules of formation, and the final scope is to establish the relations between the four rules of formation in order to map the discourse.

This is all very abstract. Indeed, the main problem to me is to make the discourse analysis fruitful in the interaction with the source material and my hypothesis as mentioned in the introduction. At present, I work with three major research questions that reflect the methodological aspects of discourse, contrasting systems of knowledge, the main hypothesis and a discourse analytic approach:

- Which were the different discourses that affected the ideas on the public library?
- How did they talk about the (public) libraries (the object), from which positions? Which concepts and strategies have been connected with the (public) libraries?

- What aspects of power and discipline can be identified in the Danish library movement?
- Individualization of a discourse on the public libraries—how is the object (the public libraries) connected to the subject positions, concepts and strategies?
- How was the role of the state?
- How did the state talk about the public libraries—which concepts and strategies were related to the object?

The methodological framework of my project involves a connection between a Foucaultian-inspired discourse analysis and the traditional critical approach to the sources. In order to investigate the above-mentioned main themes of my analysis I intend to analyze the different ways in which the idea of the public library was discussed. By examining articles in journals, magazines and newspapers related to the folk high school movement, the labor movement, the bourgeoisie and the new progressive cultural intellectuals, it would be possible to analyze how the public libraries were related to, for example, Bildung and state in these different discourses. The result is a broad view of different discourses related to an idea about public libraries. From being part of other discourses the idea of the public library more and more became a "space" of its own—it was still less a part of other discourses. One could put it that way, that the idea of the public library became "individualized."

The central points of this inquiry are made up by the discussion of the notion about good (and true) Bildung and for whom it should be— that is, how the concept of Bildung was used. It should also be possible to analyze the objects and subject positions connected to the public libraries, and how the concepts and strategies (perhaps) changed during the period of inquiry. A possible object of the public library movement could be the organization of the public libraries,[40] and the involved subjects can hold positions inside the library "world" and thus act like experts. Possible positions can be held outside the library "world" as well, but still with the possibility of articulation—as, for instance, the teachers. The concepts in play are first of all the concept of Bildung, but also democracy, reading and culture are possible concepts whereas possible strategies concern the construction of a morally healthy population for securing democracy; an attention to the social problems and more specifically strategies as centralization, harmonization or even decentralization. Of great importance is to establish the relations between the different categories, which would map the discourse.

The analysis of the second research question addressing power and discipline is mainly to be executed after the "individualization." In 1905, a special Danish library journal—entitled *Bogsamlingsbladet*—started appearing. Through the discourse analytic approach it would be possible to follow the defined discourses concerning possible changes in their use and how the library movement absorbed them. In the end, these discourses established a discourse on the public libraries and consequently served as an exclusion of other ideas on the public libraries. An examination of books, articles and other writings by the involved persons in the periodical *Bogsamlingsbladet* would allow a study of the mechanisms of discipline inherent in the concept of library and how they affected the construction of the user—elementary in this perspective would be the rules of conduct in the reading rooms, how to treat the books but also the introduction of cataloguing and classification techniques as a way of organizing knowledge. In this respect, Kasper Graarup's article on the problems of the universal classification system is interesting because it considers the principle that inherent assumptions are basic when constructing a classification system.[41] The physical arrangement of the library—especially the reading room—is also a possible method of disciplining. The mechanisms of control that were at play in the cause of public libraries are—in my opinion—concerned with the desire for disciplining the reading habits of the population: Talking about democratization of the reading culture also implies the possibility of controlling it. This is an implicit part of the entire discussion on the concept of Bildung, which went on within the library movement. The increasing efforts aiming at centralization, harmonization and professionalization are possible methods of disciplining, and the claim for this discipline was gradually taken over by the state. An analysis of this gradual taking over the structures of power would also be of relevance.

These methods of disciplining seem to have a very logic explanation, which is related to the everyday practice of public libraries. No sophisticated theoretical concepts are needed to explain this. The crucial question is, however, how these methods of disciplining are related to a discursive level and how they shaped the notion of the public libraries and of the user.

The third research question considers how the state was involved in the field of the public libraries. At this early stage of my research project my ideas on how to examine the role of the state are very vague. At the moment, my considerations concern the possibilities of establishing a consistency in the argumentation throughout the period 1880-1920 in the annual reports on the granting of subsidies. In this respect the State Committee for Book Collections (*Statens Bogsamlingskomité*) and its predecessors assume a central position in the examination. The examination also includes an analysis of the Public Library Act of 1920, the preliminary hearings and the internal case records from the Department of Education under which the public libraries belonged. This will be done by looking at possible relations between the objects of the different discourses (e.g. Bildung, rationalizing, professionalization) and by identifying the strategies and concepts with which they are connected.

The inquiry should also expose the intentions of the state in participating in the development of public libraries as a project of educating the population. Involving a Foucaultian concept of power which stipulates that power is everywhere and not the possession of a specific class or institution,[42] it would not be sufficient to say that the state wanted to integrate the working classes. At the same time, it would be obvious to focus on the ever-increasing exclusion of the part of the library movement that did seek to preserve the privately based library out of state control. Indeed, the aspect of power has to do with not just the relation between the state and the public libraries. Power is also present within the library movement. Therefore, the Foucaultian notion of social control is not only connected to the strategies of government institutions or the establishment in order to prevent social instability— for example, the ability of public libraries as integrators of deviant groups in society. But by using the Foucaultian notion of social control, one has also the possibility of examining the construction of (the notion of) the users and how these users are disciplined. This is, however, not a strategy of the state or the establishment but is inherent in the concept of public libraries and it influences everybody.

A Critical Perspective

An analysis of the history of the Danish public libraries based on a Foucaultian inspired discourse analysis focuses on the questions: How could the public libraries become an issue at the turn of the century and what aspects of power and discipline could be found in the library movement? How was the concept of Bildung used and, finally, which other discourses did affect the notion of the public libraries? The personal aspect is not of great importance to a discourse analytic approach. Nevertheless, Foucault does not deny a writing and inventing individual[43]—the individual is only of relevance as far as its access to the subject positions is concerned. A question for further consideration is whether, and (if at all) how, to involve the personal element in spite of the minor importance given to the persons involved when analyzing at a discursive level. Whereas Emerek's presentation has a very strong focus on one aspect of modernity, that is, the concentration on the self, its emancipation and progress, my analysis would focus on control, surveillance and discipline. These aspects do not directly originate from the desire of the state to integrate the working classes, but they are inherent mechanisms of discipline in the discourse on the public libraries.

This perspective, which focuses on the mechanisms of control, surveillance and discipline, seems to have some very negative connotations. The reason is probably that the subject—the human being—is left without any influence whatsoever and that we do not like the idea of being controlled "by unknown forces." Furthermore, we have a strong feeling of progress in history—of evolution from a lower to a higher stage. Hence, the Foucaultian perspective ruins these assumptions and is regarded as pessimistic and misanthropic—some would believe this to be a more realistic perspective. I would definitely stress the critical aspect. With the Foucaultian perspective, one questions the library world's notion of . . . the library world. Although I name this aspect critical, I do not intend to be critical in the normal sense of the word, that is, claiming that the existing self-interpretation of the library world is all wrong and too idealistic. This would have no relevance at all. Instead I understand the critical aspect as a way of questioning self-evident categories and practices in order to give a broader picture of the history of the public libraries and not constantly compare the utopian perspective with the controlling perspective in order to find resemblances or differences.

As a contribution to the existing research, an examination of the Danish public library history from this perspective is relevant because of the focus on the changes in discourses and on the social control. In my opinion, other theoretical frameworks do not to the same extent incorporate these two parameters. One finds research traditions whose focus would be on economic, social and "mental" structures and not "event" history, but these traditions would neither be able to explain the changes in discourse nor the social control.

Final Remarks

Some general remarks should end this article giving a brief summing up of the different aspects that have been mentioned here. The focus was at the beginning turned towards two different ways in which Danish library history has been written and then shifted towards how I intend to carry out my research project. A strong impulse comes from the articles by Alistair Black, who specifies three different ways of approaching library history: (1) the traditional history of the institution, (2) a theoretically based approach involving the idea of modernity and (3) a theoretically based approach involving ideas on control and surveillance. In a Danish context the normal tradition was to describe the institution, which has been done by Hvenegaard Lassen. Emerek provides the Danish history with the aspects of modernity and the emancipation of the bourgeois self. The third way places emphasis on the disciplining and controlling function of the public libraries—an aspect which I found has not been exposed in the field of Danish public library history. I then concentrated on establishing a framework in order to expose these aspects of the public library history and found inspiration in the theories of Michel Foucault. From my point of view it is of great importance to present this inspiration to the readers in order to explain why I am doing my research in this way.

Three different perspectives will of course result in three different analyses with their separate focus. Two perspectives have a theoretical basis. This raises the question about the importance of theory in order to analyze the history of the public libraries (or history in general) especially regarding the Danish library history tradition, which has, to no great extent, adopted and relied on theoretical frameworks. A theoretical context is not indispensable, but theories contribute to those considerations which are involved when working with source material. This results in—if not new knowledge—then new perspectives on the topic. Theories are good to think with; they can open your eyes and call attention to new ways of interpreting the historical material.

The field of library history offers a lot of possible perspectives for research. In my opinion, none of these perspectives alone tells the "truth" about the history of the public libraries. But brought together they reveal still more new knowledge in this field. This is how I would like to see my own inspiration from Michel Foucault: It is not an attempt to find the ultimate truth about the foundation of the public libraries but an attempt to expose an aspect of this history. An aspect which, to my knowledge, has not yet been exposed in the field of Danish public library history.

Essential to the considerations on the application of a theoretical perspective is the desire to write a history of the public libraries, but in this case not just for the library world.

Notes

1 Martin Dyrbye, "Foreign Influence on the Development of the Danish Public Libraries with Emphasis on the Association Denmark's Popular Book

Collections, 1905–1919" in *New Frontiers in Public Library Research*, ed. Leif Kajberg and Carl Gustav Johannsen (Lanham, Md.: Scarecrow Press, 2005). Included as a chapter in the present book.

2 Nan Dahlkild, "Architecture and Design of Danish Public Libraries, 1909-1939: Between Tradition and Modernity" in *New Frontiers in Public Library Research*, ed. Leif Kajberg and Carl Gustav Johannsen (Lanham, Md.: Scarecrow Press, 2005). Included as a chapter in the present book.

3 Harald Hvenegaard Lassen, *De danske folkebibliotekers historie 1876-1940* (Copenhagen: Dansk Bibliografisk Kontor, 1962). There is no English translation of this book.

4 Leif Emerek, "At skrive bibliotekshistorie: Om grundlæggelsen af det moderne folkebibliotek i Danmark" in *Det siviliserte informasjonssamfunn: Folkebibliotekenes rolle ved inngangen til en digital tid*, ed. Ragnar A. Audunson and Niels W. Lund (Bergen: Fakbokforlaget, 2001), 88-117. The article is not published in English.

5 An appropriate English term for the Danish concept of "dannelse" is difficult to find—one suggestion could be the concept of "liberal education." I am using the German word *Bildung* for this kind of education since it stresses the ideological foundation and that it should not be seen as a practice. The use of the German term in English steadily becomes more common. See, e.g. Guri Jørstad Wingård, "History and Bildung: The Political and Pedagogical Relevance of History within a Changing Scientific Discourse" in *Mod nye historier*, ed. Carsten Tage Nielsen, Dorthe Gert Simonsen, and Lene Wul (Århus: Jysk Selskab for Historie, 2001), 178. Though the project gives an analysis of the role of the state high priority, a more explicit definition of the state has not been provided yet.

6 Hvenegaard Lassen, *De danske folkebibliotekers historie 1876–1940*, 9, my translation.

7 Alistair Black, "Information and Modernity: The History of Information and the Eclipse of Library History" in *Library History* 14, no. 1 (May 1998): 39; Alistair Black, "New Methodologies in Library History: A Manifesto for the 'New' Library History" in *Library History* 11 (1995): 76-78.

8 Black, "New Methodologies in Library History: A Manifesto for the 'New' Library History," 80ff.

9 Black, "New Methodologies in Library History: A Manifesto for the 'New' Library History," 81.

10 Black, "Information and Modernity: The History of Information and the Eclipse of Library History," 39-40.

11 Hvenegaard Lassen, *De danske folkebibliotekers historie 1876-1940*, 119-20.

12 Hvenegaard Lassen, *De danske folkebibliotekers historie 1876-1940*, 339.

13 I distinguish between the two types of libraries: the public library as the new type of libraries for which the pioneers advocated and the old type of libraries that I then call popular book collections. This is, however, not an adequate translation of the Danish term *sognebogsamling*. A direct translation

into Danish of the English "parish library" would indicate a stronger relation to the church, which not always did exist.

14 Hvenegaard Lassen, *De danske folkebibliotekers historie 1876-1940*, 21, my translation.

15 Hvenegaard Lassen, *De danske folkebibliotekers historie 1876-1940*, 32-36 and 194-201.

16 Hvenegaard Lassen, *De danske folkebibliotekers historie 1876-1940*, 21ff.

17 Hvenegaard Lassen, *De danske folkebibliotekers historie 1876-1940*, 132, my translation.

18 Hvenegaard Lassen, *De danske folkebibliotekers historie 1876-1940*, 183 and 187.

19 Emerek, "At skrive bibliotekshistorie: Om grundlæggelsen af det moderne folkebibliotek i Danmark," 89.

20 The Danish folk high school had as its main purpose to spread the notion of the Danish national culture among especially the peasants. The pedagogical principle was education through the spoken word.

21 Emerek, "At skrive bibliotekshistorie: Om grundlæggelsen af det moderne folkebibliotek i Danmark," 94.

22 Emerek, "At skrive bibliotekshistorie: Om grundlæggelsen af det moderne folkebibliotek i Danmark," 90.

23 Emerek, "At skrive bibliotekshistorie: Om grundlæggelsen af det moderne folkebibliotek i Danmark," 112 and 110.

24 Emerek, "At skrive bibliotekshistorie: Om grundlæggelsen af det moderne folkebibliotek i Danmark," 110.

25 See, e.g. the review by Thorkild Kjærgaard, "Krigen mod kopper," *Weekend-avisen*, no. 38 (21-27 September 2001): 1-2.

26 Michel Foucault, *The Archaeology of Knowledge* (London: Tavistock Publications 1972, 2001), 175ff.

27 Michel Foucault, *Die Ordnung des Diskurses* (Frankfurt am Main: Fischer Taschenbuch Verlag 1972, 2000), 22-25.

28 Jeffrey Weeks, "Foucault for Historians." *History Workshop Journal*, no. 14 (1982): 111.

29 Norman Fairclough, *Discourse and Social Change* (Polity Press, 1996), 50.

30 Foucault, *The Archaeology of Knowledge*, 6ff.

31 Hvenegaard Lassen, *De danske folkebibliotekers historie 1876-1940*, 185.

32 Foucault, *The Archaeology of Knowledge*, 38.

33 Foucault, *The Archaeology of Knowledge*, 40-50.

34 Foucault, *The Archaeology of Knowledge*, 50-55; Foucault, *Die Ordnung des Diskurses*, 22.

35 Fairclough, *Discourse and Social Change*, 44.

36 Fairclough, *Discourse and Social Change*, 45.

37 Foucault, *The Archaeology of Knowledge*, 56-63.

38 Jan Ifversen, *Om magt, demokrati og diskurs: Diskuteret i lyset af den franske revolution*, vol. 2 (Århus: University of Aarhus, Centre for Cultural Research, 1997), 483.

39 Foucault, *The Archaeology of Knowledge*, 64–70.

40 Hans Ostenfeldt Lange, *Bibliotekssagen uden for København* (Copenhagen: Høst, 1909), 3.

41 Kasper Graarup, "Classification of Religious Literature: Some Thoughts on the Dilemmas of Universalism" in *New Frontiers in Public Library Research*, ed. Leif Kajberg and Carl Gustav Johannsen (Lanham, Md.: Scarecrow Press, 2005). Included as a chapter in the present book.

42 Michel Foucault, "Afterword: The Subject and Power" in *Michel Foucault: Beyond Structuralism and Hermeneutics*, ed. H.L. Dreyfus and P. Rabinow (Chicago: The University of Chicago Press, 1982), 224.

43 Foucault, *Die Ordnung des Diskurses*, 21.

Part V

PROFESSIONAL IDENTITY

The Meaning of the Public Library in People's Everyday Life: Some Preliminary Results from a Qualitative Study

Ellen-Merete Duvold

Traditional quantitative user surveys are being challenged by qualitative everyday life studies focusing not only on use and motivations for use but also on the various contexts that surround the actual use. In her article, Duvold criticizes the "information paradigm" in user studies for being theoretically insufficient. Instead, she argues that the concept of knowledge is better for understanding the meaning of library use for the user. Based on observations and interviews, she emphasizes that the use of public libraries is often connected to serious existential projects in life—studies, work, search for roots and identity and so forth.

Walking in the woods and seeing a man chopping wood, the observer can watch the behavior and have an "observational understanding" of the woodchopper. But what the observer understands as a result of his observation may not be at all consistent with how the woodchopper views his own behavior. To understand the woodchopper's behavior, the observer would have to gain access to the woodchopper's "subjective understanding," that is, know what meaning he himself made out of his chopping wood. The way to meaning, Schutz says, is to be able to put behavior in context. Was the woodchopper chopping wood to supply a logger, heat his home, or get in shape? (Alfred Schutz, quoted by Seidman)[1]

Introduction

The public library is open to all members of the community, and from the user's perspective it is free, voluntary and without obligation. The limits of its conduct are rather loose; there are no fixed borders as far as its offers and services are concerned.[2] Factors like enlightenment, education and culture are all mentioned in section 1 of the Norwegian Public Libraries' Act, and transmission of culture, knowledge and information are usually regarded as the most important tasks of the public library.[3] Among the many possible roles of the public library in the local community, I will emphasize the following: cultural center, knowledge center, information center, social center and also meeting place.[4] Usually all these roles are operating in parallel in the contemporary Norwegian public library, as they are both "quiet oases" and "local windows towards the world."

In our postindustrial society, the questions about the role of the public library in society are actualized by the increasing significance of information, technology and documents as resources. One may formulate a contrasting hypothesis about the need for the services of the public library in such a situation. On one hand, people have more sources of information than ever; we live in a "media society" where lots of different media compete for attracting our attention and where citizens in many ways are bombarded with information. When media to an ever-increasing degree are entering our private living rooms, do we then need the public library? On the other hand, we also live in a more brittle and "looser" society compared with a few generations ago, with lesser village pumps and fewer open meeting places in the public sphere.[5] Thus, social networks to a lesser extent offer relevant information about rights and duties and the minor and major problems in everyday life—about food receipts, gardening and treatment of fruit trees, social security rights and so forth. If the latter hypothesis (or "diagnosis") is true, the need for the public library should increase rather than decrease—not only because it is a center of information but also because it represents one of the few remaining public spaces not dedicated to shopping.

In this paper, I will analyze what role people themselves ascribe to their use of the public library in their everyday lives. I intend to apply a microperspective, a perspective "from below," with its point of departure in the users' phenomenological experience of reality. I ask: What do people use the public library for—and in what social situations? What makes people visit the public library? What kinds of knowledge do they seek—is it practical knowledge, professional knowledge, scientific knowledge or artistic knowledge?[6] And how is this need for knowledge embedded in their everyday lives? Do people come to borrow media products they otherwise would have bought or media that are perhaps not longer available? Do people come due to private concerns or due to work or formal education concerns? Do they appear on behalf of others, privately or professionally? Can we identify a longing for "adventure" or entertainment from people's uses of the public library? Perhaps the visitors only want to find out "what exists." We have little knowledge about this, and the need for knowledge of this type is not reduced by the development that gradually "opens" the library field to new types of use.

I want to analyze the reasons and motivations that lead people to the public library in the first place, and also what "outcome" they get from the use (in the widest possible sense: in the context of everyday life). Important here is the form and content of the various media and the *contexts* that surround the actual use. Traditionally, the public library has tended to draw a sharp and somewhat misguided distinction between fiction and nonfiction, where fiction is seen as belonging to the sphere of culture while nonfiction belongs to the sphere of knowledge. A novel is considered as fiction, despite that it might just as well work as specialized literature to a student. On the shelves of the public library and in official statistics an illustrated cookery book will be classified as specialized literature, but to a user it may just as well function as entertainment (glossy pictures of colorful ratatouille in picturesque Provencal surroundings can also feed dreams . . .). To another user, the same book may provide the recipe (ratatouille) needed in his or her job, as, for example, a cook in a restaurant or a teacher in domestic science. The contents may be found in printed form, on video or in auditive format. By approaching the use of the public library in a wider everyday life context as this, we are in a position to answer the question "Why do people go to the public library?" in a way that hitherto has been relatively unusual, at least in Norway.

The paper is structured as follows: First, I outline the "information paradigm" that currently dominates in research on public library use. This approach has its point of departure in models that emphasize users as acting on the basis of relatively well-defined "needs." Users are presumed to go to the public library with an intention of overcoming an "information gap" related to a current issue (or situation) they may be grappling with. I criticize this approach for involving a too narrow view of what library use means to many users. It cannot fully cover the variety of public library use. I justify this argument in the second section of the paper by presenting a phenomenological perspective inspired by Alfred Schutz that I consider better suited to outline how public library use is about construction of meaning in users' everyday life. By treating everyday life as a totality, and connecting the use of the public library to the concept of knowledge (rather than the concept of information), I show how the use may be embedded in a wider (and culturally "deeper") context. This context is related to concrete elements of the life-world, earlier experiences in life (which if fact may date from far back in time), current projects and life circumstances as well as political and cultural values related to print culture and general culture use. This also involves an aim to show how the public library functions as public space in the local community. The third section briefly outlines some crucial methodological strategies and problems connected to the analysis of these questions before I finally turn to face the problem empirically, by presenting some preliminary findings from a qualitative analysis.

The "Information Paradigm" in User Studies

Let me first provide some biographical information. When I was educated as a public library librarian early in the 1980s, "information" in public libraries was not as much discussed as it is today. It was simply taken for granted that our task was to transmit culture and information. What we learned about "information" in the public library was basically about public information, or the public library as a so-called "information center." Information was primarily about organization of knowledge, what we called "the tools," namely, storage and retrieval of information.

Then I was away from the library field for more than ten years. When I returned to the field in the mid-1990s, with sociology as new ballast, I discovered that information and users needs' were ranked markedly higher on the agenda. Information was now about "user needs" and "information behavior." Traditional user studies—surveys emphasizing the relationship between use and demographic background variables—were no longer the dominant approach. Instead, factors related to the individual, and factors related the contexts the individual was situated in, had become important. What was in focus was the information-seeking process of the individual. User needs and user studies were new and exciting perspectives to me.

During the period I was away from the library field, important developments took place, both in society in general—in terms of technological development and in an enormous increase of education—*and* in the library field. The term *information* may of course be important as shorthand for describing this development. Yet I found it surprising having to relate to the concept of information as *the* crucial concept in user studies. I also find the information paradigm theoretically insufficient, which means that it should, at least, be supplemented with other perspectives. Let me justify this claim in some more detail.

What is common to recent user studies is their point of departure in user needs and the information-seeking process. One variant is studies of "reference questions": What do users ask for, and what kind of information do they seek according to this source? Users' enquiries to librarians are categorized and classified. The more advanced studies focus on information seeking as a process. Here, information needs do not exist as such, as a separate category of "needs." Instead, other needs are treated as the cause of information-seeking behavior.[7] It is necessary to find out what are the preceding needs that lead people to the public library; information seeking and information needs are here seen in context.

Yet user studies seem to have become synonymous with studies about user needs, and hence with how users seek information to satisfy their needs. My first question then is: Does all use of the public library arise from needs? The next question is logically derived from the first one: Are these needs recognized? Are all users rational players who know what they need or what they want? How consciously aware are people in their seeking inside the public library? Geir Vestheim calls them "users standing by the counter claiming."[8] But do all people really have a rational intention with all their use of the library? And if so, how specific is this intention? My third question is if all user needs can be satisfied by information alone. Is it really information people seek or need to be satisfied? I doubt if this is always the case.

Let us reflect one moment about what may happen inside a public library: What about the small group of immigrant boys about twelve years of age who come to play data games. Would this be an expression of "information needs"? What about the man who has popped in together with his kid on a rainy day while waiting for the bus? Is this "information needs"? And what about the woman who visits the library to get a "time-out" from her Christmas shopping, to relax with a classical work of music which she loves and which makes her calm down? Is this information needs? But this may be the very same overture that another user wants to listen to because he heard some of it on the television program "Kontrapunkt" the evening before. The latter may be said to seek information, he had a well-defined "information need"—but the woman who just wanted to relax, would that correspond to an "information need"?

And do users always have a clear intention with all of their use? When a user pops in to leaf through some magazines, does he necessarily have an intention with it? Or if, on a rainy day, a man wants to check out if the public library has a CD with a classical piece played in "Kontrapunkt," does the man then have an intention? What about spontaneous impulses? Many librarians have their professional tricks to offer the user something he had not planned on beforehand, for example, by putting books on a trolley close to the counter, thematic exhibitions and exhibitions of new books. (The librarian: "What about a talking book?" The user: "Yeah, that was a good idea.") Does our research merit from considering spontaneous use like this as "information"? I would rather dare to ask if we do not become a little bit more "poor" by these attempts to define as many human activities as possible as "information." Don't we then loose many aspects of cultural manifold? What about the genealogist, who comes to the public library, she may indeed have a well-defined need for information—but she may also seek her "roots" and her cultural identity. Her search for roots may in fact be of uttermost importance to her, but this aspect of her conduct disappears when information seeking is made the prominent term.

In addition to pointing out how questionable it may be to consider many of the activities that take place inside the public library as "information exchange," the information paradigm may also be criticized on theoretical grounds. I consider "information" as a manufactured product, a "message" that a "sender" wants to pass on to a "receiver" in a linear information (or communication) sequence. To me, information is something we consume, something that does not invite reflection. Such a one-dimensional information sequence does not incorporate the dynamic interaction relationship between the "text" (the message) and the users. Exactly this dynamic aspect, where human beings are considered as an active and meaning-creating creature, disappears in such a one-dimensional information model.[9] As a sociologist, I miss this communicative aspect of public library use as cultural practice, that is, information seen in a transactional perspective.[10] Human beings are seekers of knowledge and meaning, and the way people seek and use texts—for example, in a public library—is one of several ways to create meaning in everyday life.

I consider the concept of information in its general application as isolated from cultural context.[11] Knowledge, however, is constructed and produced by people; it cannot be seen as isolated.

The Role of the Public Library in People's Everyday Life

Knowledge in Everyday Life

I will argue that the concept of knowledge is better able to grasp what people use the public library for. Knowledge is something people themselves must acquire, and add to, in the process; knowledge is not automatically transmitted, it must also be worked on. Even factual knowledge will be marked by the communicative process, like every teacher does when she transfers knowledge to the pupils. The concept of knowledge does also have room for experiences and further refinement of knowledge.

Knowledge may be divided into several forms: professional knowledge, practical knowledge, scientific knowledge or artistic knowledge.[12] Some forms of knowledge are contribution to skills, others to human imagination. The concept of knowledge incorporates the need we have in everyday life for "cookbook knowledge," and it also incorporates people's need for knowledge about the serious and moral dimensions of existence, like life, death and love.

In everyday life several areas and dimensions in life meet. Thus, an "everyday life perspective" implies a holistic perspective with its point of departure in the notion that people actually experience daily life as a whole. For the individual, "everyday life" emerges as the sum of all the different roles one engages in (be that worker, student, parent, house builder, manager of housing cooperative [*Borettslagsformann*], social security recipient, politician, fellow being, etc.), and all the situational interactions he or she participates in during a certain period of time. In relation to library use, the point is that the distinction between literature meant for either entertainment, information or knowledge becomes less relevant, since the "whole" human being is what counts. Nor should we investigate, for example, leisure reading isolated, or information seeking (narrowly defined) isolated (as, e.g. in the sense of "students' information seeking").

Admittedly, everyday life may be analyzed in several ways. In my project, where I focus on the meaning of the public library, it is likely to apply an approach based on everyday life understood as *experience* and *life-world*, as seen "from below."[13] This is the public library as seen from the users' perspective. What is crucial is how the use of the public library is involved in everyday life projects of individuals, and how the meaning of the use of the public library is in comparison with other daily tasks. *Meaningful action* is an important notion here, which refers to phenomenal qualities of library use that quickly may be losing their essence by being quantified into statistics.

The Public Library as Public Space

The Danish cultural sociologist Dorte Skot-Hansen[14] has proposed the notion of the "culturally liberated" library as an approach to analyzing the contemporary public library. The notion implies that the public library institution has been "set free" from earlier dominating norms and values about the public library in society. According to Skot Hansen, this involves new possibilities for the public library to reconsider its activities—including serving to co-construct new local identities. She views the public library as a local resource, and claims that the public library today finds itself in a "squeeze" between mediation of culture and transmission of information.

On this basis, she has created a model of the different roles of the local public library: The public library as a *cultural center* emphasizes the public library as contextual frame for cultural and artistic experiences and performance, including arrangements, exhibitions, workshops, assembly room and rehearsal room (thus, culture as *expression*). The public library as a *center of knowledge* views the public library as contextual frame for education and general enlightenment, including facilities for studies, goal-oriented library supervision and seeking (relevant today due to educational reforms). The public library as *information center* sees the public library as an arena for information directed towards the general public as well as the rational user. This includes reference work, social information, information about the job market and the economy, tourist information and so forth, while the public library as *social center* focuses the public library as context for social encounters in everyday life, including residence, counseling, services to certain marginal groups and service to social institutions.

In my project, I have redefined the last category, and I call it the *public library as meeting place*. This is first and foremost because I am concerned with considering the public library as *public space*. This is also in line with current terminology; my impression is that it is quite common today to talk about the public library as "meeting place."

Anyway, all these roles exist side by side in the public library, but different libraries can of course choose to give priority to different roles. For me it is interesting to see how *users* use the public library and to what extent people themselves experience or think about the public library in terms of it being a "cultural center," a "knowledge center," an "information center" or a "meeting place."

As a sociologist, I am interested in what people use this public room for. The public library is a public space filled with documents, a public room without obligations which is open to anybody. Here people may come with their everyday "worries" or everyday wishes or everyday needs—in short, the "whole" of their everyday life. They may seek information or knowledge, go to the toilet, relax, recreate, participate in "adventure," meet other people, see an exhibition, surf the Internet and so on.

"In-Order-To" and "Because" Motives

To grasp what people in fact do inside this public space, the concept of action, as theorized by Alfred Schutz, is well suited. "What distinguishes action from behavior is that *action is the execution of a projected act . . . the meaning of any action is its corresponding projected act*."[15] Action is designating human behavior, developed by the actor in advance; namely, being conduct that is based on a "project." If one is to grasp the "meaning" of people's use of the public library in everyday life, such a concept of action should be applied. A person may have a project of listening to talking books at work; he thus borrows some books once a week on his way home from work. Or she may be involved in a project of mapping the family.

People as subjects may in various ways justify their projects. *In-order-to* motives refer to motivation such as "Let us get started." Seen from the viewpoint of the actor, this class of motives refers to the future.[16] *Because* motives, on the other hand, refer to the actor's previous experiences. If the user has been motivated to use the public library from childhood on, we may call this a pure because motive. But if one can say that the motive for his use is to write down genealogy, it would rather be an in-order-to motive.

Public library use is often explained in terms of because motives, for instance in relation to social background. People use the public library *because* they have done it from childhood on, *because* the public library building is located nearby in the community, *because* people have higher education, *because* they are students and so forth. Or, in other words, in experience or motives found prior to use. Admittedly, this model of explanation is what one ought to apply as long as the use is analyzed from the "outside" (externally), for example, when what one knows is that the user is a person with certain demographic traits (as in analysis of survey data). However, observation of actual use may also give suggestions of motivations in the future.

If one is to provide a because explanation of public library use, one obviously needs to ask people about their motives of the use. In my research, I have asked people about what they consider their main project in life and tried to find out what the aims of their use are.

Some Methodological Considerations

Choice of Library

How do people use the public library? How do users experience the public library? How do they interpret their use? In brief: What is the meaning of the use? Amount of use (number of visits or media borrowed) is not what is important or relevant here. Rather, what are important are the *qualities* of use. I emphasize that it is the modern library, made for contemporary uses, that concerns me here. As previously mentioned I am interested in the "culturally liberated" public library, a public library opened to various forms of use.

These premises meant that the public library in which I was to undertake observation and data collection had to be a "pleasant" place, a public space that invites many forms of use. It should also be located centrally in the community; the location must contribute to making it the public living room it aims to be (or at least have such a potential). I had to choose a public library that met these demands.

"My" public library is rather new, about three years old. Its news value has now calmed down; the use has stabilized—on a fairly high level. (It should be mentioned that the previous location was outside the center, and it was a dark and narrow library.) My public library is now located in the center of town, more precisely at the town square (the "marketplace"). The door "pulls" one inside; in a sense, one is not in doubt that one is allowed to enter—even if one does not have a particular errand there. This is not a building that demands that visits there must necessarily be legitimized. Inside the public library building one has a view out towards the town square (and with that, "the world"); outside the library building, one has a view in. This is how a public library should be, it should provide a view towards the outside world and it should yield insights.

Inside the building, there is much open space but also many small corners. In the middle, there is an inviting staircase, where people meet. The public library has three main floors plus a "semi-floor." A good view can be gained from several places inside the public library; one can easily drop in to look for friends and relatives, and there are many obvious meeting places.

The First Observations . . .

Since users use the same building in many ways simultaneously, I began by observing the users—for hours, and in systematic ways. Despite that it was autumn and quite cold, wet and windy, every morning a small crowd of about fifteen people were waiting to enter the building at one minute to 10 a.m. (To some there almost seemed to be a kind of competition to be the first to enter.) Five minutes later, the public library was filled with people and put to use. There were people to be found in almost all corners of the library, and the first fifteen people had been joined by a steady flow of users during the first opening minutes. Newspapers were read, computers had been logged into, the first users of the reading room had found their seats, the microfilms had been put to use, and people were padding about the shelves. To me this was somewhat surprising, as I had expected a rather silent period during these first hours of the day.

I observed. Who *were* these users and what did they *do*? At first, there were many old or retired people, later in the day school pupils arrived. There were students in the reading rooms, old women by the shelves filled with novels, old men reading newspapers, old men with the microfilms and immigrants on several places. Some users were regular. In the little crowd outside the building just before 9:55 a.m. there were some familiar faces. Did the retired simply want to kill time? Or perhaps they could not afford their own newspapers? And who were the immigrants? What else did they do in life, apart from sitting in front of the PC in the public library? The school pupils—did they do homework, did they meet here or did they lack a PC at home?

Several questions like this were arising. To answer them, I had to talk to users, or else my prejudices would govern my interpretations. What insights do we gain from simply watching old ladies looking at books by the shelves? And what knowledge about library use among immigrants do we gain from observing a dark-colored man in front of the PC? What kind of knowledge do we gain from observing students who read in a reading room? Reading a novel, sitting in front of the PC, reading the newspapers, picking up a preordered document, reading a microfilm and so on all have a certain meaning for the users. This meaning was what I wanted to study. By interviewing them, I would get a more detailed impression. The meaning of the use was not given; it could not be automatically read from the observations. The use must be seen in contexts, which again need to be articulated.

The Interviews

By means of observation I was able to form an idea of what kind of users I should interview. I wanted informants representing all of the locations I had observed: PC users, microfilm users, reading room users, novel shelf users and so on. To attain good and informative interviews, I needed quite competent and fluid users. The librarians helped me find and get in contact with actual users. This method of selecting the sample has obviously involved an "overrepresentation" of heavy users.

I conducted all the interviews myself. I chose "open-focused" interviews and in most cases they lasted about one hour. The idea was to orchestrate a kind of everyday conversation. I used an interview guide primarily meant as a checklist.

The interviews were tape-recorded. I have also transcribed the interviews myself, but they are only roughly analyzed yet. Hence, what follows are some preliminary "early" thoughts on use of the public library. I shall provide some small tastes of these rather raw data.

"Preanalysis"

It seems that the use of the public library may often be connected to serious existential projects in life—what people usually consider as the *most* important projects in their lives, be that studies, work (and the quality of performance at work), search for roots and identity, the struggle to find *new* roots or coherency of meaning in life, or it could be related to other forms of self-realization.

Admittedly, the student used the public library as his reading room, but not due to lack of alternatives. Database searches of literature he undertook at home, and orderings of literature were organized through his university. But he used the public library as an "office." Here he could sit in peace, while he also, on one side of the reading room, could follow life on the street, and, on the other, the silent life of the public library.

The old people were not necessarily retired as I thought at first. One of the newspaper readers who I presumed was a retired person turned out to be a journalist. He simply preferred the library as location for his daily work routine of scanning the newspapers to the locales of his own newspaper.

Immigrants varied considerably. Some had just arrived in the country; others had been here for a long time. Some wanted to stay; others wanted to go home. Some were applying for political asylum; others were refugees. Others were married into Norwegian families. And their use of the public library was almost just as heterogeneous! In addition: How can we infer that people are immigrants simply by watching them? Norwegians may also be dark looking, and adopted people are just as Norwegian as those individuals who are born in this country.

A person who was seeking political asylum came to check his e-mail, read newspapers, and to borrow children's books to train his skills in the Norwegian language. He also preferred to use the computer at the public library rather than the one at the reception camp for refugees. The public library is located in the center of town, while the reception camp is outside of town. At the public library he could also see friends. The routine of visiting the public library on a daily basis was also important to him. Another immigrant collaborated with the public library on a project of drama for children. The school pupils were using the computers to chat, sometimes with each other, sometimes with others. As one girl said, "It is sort of different to write than to talk." They were sitting quietly by the computers, while they in fact were communicating with each other, the content of this communication, however, being invisible to me as observer.

To many of those I talked to the use of the public library was connected to routine. Reading newspapers, checking e-mail, using the reading room as an office or dropping in on the way home from work. Many had fixed hours they arrived, fixed routines for their public library use.

Most of them had "always" used the public library, if not always from early childhood on. And no one had used the old public library as much as the new one. The new locales were obviously important to these users—it should be added, however, that the old ones were rather sad!

For the "heavy users" it was often dramatic events that had provoked their intense use of the public library. Dramatic events like death, illness and escape had influenced their use of the public library.

Most of them had books at home—and computers too; they had friends and relatives. Nevertheless, to them the public library represented a place to be alone together with others. As one informant said, the public library offered gluttony; she could bring home whatever she wanted without having to worry about costs. "My other home," several informants actually stated.

What if the public library did not exist? I asked. It would be very sad, they all said; life would not be the same without it. Obviously, they could have managed without it, but it would probably be very sad even though they had books at home (and computers, too). For some, life would have been quite *different*, and their life projects would have been considerably more difficult to run, as in the case of the genealogist.

Most of them found the contact with the librarians to be of relatively little importance. All of them were complimenting the librarians, and said that they were very nice and helpful. Yet according to themselves they seldom asked the librarians for advice. They preferred to operate on their own but felt safe that help could be gained if they were to ask for it.

Also, the public library is obviously used as a *meeting place* for many users at various times of the day and week. Many school pupils do their homework together, or they are engaged with group projects. Some of the younger users read. One of those I talked to mainly spent most of her time there in front of the computer, but on occasions when there were no computers available, she read a book from the shelves instead—a book that she never took home; she only read in it in-between computer activities. Users of the reading rooms often used the room with newspapers and periodicals as a resting room. These two rooms were actually located on different floors. In the newspaper room, a coffee machine and newspapers serve as fitting relaxation for the users of that reading room. In-between the shelves I found breastfeeding mothers. And on Saturday mornings, the public library obviously functioned as a meeting place for people on a trip to town. On the other hand, on weekdays the public library was largely a meeting place for school people and for some immigrants.

These are some small pieces from my relatively raw data.

Final Remarks

The public library means various things to various users. Even if they are present in the same room, where the same media are found, the public library represents different roles (or functions) to them.

For some, the public library is an *office*—this is a place where they occasionally work. For others it is a room that can be applied for *drama or exhibitions*. Some meet *people* at the public library, whether in real life or virtually. Some again go to the public library to *borrow books* in the old-fashioned way, while others use the documents inside the locale only. Furthermore, it seems like the use of the public library in many cases is part of the realization of a life project, be that passing an exam, doing a better job performance, finding one's roots or one's future, or it may simply be about attempting to create a better life!

The same use of the public library service, like borrowing a children's book, may have different meaning for different users. To a refugee, it may mean language training; for a teacher, it may be for reading aloud; for a child, it may be pure entertainment. The same document may, for one user, provide adventure and feed dreams, for others it may provide crucial information.

This is a type of knowledge that the numbers of the public library statistics do not carry, and that illustrates the need for qualitative analysis.

Further Plans for Analysis

My analytical point of departure is inductive, which means that I will attempt to develop an image of people's use of the public library and the significance of the public library in their everyday life. In other words, I will first and foremost "let the data do the talking"; consequently, my approach will be close to the empirical. My conceptual approach is relatively open. I do not want to consider the user as an *information seeker*, because I fear that this may block other aspects of use. Hence, my approach to defining the user will underscore the user as a seeker of meaning. The aim of the analysis will be to better understand the meaning of the use in the context of the meaning it has for the user. To avoid an impressionist analysis of the data, I will in my further work try to apply *grounded theory*: "The grounded theory approach is a qualitative research method that uses a systematic set of procedures to develop an inductive derived theory about a phenomenon."[17]

Notes

1 Alfred Schutz, quoted by Irving Seidman, *Interviewing as Qualitative Research: A Guide for Researchers in Education and the Social Sciences*, 2nd ed. (New York: Teachers College Press, 1988), 3-4.

2 *Borrowed Time? The Future of Public Libraries in the UK* (Stroud: Comedia, 1993).

3 *Bibliotek i Norge: For kunnskap, kultur og informasjon—utredning fra et utvalg oppnevnt ved kongelig resolusjon av 7 september 1988* (Oslo: Statens Forvaltningstjeneste, Sektion Statens Trykningskontor, 1991).

4 Marianne Andersson and Dorte Skot-Hansen, *Det lokale bibliotek: Afvikling eller udvikling* (Copenhagen: The Royal School of Librarianship, Danish Research and Development Centre for Adult Education, 1994).

5 Richard Sennett, *The Fall of the Public Man* (New York: Vintage Books, 1977).

6 Emin Tengström, *Myten om informationssamhället: Ett humanistiskt inlägg i framtidsdebatten* (Kristanstad: Rabén & Sjögren, 1987).

7 Carol C. Kuhlthau, "Inside the Search Process: Information Seeking from the User's Perspective," *Journal of the American Society for Information Science* 42, no. 5 (1991): 361-71.

8 Geir Vestheim, *Folkebibliotek i forvandling* (Oslo: Samlaget, 1992).

9 Some prefer the term *enlightenment* as an alternative to information, since enlightenment to a greater extent presupposes *active* users, *seeking* enlightenment. However, this term also lacks the communicative aspect. Even if focus here is moved to the recipient, enlightenment is still a term that sees the communication process as linear.

10 The influential Brenda Dervin is aware of this point, but she may still be criticized for drawing too heavily upon "rational actor" theory, in the sense that the meaning of the public library use is reconstructed in terms of means/ end relations. See Ellen-Merete Duvold and Gunnar Sæbø, "Tilnærminger til studiet av folkebibliotekets rolle i menneskers hverdagsliv" in *Det siviliserte informasjonssamfunn: Folkebibliotekets rolle ved inngangen til en digital tid*, ed. Ragnar Andreas Audunson and Niels Windfeld Lund (Bergen: Fagbokforlaget, 2001), 171-87.

11 George Gerbner, "Telling Stories in the Information Age" in *Information and Behavior*, ed. Brent D. Rubin (New Brunswick, N.J.: Transaction Books, 1988), 3-12.

12 Tengström, *Myten om informationssamhället: Ett humanistiskt inlägg i framtidsdebatten*.

13 Marianne Gullestad, *Kultur og hverdagsliv* (Oslo: Universitetsforlaget, 1995), 19.

14 Andersson and Skot-Hansen, *Det lokale bibliotek: Afvikling eller udvikling*.

15 Alfred Schutz, *The Phenomenology of the Social World* (Evanston, Ill.: Northwestern University Press, 1967), 61.

16 Alfred Schutz, *Hverdagslivets sociologi* (Copenhagen: Reitzel, 1975), 36.

17 Anselm Strauss and Juliet M. Corbin, *Basics of Qualitative Research: Grounded Theory Procedures and Techniques* (Newbury Park, Calif.: Sage, 1990), 24.

The Public Library as a Social Field

Henrik Jochumsen and
Casper Hvenegaard Rasmussen

The authors reflect upon the public library in a greater sociological perspective. Using Pierre Bourdieu's concept of social fields, they discuss a set of issues related to the development of the public library, particularly the development in the historically conditioned ideological concepts, which characterize the librarians; the battles, which generate a kind of internal institutional dynamics; and the scarce autonomy allowed the public library in relation to its environment. Illustrations from recent Nordic public library research are presented.

Introduction

"Excuse me, is this a library?" is probably a question few librarians have ever come across. The modern public library represents a great variety of services, but even so the local library looks very much the same as it always has, just as for most people the public library is associated first and foremost with borrowing books. In a world of change the public library might even appear as quite a stabilizing element to its users. For the librarian, as well as for other library professionals, it is, however, quite a different situation. The public library today has to deal with an explosive development in technology, media and forms of mediation, while at the same time its tasks have become diversified and are no longer exclusively associated with enlightenment and promotion of "the good book." On the contrary, the concept of a mononational cultural canon is today being challenged,[1] and the individual library as well as the individual librarian must to a greater extent orientate themselves towards a diversity of culture. And as the Danish library scholar, Leif Emerek, points out, this emancipation is counterbalanced by defining a firmer institutional identity.[2]

As external changes increase, so the demand for internal changes grows, resulting in institutional and organizational analyses being applied to a greater extent in the public library. A tool, which at the same time can be applied to unearth important characteristics about the public library as an institution and about the relations which exist between the institution and the surrounding world, is the recently deceased French cultural sociologist Pierre Bourdieu's concept of different *social fields*, that is, social "microcosmos" with particular codes of practice, values and interests. In this article we intend to apply Bourdieu's field concept as the basis for a discussion of a number of topical problems associated with the development of the public library, hoping in this way to contribute to a qualification of the debate on conditions and opportunities for the public library on the threshold of the twenty-first century. By way of introduction we shall delimit the public library from other social fields. Next, we want to identify the ideological concepts, which influence the public library, and in this context discuss the dynamics, which guarantee development within the institution. On the basis of thoughts on the public library's autonomy in relation to other fields, we will subsequently relate the library to the surrounding world. Finally, we will discuss a number of current development tendencies. We shall include recent Nordic library research, not least thoughts and results from our own research project *Library Usage between the Individual and the Institution*,[3] in which we describe and analyze the public library's institutional identity and appearance vis-à-vis the public and the way in which the public library forms part of the population's everyday lives.

It is important to stress that this article will in no way represent an exhaustive field analysis. Thus, the appearance and historical development of the field is only touched upon indirectly and sporadically. This is partly due to lack of space and partly because we consider Bourdieu's theoretical framework as a kind of "toolbox" to delve into for various analytical tools as the need arises. An approach which, by the way, is quite in accordance with Bourdieu's own very pragmatic attitude to other theorists and their works.

What Is a Public Library?

According to Bourdieu, society consists of a number of more or less independent fields, each with their own specific codes of practice, values and interests, and with different groups fighting for what should constitute the overall norms for the field. In this way a field may be regarded as a microcosmos[4] where a specific human practice takes place according to a logic which is relatively autonomous in relation to the logic of other fields. A field can, according to the focus one applies, be perceived either as a field of consumption or a field of production. In his work *The Rules of Art: Genesis and Structure of the Literary Field*[5] Bourdieu focuses on the field for artistic and cultural production in the form of an analysis of relations and positions within the literary field. A similar analysis, this time within the academic field, forms the basis for the book *Homo Academicus.*[6] Conversely in *Distinction: A Social Critique of the Judgement of Taste*[7] he directs his gaze at the consumption of art and culture, analyzing the relation between society's social structure and different classes' lifestyles and tastes. In our book *Gør biblioteket en forskel?* (Does the library make a difference?)[8] we too place the main emphasis on the use of the library, thereby examining the public library as a field of production. In the following, focus will first and foremost concentrate on the public library as a field of production.

In order to talk about an independent social field at all, an idea or a collective awareness must exist as to what belongs to the field and what lies outside it. The libraries are included as one of several activities associated with the concept of Enlightenment. Within this major cultural field the libraries can be seen as part of a smaller field which deals particularly with preservation and mediation and which, apart from the libraries, also includes archives and museums. Between these institutions there exists a roughly defined division of labor, which helps to distinguish them from each other: The archives have case documents as their primary material, while the museums have the object and the library the book.[9]

The public libraries can again be distinguished from other types of libraries whose task it is to fulfill special obligations, defined by the libraries' mother institution such as, for example, education, research or production. In the words of the Norwegian public library scholar, Ragnar Audunson,[10] the public libraries have a special history, which at the same time separates them from other libraries and creates a fundamental ideological basis. Together with other institutions, such as schools, adult education associations and cultural historical museums, the public libraries are built on ideas about democracy, public enlightenment, cultural welfare development and, at times, even about social emancipation. This political and value-based legitimization, which goes back to the establishment of the public library in the nineteenth century, forms, according to Audunson, the background for the public librarian's self-perception which is still closely associated with the role of supporting those lacking resources in relation to participation in a democracy and social mobility. Among many concrete examples of this is the librarians' view of the public libraries as key players in endeavors for a democratization of both access to and use of information technology.

Another important demarcation of the field in relation to the public library is the one towards other public organizations. Like these, the public libraries are political instruments, which have been established in order to further various political goals within cultural, educational and information policy. However, when comparing the public library with other public institutions we do observe certain marked differences.[11] First of all, the public libraries are totally dominated by a single professional group, namely librarians. This means that perspectives and ways of thinking which originate from other professions are not built into library organizations. Second, the public library does not only deliver specific products, services or solutions, but also "contextuality" which helps support the ideology-based self-perception mentioned above.

Looking at the public library from a user angle, it is interesting to note that although the public library today contains many media apart from the book, just as it has a large number of functions in the local community,[12] it is still the book collections that basically constitute the public library in the minds of the users. In the book *Gør biblioteket en forskel?* we examine people's perceptions of the public library, based on thirty-two qualitative interviews with users and nonusers. It turned out that, above all, our interviewees associated the public library with books. But at the same time it was also evident that the public library represented something else and more. Some associated the public library with more abstract and ideological concepts such as public enlightenment thought or free access to information, while others thought of the public libraries in terms of cultural activities or as a meeting place for the local community. When asking our interviewees to compare the library with other places or institutions, the following four categories emerged:

- cultural institutions, such as culture centers and museums;
- places of information and knowledge, for example, the public schools and booksellers;
- public offices, such as those for technical administration and Social Security; and
- social meeting places, for example, village halls, clubs and day centers.

In this light it was also interesting that nobody compared the public library with the Internet; as apart from being public, the Net—like the public library only in a virtual sense—also mediates information, knowledge and experiences. When this was not the case, it is probably due to the fact that the library is of great importance as a *physical* place. Thus, to the population it is the overriding concept of the library as a physical place where one borrows books which distinguishes the public library from other social fields.

Specific Characteristics of the Public Library as a Field

Apart from the specific characteristics of the public library which we have outlined already, all production fields have some overall characteristics which transverse the different fields. In order to be able to talk about an independent production field, there must be associated a specific *case logic*, that is, a specific way of relating to the activities within the field. Moreover, there will as a rule be one or more *educations*, directed at the field and which help to support a common *work ethic*. These three characteristics are both instrumental in delimiting a field in relation to its surroundings and give the field a certain kind of autonomy—the fact that the players in the field have a relatively great influence on the rules that apply within the field in question.

The common case logic attached to the public library can be observed both in relation to particular work practices in the library and to the way in which the library is run. Looking at classic library work practices such as storage, retrieval and mediation of information and knowledge, these have to a great extent become standardized in Danish public libraries. Classification and cataloguing are done according to the same rules, with each library buying the main part of their catalogue records from the same semipublic supplier, *Dansk BiblioteksCenter* (Danish Library Center), which also delivers library systems, book résumés for librarians and materials ready to be put on the shelves. All this helps to create a kind of uniformity, which is also reflected in the physical design. The basic distinction in classification between fiction and nonfiction is, for example, also a structuring principle for the organization of the libraries, as most libraries have a centrally placed counter, a reading room and a children's library. The development of this particular case logic goes back a long way and has also helped to delimit the field in relation to its environment.

The development of a common case logic originates in the ongoing development of library education. The first publicly supported courses for librarians started in Denmark in 1918. These courses lasted for three months with three to four weekly lessons, with focus on practical matters such as the design of library premises, choice of books and how to deal with the books from purchase to placement on library shelves.[13] Since then the training has been extended and changed quite radically. The latest example is the passing of the new act regarding the Royal School of Library and Information Science in 1997, where the educational program is adapted to a university structure with bachelors, postgraduates and Ph.D.s. On one hand, these changes in library education might in time alter the case logic in the libraries, as the former professional education is replaced by an academic education, while on the other hand the changes and the extension of the education can be seen as a long fight for the acknowledgement of the library profession.

At the same time, an educational program directed towards the field helps support a special work ethic among the professionals in the field. A special "public librarian ethic" does exist according to a quantitative Nordic study from 1994, which shows that the responding Danish librarians, like their Nordic colleagues, strongly reject user payment for the library's basic services and political interference in the literary choice of materials.[14] The aversion towards political interference in the libraries' choice of materials is not only an ideological reasoning in the minds of the librarians but very much apparent in practice, and there are both Danish as well as other examples from abroad of this. In Denmark one has to go back to 1977 when the cultural affairs committee in a rural local authority banned a book (for young adults, which the committee found to be of poor literary quality), from being accessioned into the library's collection. This created immense indignation on behalf of the librarians at national level and the Librarians' Union brought legal action against the local town council, stating that the council was in breach of the library act. The town council was acquitted, but since then there has been no political interference in the libraries' choice of materials in Denmark.[15] For a number of libraries in Southern France the situation is at present rather more aggravated. From 1996 and up until today, the right-wing radical party *Front National*, which holds a majority in a few Southern French municipalities, has been dictating the local libraries' choice of material. In practice this has meant that, for example, books about Jewish matters and by left-wing authors have been removed from the libraries' shelves, just as the right-wing radical municipal government has demanded that the libraries purchase more materials which disseminate anti-Semitic and right-wing views. This has provoked protests from national as well as international players in the library world—for example, the French union of librarians, the *Association des Bibliothécaires Français*, and the *European Bureau of Library, Information and Documentation Associations* (EBLIDA)—a sign of the international character of the librarian work ethic.

However, the ongoing battles for the right to personally choose the materials are not based solely on noble motives such as democracy and minority rights, it is also a fight for maintaining and extending the libraries' autonomy. In the same way, the "ventures into academia" of library education is not only a question of keeping abreast of the information society or similar statements which are often aired on festive occasions; the extended education does add more prestige to the field and provides its players with better cards in the fight for securing the field's autonomy—for example, in relation to also in the future being able to define the field's case logic internally.

The Library Doxa

A (professional) education, a particular work ethic and a certain autonomy together form the basis for what Bourdieu calls *doxa*: a field's ideological foundation which is above discussion and is therefore completely accepted by the field's central players. In other words, the axiom which is the basis for the activities of the entire field. Doxa is at one and the same time instrumental in creating solidarity within the field and acts as a shield against threats from outside the field.

An important element in the library doxa is the idealized concept that the whole population should be using the library. The reasons for this view are probably manifold: As touched upon earlier, the public library is part of enlightenment thought and was established at the beginning of the nineteenth century as an institution which could qualify the individual as citizen, subject and human being to live in modern society by offering information, knowledge and education to the entire population.[16] At the same time, the development of the public library—not only in Denmark but also in the other Nordic countries—was founded on inspiration from English and American libraries where the principles of state subsidy, rational administration and organization of the libraries went hand in hand with the concept of the whole population being the target group.[17,18] Finally, it should not be overlooked that the concept helps legitimize activity within the institution as well as in relation to the authorities empowered to award grants. The concept of the public library for all the people is manifested in those mediation strategies that have characterized the public library over the years. The librarians have increasingly tried to accommodate the users by breaking down barriers, by incorporating more popular cultural forms of expression in the choice of materials and by making the mediation altogether more user- rather than material-orientated.[19]

The Norwegian culture and library scholar, Geir Vestheim, singles out three central examples of doxa, which are in fact all closely associated with the concept of the library being for everyone: The first is the concept that the public library is an absolutely essential institution for the well-being of a democracy. The second is the concept that reading and public enlightenment have an irreplaceable value of their own, which is a welfare benefit both for the individual and for society as a whole. And the third is the concept of the public library's services being free of charge, as this, in Danish called "principle of gratis or for free," is a preconception for the public library's public enlightenment function. Particularly the last point is described as the crux of the matter in the library cause:

> The democratic and cultural political legitimacy of the public library has above all been associated with the gratis principle and being a doxa for the field it has a strong symbolic value. The symbolic importance is considerable within the field, but it is important not least in relation to society outside, which has to contribute resources to the field and benefit from the services, which the field produces. The gratis principle touches the primary interests in the field, and therefore there is a system's logic in the fact that the practitioners of the profession have been guarding this principle.[20]

The library doxa came to the fore a few years ago when a committee in the most recent Danish report on the public libraries suggested introducing user payment for a number of services. The objection in library circles was so massive and a priori that one can almost speak about a "librarian theology" which rendered impossible a discussion of the more complex aspects involved in various forms of user payment.[21] We have ourselves experienced the library doxa several times during our research, including a distinct wish by the Danish Library Association that focuses on attitudes towards the public library among the 35 percent of the population who, according to statistical investigations[22,23] do not use it,[24] should be given a higher priority than has been the case earlier.

The Battle about Doxa

A social field is marked by consensus as well as fighting between the various players within the field. In practice this can be deduced from the fact that most active players within the field are fighting for the public library to maintain and extend its position as a societal necessity, while there is some disagreement as to how this can be done in practice. The ever present discussions about quality in relation to choice of materials, the ever prominent debate on new media in the public library or discussions about introducing user payment for the public library's various services, which appear at regular intervals when the Realm is in want of money, can all be seen as a sign of various fights within the field. At any rate, the latent overall premise is that the public library plays an important societal role, while there is some disagreement as to what shape the role should actually take.

A trait common to all fields is the conflict between the established within the field and its new players. The new players always represent a certain *heterodoxy*, while the older ones, having a position to defend, primarily represent the doxa of the field. In Denmark, this became very apparent in the mid-sixties when a group of younger librarians in the periodical *Biblioteksdebat* challenged the established public library world represented by the Danish Library Association, the State Inspectorate for Public Libraries and the Librarians' Union. At the beginning, it was first and foremost a criticism directed at an old-fashioned and undemocratic library system, and the demands of the younger librarians were therefore concentrated on the introduction of democracy at work. In the late 1960s the attention turned towards the public libraries' choice of materials in the shape of a national and monocultural value system and an antipathy against a traditional (and bourgeois) literary concept. On the basis of this the group pleaded for the introduction of new genres and media into the library, such as popular literature, science fiction and beat music.[25]

Through the periodical *Biblioteksdebat* and those associated with it, the youth revolution had also broken through to the public library, and during the 1970s the rather traditional enlightenment concept, which had until then been characteristic of the public library, was now supplemented by a politicizing and sociological rationale, where the object is an emancipation of oppressed groups in society. In practice this means that librarians now begin to take into consideration the different social and cultural backgrounds of the users by focusing on possible barriers embedded in the library in relation to different target groups. This means that the mediation activities, as described earlier, move away from material- to user-orientated while at the same time the public library starts to open up for the purchase of previously rather despised popular culture.

According to Bourdieu, it is this kind of fight that guarantees a certain dynamics in the field. However, the fights are not only about different views on practice within the field but, more subtly, also about which *forms of capital* should be regarded as legitimate. Bourdieu's concept of forms of capital is closely related to what he calls the *social room*. With this concept Bourdieu replaces our intuitive perception of society with a multidimensional geometric room where individual groups of society can be seen as positions that are connected to each other. In *Distinction: A Social Critique of the Judgement of Taste*[26] one finds the most thorough description of the social room—the social room is primarily to be seen as a two-dimensional room where the position of the groups is to a great extent constituted by *economic capital*, which refers to property, income, capital and other money-related possessions, and *cultural capital*, which can be defined as the ability to master the legitimate culture's manifestations, acquired via social background and the education system.

How the different trade or professional groups are placed in the social room depends on the size of the group's share in one or the other type of capital. Those who are "at the bottom" of the social ladder have little economic and cultural capital, while those who are placed "at the top" have plenty of both. However, as a rule it is the degree of either economic or cultural capital that dominates and determines the exact position for the different professional groups. According to Vestheim, the social position associated with librarians as a professional group is first and foremost dependent on a relatively large volume of cultural capital acquired through education, as it is precisely this which gives prestige and status in society.[27]

According to Bourdieu all fields basically have a structure corresponding to the structure in the social room. At the same time the individual fields do have a relative autonomy, as they have a specific logic and require a specific constellation of capital—in Bourdieu's terms, the symbolic capital which is acknowledged or legitimate within the field. If one considers the individual public libraries as analogous to the social room, the librarians no doubt find themselves in a dominant position, as apart from being the largest professional group they also possess more capital, cultural as well as economic, than, for example, clerical staff and janitors. Especially the cultural capital is of particular importance as training as a librarian is a prerequisite for influential positions in the public libraries. In other words, cultural capital is a prerequisite for being able to enter the field as a principal player in the field, while the symbolic capital is related to the continuous fight for recognition within the field.

The fights within the field are therefore a question of the already established, who have already gained maximum amounts of acknowledged forms of capital in the field, attempting to freeze time and stop the development, so that exactly their special understanding of capital goes down in history as permanently valid.[28] The changes following in the wake of the journal *Biblioteksdebat* represent a change in the symbolic capital, which until then had primarily been founded on a national monocultural understanding,[29] now supplemented with a more relativistic attitude towards the library's materials and a sociological understanding of the relation between dissemination and user. A shift in the symbolic capital, which had gradually embedded itself in the prevailing preferences of taste within the field. This is apparent in a Norwegian study of the literary taste of public librarians in that they have a sympathetic and solidary attitude towards the tastes of the general public, while their attitude towards the academic taste is more reserved.[30] Here it is rather more a question of the previous symbolic capital in the shape of the national monoculture, as a result of continuous fights within the field, having been transformed into a more marked user orientation. But heterodox revolutionary thoughts will typically at some time become orthodox and conservative, and in this connection it is quite characteristic that key persons from the group of younger librarians associated with *Biblioteksdebat* today are all centrally placed in the Danish library world.[31]

A new "revolution" which turns the field's symbolic capital in the direction of the market-orientated becomes apparent when two young librarians, referring to a Danish futurologist's assertion that the image of a product will in future be as important as the product itself,[32] argue in favor of a new and different "lifestyle library," as, for example, "the erotic library" with cafés, exclusive coffee, Belgian chocolates and Italian magazines as one of several possible lifestyle libraries.[33]

How Autonomous a Field Is
the Public Library?

To talk about a social field in a Bourdieuan sense it has to possess a certain degree of autonomy. And as we have pointed out already, the public library is characterized by this as well. The internal fights between conservative position holders and new players in the field towards the end of the 1960s signal a certain kind of autonomy, as the fight for the right to define the field's doxa at this time took place internally in the public libraries. Likewise, the librarians' current international fights for the right to personally take care of the choice of materials can be seen as a global field's fight for maintaining and extending the public libraries' autonomy. Add to this that the minimum demand for becoming a professional player in the field is that one has obtained an acknowledged educational qualification whereby one as a student has been both introduced to and socialized in the field's doxa, just as the individual library itself makes the decision among applicants for a position advertised in their library. But according to Bourdieu, a field cannot act totally independently of its surroundings as these, in fact, define the frames of the field, while different fields, to a varying degree, have the power to expand these. Thus, the library act in Denmark provides the framework for the libraries' activities, while the individual libraries themselves can choose how to fill in these frames—for example, as regards profile, choice of materials and design.

So, there are a number of indicators that the public library field possesses a certain degree of autonomy, but not how pronounced this is. The crux of the matter is therefore to pinpoint the public library's degree of autonomy, as this seems to be a decisive factor as to what extent and in what way the surrounding world brings influence to bear on the public library.[34] And here there are many indicators that the Danish public libraries are characterized by a relatively lower degree of autonomy than the fields which Bourdieu himself has been dealing with. In concrete terms it is a question of:

- the position in the social room of the players of the field and
- the structure for the appropriation of funding to the public libraries.

As regards fields such as science and art with which Bourdieu is typically preoccupied, the central players within the library field—the librarians—are characterized by a lower volume of capital, culturally as well as economically, than is typical for players within the aforementioned fields. This relatively inferior position in the social room in which the field's central players find themselves makes the librarian vulnerable to criticism from outside. An obvious example of this is the libraries' choice of fictional material, which the literati have continuously criticized as being too demand-orientated and too inferior in quality.[35,36] It is, of course, debatable to what degree the libraries have given in to this criticism and therefore how autonomous the field really has been in relation to criticism from outside. But it is characteristic for the library as a partial field within a larger cultural field that it is players outside the library world also who determine the agenda. On the other hand, it happens very rarely that research is questioned by people outside the scientific field, or that the arts debate is influenced by players outside the ranks.

Another example of how players from outside qua their relatively high cultural capital can join and act within the library field, and moreover be able to set the agenda, is the latest Danish white paper on the public libraries.[37] The paper has been prepared by a committee consisting of eight members, only two of whom come from a library professional background, while the remaining six members were not working within the field. If one looks at the composition of other committees, councils and boards within the cultural sphere, things are very different. Here it is primarily players within the field itself who are represented. Again a plausible explanation can be that the librarians' relatively low volume of capital means that the field receives a relatively lower autonomy.

A similar tendency can be observed in the way in which the appropriation of funding takes place. Once again drawing comparisons with the fields of science and the arts, which Bourdieu has been doing, the universities have had a long tradition of self-determination, which has given them a greater degree of autonomy. Likewise, Danish arts policy, as in most other countries,[38] has been based on the arm's length principle—that politicians on behalf of the government apportion grants, while selected players within the various art forms (fields) distribute the money. A principle which clearly and unambiguously has as its objective that the field does not just distribute the means but also has the possibility of defining itself and apportion recognition internally. Although the official Danish cultural policy sets out the guidelines for the public libraries' activities in the current library acts, the libraries are governed by the local authorities in terms of financial grants, which means that they are in competition with other cultural institutions and activities. As far as the public libraries are concerned, the conclusion is once again that in relation to art and science they are, to a greater extent, subject to the (local) political agenda with the result that their autonomy is weakened. This is in fact a rather paradoxical situation for the libraries, considering that they do not receive as much public attention as, for example, art and science.

Status of the Public Library

A field's degree of autonomy is closely connected with the status given to it by the surrounding world. When science and art are two fields with a relatively high degree of autonomy, it is due to the players of these fields, qua their relatively high volume of capital, having been dealt a good hand to enable them to argue in favor of the field's societal influence and also that they possess the professional weight to maintain and extend the players of the field's right to define the field themselves. But whatever a field's degree of autonomy it will not be able to survive unless it can gather legitimacy from the surrounding world—which is particularly true for fields such as the public library, which are almost exclusively financed by the public sector. It is therefore the public libraries' social context that gives the activities within the field a high or a low status. In the following we examine the degree of recognition which the public libraries are afforded within three important areas: the public's expectations from the library, the influx of new professionals to the field and the politicians' appropriation of funding.

The "Ordinary" Library

A balanced, but not representative, picture of the public's view of the public library can be found in our own, previously mentioned, study *Gør biblioteket en forskel?* Here the interviewees are for the most part positive in their views, one of the major reasons being that the library is perceived as being a place for everyone—or for both the punk and the pensioner, as one of the interviewees puts it. The feeling that the library is a nonexclusive cultural institution is explained by the fact that the library appeals to and has something of interest for the general public as a whole—the library is seen as being completely "ordinary." One does not "stand out" by visiting the library where all members of society gather. But the library is also ordinary in the sense that most people do not even question its existence—it is just there. In other words, the library today is looked upon as a welfare benefit on a par with, for example, schools and health.

These consistent and common perceptions also influence the status which the public library is given. In order to further examine the status of the library, our interviewees were asked: Imagine the library is a car—which car would it be? Two types of cars featured prominently. The library was either compared to an older but reliable family car (e.g. a Toyota Corolla) or a bus—both vehicles regarded more as functional means of transport than status symbols. As opposed to this, museums—and particularly art galleries—as well as cultural centers were compared to more exclusive types of car such as Mercedes and Jaguar. The less-educated interviewees typically explained this by saying that these types of cars were beyond their economic means, while the well-educated motivated it by a difference in quality. On one hand it seems that the library's strength is its accessibility for every section of society, while on the other this means that the library appears less exclusive than other cultural institutions.

From Library Spinster to Knowledge Specialist

The status of the public library can also be deduced from the influx of new, professionally trained players into the field. The Royal School of Library and Information Science in Denmark, the only institution in Denmark which can award degrees in the field of librarianship and information science, has recently been conducting questionnaires in which new students have been asked about their future job expectations. There seems to be a shift in the students' prioritizations, as previously the most prevalent wish was for a job in a public library, whereas today a job in the private sector is at the top of the list.[39] One explanation of this change of attitude is the image which the public library projects to the students. A hint of this is given in the students' welcome to new students in *Rushåndbogen 1998*—an introduction to new students—from the Royal School of Library and Information Science in Copenhagen. In the words of two students:

> The role of the librarians has changed over the years. The classic image of a middle-aged woman with her hair in a bun and well-worn sensible shoes is crumbling and replaced by the image of knowledge specialists with the ability to navigate in the chaos of the information overload.[40]

This vivid description of the modern librarian's role is something more than a description of reality. It is also an indication of the wish to reformulate the image of the typical librarian—no longer do the students wish to fulfill the role associated with the classic librarian, they want to create a new and more attractive image for themselves. And in relation to this new self-perception, the work as information specialist in a private company fits in much better than a job as librarian "on the floor" in a municipal branch library.

Decentralization and Instrumentalization

The political debate does not leave a lot of room for libraries. Very rarely do libraries make the front pages of the papers, and only infrequently do they feature in the papers at all. This does not mean, however, that the libraries don't hold a certain status with the politicians. At the national level in Denmark, there is broad political consensus on the libraries' social importance. Traditionally, great importance is attached to the public library's influence on the development of democracy, as expressed in cultural political white papers and reports, and this importance has not diminished over the past few years of information technological development.[41] As it is not easy to determine the status of the public libraries from the political debate, we will examine more closely the development of the public library grants. Over the past twenty years the Danish public library policy has become decentralized, resulting in a marked differentiation of government grants to the local libraries. In 2000, the average annual grant to the public libraries was DKK 410.00 (≈$50) per inhabitant, but this figure covers considerable variations in expenses to the libraries from municipality to municipality—from DKK 47.00 (≈$6) to DKK 807.00 (≈$98) per inhabitant.[42] So it is a case of local politicians prioritizing very differently.

On top of this increased influence of local government politicians on the public libraries' activities, local cultural policy in Denmark has changed since the 1980s. Before this, local cultural policy was primarily part of a general welfare policy which aimed to make cultural opportunities available all over the country and to the entire population. With fewer public resources in the 1980s, combined with a general goodwill towards cultural life and increased "culturalization" where almost everything becomes culture,[43] current local cultural policy had to be legitimized in new ways. The result was that local cultural policy has had, to an ever greater degree, to be economically viable. The basic idea in this instrumentalization of cultural policy has been that grants destined for the cultural area should not only be viewed as expenses but rather more as cultural investments where an attractive cultural life will attract tourists, sound taxpayers and businesses.[44] This is also reflected in the municipal cultural budgets, where grants for public libraries stagnated during the period 1980 to 1995, while other cultural areas in reality have experienced considerably increased grants.[45] The status of the public libraries can therefore be said to be declining in the eyes of the local cultural politicians, just as the libraries experience increased competition from other more conspicuous local cultural institutions and events. On this basis it is hardly surprising that a new Danish investigation shows that the library directors consider the "exposure" of libraries in the political system as the major challenge in the future.[46]

Concluding Discussion and Perspectives

By way of introduction we briefly mentioned that society as well as the public library today are characterized by swift changes. And for the public library as well as for many other institutions this means that they have difficulty in defining a firmer institutional identity, as the question of what a public library is not as easy to find the answer to as it was thirty years ago. So for the libraries, too, it is necessary to take a step back and reflect upon the activities of the institution. One of several possible tools in such a process is Bourdieu's concept of the social field such as we have tried to apply to the public libraries in this article. On the basis of this we want to conclude by briefly discussing three central problems for the public libraries, which have been encapsulated through Bourdieu's field concept.

The first problem is concerned with the context of the public libraries. Here it can be ascertained that the world outside the library—that is, the population, potential new players and politicians—does not question the societal necessity of the library, while at the same time the status applied to the library is yet relatively low. New students at the Royal School of Library and Information Science prioritize other job possibilities at the expense of the public libraries, while politicians as well as the population as a whole consider other, particularly highbrow, cultural institutions as being more exclusive. At the same time there is a crucial difference in the way the public library's status is interpreted by politicians and population, respectively. In connection with the increased instrumentalization of publicly supported local cultural life, cultural centers, festivals and spectacular designs seem to be more useful for positioning oneself than do the public libraries. As we have mentioned earlier, the libraries are seen by the population as being functional and ordinary, just as they are taken for granted, which does not fit well into a cultural policy increasingly concentrating on image— and a Jaguar is more likely to create an image than a bus. The demands on the libraries are thus rather contrary: Politicians are looking for an image-creating cultural policy while the population basically considers the library's strength and justification to be due to the fact that it is a nonexclusive cultural institution which appeals to and has something of interest to offer to every section of society. One of the most important future challenges for the public libraries is therefore how to act in response to this complex surrounding world. This is going to be no easy task, as the relation between general necessity and the exclusive seems to be inversely proportional.

Another central problem, illustrated by the field analysis, is the identification of the prevailing consensus on the field's ideological foundation as expressed in the concept doxa. Basic attitudes, which are common to all players in the field, in the case of the public libraries result in an unshakeable faith in the inherent value of reading, the library's importance in relation to democracy and the gratis principle. Although doxa is characterized by languor and stability it should not be looked upon exclusively as an unalterable entity. On the contrary, it is a result of players having obtained a maximum volume of the recognized forms of capital in the field, attempting to have their special composition of capital forms go down in history as eternal, while at the same time new players in the field are predisposed to oppose the dominant positions if they want a dominant position themselves. A condition common to all fields of production which, as far as the public libraries are concerned, shows itself most clearly around 1970, when some of the new generation of librarians challenged the prevailing symbolic capital in the field. This took the shape of a revolt against the national monocultural focusing on the literary canon's representation in the library's materials, which on the initiative of the young librarians has been replaced by a more pluralistic quality concept and greater focus on the users and their preferences. Thus, user orientation has today become part of the librarian doxa. According to Bourdieu, it is this continuous fight between domineering position-holders (the orthodox) and new players (the heterodox) that guarantees the field a certain dynamics. But looking at the public library in the early 1970s, such internal conflicts concerning the field's symbolic capital might be difficult to discern. Although younger librarians have argued in favor of a new and more image-creating library, and although since the 1980s more focus has been directed at the market-orientated—for example, the libraries' services to business in the private sector—such debates and initiatives within the field must be considered more as a sideline than a true fight for the right to define the field's symbolic capital. One explanation for the lack of internal conflicts, and thereby also dynamic, might be that the influx of new librarians into the field since the 1980s has been limited, with the result that the librarians presently employed in the public libraries form a very homogeneous group. There are some indications, however, that we shall witness increased internal fighting for the public library's doxa. First of all, quite a substantial number of librarians will be retiring within the next ten years. Second, the fact that library professional education now has the same status as a university education. An increased influx of new players into the field with a different educational background could mean renewed internal fights about the field's doxa. And third, the most recent Danish library act has made it possible that library directors no longer need to be qualified librarians—which means that new players with a dominant position can enter the field with an ideological foundation different to the one into which professional librarians have been socialized.

A third central problem in relation to the public libraries that becomes more perceptible through Bourdieu's field concept is the question of the libraries' relative autonomy. The field public libraries are characterized by a relatively low degree of autonomy, as the central players of the field, the librarians, are characterized by a relatively low

volume of capital, while at the same time the structure for the appor-
tioning of financial means has brought the public libraries into increased competition with other local cultural initiatives. The consequences of a certain lack of autonomy have meant that the public
libraries in relation to other fields, such as science and art, have found it
more difficult to define their activities themselves. This might also
partly explain why there have been no major fights for the right to
define the field's symbolic capital since the generation feud around
1970. The public libraries have been under pressure from the outside
world, which has initiated many and diversified changes like the introduction of new information technology, altered administrative practices
and an instrumentalization of the cultural policy. These changes
brought about from the outside have demanded considerable resources
and qua their relatively low volume of capital librarians have found it
hard to put their personal mark on these changes. This tendency seems,
however, not to be purely a Danish phenomenon, as the Norwegian
library scholar, Ragnar Audunson, concludes in a study of processes of
change in a major Norwegian, Swedish and Hungarian public library,
respectively: Environmental changes decide, but field-norms count.[47] If
one therefore wants both to understand and to discuss changes in the
public libraries in the future, it is important to further investigate the
field's relative autonomy, as it is imperative both in a scholarly context
and for the actual players in the field to know which game is being
played and which rules actually apply.

Notes

1 Ragnar A. Audunson, "Folkebibliotekenes rolle i en digital framtid:
Publikums, politikernes og bibliotekarenes bilder," in *Det siviliserte
informasjonssamfunn: Folkebibliotekenes rolle ved inngangen til en digital tid*,
ed. Ragnar A. Audunson and Niels Windfeld Lund (Bergen: Fagbokforlaget,
2001), 206-24.

2 Leif Emerek, "At skrive bibliotekshistorie: Om grundlæggelsen af det
moderne folkebibliotek i Danmark," in *Det siviliserte informasjonssamfunn:
Folkebibliotekenes rolle ved inngangen til en digital tid*, ed. Ragnar A.
Audunson and Niels Windfeld Lund (Bergen: Fagbokforlaget, 2001), 88-117.

3 Part of this is published in: Henrik Jochumsen and Casper Hvenegaard
Rasmussen, *Gør biblioteket en forskel?* (Copenhagen: Danmarks Biblioteks-
forenings Forlag, 2000). For a summary in English, see Henrik Jochumsen and
Casper Hvenegaard Rasmussen, "Does the Library Make a Difference? New
Danish Study on the Impact of the Public Library," *Scandinavian Public Libraries
Quarterly* 33, no. 4 (2000): 19-22.

4 Pierre Bourdieu, *Practical Reason* (Cambridge: Polity Press, 1998).

5 Pierre Bourdieu, *The Rules of Art: Genesis and Structure of the Literary Field* (Cambridge: Polity Press, 1995).

6 Pierre Bourdieu, *Homo Academicus* (Cambridge: Polity Press, 1988).

7 Pierre Bourdieu, *Distinction: A Social Critique of the Judgement of Taste* (London: Routledge, 1986).

8 Henrik Jochumsen and Casper Hvenegaard Rasmussen, *Gør biblioteket en forskel?* (Copenhagen: Danmarks Biblioteksforenings Forlag, 2000).

9 Geir Vestheim, *Kultur, fornuft og velfærd: Ein Historisk-sociologisk studie av norsk folkebibliotekspolitik* (Oslo: Det Norske Samlaget, 1997).

10 Ragnar A. Audunson, *Change Processes in Public Libraries: A Comparative Project within an Institutionalist Perspective* (Oslo: Høgskolen i Oslo, 1996).

11 Audunson, *Change Processes in Public Libraries: A Comparative Project within an Institutionalist Perspective.*

12 See, for example, Dorte Skot-Hansen, "The Local Library: Its Profile and Anchorage." *Scandinavian Public Library Quarterly* 29, no. 1 (1996): 4-7.

13 Ole Harbo, *Bibliotekaruddannelse i Danmark i 75 år: 1918-1093* (Copenhagen: Danmarks Biblioteksskole, 1993).

14 Johannes Balslev and Kerstin Rosenqvist, *Bibliotekaren og samvittigheden: En rapport om nordisk bibliotekar-etik* (Fakse Ladeplads: JB information management, 1994).

15 Poul Andersen et al., *Fra Thisted til Christansborg: En absolut underlødig historie* (Copenhagen: Bibliotek 70, 1979).

16 Leif Emerek, "At skrive bibliotekshistorie: Om grundlæggelsen af det moderne folkebibliotek i Danmark," 88-117.

17 Gunhild Salvesen, "Hva kjennetegner kvalitetsarbeidet i norske folkebibliotek?," in *Det siviliserte informasjonssamfunn: Folkebibliotekenes rolle ved inngangen til en digital tid*, ed. Ragnar A. Audunson and Niels Windfeld Lund (Bergen: Fagbokforlaget, 2001), 246-68.

18 Lis Byberg and Øivind Frisvold, "Hvorfor folkebibliotek? Et tilbakeblikk på bibliotek og politisk legitimering ved tre hundreårsskifter," in *Det siviliserte informasjonssamfunn: Folkebibliotekenes rolle ved inngangen til en digital tid*, ed. Ragnar A. Audunson and Niels Windfeld Lund (Bergen: Fagbokforlaget, 2001), 63-85.

19 Bruno Kjær and Anders Ørom, "Forvandlingsbilleder og biblioteks-kulturelle identiteter: 1. del," *Biblioteksarbejde* 12, no. 34 (1991): 33-43.

20 Geir Vestheim, *Kultur, fornuft og velfærd: Ein Historisk-sociologisk studie av norsk folkebibliotekspolitik* (Oslo: Det Norske Samlaget, 1997), 422. Our translation.

21 Charlotte Egholm and Henrik Jochumsen, "Perspectives Concerning User Fees in Public Libraries." *Library Management* 21, no. 6-7 (2000): 298-306.

22 Torben Fridberg, *Fra eliteforbrug til masseforbrug: Interessen for kultur 1964-1993* (Copenhagen: Socialforskningsinstituttet, 1997).

23 Torben Fridberg, *Kultur- og fritidsaktiviteter 1998* (Copenhagen: Socialforskningsinstituttet, 2000).

24 There is no doubt that the "nonuser" as a rule within the field is seen as locked in social poverty and intellectual darkness because of his lack of knowledge as to the possibilities that the public library offers. In this connection it must be said, however, that our study of the importance of the public library in people's everyday lives shows that the group of nonusers in Denmark is not a definite and socially stigmatized quantity, as the use of the library may in fact vary greatly during different phases of one's life. See Jochumsen and Hvenegaard Rasmussen, *Gør biblioteket en forskel?*

25 Claus Secher, "Folkebibliotekerne og den litterære kvalitetsdebat i Danmark," in *Litteratursociologi*, ed. Erland Munch-Pedersen (Ballerup: Dansk BiblioteksCenter, 1995), 150-72.

26 Bourdieu, *Distinction: A Social Critique of the Judgement of Taste.*

27 Geir Vestheim, "Bibliotek som sosialt felt." *Syn og Segn* 100, no. 1 (1994): 65-75.

28 Margaretha Järvinen, "Pierre Bourdieu," in *Moderne og klassisk samfundsteori*, ed. Heine Andersen and Lars Bo Kaspersen (Copenhagen: Hans Reitzels Forlag, 2000), 342-63.

29 In Denmark, as in the other Nordic countries, there has not traditionally been a sign of equation between the formation culture and the so-called highbrow culture. As opposed to, for example, France, the legitimate formation culture has been integrated into a mutual cultural understanding based on a democratic bearing where cultural currents outside the highbrow culture have been incorporated (see Vestheim, *Kultur, fornuft og velfærd: Ein Historisk-sociologisk studie av norsk folkebibliotekspolitik*, 1997). Examples of this are various cultural expressions related to both labor movement and the public enlightenment tradition inspired by the Danish priest and author Grundtvig.

30 Jofrid Karner Smidt, "Bibliotekarens smak og litteraturformidlingens normer," in *Det siviliserte informasjonssamfunn: Folkebibliotekenes rolle ved inngangen til en digital tid*, ed. Ragnar A. Audunson and Niels Windfeld Lund (Bergen: Fagbokforlaget, 2001), 292-317.

31 Pierre Evald, "Biblioteksdebat 1965-1970: A Library Journal for the Danish Anti-Establishment Movement." *Journal of Swedish Library Research* 14, no. 3 (2002): 146-55.

32 Rolf Jensen, *The Dream Society* (New York: McGraw-Hill, 1999).

33 Bettina Graabech and Susanne Gilling: "Fremtidens bibliotek." *Danmarks Biblioteker* no. 7 (September 2000): 4-5.

34 Pierre Bourdieu, *Af praktiske grunde: Omkring teorien om menneskelig handlen* (Copenhagen: Hans Reitzels Forlag, 1993).

35 Anne Lise Japsen, *Biblioteket og den gode bog* (Copenhagen: Gyldendal, 1992).

36 Claus Secher, "Folkebibliotekerne og den litterære kvalitetsdebat i Danmark," 150-72.

37 Kulturministeriet, *Betænkning om bibliotekerne i informations samfundet*. Udvalget om Bibliotekerne i Informationssamfundet (UBIS). Betænkning nr. 1347 (Copenhagen: Kulturministeriet, 1997).

38 Harry Hillman-Chartrand and Claire McCaughey, "The Arm's Length Principle and the Arts: An International Perspective—Past, Present and Fu-

ture," in *Who's to Pay for the Arts? The International Search for Models of Arts Support*, ed. Milton C. Cummings Jr. and J. Mark Davidson Schuster (New York: ACA Books, 1989), 43-80.

39 Charlotte Egholm, *De nye bachelorstuderende årgang 2000* (Copenhagen: Danmarks Biblioteksskole, 2001).

40 *Rushåndbogen 1998* (Copenhagen: Danmarks Biblioteksskole, 1998), 5.

41 See, for example, Kulturministeriet, *Betænkning om bibliotekerne i informationssamfundet*.

42 Biblioteksstyrelsen, *Folkebiblioteksstatistik 2000* (Copenhagen: Biblioteksstyrelsen, 2001).

43 Hans Fink, "Et hyperkomplekst begreb: Kultur, kulturbegrebet og kulturrelativisme I," in *Kulturbegrebets kulturhistorie*, ed. Hans Hauge and Henrik Horstbøll (Århus: Århus Universitetsforlag, 1988), 9-23.

44 Dorte Skot-Hansen, "Between Identity and Image: Holstebro as a Model for Cultural Policy." *The International Journal of Cultural Policy* 5, no. 1 (1998): 149-67.

45 Finansministeriet et al., *Folkebibliotekernes økonomi 1980-1995: En undersøgelse af statens og (amts-)kommunernes udgifter til folkebibliotekerne og kulturområdet generelt i perioden 1980-1995* (Copenhagen: Kommune-information, 1997), 20.

46 Carl Gustav Johannsen and Niels Ole Pors, *Ledere og ledelse i danske biblioteker* (Copenhagen: Bibliotekarforbundet, 2001).

47 Ragnar A. Audunson, *Change Processes in Public Libraries: A Comparative Project within an Institutionalist Perspective*.

Users' Library Discourses[1]

Sanna Talja

Using a discourse analytic research approach, users' interpretations of the social and cultural role of music libraries are examined. Three interpretative repertoires were identified from interviewed users' talk: the general education repertoire, the alternative repertoire and the demand repertoire. Diversity, quality and equality are central concepts in all library talk, but their meaning is contextually and ideologically defined. It is concluded that the library is as multifaceted an institution for users as it is for librarians, which poses a problem for the planning of user-centered library services.

Introduction

The majority of librarians nowadays emphasize that libraries should focus on the needs of their users and communities.[2] However, users' views of how public libraries should operate, of what users regard as good library service and selection principles, have received surprisingly little attention. There are a number of studies which tap user responses to library services of all kinds, but users are usually asked to evaluate services "as they are." User studies tend to concentrate on aspects such as user satisfaction, service quality, and, most commonly, information needs. Susan Edwards and Mairead Browne[3] note that although it is generally considered as important that users are asked for their views, it is usually on terms dictated by librarians.

While service quality, user satisfaction and user needs are all undoubtedly important and legitimate research interests, such conceptualizations assign users but limited roles and responsibilities in relation to library services. Michael Harris[4] points out that the professional discourse of the library field rarely questions librarians' professional autonomy in the definition of service principles. It is not assumed that users would want to, or have the competence to, discuss library policy and practice.[5] Similarly, Gary Radford states that in the professional discourse of library and information science, "Library and user are separate domains; the library is the domain of order and the user the domain of ambiguity."[6] There is a need for research which looks at libraries and librarians from the users' viewpoint. This article reports the results of a qualitative interview study that examines how music library users interpret the social and cultural role of music libraries.

In this study, library users were assigned the role of cultural experts in relation to library services. This means that the participants were asked the same kinds of questions one would normally ask a librarian (e.g. "What in your opinion should be taken into account when selecting records for the library collection?"). Moreover, users' interview talk is analyzed as serious speech acts.[7] As producers of research data, users are not seen as "just" users whose opinions are in themselves interesting but not based on specialized knowledge about the library institution. Users are in the role of competent interpreters of library culture and music culture.

This article also compares users' library discourse to professional library discourse. The claims made about librarians' professional discourse are based on official and semiofficial music library policy statements, studies made on music librarians' conceptions of music libraries' role and purpose[8] as well as an extensive collection of texts representing professional library discussion in Finland in the 1980s and 1990s. There are no important differences in the professional library discourses of Nordic countries and the United States, as the professional norms and standards of Scandinavian libraries imitate those of their Anglo-American sister institutions.[9]

This study was conducted in the Finnish music library setting. The results of the study, however, are for several reasons of greater general interest. First, the interview talk described in this article represents culture talk indicating how library users define the cultural values that should guide library collection development. Second, although the interview talk reported in this article concerns music and records, the same distinctions and categorizations (e.g. commercial/noncommercial) are utilized in all fields of art. Thus, the same distinctions and starting points emerge in discussions on book selection.

Third, in qualitative research, the generalizability of research results does not depend on the sample and data-gathering procedures but on the method of analysis and the formulation of research questions.[10] The questions put to nonrepresentative samples must, in themselves, contain a generalizing operation so that the interpretative framework developed to explain the research results can be applied also to other cases.[11] In this study, the user interviews are analyzed from a macrosociological perspective, which means that the principal unit of analysis is not the individual but linguistic forms. The analysis concentrates on users' ways of talking in order to identify and systematize the interpretative repertoires through which users give meanings to the music library. The purpose of this paper is to identify the discourses present in users' library talk.

The first section of the paper describes the research setting, the selection of participants and the method of analysis. The second section describes the three interpretative repertoires identified from users' library talk: the general education repertoire, the alternative repertoire and the demand repertoire. The third section discusses the implications of the findings for public library planning.

Research Setting

In Finland, the expression music library generally refers to public libraries' music departments, whose service principles correspond with those of public libraries in general. Finnish public libraries' music departments or music collections consist of records and sheet music acquired for lending purposes, often accompanied by reference collections, reference services, and listening facilities.

The users who participated in the study are regular music library users, most of whom have visited more than one music department. The study's limitation is that no nonusers were included in the sample. On the other hand, the participants represent a socially heterogeneous group. In the selection of interviewees, my objective was to ensure that as wide a range of musical, educational and age backgrounds as possible would be represented in the sample. I selected the interviewees strategically by observing users in the library and by asking suitable "targets" to consent to being interviewed. The majority of the twenty-three participants are "ordinary" music library users. Six of them are more professionally involved with music. The sample includes rock fans, opera fans, occasional listeners, music students, musicians, journalists, teachers, workers at a nearby postal center, unemployed people, nurses and so on.

In order to further ensure variability in the sample, I conducted the interviews in two different music departments of the Helsinki City Library. The Töölö branch library is the oldest music library in Finland. It is frequented by music students due to its extensive reference collections of records and sheet music. The Pasila music department was founded in the mid-1980s and is mostly used by youthful borrowers of CDs.

The interviews varied in length from half an hour to one-and-a-half hours. I conducted them in the two music departments' listening rooms, recorded and later transcribed them. I first asked the participants to describe their personal music library experiences and their patterns of music library use. Thereafter, I asked them to state their views about music library service principles. In the second part of the interviews, I asked the participants about their personal relationships to music and about their opinions on music culture and musical life. In this article I analyze the interviewees' ways of talking about library service principles. However, the participants' statements about music, music culture and musical life have also influenced my interpretations. The participants, in turn, viewed the interview as a welcome opportunity to influence the two music departments' material selection. The interviewed users turned out to have measured and clear views of library policy and practice.

Discourse Analysis

The terms *interpretative repertoire*[12] and *discourse*[13] are near synonyms. The identification of interpretative repertoires is the aim of discourse analysis, and a repertoire is a named discourse.[14] The concept "interpretative repertoire" is important because it distances us from the way we have learned to interpret people's talk in normal everyday life. Library users' opinions are many times in themselves interesting, but they still should not be interpreted as straightforward reports about how users really think.[15] Discourse analysis differs significantly from more familiar methods of analyzing qualitative interview data, as it does not aim at capturing individual participants' meanings, opinions or attitudes.[16]

Interview talk basically represents participants' interpretation work concerning the topic in question, and this interpretation work is much more variable and multidimensional than is normally recognized in handbooks of qualitative research.[17] When talking about the library, participants do not only produce a neutral description and express their opinion. They produce a version of the library, and this version contains an evaluation.[18] Thus, the library does not exist as a neutral, stable entity of which different users simply have different opinions and experiences. Speakers construct "the library" in their interview talk as a specific kind of institution, and their opinions and attitudes concern these specific formulations, context-dependent versions of the library.

Descriptions, evaluations and large-scale cultural models of accounting are inseparably bound together.[19]

Over an entire interview, it is often exceedingly difficult to reconstruct or summarize the participant's view,[20] because not only do different actors tell different stories but, as Bernd Frohmann[21] has shown in his analysis of Melvil Dewey's writings, each speaker has many different voices. Interview talk is the weighing of different views concerning the topic in question, and in a longer interview, the speaker takes variable viewpoints into consideration and, in their connection, expresses variable views. When the same phenomenon is approached from different angles, different aspects of it come into sight and assume a privileged position. Thus, the variability of interpretations does not mean that there is no regularity at all in participants' discourse; it only signifies that regularity cannot be pinned down at the level of the individual speaker.[22] In similar conversational contexts, similar arguments and explanations tend to be used. At a certain point in history, the meanings that can in reality be produced are limited. As interview answers are produced with the help of shared linguistic resources, they are cultural and collective phenomena.

In discourse analysis, the researcher abandons the assumption that there is only one truly accurate version of participants' views. The basic research strategy of the analysis of interpretative repertoires is the systematic examination of context-dependent variability in talk and texts.[23] The discourses existing in a particular field can be discerned on the basis of the interpretative conflicts, or points of incompatibility, present in the texts under study.[24] The search for the pattern of repertoires includes three phases. The first phase consists of the analysis of inconsistencies and internal contradictions in the answers of one participant. The second phase consists of the identification of regular patterns in the variability of accounts: recurring descriptions, explanations and arguments in different participants' talk.[25] The end-point of analysis is the systematic linking of descriptions, accounts and arguments to the viewpoint from which they were produced, and the naming of the different interpretative repertoires—usually by concepts recurring in participants' talk and tending to be used when the topic is approached from a particular angle.

According to Michel Foucault, we can speak of a discourse when we can discern a limited viewpoint on the basis of which the objects and themes of talk are selected and common concepts are defined.[26] The term *discourse* refers expressly to perspectives. Discourses do not consist merely of single meanings or interpretations: they are knowledge formations, entities that provide an effective and limited lens for producing knowledge about a topic.[27] Analyzing discourses means analyzing background assumptions which are rarely voiced but are implicitly a part of a particular way of talking about things.[28]

The different starting points of discourses are discernible from the way common concepts are understood and defined. Language contains only a limited number of concepts, and words like *demand, civilization* or *culture* have divergent meanings in different discourses and contexts of speaking.[29] Terms that have been linked together on a basis of a particular background assumption lose their link on the basis of a different assumption and are linked to other words.[30] Analyzing discourses involves analyzing the selection, linkage and ordering of terms.[31]

In discourse analysis, interviews are thus not interpreted as stories having a clear message and meaning, instead all the descriptions and accounts produced by the participants are taken into consideration and analyzed in order to identify significant patterns of consistency and variation in ways of classifying and categorizing phenomena.

Findings

Diversity Ethics

On the surface level, participants' talk about the function and service principles of the music library is uniform and represents what I call diversity talk. When participants are asked on what grounds they think music materials should be acquired for the library collection, they stress without exception that no group should be excluded from library services, and that all musical genres and all possible tastes should be represented in the collection. Participants generally take music libraries' historical "classical line" as the object of comparison against which they formulate their own stands. The "classical emphasis" is either opposed, or the strong position of classical music is considered self-evident and natural. Even in the latter case, participants emphasize that the centrality of classical music may not mean the undervaluation of other musical genres.

> *Question:* What do you think should be taken into account when records are selected for the collection?
> *Answer:* Of course, all kinds of music should be acquired. It is not possible to draw limits "this isn't needed, this is needed more," there must be everything. Because there are all kinds of us people, and we listen to all kinds. (Interviewee 21)

The diversity principle is so consistently stressed in users' library talk that it may even be called diversity ethics. Users make as clear a division between their own private tastes and preferences and more general service principles, as do librarians. The contradiction between private desires and interests (the personal wish for a "deep" collection in the user's own interest area) and the diversity principle is without exception resolved by giving priority to the diversity principle.

The participants, however, understand well that as library funds effectively preclude having everything, it is necessary to take a stand on what kinds of materials are essential and less essential in the library collection. In different contexts of discussion, the prioritizing is done from different angles, and the library's cultural role is defined differently. Closer analysis of participants' talk reveals that despite the principled pluralism and tolerance of diversity talk, users, in fact, hold different views about what a "diverse" and "balanced" collection is like.

Librarians similarly emphasize that collections should be balanced.[32] In fact, *diversity*, *equality* and *quality* are words that are consistently used in the description of library service policies. Generally, when these words are used in professional library discourse, it is assumed that their content is self-evident, that all discussants understand their meaning in the same way. Otherwise it would make no sense, for instance, to state that "music libraries offer qualitative diversity for those in need."[33] When library policy documents state that "libraries must contain a diverse collection of music,"[34] or that "quality music from every genre must be selected to the library collection,"[35] they manifest an assumption that after reading these statements, it is clear for everyone what kind of music is selected for the collection.

"Diversity," "equality" and "quality" are "essentially contested concepts"—the same positively loaded words are used to crystallize and legitimate heterogeneous ideas about collection development.[36] For instance, in the music library policy statements of the late 1950s and early 1960s, diversity meant providing the audience a full picture of the breadth and length of "the giant tradition of Western concert music."[37] Forms other than classical, folk and "good jazz" were classified as entertainment music to be excluded from the library collection. It was considered that as the Library Law defined the library's task as the "fulfillment of the general need for education," government subsidies could not be used for the acquisition of "music material of inferior value."[38] By contrast, in the 1986 Handbook of Music Library Activity[39] the diversity principle meant that the objective of the music library is to make visible the diversity of the field of music. In the following, I focus on the way the common concepts of diversity, quality and demand are defined when music libraries' role is approached from different viewpoints.

The General Education Repertoire

In the general education repertoire, music library work is approached from the viewpoint of music education and study. In this context of discussion, the history of music provides the central material for collection building. The central idea in the general education repertoire is the existence of a "basic repertory" or "basic collection." The nature of music library collections is understood to be such that they contain "the central pillars and artists" of each musical genre.

> *Question:* What, in your opinion, should be taken into account in selecting records for the library collection?
> *Answer:* Of course, in the record collection and in the service, there are certain educational considerations librarians can influence what kind of music people come to know. And it is pretty essential that because of the structure of the collection, the user would tend to gain a sensible conception of musical styles and types and how they have evolved throughout the ages. A lot of people probably come here just looking for something nice to listen to, light entertainment. That need cannot necessarily be satisfied that well, because it is not the music library's most essential task. Those kinds of users are pretty frustrating because the records are such that they are left in the shelves; nobody wants to listen to them later. If we think about the general education necessary for people—then there should be an extensive basic collection in all categories. Librarians should know the central pillars and artists that at least should be in the collection in order for it to be representative and library-like. And of course, it is part of the library's role that all recordings of domestic contemporary music are acquired. Instead of all the surface phenomena, which are probably frequently requested by the clients. Popular music is such an immensely huge field, that it is pretty difficult to realize all the users' wishes. In light music, after all, the important records live longer, and it cannot be known when the record is released what its meaning is going to be. And the library sector is not the kind to be most in keeping with the times. It is not the library's task at all to operate on a monthly schedule. (Interviewee 4)

The general education repertoire contains a culture historical perspective on collection work. When participants approach music libraries as history institutions, they typically stress the need for strict material selection principles. The music library's role is to "offer the taxpaying population at least some kind of cultural basis." It is an institution that "educates by its very existence" and "is about being uplifted and looking for something higher." The music library is defined as a cultural and educational institution whose purpose is not only to meet users' demands but also to "guide them towards higher destinations." The library's social role is viewed through the ladder theory[40] according to which individuals become socialized as library users via materials that are familiar to them, and gradually develop the cultural competence to select more versatile and demanding materials.

When this repertoire is used, participants typically argue that other channels (radio, music stores) serve sufficiently well those whose listeners whose musical taste and need is one-sidedly oriented towards the music of the day. Demand is assumed to focus primarily on commercial "surface music." A central feature of the general education repertoire is the assumption of the existence of a conflict between demand and quality. It is considered that the attempt to satisfy demand on a larger scale would take place at the expense of the quality and endurance of the collection.

> One possibility would of course be that the library would ask the users "what do you want" and act according to that. In that case the collection would surely be quite different than it is now. It is certain that classical music would not do well. Another possibility would be to see to it that of all the music that is made, users can follow what happens and what has happened in history. (Interviewee 13)

In the general education repertoire, classical music is considered to be the most important form of music culture. This does not entail a conception that, for example, jazz and rock music do not represent culture or art. Altogether seven of twenty-three interviewees were of the opinion the proportion of classical music in acquisitions should be 50 percent or more. The classical emphasis is natural when music library work is approached from the viewpoint of music education and study, as the training provided by state-supported music schools and institutes primarily (although not exclusively) focuses on classical music. In the general education repertoire the music library is viewed as an institution that is an essential part of the system of music education. The music library's task is to function as a "study material center," and meeting the needs of music students is considered more important than meeting "the demand for entertainment."

In the general education repertoire, the music librarian is perceived as an expert on music. In this discussion context participants usually assume that music librarians are required to have a degree in musicology. In this repertoire they also assign music librarians an instructive role in relation to music library clients. Librarians should, in principle, actively market high-quality materials. Users' demand is viewed as a question of personal preferences, while librarians, by virtue of their professional training, are understood to have the ability to distinguish quality music from surface music. The concepts "basic collection" and "classics" contain the assumption that the lasting value of a cultural phenomenon or product will be proved by history. Conclusions about the quality and cultural value of cultural products are, as it were, inevitable and indisputable historical facts.

The Alternative Repertoire

The alternative repertoire appears in users' interview talk in a context in which the library's material selection principles are compared to other channels' music supply. In this repertoire, the music library's function is to supplement other music provision channels. The music library is spoken of as a "cradle of counterculture," a "counterbalance" and an "alternative to mass culture." In this repertoire, the music library has an alternative nature in relation to the supply of commercial channels, which is considered to be narrow. The task of music libraries is to fill the gaps left in the general supply of music by taking care of the availability of rarer and marginal music. Music libraries offer people the opportunity to become acquainted with the picture of music as a whole, and thus guarantee that "people really can choose."

In the alternative repertoire, too, the object of comparison and opposition is the vision of a music library in which selection follows the current supply and the majority's musical tastes. In this repertoire it is presumed that both the general supply and consumption of music are clearly weighted towards the music that is most publicized, easily available through the radio, Music Television (MTV) and record stores. The alternative repertoire is characterized by its emphasis on "counter cultural" and "minority" phenomena.

> *Question:* How do you find this collection as a whole?
> *Answer:* What kind of bothers me is the happy mean, that you can't easily find different things. There is less newer music, experimental music. One would wish more ethnic music, world music, more special—not the mainstream.
> *Question:* According to what principles do you think recordings should be chosen for the collection?
> *Answer:* At least one principle should be the demand. It must not all be like that, somehow educational or representing good taste, that it would be only classical music, or classics. Let's say maybe half of this that has the most demand, and half of this more special music from different areas that cannot be easily found in stores and is not publicized much. Because, for instance, from the radio you can nowadays hear so much and any kind of music, and what you hear

less is—indie bands or those outside the mainstream. It would be a good choice of line for the library, if it could supplement this supply, because rock and classical can be heard ears full. There are some essential things not seen here—I'm again speaking of—if we think about rock music, bands that do not represent big record companies—that are independent or even privately published. (Interviewee 2)

In this context, quality is linked with experimentality and novel phenomena. The supply of "the happy mean," a line of selection that is based on "instructive" and "conventional" choices, on familiarity and predictability, is criticized. Libraries should "take risks" and "provide surprises." In addition to mainstream music, "the classics" of classical and rock music are mentioned as the music that could be acquired less because of their familiarity. However, speakers who prioritize the provision of "rarities" and "specialities," without exception, state that music favored by the majority should also be offered. "Demand" is constructed as something that is likely to follow the trends of media publicity, but it is considered that too extravagant a supply of alternatives would banish the youth and more passive listeners from the library. "Diversity" means balancing between the structure of the clientele's interests and quality criteria. This repertoire, too, is based on the supposition of the existence of a contradiction between quality and demand— users' demand is believed to concentrate on hit music and mass music, whereas quality music is alternative and minority music.

The music library's purpose in this repertoire, too, is to broaden the users' musical horizons, but it is based on a different idea of "culture" than the general education repertoire. The ideal is that "people find their own thing," become specialized fans rather than passive receivers of "predigested" music. It is considered that music libraries can play a role in the strengthening of the music listener's "cultural identity."

As there are marginal areas in each musical genre, there is no clear consensus among the participants on what is "alternative" and "special." For instance, some interviewees say that as classical music is not commercially successful, it is in a minority position in music culture and should be supported. However, the alternative repertoire differs from the general education repertoire in that it sets the commercial culture against authentic music culture. For instance, ethnic music and world music are understood to represent the genuinely authentic (uncorrupt) music of indigenous cultures. Mainstream music is understood to be commercially calculated and produced by big record companies, while alternative music is assumed to be produced by small and independent record companies.

Although the speakers do not make any explicit assumptions about
the nature of music librarians' professional competence in this repertoire, it is considered that in comparison to commercial music distribution channels, music libraries' task is not to court the audience but to
choose music expertly. Like the previous repertoire, this one, too, pos-
its an expert status for librarians. Librarians' evaluations are assumed to
have a more objective basis than users' tastes and opinions.

The Demand Repertoire

In the demand repertoire, collection development is approached from
the viewpoint of citizens' cultural interests and engagements. The
music library is assigned a responsive role: its task is to satisfy user
needs. Collection development should be grounded upon social
knowledge concerning "musical behavior." The library's role is viewed
as something which largely depends on its local environment. It is
stressed that planning and collection development requires knowledge
about the community to be served.

> *Question:* On what grounds do you think music should be selected
> for the collection?
> *Answer:* I would really build it according to the demand. I would map
> the situation. One way, if there is no computerized system, would be
> to make an investigation of the users. I don't know how that
> information is registered now that you have computerized systems.
> But the ideal situation would be, even socially, to know about
> musical behavior, that is, to outline what is needed. That is the only
> ground on which to make meaningful acquisitions.
> *Question:* Are there other aspects you think should be considered in
> the selection? Do you think this other supply, for instance what you
> hear on the radio, matters?
> *Answer:* Not in my opinion. Because the most essential is the
> planning according to demand. After all, what is offered on the
> radio—it is not necessarily at all in accordance with the listener's
> musical taste, and then the need is not satisfied. In these circum-
> stances, I don't think they have anything to do with each other.
> *Question:* Would there be other criteria then?
> *Answer:* Of course, it also depends on the library's location. To be
> sure, the part of town affects the demand. So that the building of the
> collection should after all be founded on the need.
> *Question:* Do you have a view of how music libraries in general
> relate to music culture or musical life? Or what should their
> relationship to musical life be like?
> *Answer:* The responsibility of the music department is not to
> represent—it absolutely may not represent any school or any trend in
> music in particular, or to make acquisitions just because we want to

guide musical tastes. In my opinion it is not—it must be based on the demand. It must answer this need, the user's need. (Interviewee 22)

The main characteristic of the demand repertoire is the requirement that collection development should be based on the systematic investigation of user needs. It is stated that the needs of the local users cannot be known as a matter of course; demand is not considered as obvious. Suggested aids for collection development are loan statistics, which show how much demand there is for particular kinds of materials, user surveys, monitoring general studies on musical tastes and behavior and following the charts. Monitoring loan statistics also reveals what is not worth acquiring. The music that "just stands on the shelves" is named as the object of discarding. In the demand repertoire it is thus not only considered important that users' acquisition wishes or the majority's tastes be taken into consideration, it is stressed that the selection of materials ought to quantitatively reflect the structure of local users' interests.

Question: If you had to choose material for the collection, on what grounds do you think this should be done?
Answer: According to the demand, what is requested and how much. Probably in the library, too, the most demand comes from these youngsters, and that is then rock. And those who are interested in classical music are a little older bunch, and smaller. (Interviewee 26)

In the demand repertoire, the music library is defined as a "social service." Unlike many other cultural institutions and institutions of higher education, the library is not exclusive, nor does it carry elitist overtones—it serves "real people," "ordinary people," and acts as "a treasure chamber of the working class." The target of criticism is a line of selection, which aspires to guide musical tastes and to advance "elite culture" in which "only a small but influential minority" is interpreted to take an active interest in. Music libraries should offer the music that "Finnish people love" (interpreted to consist of rock bands and popular singers who "have stayed on the scene for decades"). In this repertoire, culture is divided into popular and nonpopular, and popularity is constructed as an achievement, as a sign that music has succeeded in its attempt to reach the audience, while nonpopular music is characterized as "dead music."

The general education repertoire prioritized the objective need for musical information over users' (changing) preferences, and the alternative repertoire was built on the conviction that regardless of demand, there is, objectively, more need for music that is not easily available in record stores and on the radio. In the demand repertoire, needs are not distinguished from wants and preferences, or objective information needs from subjective demand. As commerciality and noncommerciality are not the determinants of quality culture in the demand repertoire, the audiences are not considered to be wrong, inexpert, or passive in their preferences. Neither is "demand" considered to be one-sidedly oriented towards certain kinds of music. For instance, "list music" is considered to consist of diverse trends appealing to different groups. It is argued that the fragmentation of tastes is mirrored by radio channels' specialization and segmentation.

In the demand repertoire it is emphasized that "there are a thousand opinions on what is good music," and that librarians should not rely on their own expertise in selection because they look at culture from a certain viewpoint and cannot divest themselves of earlier experiences, age, affections and partialities any more than users. In this repertoire, the librarians' professional competence consists of the ability to analyze and identify different user and audience groups and their specific needs.

Discussion

The interpretative repertoires of the music library were distinguished by paying attention to variation and inconsistencies in participants' accounts. The analysis of users' library discourses concentrated on the perspectives and implicit background assumptions that participants adopted when discussing music library service principles. The different "music library versions" are summarized in the table.

THE INTERPRETATIVE REPERTOIRES OF THE MUSIC LIBRARY

	General education repertoire	Alternative repertoire	Demand repertoire
Music library's role	Cultural institution	An alternative to other provision channels	Social service institution
Idea of collection building	Collects the basic repertory of each genre	Reflects the diversity of music	Responds to users' needs
Target of criticism	Line that follows demand and concentrates on novelties	Line that follows mainstream supply, instructive line reflecting "good taste"	Line that emphasizes high culture and abstract quality
Selection criteria	Historical significance	Marginal areas, experiments, new trends	Systematic following of local demand
User categories	Music students / entertainment listeners	Passive listeners / specialized fans	Users / non-users, rock generations / older age groups
Music categories	Serious / light, lasting / superficial, classics / mode music	Mainstream / marginal, commercial / noncommercial	Popular music / rarities, underused materials
Materials not to be acquired	Novelties, mode music, superficial pop, entertainment	Chart music, basic rock, basic classics	Rarely used materials
Distribution among styles	Half classical music, half light music	Half according to demand, half rarer and lesser known music	On grounds of loan figures, the share of classical music must not exceed demand
Expertise required in selection	Expertise in music, degree in musicology or music training	Awareness of marginal areas, familiarity with independent and small record production	Knowledge about users' and potential users' needs
Library's ethical quality	Provides a chance for all to develop, train and cultivate themselves in the field of music	Guarantees opportunities for musical experimentation, supports noncommercial alternatives	Satisfies musical needs without evaluative attitudes

As John M. Budd and Douglas Raber[41] observe, professional library discourse presents a conflicted state. Library users' discourse manifests the same kinds of conflicting views of the purpose of library collections as professional library discourse. Library history conventionally presents library ideals and philosophies as the creations of librarians as a professional group, or even as particular individual thinkers', library pioneers', creations.[42] This article demonstrated that the discourses concerning the principles of library work are a part of our common cultural heritage. They are based on conceptions of culture, art and civilization which are important not only in the library context but have had an important formative function in society.[43] The coexistence of competing library repertoires can be explained as the parallel existence of equally well-established but mutually contradictory ways of understanding what "culture," "art" and "civilization" are.[44] Novel conceptions of culture, art and civilization have evolved as corrections to prior discourses, which have begun in some aspects to seem limited and one-sided. Historically strong discourses do not, however, disappear with the emergence of alternative discourses. There is no linear development in which "postmodern" library conceptions would displace "modern" or Enlightenment conceptions.

The general education repertoire closely corresponds to what Alistair Black and Dave Muddiman,[45] in their analysis of British libraries' service principles and philosophies, call the heritage perspective. In this perspective, the library is a socially neutral collector, preserver and disseminator of knowledge. Library users are placed in the role of citizens, whose level of culture and education must be elevated to a level corresponding to the requirements of modern society. This discourse is characterized by the absence of gender, age, social and cultural differences. The "objective" need for information and culture is a need for a "cultural basis," humanistic all-round education. "Subjective" needs are needs for entertainment, recreation and relaxation. The same ideal of civilization is considered valid for everyone, everywhere and at all times.[46] When "culture" is linked with the term *education*, it is conceptually separate from the real individuals and groups supporting it.

According to Black and Muddiman,[47] the heritage perspective is historically bourgeois-directed, hegemonic, socially controlling, elitist, paternalistic and censorial. However, as they also point out, in effect libraries, among other institutions, do serve as museums of literary and music culture.[48] Second, libraries have always also supported education and self-education in all fields of knowledge. Thus, rather than simply renouncing the general education repertoire as elitist, it should be noted that the repertoire is rather inevitably used in discussion contexts where libraries are considered as financial investments of the state for the provision of education and knowledge to its citizens.

In the professional discourse of library and information science, the alternative repertoire is more often used than analyzed. Speakers who take distance from public libraries' historic educational ambitions, who emphasize pluralism, the acknowledging of differences and diversity, often simultaneously criticize "postmodern" culture and libraries' "consumerist market orientation" or "userism"—their (alleged) capitulation to market forces in the name of user-friendliness. This discourse also typically prioritizes the public library's status as a "public service," as an institution autonomous from market forces, ideologically committed to the provision of true information and to the support of risk-taking, experimentation and alternative cultural movements.

This perspective can also be called the cultural industry theory because it links the production and consumption of culture to the capitalist market and pursuit of benefit. The expressions "mass music," "market forces" and "consumerism" imply that the choices of the public at large are market-guided, and that technological development and industrial production lead to the standardization and degradation of culture instead of expanding the range of cultural choices. Zygmunt Bauman[49] notes that the view of postmodern culture as a "postculture" represents legislation nostalgia, nostalgia for universal criteria of truth, judgment and taste. In the alternative repertoire, the authenticity or alternative character of music justifies the financial investments in it. The content and meaning of cultural products are understood as facts, which exclude the analysis of concrete audiences and their sense-making practices. The public service ethos also assigns libraries a prioritizing, judging and discriminating role in relation to culture, and an "illuminating" role in relation to users.

The demand repertoire, or what Budd and Raber[50] call the customer service discourse, in turn privatizes the civilization project and welcomes the crumbling of the welfare state's paternalistic and custodial role in the field of culture. It is typical for library policy documents[51] that emphasize the transition from a librarian- or collection-centered viewpoint to a user-centered viewpoint to construct the responsive role as more humane, dynamic and serving than libraries' traditional role as agents of civilization and social change. The leisure ethos[52] implies a trust in the wisdom of users' momentary fancies. Public libraries' task is to provide better leisure opportunities, and that way increase users' quality of life. "Culture" manifests itself as a spontaneous process which flourishes best in the absence of restricting administrative plans and is best advanced by the decentralization of power. "Culture" is disconnected from the concepts of education and civilization and linked to words like connectedness, identity, affect and mastery of life.

Conclusions

The findings of this study indicate that library users not only want public libraries to satisfy their own needs, they also view the library as an institution fulfilling more general tasks. Users are as sensitive towards the needs of "others" as librarians. A study that enables users to display the full range of their cultural and library expertise undermines the librarian-centered viewpoint, but, paradoxically, it also reveals that there are some problems, or generally neglected issues, in the user-centeredness discourse. This discourse ignores the fact that in the identification of user needs and user groups, library professionals have to lean on specific current theories about needs, audiences and cultural megatrends—which may or may not be pertinent in the library context. It is implicitly assumed that communities and user groups already exist as clearly defined entities, and that the tailoring of service to user demand by using methods such as community analysis is a relatively straightforward task. The findings of this study imply that while interviews, qualitative user studies and use studies may successfully capture the subjective dimension of people's library and cultural experiences, the results may not necessarily be easily applicable in practice.[53] In fact, they do not necessarily provide any guidelines for the planning of activities. Cultural audiences are also open potential to be conquered with supply. Public libraries, as cultural and historical institutions, not only serve previously existing audiences and user groups but also produce certain kinds of audiences and users with their traditions and current supply. There are conflicting views of library collections' purpose, and the same kinds of conflicts exist in users' expectations.

When we have a clearer view of the underlying tensions and conflicts in library discourses, we may be in a better position to adopt a reflexive view of public library planning, policy and practice. Since the end of the 1980s, user-centeredness, profiling, customization, community analysis and total quality management have been the central catchwords in library discussion and have been accorded the status of professional and systematic planning. This article has demonstrated, however, that the public library is for users as multifaceted an institution as it is for librarians. The important lesson of the analysis of users' library discourses is therefore that there is no single scientific or rational principle on which to rely in the planning of library activity. The competing nature of library discourses reflects the fundamental ambivalence of cultural values. This ambivalence is a permanent part of our cultural reality, and the challenge we face is how to discuss and develop public library policy and practice in a way that fully acknowledges it.

Notes

1 This article is based on my book *Music, Culture, and the Library: An Analysis of Discourses* (Lanham, Md.: Scarecrow Press, 2001) and published with the permission of the publisher.

2 Alistair Black and Dave Muddiman, *Understanding Community Librarianship* (Aldershot: Avebury, 1997), 102.

3 Susan Edwards and Mairead Browne, "Quality in Information Services: Do Users and Librarians Differ in Their Expectations?" *Library & Information Science Research* 17, no. 2 (Spring 1995): 163-82.

4 Michael H. Harris, "State, Class, and Cultural Reproduction: Toward a Theory of Library Service in the United States." *Advances in Librarianship* 14 (1986): 211-52.

5 Harris, "State, Class, and Cultural Reproduction," 216.

6 Gary Radford, "Flaubert, Foucault, and the Bibliotheque Fantastique: Toward a Postmodern Epistemology for Library Science." *Library Trends* 46, no. 4 (Spring 1998): 616-34.

7 Bernd Frohmann, "Discourse Analysis as a Research Method in Library and Information Science." *Library & Information Science Research* 16, no. 2 (Spring 1994): 119-38.

8 Sanna Karttunen, *Musiikkikirjastonhoitajien musiikillinenmaailmankuva* [Music Librarians' Musical Worldview] (Helsinki: Suomen Musiik-kikirjastoyhdistys, 1990); Päivi Rautavuori, *Popmusiikin kokoelmatyö* [Collection Work in Pop Music] (Helsinki: Suomen Musiikkikirjastoyhdistys, 1991).

9 Ragnar Audunson, "Between Professional Field Norms and Environmental Change Impetuses: A Comparative Study of Change Processes in Public Libraries." *Library & Information Science Research* 21, no. 4 (1999): 523-52.

10 David Silverman, *Qualitative Methodology and Sociology: Describing the Social World* (Aldershot: Gower, 1985).

11 Pertti Alasuutari, *Researching Culture: Qualitative Method and Cultural Studies* (London: Sage, 1995).

12 Nigel Gilbert and Michael Mulkay, *Opening Pandora's Box: A Sociological Analysis of Scientists' Discourse* (Cambridge: Cambridge University Press, 1984); Jonathan Potter and Margaret Wetherell, *Discourse and Social Psychology: Beyond Attitudes and Behaviour* (London: Sage, 1987),

13 Margaret Wetherell and Jonathan Potter, "Discourse Analysis and the Identification of Interpretive Repertoires," in *Analysing Everyday Experience: A Casebook of Methods*, ed. Charles Antaki (London: Sage, 1988).

14 Michel Foucault, *The Archaeology of Knowledge* (London: Routledge, 1972).

15 Sanna Talja, "Analyzing Qualitative Interview Data: The Discourse Analytic Method." *Library & Information Science Research* 21, no. 4 (1999): 459-77.

16 Talja, "Analyzing Qualitative Interview Data."

17 Potter and Wetherell, *Discourse and Social Psychology.*

18 Gilbert and Mulkay, *Opening Pandora's Box.*

19 Potter and Wetherell, *Discourse and Social Psychology.*

20 Potter and Wetherell, *Discourse and Social Psychology.*

21 Gilbert and Mulkay, *Opening Pandora's Box.*

22 Bernd Frohmann, "Best Books and Excited Readers: Discursive Tensions in the Writings of Melvil Dewey." *Libraries & Culture* 32, no. 2 (Spring 1997): 349-71.

23 Wetherell and Potter, "Discourse Analysis and the Identification of Interpretive Repertoires," 172.

24 Wetherell and Potter, "Discourse Analysis and the Identification of Interpretive Repertoires."

25 Foucault, *The Archaeology of Knowledge*, 65; Ian Parker, *Discourse Dynamics: Critical Analysis for Social and Individual Psychology* (London: Routledge, 1992), 13.

26 Wetherell and Potter, "Discourse Analysis and the Identification of Interpretive Repertoires."

27 Foucault, *The Archaeology of Knowledge.*

28 Foucault, *The Archaeology of Knowledge.*

29 Parker, *Discourse Dynamics.*

30 Valentin Volosinov, *Marxism and the Philosophy of Language* (Cambridge, Mass.: Harvard University Press, 1986); Stuart Hall, "The West and the Rest: Discourse and Power," in *Formations of Modernity*, ed. Stuart Hall and Bram Gieben (Cambridge: Polity Press/Open University, 1992).

31 Talja, "Analyzing Qualitative Interview Data."

32 Cf. Donald G. Davis Jr., "Wars in American Libraries: Ideological Battles in the Selection of Materials." *Libraries & Culture* 33, no. 1 (Winter 1998): 40-46.

33 *Musiikkikirjastotoiminnan käsikirja* [Handbook of Music Library Activity] (Helsinki: Kirjastopalvelu, 1986), 30.

34 *Musiikkikirjastotoiminnan käsikirja*, 30.

35 *Musiikkikirjastotoiminnan käsikirja*, 30.

36 Michael Harris and Stan A. Hannah, *Into the Future: The Foundations of Library and Information Services in the Post-Industrial Era* (Norwood, N.J.: Ablex Publishing, 1993); John M. Budd and Douglas Raber, "The Cultural State of the *Fin de Millenaire* Library." *Library Quarterly* 68, no. 1 (January 1998): 55-79; Shirley H. Wiegand, "Reality Bites: The Collision of Rhetorics, Rights, and Reality in the Library Bill of Rights." *Library Trends* 45, no. 1 (Spring 1996): 75-86.

37 Seppo Nummi, "Musiikki ja kirjastot" [Music and Libraries] in *Musiikkikirjasto-opas* [Music Library Guide], ed. Ritva Piispanen (Helsinki: Suomen Kirjastoseura, 1964).

38 Kaarina Ranta, "Musiikkikirjastojen hallinnosta" [About the Administration of Music Libraries] in *Musiikkikirjasto-opas* [Music Library Guide], ed. Ritva Piispanen (Helsinki: Suomen Kirjastoseura, 1964), 22.

39 *Musiikkikirjastotoiminnan käsikirja*, 50.

40 Catherine Sheldrick Ross, "Metaphors of Reading." *The Journal of Library History, Philosophy, and Comparative Librarianship* 22, no. 2 (Spring 1987): 147-63; Catherine Sheldrick Ross, "If They Read Nancy Drew, So What? Series Book Readers Talk Back." *Library & Information Science Research* 17, no. 3 (Summer 1995): 201-36.

41 Budd and Raber, "The Cultural State of the *Fin de Millenaire* Library," 77-78.

42 See also Laura Henriette Christine Skouvig, "Institution, Modernity and Discourse: Three Perspectives on Public Library History," in this volume.

43 Terry Eagleton, *The Ideology of the Aesthetic* (Cambridge: Blackwell, 1990).

44 Sanna Talja, *Music, Culture, and the Library: An Analysis of Discourses* (Lanham, Md.: Scarecrow Press, 2001).

45 Black and Muddiman, *Understanding Community Librarianship*, 116.

46 Zygmunt Bauman, *Legislators and Interpreters: On Modernity, Postmodernity and Intellectuals* (Cambridge: Polity Press, 1987), 151.

47 Black and Muddiman, *Understanding Community Librarianship*, 121-22.

48 Black and Muddiman, *Understanding Community Librarianship*, 116.

49 Bauman, *Legislators and Interpreters: On Modernity, Postmodernity and Intellectuals.*

50 Budd and Raber, "The Cultural State of the *Fin de Millenaire* Library," 74.

51 *Muuttuva kirjasto: Kirjastoverkkotyöryhmän raportti* [The Changing Library: Report of the Library Network Workgroup] (Helsinki: Helsingin kaupunginkirjasto, 1991).

52 Robert Snape, *Leisure and the Rise of the Public Library* (London: Library Association Publishing, 1995), 141.

53 See also Ågot Berger, "Usability Studies and Focus Groups as Methods for Developing Digital Public Library Services in a Multiethnic Society," in this volume.

Part VI

ISSUES AND
PERSPECTIVES

The Heritage of Public Librarianship

Michael K. Buckland

Public library research is seen as fragmented and in need of a more coherent sense of context and a more unified understanding. Three questions are addressed: What kind of work do we do? How can we do our work? Why do we do our work? Libraries are based on documents, which can affect us aesthetically and emotionally. Public libraries are concerned with culture, ideas and complex problems. Every public library enacts a cultural policy. Public libraries are important because it matters what people know.

Introduction

The call for papers for this seminar says that "current public library research seems to be fragmented across countries, institutional contexts, and academic communities." This statement implies a need for a more coherent sense of context and a more unified understanding of what we do. So I will talk in general terms about three questions:

1. What kind of work do we do? In effect, what have we been doing? What is our heritage?
2. How can we do our work?
3. Why do we do our work?

What Kind of Work Do We Do?

What kind of work do we do? Or, rather, what have we been doing? What is our tradition, our heritage? I use the word *heritage*, not history. Heritage is the present effect today of the past. One speaks of cultural heritage, of patrimony. Heritage is what one inherits, what one receives from one's parents when they die. Some of it is useful; some of it is not. The challenge is to make the best use of it.

When we look at what we have been doing, what can we say about our activity in librarianship? We can say that we are concerned with documents: texts, images, sounds, statistics, books, newspapers, databases, music recordings, manuscripts, any thing of any genre and in any form regarded as signifying something worth collecting. Society is full of documents. Educators use textbooks and instructional media to change what students know. Lawyers and law courts use documents as evidence to decide whether or not we are guilty of a crime. Scientists use documents (articles, datasets, laboratory notebooks) as an archive of achievement and for personal status. The mass media use documents to persuade. Governments use documents to exercise social control. Religions use documents to assert authority and to make us change our behavior. Artists use documents (images) to challenge and to inspire us. Commerce depends on documented transactions. Modern society exists on a foundation of documents. Libraries are based on the use of documents, and public libraries have been hospitable to different forms, such as music recordings, maps and games.

The high social prestige of the mathematical and natural sciences has encouraged researchers to turn away from social and cultural traditions of scholarship and to make algorithmic and quantitative approaches their scientific ideal. As a result, the desire to be respectable and "scientific" steers attention towards what is quantifiable and away from important human and social aspects. Librarians who work in public libraries understand better than other librarians, and better than most theorists of information, that documents, signifying objects, are not simply a form of recorded, objectified knowledge from which we may learn. Documents also can affect us aesthetically and emotionally. This "affective" aspect of documents, and, therefore, of libraries seems to have been neglected among researchers. The pressure on researchers to be "scientific" limits their range.

Culture is built through communication, through the sharing of experience and the negotiation of shared meaning through communication. For this reason, communication, whether discussion or the exchange of documents, is constitutive of culture. The use of documents is invariably a cultural activity, and every public library enacts a cultural policy. That is why there are so many controversies over documents. Any document may change belief and behavior, which brings us to ideas.

Ideas

Libraries, especially public libraries, are concerned with ideas, beliefs and feelings in three ways:

1. We are concerned with documents and documents would not be documents if they did not signify something. That is to say, they are perceived as meaningful. They are related to ideas.

2. There are many documents and many different kinds of documents. Our responsibility is to organize documents in the most meaningful way. We can ask, meaningful in relation to what? We select, collect, arrange and recommend documents. Vesa Souminen, in his book, *Filling Empty Space*,[1] asks the question: What does it mean to be a good librarian? His answer is that a librarian's task is to create arrangements of documents that are meaningful for readers. This implies that the arrangement should be related to the users' ideas. A good librarian is, quite simply, a librarian who does that well.

3. Those who do research, and those who teach, as I do, should think about the nature of what we teach about. What kind of activity is librarianship? What does "information service" mean? There are thousands of books on *how* to do things, but not enough on the nature, character and purpose of what we do. Developing theory is difficult and those who try tend to receive little recognition. But there are a few people who make the effort.

Writing history, making narratives, is a kind of theorizing. But the historiography of our field is very incomplete. There is good work on the history of libraries and on the biography of librarians, but not enough on the history of ideas, on the history of techniques or on the social, interpersonal networks by which ideas and influences emerge, spread, change or become forgotten. (We welcome the efforts of the Special Interest Group in the History and Foundations of Information Science of the American Society for Information Science and Technology, for example, T.B. Hahn and M. Buckland;[2] M.E. Bowden, T.B. Hahn and R.W. Williams.[3])

Complex Problems

Anyone who is interested in what human beings know is necessarily dealing with very complex matters: human understanding and belief, information technology, social policies and human behavior. That is why even the smallest public library deals with complex matters.

There are important consequences here for the schools of library, information and documentation studies. Disciplines are defined by the problems they try to solve. We deal with the socially important problem of assisting in the creation, distribution and use of knowledge and any convincing definition of knowledge includes beliefs and attitudes. For this we need to have a wide range of techniques. Our discipline is broadly based. Rhetoric about how we are interdisciplinary can distract us from the unity of our purpose and from the important question: What range of expertise do we need and can afford? Instead of saying that we are interdisciplinary, we should say that we are multitalented.

How Are We to Do Our Work?

How we are to do our work is a question for everyone, including the schools of library, information and documentation studies. The schools need to define their curriculum. We typically find four basic components: organization of information, information in society and information policy, technology for information services, management of information services.

Organization of Information

The organization of information, or, as I prefer, of documents, has two aspects: (1) Selecting and collecting, which is the privileging of some documents over others, either because people will ask for them or because you decide that some documents are better than others for the purposes of your library; (2) Organizing, arranging, categorizing, indexing and providing support for filtering and retrieval.

There are important needs here. Webpages, for example, are documents. Websites are collections of documents. Webpages need the same kind of selection, arranging, indexing and support for searching as other collections. If we see the World Wide Web as a kind of publishing universe, then the people who need books also need guidance in finding the best relevant webpages. A guide to websites is a bibliography. A selection of links is a kind of library.

Birger Hjørland rightly stresses the existence and the importance of specialized communities of discourse.[4] Any broad bibliography or general collection includes smaller domains of discourse, each with the stylized language of that specialty. At Berkeley we have been experimenting with the creation of multiple indexes for the same collection, with different indexes for different communities of user. Preliminary results show that searching can be significantly improved in this way.[5,6]

Information in Society and Information Policy

The two topics, information in society and information policy, go together because information policy is concerned with efforts to influence the distribution and use of information in society. I take information policy to include all the different kinds of decisions, especially government decisions, that influence what people know and what they do not know. Many groups have an interest in influencing what you know. Public libraries, serving a community, have an important role to play in complementing and balancing the effects of the information policies of other groups.

Technology

Librarians have always been interested in technology and have often been early adopters. New technology offers new possibilities for providing new kinds of service and also specialized services for special groups, raising new questions about our priorities. A challenge is to remember the difference between means and ends, between process and purpose. There is also a basic difference between *invention*, which is the designing of new methods, and *innovation*, which is the managerial challenge of selecting and implementing new methods. Being a librarian today is made more exciting by the arrival of new methods. We are in a position not only to perform existing services differently but also to develop different, better services. We are in a situation to redesign library services, but this is as much a management challenge as it is a technological challenge.

Management

Management includes specific skills such as budgeting and project management, but it is also the art of achieving results through other people and how to survive and thrive in a political and economic environment.

A significant example of public library research was conducted in California after a financial crisis in local government. Some public libraries were closed. Others had their budgets greatly reduced. The researcher, Snunith Shoham, found that the most important factor in the economic health of the public libraries that she studied was political—the relationship between the public library, especially the director, and the community.[7] The more actively the library and its director were involved in the community and in the rest of local government, the better the library's budget. The more separated and isolated the library was, the weaker it was in a financial crisis. This is a very simple lesson for all of us.

Looking Forward: Why Does It Matter?

Why is our activity important? Why should we have public libraries? And why have schools of library, information and documentation? Is it because there are so many documents? Is it because information services and information technology need to be managed? My answer is that *it matters what people know*. When you need a doctor, a lawyer or an automobile mechanic, do you want one who is ignorant? Your business will not succeed if you do not know what you need to know. Teachers should understand what they are supposed to teach. In California there is a slogan: "If you think education is expensive, consider the cost of ignorance." What people know is important to the individual, to an organization and to society. Public librarians understand that there are different kinds of knowledge. They try to support not only technical knowledge but also cultural understanding, aesthetic insight and affective experience. So our concerns are important, but we do not have a monopoly. School, museums, the media, governments, publishers, commerce and many others have an interest in what people know: to help them, to influence them, to control them and to exploit them.

Librarians and information managers have a particular role to play. We are concerned with understanding. One can think of three kinds of memory: private memory; social memory, that part of culture that is shared, the stories that we tell and share to create our shared identity; and external memory—the records, documents, texts and so on—which is our specialty. And our purpose is to serve some community, which means that we must relate to the priorities and values of our role in the community, our political and economic purpose.

So we have a history, a heritage and professional skills, and we need to study all three. We need to know why libraries and librarians are important and we need to explain that to others. We are at a wonderfully interesting situation in which changes of technology allow us to redesign what we do, yet technology is only a means to our ends. There is a wonderfully rich agenda for public library research.

Notes

1 Vesa Suominen, *Filling Empty Space: A Treatise on Semiotic Structures in Information Retrieval, in Documentation, and in Related Research* (Oulu: Oulu University Press, 1997). (Acta Universitatis Ouluensis Humaniora B27.)

2 Trudi Bellardo Hahn and Michael K. Buckland, eds., *Historical Studies in Information Science* (Medford, N.J.: Information Today, 1998).

3 Mary Ellen Bowden, Trudi Bellardo Hahn and Robert V. Williams, eds., *Proceedings of the 1998 Conference on the History and Heritage of Science Information Systems* (Medford, N.J.: Information Today, 1999).

4 Birger Hjørland, "Domain Analysis in Information Science: Eleven Approaches—Traditional as Well as Innovative." *Journal of Documentation* 58, no. 4 (2002): 422-62.

5 Michael K. Buckland, Aitao Chen, Michael Gebbie, Youngin Kim and Barbara Norgard, "Variation by Subdomain in Indexes to Knowledge Organization Systems," in *Dynamism and Stability in Knowledge Organization: Proceedings of the Sixth International ISKO Conference, 10-13 July 2000, Toronto, Canada*, ed. Clare Beghtol, Lynne C. Howarth and Nancy J. Williamson (Würzburg, Germany: Ergon Verlag, 2000), 48-53.

6 Michael K. Buckland, Hailing Jiang, Youngin Kim and Vivien Petras, "Domain-Based Indexes: Indexing for Communities of Users," in *3e Congrès du Chapitre français de L'ISKO, 5-6 juillet 2001. Filtrage et résumé informatique de l'Information sur les réseaux* (Paris: Université Nanterre Paris X., 2001), 181-85. http://metadata.sims.berkeley.edu/papers/ISKObuck.pdf

7 Snunith Shoham, *Organizational Adaptation by Public Libraries* (Westport, Conn.: Greenwood Press, 1984).

Research Perspective

Sandra Parker

Sandra Parker was asked to sum up the Nordic Seminar on Public Library Research at the Royal School of Library and Information Science, Copenhagen, 10-11 December 2001. Her perspective is that of the researcher. Parker was given with the task of characterizing the range of papers presented to the seminar emphasizing the theoretical perspectives and drawing comparisons between the situation in the Nordic countries and in the United Kingdom.

The public library research seminar was a stimulating and exciting event. Overall, from a UK perspective the seminar was intellectually challenging with many thought-provoking papers. It was refreshing to examine the theoretical and philosophical perspective of the public library service within the context of changing political situations. The themes that were addressed were varied, as could be expected. The papers fell into several categories:

1. The role of libraries
2. Public library developments
3. Users
4. Delivery of library services

Michael Buckland gave the keynote address that helpfully examined the nature of research in our area. He pointed to the culture of fragmentation within the sector and our inability to use appropriate transferable and testable methodologies in our research. We had not even successfully defined our own discipline and thus research in the subject was hampered. To some extent, our interdisciplinary nature provided obstacles. However, he said that we were concerned too much with means and methods and not enough with objectives, too much concerned with process and not enough with purpose. What was needed was a more coherent framework within a social science context. We need to undertake more qualitative work and follow the lead of medicine with some evidence-based practice, which is capable of being replicated and validated. These were timely comments for the audience, who were largely practitioner researchers.

The Role of Libraries

Svanhild Aabø from Oslo University College examined the benefits of the public library and discovered that the overwhelming majority of the Norwegian population perceived that they have property rights to public library benefits. This echoes research done in the UK where the public library is normally ranked very high, together with emergency services such as ambulance and fire brigade in the services that people perceive as being of a direct benefit in exchange for their taxes. They may not use the service themselves but believe that it should exist and be well funded for the benefit of their children and/or other people in the community.

Sanna Talja from Finland stressed the importance of engaging with and maintaining a dialogue with users. Within the context of a music library she provided details of library users' interpretation of the social and cultural role of the public library. She found that users were informed, informative, supportive and able to view collections dispassionately and to effectively contribute to service development. A major flaw in the methodology was that the opinion of the nonusers was not solicited.

Public Library Developments

These papers were much exercised with the move of the public library into the electronic environment. This research echoes the work in the UK where a "People's Network" is being created by using money from our lottery system to fund such large projects via a New Opportunities Fund (NOF). All schools, colleges, universities, hospitals and libraries are being networked. Public access to the Internet is being provided by funding the installation of PCs in public libraries together with providing the training of the staff to use the technology effectively. Ulla Arvidsson provided a study in Southern California of librarians' experience of introducing the Internet in the public library. Experiences of this process must be the same all over the globe, and it is good to reflect on how common the issues are, nationally and internationally. Marianne Hummelshøj continued this theme with her "Web-Based Information Services: The Role of the Public Library." She had surveyed Norwegian, Swedish and Danish library websites examining the provision of community information and suggested a useful model for a strategic developmental approach. Trine Schreiber of the Royal School of Library and Information Science in Copenhagen looked at designated websites—"networked study rooms" and their provision by Danish public libraries.

Librarians have been concerned with issues surrounding classification since the days of the Alexandrian library in ancient Egypt. Kasper Graarup of the Royal School of Library and Information Science in Copenhagen posed the interesting problem of the Christian bias of UDC.

Users

Services to ethnic and cultural minority users and the public library services have long been a concern in the United Kingdom and the Nordic countries, and are increasingly so. Thus, they are the subject of much research. Hans Elbeshausen and Charlotte Werther looked at ethnic minority users in Denmark. As in the United Kingdom, their conclusions were that the public library is often seen as a forum or refuge and that usually a very high standard of service is offered. However, they raised the questions: Do the high standards of services offered and high level of user satisfaction necessarily equal integration? and To what extent and in what ways are public libraries supposed to contribute to that process? These questions might be answered by research currently being undertaken by Bo Skøtt of the Royal School of Library and Information Science in Aalborg, where he is looking at role of the public library in the multicultural society, which started to develop in 1960s.

Casper Hvenegaard Rasmussen and Henrik Jochumsen, also from the Royal School of Library and Information Science in Copenhagen, developed this theme in a very philosophical paper examining the historical role of the public library. They suggested a strategy for change in an era of cultural diversity. The research was based on responses to reference enquires.

Delivery of Library Services

Laura Skouvig looked at different perspectives on the history of Danish public libraries from 1880 to 1920, using the analytic approach of the French sociologist Michel Foucault. Nan Dahlkild examined library architecture and design and how it represented the cultural debate in Denmark in the period 1919-1939. There was an expressed concern that the library as public space will not survive the electronic revolution. Tord Høivik, in "A Poem Lovely as a Tree?," examined the uses of technology in creating new ways of organizing, studying and improving reference work.

The management of libraries, their quality, performance and impact is an area for much research in the United Kingdom and the United States. Niels Ole Pors and Carl Gustav Johannsen presented some results from a comprehensive survey conducted in 2001 into leadership and management in Danish libraries. The broad concepts of new public management theory and value-based management were outlined. The findings revealed that the actual use of quality management tools is very traditional and is influenced heavily by external requirements. This is reflected in the UK, where the government now imposes quality and performance evaluation of public libraries every year.

A similar conference in the UK would perhaps have drawn on different issues. Major themes currently are the nature of e-government and libraries' role in that, lifelong learning, social inclusion and neighborhood renewal. The government increasingly sees libraries as part of a wider cultural service together with museums and archives and thus research is tending to span the three sectors. The culture of accountability seems to be more advanced in the UK, with public libraries being scrutinized to ensure that they are providing "best value" to the community for the investment made and, as a result, there is much research on performance measurement.

Libraries throughout the world are on the cusp between the heritage of Gutenberg and the challenges of the electronic revolution. There are few areas of the library service that not affected by these rapid developments and the fields of research reflect this largely discontinuous change. As Michael Buckland said, we need to have a very strong framework and methodology to reflect the changes adequately. A conference of this nature is ideal in bringing together practitioner researchers and academic staff to respond to the challenges that surround us. It was a privilege and a pleasure to be invited to attend.

Summing Up: Practitioner's Perspective

Ruth Ørnholt

Ruth Ørnholt was asked to sum up the Nordic Seminar on Public Library Research at the Royal School of Library and Information Science, Copenhagen, 10-11 December 2001. Her perspective is that of the practitioner. Thus, based on her own experiences as head of Hordaland County Library in Norway, Ørnholt points out the most important problems and issues facing Norwegian public libraries and details the strategies that are formulated to provide an answer to these challenges. She also comments on selected articles from a practical point of view.

I have never before attended a seminar devoted entirely to library research, but the research program we have carried out in Norway during the last five years has led to a marked improvement in the professional content of conferences and seminars, both nationally and regionally. For me, this seminar has shown how much interesting research is taking place at present in the Nordic countries.

I am head of the County Library in Hordaland, a county with a population of 435,000 distributed among 34 municipalities. The smallest of these has only 385 inhabitants, while the largest, Bergen itself, has 230,000. Although we cooperate closely with the main public library in Bergen, our activities are mainly concentrated on the 33 other municipalities.

The county library's twelve members of staff devote half of their time to statutory duties such as interlibrary lending, advisory services to the municipalities, course programs and the management of a library boat. The rest of the time is taken up with development work. The nature of this work is dictated by a library plan drawn up by the county council and later approved by the Norwegian Department for Policy Planning and Research.

This plan is the product of a process involving all aspects of library activity in the county, including academic and special libraries, the public library sector and the relevant cultural-political bodies. In the recent plan, in order to keep in step with national developments, we also bring in representatives from the archive and museum sector.

The first library plan in Hordaland was introduced in 1994 and we are now in the middle of our third. In May/June next year the plan is due to be submitted to a comprehensive hearing before final acceptance at the county's highest political level in October.

The planning process has revealed clear signs of the main concerns among a majority of librarians, politicians and museum and archive curators in the county and what they consider important questions to be dealt with on a regional basis.

I have been given the task of summarizing this seminar from a library practitioner's point of view. It has been impossible for me to study all the contributions in advance and I have wondered about the best method to apply, but I believe I have arrived at a practical and simple approach.

In light of what I know to be the greatest problems at the moment among small and medium-sized municipalities along the western coast of Norway, I have compared the various presentations to the seminar against the strategies and initiatives contained in our new library plan.

The primary aim of the plan is to ensure that all libraries throughout the county function as an efficient and coordinated network, giving the needs of library users a central place in the management and accessibility of information. The aim of the library sector shall be to make available to all inhabitants services of high quality in the areas of public enlightenment, education and culture in general.

The main topics of this seminar—the fundamental philosophy behind the establishment of public libraries, the historic role and function of libraries, the place of the library system in today's society, its value to the community, public library management, the place of the public library and public library services—are all of interest in the light of our plans for the county. I have no hesitation in stating that the seminar's choice of topics very much reflects our own concerns.

We have developed six different strategies in order to achieve our aims and have attempted to establish concrete initiatives within each strategy. Some of these initiatives are pure development projects, while others are of a more administrative or technical nature.

Our first strategy is to improve library structure and to coordinate resources with the help of new technology. In a county with many small municipalities and a large number of libraries with very limited resources, both professionally and financially, cooperation is vital. We are particularly interested in research aimed at evaluating the benefits to be gained from intermunicipal cooperation between two or more municipalities. Cooperation of this type can range from a single, specific practical agreement to the administration of several libraries in the same region.

We also need more information on broadband technology. Government authorities have granted funds towards the introduction of broadband in as many libraries as possible. Now county libraries throughout the country are pondering the same questions. How great a capacity do we require? Two or one hundred megabytes? What services can we offer on different bandwidths? Which library services are best suited to broadband technology? We need insight not from the broadband providers but from people who understand the nature of a public library.

Our second strategy concerns the improvement of expertise among library staff, teachers and users. We wish to determine the type of expertise required and how great the need is for further training and education. We intend to arrange courses, carry out quality control and educate the library owners, that is, the municipal politicians and administrators, in how a library works.

We would like research on, for example, how the training of librarians relates to their actual working duties in a library. I should also like to see some analysis of the expertise required.

All the county libraries in Norway arrange regular meetings and short courses each year for library staff throughout the county. These meetings provide an excellent opportunity to discuss library research, put it into practice and hear what staff members are most concerned about in their day-to-day work. Researchers must become more active in presenting their findings to the library sector, while at the same time adopting a more popular approach.

Our third strategy aims at bringing to public notice the value of libraries as providers of unique services and as attractive meeting places. In this respect several of the papers in this seminar have been very interesting, both with regard to public libraries as multicultural meeting places and as providers of information to the community. Much interesting research also exists on the public library as an arena for democracy. I should like to see these results converted into concrete strategies, which we can use in order to be seen and heard by both the politicians and the public.

We also try to persuade new groups within the local community to make use of our information expertise. One of our projects involves supplying local business and industry with tailor-made information. The municipal library registers details of local businesses in a special database. The librarian distributes EU documentation and other relevant information according to the profile in the database and without the companies concerned having made any approach. We call this "pro-active information." I feel sure that this can help to improve the competitiveness of small and medium-sized businesses, but also here I should be grateful for some facts.

Our fourth strategy is based on establishing cooperation with the archives and museums sector. Unlike the national scheme for joint organization, we limit our proposals to considering various forms of cooperation and to establishing common ground with the county archives and museums. We intend to work together on initiatives aimed at the public, joint courses and so forth. There seems, however, to be a lack of research to show us the best way forward.

The program for library research in Norway recently held a conference in Oslo where development and research within the archive-library-museum field was high on the agenda. I was not able to attend the conference myself, but I understand that several interesting proposals were made for research in this area.

In Hordaland, we have for many years worked on developing the public library as an arena for lifelong learning, and our fifth strategy concerns making the public library sector a resource factor for all those seeking further education, regardless of age or situation. In the same area, there is also great interest in possible interaction between school libraries and the municipal public library system. In one municipality we hope to try out a form of cross-sector cooperation by combining school libraries and public libraries into one administrative and professional unit.

Relevant in this respect is the research carried out on reference services in public libraries. The paper on Internet-based study rooms is also a useful contribution. There seems, however, to be a need for more widely based research in this field.

For many years I have maintained that in the case of adults seeking further education, the public library system has a much lower threshold than the school system. Is this correct? Are public libraries good centers of learning, or do they function best as learning resource centers? How desirable is it that librarians should act as supervisors of lifelong learning? How profitable is it for a municipality to organize school libraries and the public library system as one unit? Is there only a financial gain, or do library users also benefit? There are many possibilities for research in this area.

The final strategy we have developed towards achieving our aims is to strengthen the image of the libraries in our county in both a national and an international context.

That is partly the reason why I agreed to present this summary. We are interested in learning from the experience of others and in cooperating with others on various projects. I should like to see some comparative studies on the various problems faced by the library systems in the Nordic countries. Why is the library system in Finland so different from the Norwegian, considering the similarity of our situations? Why among the Nordic countries do the Finns read the most?

Research Commissions

Central to our planning is the financing of development work in the municipalities. Since 1994, when the first library plan was approved, we have obtained state funding of almost 6.5 million Norwegian *kroner* for various projects. This does not include the funds the municipalities have raised on their own account nor the fixed annual sum of 300,000 *kroner* granted by the county authorities in order to implement our plan.

Limited resources in most of the municipalities make it difficult for them to carry out independent development work. The initiative must be taken elsewhere, and they need help in obtaining funds.

Some of the funds available to us have been used for hiring the expertise of certain research institutes. During the past month I have initiated two projects of this type.

The research department of the Oslo College of Higher Education, which has presented six papers at this seminar, has been commissioned to compile a report on alternative modes of cooperation between the county library and the main public library in Bergen. In addition, we want the report to outline possible new models for the organization of the county library within the system of local government.

By assigning the task to specialists who have for many years conducted research on the public library in a social context, we hope to obtain the information necessary to help us plan the way ahead. We also need good arguments to help our owners come to correct decisions governing our future tasks and organization. (The steering committee for this project consists of politicians, chief librarians from various types of libraries and the county director for regional development. Members of the committee will also act as resource persons during the compilation of the report.)

With regard to the second assignment I have recently sent invitations for tender to two institutions, the Oslo College of Higher Education and BRODD, which is a private body offering consultancy services within the library sector. This is the first time I have taken advantage of the fact that there are two expert bodies in Norway capable of taking on a task of this nature. The project is extremely interesting.

In connection with the development of library services for adults who are following a course of further education, we intend to introduce quality control and a system for the certification of libraries. The concept is taken from the Michelin guide. Based on requirements for lifelong learning, we shall compile scales to evaluate library stock, infrastructure, expertise and accessibility. Interested libraries, once evaluated, will be awarded a diploma showing their star rating. This can be displayed to their users as a guarantee of an approved standard of quality. (I have commissioned these two reports, but I should also like to mention an initiative taken by a working committee at the Norwegian Library Association. The intention is to carry out a survey among employers, including local authorities, universities, training colleges, business and industry, in order to register their views on the need for expertise and knowledge in the library sector. The Oslo College of Higher Education has been entrusted with this survey.)

I do not usually commission two projects of this kind in the space of one month. This research, however, springs directly from the problems we confront in our work, and we are happy to make use of the specialist expertise available in Norway.

Through our work on the library plan we have come upon a method to promote library development. We look at our "market," which consists of the library sector in thirty-four municipalities, and we try to see it in relation to existing regional and national objectives in addition to political guidelines. Our aim is to ensure that the plan has the greatest possible impact by being firmly based on facts. In order to achieve this aim we are looking for suitable partners within the county and in the individual municipalities. Funding can be either regional or national. Carrying out a series of projects will require top expertise, and we shall doubtless rely even more upon those already engaged in research.

I have great faith in collaboration between researchers and library practitioners. Researchers should enter into our territory, but we should also meet them halfway by thinking in a more systematic way and making ourselves familiar with existing research. However, as previously mentioned, we urgently need a simpler and more popular presentation of research results.

Personally, I snap up any research result that comes along, whether in a periodical or at a conference. Stored at random in my consciousness, they turn up again as arguments in discussions and without any reference to the source. A short while ago I read an article by Niels Windfeld Lund in a Norwegian library periodical which suggested that

Norway should pay less attention to Denmark and instead use its own actual situation as a starting point when planning for library development. This article strengthened my belief that the path we are following in my county is the right one in relation to the situation of the library sector in Norway today.

According to Ragnar Audunson and Niels Windfeld Lund in their introduction to a collection of articles called "The Civilized Information Society," which was published in 2001, library research should contribute "to a more informed attitude towards the library situation and possible choices of direction."[1] Library research, however, must also give us working methods for the practice of our profession. It is important for research to give perception a concrete form, replace guesswork with facts, explain to us what is happening and why and place our work in a social context.

There is a need for someone to provide the fuel to keep the flame alive so that we librarians can continue to burn with enthusiasm for our cause—even in the darkness of the Norwegian winter.

Note

1 Ragnar Andreas Audunson and Niels Windfeld Lund, eds., *Det siviliserte informasjonssamfunn: Folkebibliotekenes rolle ved inngangen til en digital tid* (Bergen: Fagbokforlaget, 2001).

Index

About the Contributors

Svanhild Aabø is currently associate professor at the Oslo University College, Faculty of Journalism, Library and Information Science. Her writing, teaching and research cover such themes as library valuation, information economics and information policy. Previously she was head of the library serving the Library and Information Science Program at Oslo University College. She has working experience from both public and academic libraries, publishing houses and the National Library's Planning Department.

Ulla Arvidsson is a librarian from the University College of Borås (UCB), Sweden, now living in Southern California. She is currently working on her doctorate. She has worked as a librarian, implementing the Internet and writing several articles in the journal *Swedish Library Research* on that subject. She began her professional career as a teacher.

Ågot Berger was educated as a librarian at the Norwegian School of Librarianship in Oslo. She has worked as a consultant at the Århus Public Libraries and at the Danish Central Library for Immigrant Literature. Berger is now head of the Blågården Public Library in Copenhagen. During the last ten years she has written several articles on digital library issues and on library service provision to ethnic minorities. She is author of the 2001 book (in Danish) *Mangfoldighedens biblioteker* (*Libraries of Diversity*).

Michael K. Buckland is professor of Information Management and Systems and codirector, Electronic Cultural Atlas Initiative, University of California, Berkeley. He has worked in libraries in England and the United States. His interests include library services, cultural heritages and the history of information management. He was president of the American Society for Information Science in 1998.

Andrew Cranfield is the chief officer for media and marketing at the Danish National Library for the Blind. Prior to this he held the position of library director at Slagelse County Library and has also worked as a lecturer at the Royal School of Library and Information Science in Copenhagen. Cranfield holds a B.A. in Library and Information Science and an M.A. in Cultural Studies from the University of Southern Denmark.

Nan Dahlkild graduated as a cultural sociologist from the University of Copenhagen. He is an associate professor at the Royal School of Library and Information Science, Denmark, and is in the department of Cultural and Media Studies in Copenhagen. Moreover, he is an external lecturer in art history at the University of Copenhagen. His academic interests include architecture and design, cultural policy, history of culture and town planning. Dahlkild has published widely in the field of leisure-time studies and currently is doing a Ph.D. project on *Libraries as Houses of Culture: Public Enlightenment, Cultural Debate and Architecture.*

Ellen-Merete Duvold graduated as a sociologist from the University of Oslo and is currently a doctoral student in Documentation Studies at the University of Tromsø. Her doctoral dissertation deals with the use of the public library in everyday life. She has also conducted research in demographics and in the sociology of the family. Duvold has published widely in scholarly and popular journals, among them *Scandinavian Public Library Quarterly* and *Scandinavian Population Studies.*

Martin Dyrbye is an associate professor at the Royal School of Library and Information Science, Denmark, with library history and comparative librarianship as specialties but also giving lectures about subjects such as information seeking in the humanities and collection development. He holds three master's degrees: History, Drama and Performing Arts, as well as Library and Information Science. He has published books and articles about history, history of theater, collection development, and, among other things, compiled catalogues for the Department of Manuscripts at the National Library of Denmark.

Hans Elbeshausen has been an associate professor with the Department of Library and Information Management at the Royal School of Library and Information Science, Copenhagen, since 2000. Previously he was senior lecturer at the University of Odense and the Copenhagen Business School. His current teaching includes library history, communication studies and intercultural communication; his research interests include migration processes in Danish society, intercultural communication, communication theory and contemporary German history.

Kasper Graarup is an associate professor with the department of Information Studies at the Royal School of Library and Information Science, Denmark. In 2004, he took up the post of principal at the Vraa Folk High School in Northern Jutland. He holds a master's degree in comparative religion. His writing, research and teaching activities have mainly been concerned with knowledge organization in the humanities and the social sciences, along with information ethics.

Tord Høivik works at Oslo University College, where he teaches management subjects, web design and social science methods. His main professional interests include the interplay between data technology and processes of social change—both in organizations and in society as a whole. He is currently studying the impact of digital reference services on reference work and on librarianship. Høivik graduated as a statistician (M.A., 1969) and a sociologist. He has been employed as an associate professor at the Oslo School of Library Education since 1992, after many years as a researcher and research manager at the International Peace Research Institute in Oslo.

Marianne Hummelshøj is an associate professor at Royal School of Library and Information Science. She is with the department of Information Studies, where she teaches courses in information retrieval and reference services. Previous to this appointment, Hummelshøj worked as a reference librarian in the public library at Frederiksberg, Copenhagen, and as corporate librarian. She has been an evaluator in the European Union Telematics program.

Casper Hvenegaard Rasmussen is an associate professor at the Royal School of Library and Information Science, Denmark. He is in the department of Cultural and Media Studies in Copenhagen and attached to the Centre for Cultural Policy Studies. He holds a master's degree in Cultural Studies from University of Southern Denmark and has done research in the fields of cultural theory, cultural policy and public libraries, as well as an investigation for the Danish Ministry of Culture: *The Cultural Institutions Support to a Cultural Diverse Denmark* (2001). His 2000 book, *Does the Library Make a Difference?*, examines the significance of public libraries in the lives of various types of users.

Henrik Jochumsen is an associate professor at the Royal School of Library and Information Science. He is in the department of Cultural and Media Studies in Copenhagen and attached to the Centre of Cultural Policy Studies. He graduated as a cultural sociologist from the University of Copenhagen and has done research in the fields of cultural theory, cultural policy and public libraries, as well as investigations carried out for the Danish Ministry of Education and the Danish Ministry of Culture. Jochumsen is the author of numerous articles on public libraries and cultural policy, and his book *Does the Library Make a Difference?* examines the significance of public libraries in the lives of users.

Karen Nowé is a doctoral student at the Swedish School of Library and Information Science in Borås. She teaches in Library Management and Information Management, with her main interest as information management.

Ruth Ørnholt is director of the County Library in Hordaland on the Norwegian west coast. She has various working experiences from academic, public and private sector libraries. In her current job she has a special interest in the development of public libraries. At the moment, Hordaland County Library is involved in different projects including lifelong learning, cooperation between libraries, public libraries and business partnership, the use of broadband in library services and reading. Ørnholt is also chair of the Mobile Libraries Section of the Norwegian Library Association (NLA).

Sandra Parker is currently a research fellow in the Information Management Research Institute in the School of Information Studies, University of Northumbria, Newcastle upon Tyne, U.K., having taught for many years. She is chair of the editorial board for the Northumbria International Conference on Performance Measurement, held in Pittsburgh, Pennsylvania (U.S.) in 2001, and the journal *Performance Measurement and Metrics*. Parker recently completed two research projects for Resource: The Council for Museums, Archives and Libraries—The Bidding Culture and Local Government: Effects on the Development of Public Libraries, Museums and Archives and Neighbourhood Renewal and Social Inclusion: The Role of Museums, Archives and Libraries. She was president of the Library Association in the United Kingdom in 1996.

Niels Ole Pors has an academic background in social science and history. He is employed as an associate professor at the Royal School of Library and Information Science, Denmark, and is in the department of Library and Information Management. His research interests include organizational theory, leadership studies, service quality, user studies, performance measurement and research methodology, and he has published several books and numerous papers on these topics. He has international experience running library projects worldwide and is a member of the editorial boards of several library and information science journals.

Trine Schreiber is an associate professor at the Royal School of Library and Information Science, Denmark, and is in the department of Library and Information Management. Her teaching covers such themes as knowledge management, information management and communication theory. For several years, Schreiber has undertaken research in the area of networked learning support and the librarian's role as a facilitator in computer-mediated communication. She holds a Ph.D. in sociology from the University of Umeå, Sweden.

Bo Christensen Skøtt holds a master's degree from the University of Southern Denmark. He is an associate professor at the Royal School of Library and Information Science and attached to the Department of Library and Information Management. His teaching and research covers cultural and ethnic topics and their intersection with public librarianship.

Laura Henriette Christine Skouvig took her Ph.D. degree at the Royal School of Library and Information Science, Denmark, in 2004. With inspiration from Michel Foucault, her thesis breaks with the traditional approach to Danish public libraries. She is now an assistant professor at the Royal School in Copenhagen, with her research spanning such areas as the history of the profession. She graduated with an M.A. in history and German from the University of Aarhus in 2000. Her master's thesis studied a reading circle in Weimar in the period 1830-1848. Her doctoral research project is concerned with the history of the Danish public libraries during the years 1880-1920, with the focus directed towards influential discourses concerning "Bildung" and centralization efforts.

Sanna Talja worked as a researcher on the Academy of Finland's Research Program in Media Culture (2000-2002). She earned her Ph.D. in Information Studies at the University of Tampere in 1998, and worked as an assistant professor at the department of Information Studies, University of Tampere, from 1996 to 1999. Talja is the author of *Music, Culture, and the Library: An Analysis of Discourses* (Scarecrow Press, 2001). She has published several articles and book chapters on discourse analysis as a research method in Information Studies, and on the philosophical premises of information science and information seeking research.

Charlotte Werther is senior lecturer with the department of English at the Copenhagen Business School (CBS). From 2000 to 2002 she was with the Royal School of Library and Information Science, Copenhagen, where her teaching and research included aspects of the intercultural work of Danish libraries. Previous to that she was with the Department of Intercultural Communication and Management, also CBS. Werther currently teaches British studies, and her research interests include British culture and society, intercultural communication and discourse analysis.

About the Editors

Carl Gustav Johannsen is head of the department of Library and Information Management at the Royal School of Library and Information Science in Copenhagen. He has a master's degree from Aarhus University and a Ph.D. on the application of TQM in libraries in Business Management from the Business School of Aarhus. He has been chair of the Danish Research Library Association and is visiting professor at the Aarhus Business School. Johannsen has written several books and many articles on various topics such as business information searching, special libraries, information management and library management. His recent research concerns library leadership. He has delivered numerous conference papers and held teaching sessions in many European and overseas countries.

Leif Kajberg holds a basic degree in public librarianship from the Royal School of Librarianship, Denmark, and an M.Phil. degree in Library and Information Science from the University of Wales (UK). He has been employed at the Royal School of Library and Information Science since 1970, with major areas of activity in international relations, international student mobility and research administration. Kajberg is on the editorial boards of *New Review of Library and Information Research* and *Information Research Watch International* (Bowker Saur). He is an overseas member of the United Kingdom-based Library and Information Research Group (LIRG) and has published widely in Danish and international library and information science journals.